# Princess Cultures

The Mediated Youth series is part of the Peter Lang Media and Communication list.
Every volume is peer reviewed and meets
the highest quality standards for content and production.

PETER LANG
New York • Bern • Frankfurt • Berlin
Brussels • Vienna • Oxford • Warsaw

# Princess Cultures

## mediating girls' imaginations and identities

EDITED BY MIRIAM FORMAN-BRUNELL & REBECCA C. HAINS

PETER LANG
New York • Bern • Frankfurt • Berlin
Brussels • Vienna • Oxford • Warsaw

**Library of Congress Cataloging-in-Publication Data**

Princess cultures: mediating girls' imaginations and identities /
edited by Miriam Forman-Brunell, Rebecca C. Hains.
pages cm. — (Mediated youth; vol. 18)
Includes bibliographical references and index.
1. Girls—Psychology. 2. Identity (Psychology). 3. Princesses.
I. Forman-Brunell, Miriam. II. Hains, Rebecca C.
HQ1229.P89 155.43'3—dc23 2014000841
ISBN 978-1-4331-2062-6 (hardcover)
ISBN 978-1-4331-2061-9 (paperback)
ISBN 978-1-4539-1322-2 (e-book)
ISSN 1555-1814

Bibliographic information published by **Die Deutsche Nationalbibliothek**.
**Die Deutsche Nationalbibliothek** lists this publication in the "Deutsche Nationalbibliografie"; detailed bibliographic data are available on the Internet at http://dnb.d-nb.de/.

Cover photo: Rachel Whitney-Boulanger's photograph of her daughter, Jocelyn Boulanger

The paper in this book meets the guidelines for permanence and durability of the Committee on Production Guidelines for Book Longevity of the Council of Library Resources.

29 Broadway, 18th floor, New York, NY 10006
www.peterlang.com



Printed in the United States of America

# Table of Contents

# Acknowledgements

When I was four years old, Disney's *Sleeping Beauty* (1959) stirred my interest in things princess. But only briefly. After yet another pair of recently-purchased, much longed for and poorly produced plastic slippers cracked the moment I stood up, I grew disillusioned and gave up on princess culture.

Decades later, students in a course I taught on the history of girlhood reawakened my notice of the princess. It is to my insightful students, first at Wellesely College and since 1994 at the University of Missouri-Kansas City, to whom I am indebted for inspiring me to probe the princess. At the American Play, Sports, Games, Entertainment, and Fantasy in American Culture Conference at the Strong National Museum of Play, in Rochester, New York and at the World Congress of the International Toy Research Association Conference on Toys & Culture in Nafplion, Greece, the enthusiastic audiences offered lots more excellent suggestions. I incorporated these into "The Graceful and Gritty Princess: Managing Girlhoods from the New Nation to the New Millennium," an essay published in the *American Journal of Play* in 2009. I co-authored the essay with Julie Eaton whose insights into contemporary princess culture deepened my understandings.

The outstanding contributors to this lively collection, especially Diana Anselmo-Sequeira, opened my eyes to unforeseen princess cultures. A bevy of other wonderful women made this princess project come true. My co-editor, Rebecca Hains, or "Princess Rebecca," made collaborating on this collection a pleasure.

At Peter Lang, it has been my great fortune to work with Mary Savigar and Sharon Mazzarella, who together have done more for the field of girls' studies than any other editors anywhere. Bernadette Shade and Phyllis Korper did a great job readying the manuscript for publication. I am grateful for your patience, understanding, consideration, and support during the unforeseen course of events that interrupted the timely production of this book.

Others include Rachel Whitney-Boulanger whose photograph of her daughter, Jocelyn Boulanger, is just what I wanted for the cover! Many thanks for the sharp eye, quick feet, and playful aesthetic. I also want to thank Zoe Brunell and Darcy Tepper for their millennial insights into the princess and their scholarly understandings of punctuation.

I can't thank enough: Drs. Alexander Swistell and Anne Moore at Weil Cornell and Drs. Amy Rabe, James Coster and Amie Jew at the University of Kansas hospital. They, along with the many outstanding nurses, deserve my appreciation and affection for their expertise, warmth, and meaningful conversation.

Many thanks as well to my compassionate department chair, John Herron, who negotiated a generous leave from teaching during my lengthy treatment. Also at UMKC, Amy Brost helpfully formatted, printed, copied, forwarded, and figured out all things technological.

Thank you David Formanek, Ellen Tepper, Susan Medyn, and Colette Brunell for being there; Ruth Formanek and Perry Brunell for helping me *every* step of the way; and Hagrid Meriweather Brunell for never once leaving my side. This book is most lovingly dedicated to my "happily ever after" pearl of a husband, Claude Brunell.

Miriam Forman-Brunell
Kansas City, MO

When I was a small child, Disney reigned as the supreme pop culture brand in my home. My sister and I had Mickey Mouse and Donald Duck shoes, banks, and t-shirts, and we loved *Pinocchio*, *Snow White and the Seven Dwarfs*, *Bambi*, and *Cinderella*. Princesses were just part of Disney's panoply of family-friendly characters that we knew and loved.

My family was always very musical (my father had been a member of the U.S. Navy Band, and throughout my childhood owned a music store), and we enjoyed musical theater. I frequently performed onstage myself, in Gilbert & Sullivan productions and musicals with youth groups and local community theaters. For this reason, when I was in high school and college, I adored Disney's new line of animated films that were actually musicals, like *Beauty and the Beast*, *Aladdin*, and *The Lion King*, wishing that they'd someday be set as stage productions—and was delighted when, ultimately, they were.

Much later, as a newly minted scholar of media studies, I noticed while working on my book *Growing Up With Girl Power: Girlhood on Screen and in Everyday Life* that princesses had *changed*. They were no longer on an equal footing with Disney's other characters. They reigned supreme, captivating young girls in a way that seemed new and a bit alarming. Neither I nor my friends nor the children I babysat in my youth had been dedicated to princesses in the way that girls growing up with the relatively new Disney Princess *brand* seemed to be.

Because I was so intrigued by this, when *Growing Up With Girl Power* was completed, I embarked upon my own new princess research project. I began by drawing on my performance background, going undercover à la Gloria Steinem in "I was a Playboy Bunny," seeing what it was like to *be* a princess character at children's birthday parties. Expanding from there, I conducted extensive interviews with other performers, parents, educators, and others to inform what would become my next book, *The Princess Problem: Guiding Our Girls through the Princess-Obsessed Years*—as well as my chapter in this volume.

At this time, during my background research for *The Princess Problem*, I recognized a serious gap in the literature. How could there be no scholarly anthology on princess culture? Around this time, Miriam Forman-Brunell was guest-editing a special issue of the journal *Girlhood Studies* on the subject of girls and dolls, to which I contributed an essay on girls' Bratz doll play from my girl power research. In the course of our conversations about our shared interests in girl culture, we agreed to work on this anthology together, to my great delight. I couldn't be happier about having had the opportunity to collaborate with (and learn from) such a wonderful scholar and editor as Miriam on this volume. Additionally, editor Mary Savigar of Peter Lang and our series editor Sharon Mazzarella, who has long been a wonderful mentor, have been terrific to work with once again. I am also grateful to Bernadette Shade, Phyllis Korper, and the rest of the Peter Lang team for their countless contributions to our project.

I also wish to thank several colleagues at Salem State University whose support helped make this volume possible: Michele Sweeney, Interim Dean of the College of Arts and Sciences, and her predecessor Jude Nixon; Peter Oehlkers, chair of the Communications Department, and his predecessor Judi Cook; my colleague Robert Brown, fount of endless (and entertaining) wisdom and camaraderie; and my graduate research assistants Timothy Magill, Krista Andberg, Karen Loughlin, and Irene Walcott, all of whom helped at various stages of this project: much gratitude to all.

Last but not least, I am grateful to my family for their ongoing support, including Lucie Consentino, Anthony Consentino, Sarah Jackson, Corey Jackson, and Liz Ovard: Thank you all for being there when I need you. I dedicate this book to my husband Tyler Hains and our children, Theo and Alexander, the three loves of my life, who make everything possible.

Rebecca Hains
Salem, MA

# Introduction

MIRIAM FORMAN-BRUNELL AND REBECCA HAINS[i]

Princesses are *everywhere* there are girls. Donning pink tulle dresses and sporting glittery tiaras, little princesses appear in preschools and playgrounds, backyards, and bedrooms. Many gowns and crowns are homemade while others are store-bought. Disney's pricey princess costumes (around $45.00) are among the 40,000 licensed princess products[ii] that today ornament girls from toes to tiara. Disney's "lifestyle brand"—aiming to include *everything* girls around the world could possibly *need* (including identities)—has mushroomed Disney's Princess line of merchandise into a multi-billion dollar industry. So in addition to glittering dress-up costumes, jewelry, shoes, and handbags available on line and at Target, Walmart, and other retailers, things princess also include: vanities, make-up cases, cell phones, walkie-talkies, CD players, books, kitchens, beds, comforters, cereal, toothbrushes, potty seats, raincoats, underwear, nightgowns, backpacks, bicycles, tents, TVs, rocking chairs, doggy dishes, castles, toys, games, dolls (Barbie, Bratz, others), and much, much more.[iii]

Daughters wooed by princess culture have led many parents and pundits to worry about girls' imaginations, identities, and ideals. In newspapers and magazines, on TV and radio, in blogs and on internet sites, adults have engaged in a lively public debate about the potential identity-shaping dangers of "princess culture." Peggy Orenstein, author of *Cinderella Ate My Daughter: Dispatches from the Front Lines of Girlie-Girl Culture* (2011) sees the iconic female figure as a wholly inadequate role model for well-rounded girls.[iv] Developmental psychologists Sharon Lamb and Lyn Mikel Brown similarly argue in *Packaging Girlhood: Rescuing Our Daughters from Marketers' Schemes* (2006) that commercialized princesses contribute to the erosion of girls' self-esteem.[v] In *The Princess Problem: Guiding Our Girls Through the Princess-Obsessed Years*, Rebecca Hains contends that, lacking media literacy skills, young girls are ill equipped to handle the messages princess culture conveys about consumerism, ideals of beauty, and gender and race stereotypes.[vi] Although critics acknowledge that the princess might encourage girls to feel good about their selves, they argue that the idealized figure generates a false sense of self-confidence not at all grounded in genuine accomplishments. By reinforcing the unrealistic assumption that power can only be had through magnificent clothing, fabulous wealth, and gorgeous looks, the princess fosters damaging self-scrutiny and a diminishing sense of self. One mother reported that her six-year-old daughter complained that Ariel had a prettier voice and that she wanted her skin to be as light as Snow White's.[vii]

The commercialized princess culture that has alarmed some parents, however, has simply charmed others. Among traditionalists there are those who perceive princess fantasies as perfectly "normal" for girls and a "natural" form of feminine socialization. James C. Dobson's *Bringing Up Girls: Practical Advice and Encouragement for Those Shaping the Next Generation of Women* and John Croyle's *Raising a Princess: Eight Essential Virtues to Teach Your Daughter* promote the princess as an ideal for parents and girls to work toward. These authors along with many other adults prefer innocence to the unsavory, and the fresh-faced princess to the in-your-face teen queen. Many take great pleasure in seeing a little girl dressed in a ball gown instead of sweatpants, curtsying instead of climbing, and sipping tea instead of chugging beer. "In a world where Britney goes pantyless in public and Nicole drives drunk," explained one mother, "a little princess idolatry seems a harmless thing indeed."[viii]

Still other adults believe that anything that gives girls a sense of strength is a good thing.[ix] Third-wave feminist activist Rachel Simmons argues that, "Any arena that allows [girls] access to playfulness and protects them from sexualizing themselves before they are ready" should be applauded not condemned.[x] Many experts and activists agree that "princess power" provides girls with useful skills in a sexist world.[xi] Pointing to the power and proficiencies of Mulan, Belle, and Mia, feminist critic Naomi Wolf recently advised parents and critics not worry about Disney Princesses who are "heroines of their own lives." "Don't worry if your 5-year-old girl insists on a pink frilly princess dress. It doesn't mean she wants to subside into froth; it just means, sensibly enough for her, that she wants to take over the world."[xii]

Avidly pursuing the princess across many disciplinary fields and over the decades, are a wide variety of scholars. Folklorists and feminists in the 1970s and 1980s examined patriarchal literary and cultural practices that shaped the figure of the princess in narratives that date back to ancient civilizations around the world. Since the 1990s, feminist, Marxist, poststructuralist, and cultural studies perspectives have informed critical treatments of Disney by children's literature scholars and others, as evidenced by the wide range of scholarly literature referenced by the contributors in this anthology.[xiii]

Despite the proliferation of essays in academic journals and articles in the mass media, however, there are no scholarly collections on the princess. Of course, there are books about Disney (e.g., *The Mouse That Roared* and *From Mouse to Mermaid*), and scholarly documentaries, too (e.g., the Media Education Foundation's *Mickey Mouse Monopoly*, directed by New York University professor Chyng Sun)—yet none is dedicated to the princesses that have generated billions for the global media giant. Disney Princesses do appear in the occasional piece published in girls' culture anthologies (e.g., *Growing Up Girls*), yet no collection has focused exclusive attention on the mediated figures that have played a leading role in girls' everyday lives and in constructions of girlhood for centuries. The lack of a critical text hampers attempts to scrutinize and theorize a mass culture phenomenon, especially one of likely interest to students of girlhood studies, women's studies, and media studies for whom the princess figured in their girlhoods and into young womanhood.

This is the first scholarly collection, then, to place at the center of inquiry the princess, a figure that is neither as uniform nor as immutable as popularly imagined. In fact, as the essays in this collection make clear, there is not one princess but instead a multitude of different princesses. Illustrating the broad range of princesses, this collection includes the genuine and the imagined, constructed and performed princesses—from Snow White and Princess Sissi to Jasmine and the Jewish American Princess. These princesses, along with many others, are not nearly as innocent and innocuous as we might assume. As many essays in this collection make clear, princesses of different genders, classes, races, ethnicities, ages, nationalities, sexualities, and other cultural markers have been deployed to deliver the ideas, attitudes, institutions, and practices of experts, educators, employers, and other adults who produce knowledge, construct truths, define social relations, constitute girls' subjectivities, and establish social power over girls. Yet princesses are discursive as well as disruptive figures: they also serve the interests of girls and young women in the process of expanding their autonomy and exercising their authority. The many diverse princesses who typically embody a range of notions about what it means to be a girl have provided girls with opportunities to create their own meanings as they negotiate the conflicts and contradictions inherent to girlhood. Rather than becoming passive recipients of the ideals, beliefs, and behaviors encoded in the iconic princess, generations of playful girls and young women have played princess in order to maneuver between gendered expectations and more daring identities.

Making sense of a diversity of princesses in the US and around the world necessitates a variety of perspectives for students and scholars, as well as parents, teachers, media critics, and journalists. The contributors to this multi-disciplinary endeavor hail from Australia, Austria, Canada, Ecuador, Germany, India, Portugal, Romania, and the United States. In addition to providing global perspectives, these international experts also draw upon different disciplinary habits and scholarly practices. Whether they are in traditional departments (history and English, communications/media studies, and gender and women's studies) or in post-disciplinary programs in visual studies, literacy, culture, and language education, the dozen contributors provide multi-generational and multi-disciplinary understanding of the many princess cultures examined here.

Across generations and genders, and imaginations and identities, princesses have performed cultural work, that is, transmitting the culturally constructed values, principles, attitudes, products, symbols, and practices—language, dress, rituals, social habits, songs, etc.—of distinct princess cultures. And, like the princess herself, princess cultures are anything but "uniform," "timeless," "natural," "universal," "transcendent," insulated, and insignificant. Instead, they are extraordinarily diverse, ephemeral, and shifting. Those that are more hegemonic than harmless seek to maintain social order, enforce ideals (especially about gender), and reinforce power relations (such as that between the princess and the prince). But princess cultures can be more fluid.

Providing the thematic framework of this multi-generational, interdisciplinary, and international study of the princess culture phenomenon,

diverse princessly domains are intricately imbricated with other cultures and subcultures from the traditional to the dominant. Intersecting with varieties of children's cultures (girls', boys', peer), national cultures, performance cultures, and royal cultures, some princess cultures cooperate and even collude where others—especially as they compete for dominance—occasionally collide.

## Princess Cultures and Children's Cultures

### Princess and Girls' Cultures

Late twentieth-century girls' culture provides the context for the first chapter in this book, Ilana Nash's examination of the princess in girl-centered fantasy texts. In those produced since the 1990s, the princess figure stands as the embodiment of Girl Power, the mass-culture ethos that girlhood empowerment can be achieved through pleasure, style, fashion, attitude, and athletics.[xiv] According to Nash, the notion of "specialness" in addition to other aspects of Girl

Power, informs Disney's lifestyle brand. In "The Princess and the Teen-Witch: Fantasies of the Essential Self," Nash argues that girl consumers are encouraged to feel as "special" as millennial princesses. By inheriting identities from mystical sources, fictional heroines in Disney Princess productions reinforce a sense of self that is intrinsically "special" and automatically conferred. Along with princesses, both feisty and fetching, witches who also populated girls' media at the end of the twentieth century share inborn magical powers that make them fundamentally "special." Not only does the belief in a transcendent, essential self disavow the dominant notion that identity is a social construct, it undermines important understandings about the role that choice plays in identity making. What potential danger the creed of specialness poses to real girls lies in its degradation of choice and agency.

According to Megan Condis, many Disney princesses are capable, competent, and ambitious but just what their gendered, racialized bodies can do depends heavily upon their race. In "Applying for the Position of Princess: Race, Labor, and the Privileging of Whiteness in the Disney Princess Line," Condis demonstrates that despite what the Disney Princess franchise says about the equality of its racially and culturally diverse Princesses, not all are "created equal": the lifestyle and cultural values of white girls are imagined differently from those of little Princesses of color. The social and cultural differences come into view when examining the role of labor and the place of leisure in the lives of racially different Princesses. While princesshood can only be obtained/maintained through the labor of others, Princesses of color do not experience the upper-class luxuries and privileges that come when one is wealthy enough to stop working. By sorting aspirants into different categories, Disney's bifurcated definition of princesshood reinforces racialized, gendered divisions.

## Princess and Boys' Cultures

Race and class not only influence how femininity is imagined but also how masculinity is represented. Examining the intersection between princess culture and boys' culture, media studies scholar Guillermo Avila-Saavedra argues in "Ghetto Princes, Pretty Boys, and Handsome Slackers: Masculinity, Race and the Disney Princes" that race, class, and discourses about female empowerment and the masculinity crisis inform representations of gender identity for princes of color. His discourse analysis of the performances of gender by male protagonists in *Aladdin* (1992), *The Princess and the Frog* (2009), and *Mulan* (1998) reveals that the three non-white characters or romantic interests are decidedly less masculine than all other princes from Snow White's savior prince to Rapunzel's Flynn Rider. "In the spectrum of masculinities of Disney's Princes," he argues, "within the masculine hierarchy princes of color occupy a distinctly diminished place."

The archetypical hero and the trope of the damsel in distress are the focus of Sara Grimes's chapter, which examines the intersection of princess culture and the extremely male-centric mainstream gamer culture. In "Rescue the Princess: The Videogame Princess as Prize, Parody, and Protagonist," Grimes explores the multiple functions of princesses within videogame narratives and mechanics that have appeared in popular console videogames over the past thirty years. Although the "rescue the princess" plot device has remained a central narrative convention, Grimes argues that it has nevertheless provided the materials and cultural signifiers for reinvention, deconstruction, and critique. Warrior princesses along with parodies of princesses (*Fat Princess*) defy, transgress, invert, and subvert established tropes, and creatively critique the "rescue the princess" convention.

## Princess and Peer Cultures

When kids leave home for school, they do not leave princess cultures behind them. The interaction among princess, peer, and school culture is the focus of Karen Wohlwend's "Playing to Belong: Princesses and Peer Cultures in Preschool." Wohlwend argues that preschool girls' deep knowledge of pop culture princess characters and stories can be applied to their in-school literacy learning in beneficial ways. Although attending to the problematic messages about gender and consumerism in princess texts, Wohlwend's study of princess play in preschool classrooms reveals that youngsters learn how to belong, communicate, cooperate, and develop social relationships—in ways that both align with and transgress broader discourses about gender. As a form of exploratory play, doll play creates a space in which young children can invent alternate identities. In-school doll play provides opportunities for girls and boys to develop their own productive critiques as well as ways of belonging. Wohlwend notes that in order to "effectively help young children navigate the conflicts, social relationships, and emotional attachments that constitute belonging within complex mixtures of childhood cultures" (this volume, 110), it is crucial to mediate between peer culture (play) and school culture (math and reading).

## Princess Cultures Beyond Western Cultures

In "Princess Culture in Qatar: Exploring Princess Media Narratives in the Lives of Arab Female Youth," media studies scholar Kirsten Pike studied Arab female undergraduates at Northwestern University in Qatar. In this work, she sought to amplify the Arab girls' voices and viewpoints about princess media. Pike found that in consuming Western representations of pop culture princesses, Arab girls in Qatar engage in a complex negotiation of Western and non-Western ideologies about gender, sexuality, race, class, and national identity. At the same time, they also negotiate the globalization and commercialization of children's media culture. Pike demonstrates how the media majors she studied transformed the ideological lessons they acquired from commercial princess media in their girlhoods into powerful new stories more attuned to their gendered interests and identities. By "raising their voices through cultural criticism and powerfully recasting gendered norms in their own creative works," Pike explains, "girls in Qatar demonstrate that they are active agents in the growing global march toward improving girls' media—and by extension, the cultural experiences of Arab female youth in the Middle East and beyond." (this volume, 157)

In a study of 120 girls (ages 8–10, 11–12, and 13–15) of various ethnicities from four countries (the United States, India, Fiji, and China) Diana Natasia and Charu Uppal sought to determine if Disney Princesses have surpassed monoculturalism (as Disney claims) as well as what girls have learned about multiculturalism from non-Western Disney Princesses (as presented in *Aladdin, Pocahontas,* and *Mulan*). In "Mono- or Multi-Culturalism: Girls around the World Interpret Non-Western Disney Princesses," the authors report that across the countries in their sample, girls agreed that the Princesses are physically beautiful. A key cultural difference, however, appeared in the young participants' perception of "freedom" and identification with the Princess figures. Most girls in the United States sample (regardless of ethnicity) described Disney Princesses as wealthy and "free" and expressed a desire to be like those with whom they strongly identified. However, girls in India, Fiji, and China described princesses as having many duties and, as such, not being free. These girls neither wanted to be like the Disney Princesses nor identified with them. Noting that the girls in the study "sensed few differences between the Princesses with non-Western heritage and the other Princesses in Disney animated films" (Natasia & Uppal, 136), the authors concluded that Disney Princesses have not surpassed monoculturalism. Consequently, Western elite ideals continue to predominate in Disney movies that ultimately fail to teach girls about multiculturalism.

## Princess and Performance Cultures

Girls' princessly performances run the gamut from traditional to more transgressive interpretations of femininity. The inspiration to pretend and perform is often generated by animations, movies, ice shows, birthday parties, and other commercialized and commodified forms of princess culture. Several essays focus attention on girls and young women who played professional princess roles in commercial venues. In "Blue Bloods, Movie Queens, and Jane Does: Or How Princess Culture, American Film, and Girl Fandom Came Together in the 1910s," Diana Anselmo-Sequeira examines the development of princess culture in the early American film industry—*before* the days of Disney. Historicizing the long-standing association between commodified "princess culture," female fandom, and female adolescence, Anselmo-Sequeira explores how movie fan magazines presented adolescent actresses, America's earliest movie stars, as real-life embodiments of fairytale princesses who played princesses on screen and paraded as princesses off screen. In the 1910s, the popular press that promoted teenage movie stars like Mary Pickford as rag-to-riches Cinderellas raised from urban squalor, invited girl fans to identify with the stars' mythologized biographies. "From emotive Mae Marsh to comedic Mabel Normand, and from teenage Mary Miles Minter to childlike Mary Pickford, most Thumbelina-sized female players were imagined as "Cinderella [...] girls who [...] became famous overnight when their good fairies led them into the magic light of the Kliegs."[xv] Drawing on psychology's newly formulated notion of female adolescence as excessively romantic and gullible, the film industry provided Progressive-era "New Girls" with rather regressive tropes of feminine self-betterment and fairytale romanticism.

Turning to our current context, in which princess performances are by default informed by Disney's complete dominance of that entertainment genre, Rebecca Hains considered actors' experiences performing the parts of princesses for live audiences. She interviewed women who have appeared in official Disney Princess roles on stage as well as women who have portrayed the Disney Princesses' generic, public-domain counterparts as birthday party princesses, entertaining young girls and their guests during their birthday celebrations. In "If I Were a Belle: Performers' Negotiations of Feminism, Gender, and Race in Princess Culture," Hains focuses specifically on how those women who portrayed Belle negotiated the well-known problematics of princess culture in their performances. She found that performers informed by a critical perspective engaged in microtactics that shifted the characters' portrayal. Some empowered Belle's character and conveyed more egalitarian messages (for example, by telling children at a birthday party that the prince couldn't attend because he was at home cleaning the castle). She also found that children readily accepted women of color in the role of Belle. The chapter is informative in its insights regarding the elasticity of performance cultures that enable actors to reinterpret and resist princess stereotypes.

Gender performance in everyday life[xvi] is the focus of Rebecca Starkman's study of the ways in which high-school-age Jewish girls in Toronto negotiate the

Jewish American Princess (JAP) stereotype. In "JAPpy: Portraits of Canadian Girls Mediating the Jewish American Princess and Identity," Starkman contends that rather than scripting girls' identities, the stereotype serves as a reference point for girls' individual interpretations and performances. The portraits of three participants illustrate the ways in which the girls simultaneously identify with the JAP stereotype, reject it, and apply their own unique interpretations to their identity expressions. Although elements of the stereotype apply uniformly (namely consumption patterns / materialism), Starkman carefully identifies how peer, religious, and communal experiences intersect and inform each participant's creative interpretation of aspects of the JAP stereotype. Starkman concludes that girls who creatively reappropriate dominant stereotypes alter the power of categories and redefine meanings.

## The Royal Cultures and Imagined Princess Cultures

Beginning with "Princess Sissi of Austria: Image, Reality, and Transformation," the final two essays in this collection examine the royal cultures that gave rise to narratives of princess cultures. In their co-authored essay, Phyllis S. and Helfried C. Zrzavy trace the popularity of "Princess Sissi," Princess Elizabeth of Wittelsbach, who later became Empress Elizabeth of Austria. Since the end of World War II, the media and market have fully exploited Princess Sissi's Cinderella-type image among girls in Austria, Germany, throughout Europe and beyond. National governments, too, have found countless ways to commemorate Sissi's image—through museums, memorials, and furniture collections to name a few. Rather than reflecting a reality, Sissi is, they argue, an "amalgam of societal idealizations and [a] receptacle of mirrored historical self-projections." (this volume, 235–236). The authors trace the origins of the princess's popularity to the "Sissi" movie trilogy (released in 1955, 1956, and 1957). Within the post-Nazi German and Austrian context, the idealized Sissi embodied the concept of "vergangenheitsbewaltigung," that is, the attempt to cope with the shared culpability for the atrocities committed during the Third Reich. Zrzavy and Zrzavy identify numerous points throughout the popular movies that promote a reimagining of Austria as the cultured nation it was during the reign of the Habsburgs, before Hitler came to power. The construction of Sissi's image then as now served as an effective means of transforming central Europe's past. Movie-made Sissi provided Europeans faced with their difficult recent history with "an easily embraced diversion" (this volume, 249).

Examining the origins of fairytales within the context of seventeenth-century French royal culture is Rebecca-Anne C. Do Rozario's "Dedicated to Princesses: The Marriage Market and the Royal Revelations of Ancien Régime Fairy Tales."

Do Rozario examines the early origins of fairy tales written by women who, unlike later male authors, critiqued "…issues of beauty, marital commodification, and female agency." (Do Rozario, 254) The ending of one fairy tale, for example, provided the pioneering female writer with the opportunity to affirm the suffering of women in marriage. In a tale by Perrault that brought about a shift in the fairy tale narrative, the heroine is rewarded for her obedience to the rules of marriage with a happily-ever-after ending. The "beautiful, passive, domestic heroine, rewarded for her submissive, appealing behaviour toward her prince" (this volume, 267) became the basis of the Brothers Grimm version of the Cinderella story. While Disney's Princesses are "promoted as aspirational figures for the masses" (this volume, 268), few people realize that their princessly ancestors were once the center of their own political narratives and princess cultures.

Together, these essays demonstrate that princesses *matter*—to girls, grownups, and the complexly imbricated cultures constructed by each that are defined by princesses as well as those that deploy princesses for their own powerful purposes. By unpacking the meanings of some of the many things princess, we hope that the essays prove instructive to producers and parents, skeptics and supporters. For students and scholars in media studies, childhood studies, youth studies, popular culture, history, cultural studies, women's studies, visual studies, performance studies, feminist ethnography, sociology, education—and, especially, girlhood studies, there is much more to learn from interrogating princesses and investigating their cultural domains.

## Endnotes

i Rebecca Hains would like to thank her graduate assistant Irene Walcott for her assistance with this project.

ii Giroux, Henry and Pollock, Grace. 2010. *The Mouse that Roared: The End of Innocence.* Lanham, MD: Rowman & Littlefield.

iii See PartyCheap. http://www.partycheap.com/Princess_Accessories_s/396.htm

iv Peggy Orenstein, "What's Wrong With Cinderella?" *New York Times Magazine*, December 24, 2006, pp. 34–39; Peggy Ornstein, *Cinderella Ate My Daughter: Dispatches From the Front Lines of Girlie-Girl Culture* (New York: Harper, 2011).

v Sharon Lamb and Lyn Mickel Brown, *Packaging Girlhood: Rescuing Our Daughters From Marketers' Schemes* (New York: St. Martin's, 2006).

vi Rebecca Hains. *The Princess Problem: Guiding Our Girls Through the Princess-Obsessed Years* (Naperville, IL: Source Books, 2014.

vii Melissa Fletcher Stoeltje, "Little Girls Carried Away on a Pink Wave of Princess Products," San Antonio Express-News, March 11, 2007, Life sect., 1;4.

viii Stoeltje, "Little Girls," p. 1.

ix Christopher Healy, "A Nation of Little Princesses," Salon, November 24, 2004, 2, http://dir.salon.com/story/mwt/feature/2004/11/24/princesses/index.html

x Quoted in Mary McNamara, "The Princess Principle," *LA Times*, August 26, 2004.

xi Deborah Klosky, "Princess R Us." Spot On. 7 February 2007: 2. 30 March 2007 http://www.spot-on.com/archives/klosky/2007/02/princesses_r_us.html <http://www.spot-on.com/archives/klosky/2007/02/princesses_r_us.html

xii Miriam Forman-Brunell and Julie Eaton, "The Graceful and Gritty Princess: Managing Girlhoods from the New Nation to the New Millennium," *American Journal of Play* Vol. 1, No. 3, Winter, 2009: 338–364. Naomi Wolf, "Mommy, I Want to Be a Princess." *New York Times*, December 2, 2011.

xiii Jack Zipes, "Breaking the Disney Spell," in *From Mouse to Mermaid: The Politics of Film, Gender, and Culture*, ed. Elizabeth Bell, Lynda Haas, and Laura Sells (Indianapolis: Indiana University Press, 1995), 40; Janet Wasko, *Understanding Disney: The Manufacture of Fantasy* (Boston: Polity, 2001), 136; Henry A. Giroux, *The Mouse That Roared: Disney and the End of Innocence* (Lanham, MD: Rowman & Littlefield, 1999), 102. See also Shawn Jarvis, "Feminism and Fairy Tales," in *The Oxford Companion to Fairy Tales*, ed. Jack Zipes (New York: Oxford University Press, 2002), http://www.answers.com/topic/feminism-and-fairy-tales. Tatar, Maria (ed.). *The Annotated Brothers Grimm.* (New York: W. W. Norton & Co., 2004); Maria Tatar, ed. *Classic Fairy Tales*, (New York: W. W. Norton & Company, 1999).

xiv Rebecca Hains, *Growing Up with Girl Power: Girlhood on Screen and Everyday Life* (New York: Peter Lang, 2012).

xv Shorey, Jerome. 1918. "Do You Believe in Fairies?" Photoplay (September): 47

xvi Butler, Judith, *Gender Trouble: Feminism and the Subversion of Identity.* (New York: Routledge, 2000).

# Part I
# Princess Cultures and Children's Cultures

CHAPTER ONE

# The Princess and the Teen Witch: Fantasies of the Essential Self

ILANA NASH

At the turn of the millennium, popular culture for and about girls showed a rapid growth in the fantasy genres, featuring a new emphasis on princesses and witches as the protagonists of mass-media narratives. Neither princesses nor witches were new to this period; both figures have been each other's opposites and nemeses in children's literature for centuries. But the media of the 1990s and early 2000s magnified the importance of princesses and witches in multiple media forms, to the point where tales of youth and magic became a widespread cultural phenomenon. Which conditions enable long-existing fantasy figures to suddenly find new ubiquity and profitability? Analyzing a selection of popular texts about princesses and witches from the 1990s and early 2000s, this chapter argues that these sub-genres of fantasy grew simultaneously because they participated similarly in cultural dialogues of the late twentieth century: dialogues about identity, empowerment, and the nature of good and evil.

In its discussion of princesses, this chapter focuses on the products of the Walt Disney studio. Although other princess narratives emerged in the 1990s and beyond, Disney's were the most profitable and the most influential. Children's literature scholar Jack Zipes has shown that the juggernaut of the Disney Corporation has done a disservice to the fairy tales on which it based its films, first by flattening out and distorting the meanings of classic tales (which exist in multiple versions), and then by obliterating the visibility of other versions through its domination of the marketplace (Zipes 1997). Disney further expanded its hold on the fairy-tale market in 1999, when the company launched its "Disney Princess" brand with a flood of princess-themed toys and accessories (Disney 2008), creating a widespread obsession with princesses among girls.

The witches considered in the second part of this chapter are female adolescents and post-adolescents who emerged on screen in the later 1990s, targeting young audiences. Themes of the occult had gradually been growing in mass-market teen fiction and media since the late 1980s, but the teen-witch genre took definitive form in 1996, emerging in several iterations at once. In April of that year, *Sabrina the Teenage Witch* premiered as a TV-movie on the Showtime cable network; in May, Columbia Pictures released *The Craft*, a highly profitable film about high-school witches; and in September, *Sabrina the Teenage Witch* debuted as an ongoing comedy series on the ABC television network.[1] Debuting four months later on the WB network, the critically acclaimed *Buffy the Vampire Slayer* series (1997–2003) developed a subplot about witchcraft for one of its primary characters, Willow, which grew in significance throughout the series' run. In 1998 the longest-enduring of the genre debuted in the series *Charmed*, also on the youth-targeting WB network, which ran until 2006. Some of these tales' protagonists were technically older than teenage (the sisters of *Charmed* are in their twenties), and others who began as teenagers grew out of adolescence as their series progressed. But I refer to them consistently as "teen" witches because most of them began as teen characters and all of them were primarily marketed to (but not solely consumed by) teenage viewers.[2]

## Identity, the Self, and Power in Late Modernity

Perhaps the most striking similarity between princesses and witches in the 1990s and early 2000s is that both figures exalt the power of the essential self, at a time when the truth-claims of Essentialism and other traditional systems of thought were eroding in a postmodern world. Simply put, theories of postmodernism posit that there are no objective, eternal truths; that all meta-narratives are subject to question and subversion; and that all knowledges, including knowledge of the self, can only be socially constructed and subjectively perceived. There is no stable "true self." Anthony Giddens, describing our historical moment as late modernity, has said that the loosening of old traditions calls for us actively to build our identities through a reflexive process of choice. Summarizing Giddens' theories, David Gauntlett notes:

> Even those who would say that they have never given any thought to questions or anxieties about their own identity will inevitably have been compelled to make significant choices throughout their lives, from everyday questions about clothing, appearance and leisure to high-impact decisions about relationships, beliefs and occupations. Whilst earlier societies with a social order based firmly on tradition would provide individuals with (more or less) clearly defined roles, in post-traditional societies we have to work out our roles for ourselves. (Gauntlett 2008, 105)

These ideas have been visibly enacted through the events of the later twentieth century: the Civil Rights movements, second-wave feminism, the student movements, and other social challenges of the 1960s and beyond have emphasized the rights of individuals over the oppressive authority of social institutions, and over the truth-claims of traditional ideologies.

Americans today live with an odd paradox: the rhetoric of contemporary life puts tremendous emphasis on individuality, and on personal freedom of choice, even while another condition of late modernity—global capitalism and the rise of multinational corporations—has made institutions more powerful than individuals in shaping the conditions of human existence. As Berger and Ezzy (2007) state in their overview of late modernity, "we have seen a growth in the scope and power of bureaucracies … . Within these organizations, individuals are cogs, easily replaceable and interchangeable"(47).The individual is simultaneously important and irrelevant.

Both sides of that paradox can be seen in the Disney Princess phenomenon. On the one hand, Disney's exploitation of the princess fantasy is so globally ubiquitous as to be an almost unavoidable part of girlhood. As the website of Disney Consumer Products proudly states: "Disney Princess has become a powerful lifestyle brand accounting for more than $4 billion in global retail sales, touching every aspect of girls' lives around the world." (Since 2008, when the text of that website was copyrighted, profits from the Disney Princess brand have surely risen to even greater heights). The phrase "lifestyle brand" sounds like an oxymoron, but the concept is widely used in the marketing industry to gain consumers who will, hopefully, sustain their brand-loyalty throughout their lives. As Rebecca Hains has noted, "Lifestyle brands provide identities, conferring their meaning onto the people who consume them." Through the magic of consumption, a girl can transform herself into a mass-produced identity that "touch[es] every aspect of girls' lives around the world" (Hains 2012, 390). Those consumers are countless and interchangeable.

On the other hand, Disney's corporate colonization of the childhood mind has its benefits for individuality: the princess fantasy enables a consumer to feel uniquely special. Disney's website explicitly names "transformation" as a key theme in the princess fantasy, marking each princess as supremely special:

> For a little girl, the desire to feel special is more powerful than a magic wand. She dreams of a place where clothes are spun of silk and gold, where balls are held in her honor and where princes fall in love at first sight. It is a world Disney has created — full of fantasy and romance — where a girl can feel as special as a Princess. Disney Princess — where dreams begin. (Disney)

"Feeling special" is the central commodity of this lifestyle brand. But what does "special" mean? Disney's interpretation equates specialness with wealth, which royalty certainly has. More generally, to be special is to be unusual, not common. Special girls are not just the "cogs, easily replaceable and interchangeable," that Berger and Ezzy describe. A fairytale princess is neither common nor a commoner: she stands apart from the crowd. She merits balls given in her honor; she is loveable *at first sight*, without needing to prove herself. The specialness of her inborn nature automatically guarantees the glorious transformation that signals a fairy tale's happy ending. This pattern also appears, in slightly altered form, in the teen-witch tales of the 1990s and early 2000s. Both the princess and teen-witch genres present their protagonists as supremely special: each is a paragon of qualities and abilities that surpass those of common girls. Most importantly, the heroine's specialness is portrayed as a birthright, not the result of self-reflexive choice or agency.

In these tales the heroine's choices *manifest* her identity rather than *construct* it. This, I suggest, helps explain the popularity of millennial princesses and witches. The late-modern loosening of tradition that enables us to build our own identities is certainly a form of freedom and power; but as the saying goes, with great power comes great responsibility. Actively choosing one's identity is hard work; it requires the frustration of trial and error as we negotiate contradictory messages from different sources. The labor of choice can also feel fruitless, as well as hard, if the options are either inadequate or else so plentiful as to be confusing. Wouldn't it be easier to know who you're supposed to be, to have your life-path manifest through a power other than your own weary powers of choice? Fantasy tales of princesses and witches tell us that there is, indeed, an essential self that pre-dates our consciousness and determines our destinies. What a relief.

The youngest of Disney's audience, children of the pre-school age, are not yet consciously constructing identities. At the age of four, most children do not choose their own clothes, let alone their spouses or occupations. But even these children are exposed to the conditions of late-modern life which make the Disney Princess appealing, particularly through the ideologies of education. Twentieth-century philosophies of teaching were highly influenced by John Dewey's psychological and sociological theories, Paolo Freire's political theories, and post-modernist theories (Ghiraldelli 2000). If these diverse theories could be said to have a common denominator, it would be their focus on children's subjectivity: psychologically, politically, and intellectually. In the 1980s and beyond, educators further simplified the concept of subjectivity to an emphasis on children's "self esteem." A glance at the academic database ERIC (Educational Resources Information Center) reveals that publications on the importance of children's self esteem grew sharply over the late twentieth century, spiking in the 1990s.

The self-esteem movement has also been promoted through a variety of websites made by and for teachers. At one such website, certified pre-school specialists tell us: "It is important for young children to feel good about themselves. It is never too early to teach ... the importance of having self confidence" (Child Care Lounge 2010). They recommend several activities to boost preschoolers' self-esteem, including revisions to traditional nursery songs. "I Am Special," for example, is sung to the tune of "Frère Jacques":

> I am special, I am special (point to self)
> If you look, you will see
> Someone very special, someone very special
> It is me! It is me! (point to self)

The song "Special, Special" is sung to the tune of "Twinkle, Twinkle Little Star":

> Special, special, special me
> How I wonder what I'll be
> In this big world I can be
> Anything I want to be...

Traditional nursery rhymes turned children's attention to objects in the external world, be they the bells of Frère Jacques' monastery or the twinkles of stars light-years away. In contemporary adaptations, however, the world shrinks in importance as children chant the splendors of their innate selves and desires.

It sounds nice when we tell children they can "be anything [they] want to be." But in reality, what we become depends more on abilities and circumstances than it does on simple desire. That inconvenient fact disappears in the rhetoric of fantasy and empowerment, where merely "being yourself"—a self which is automatically special because it exists—promises ultimate success. Small wonder that millennial children loved Disney's Princesses, whose essential specialness is unfailingly rewarded.

While young children were being taught to admire themselves, older girls were learning a related message through "girl power," a popular phrase and trend in entertainment during the 1990s, when girl-centered artifacts began flourishing in multiple genres of popular culture.[3] Based loosely on third-wave feminism, the girl-power messages shared a central idea that girls are "empowered" and important: worthy of attention, strong, entitled to take action to obtain their goals. Beyond that vague cluster of ideas, the meaning of "girl power" was never unanimously defined. The phrase first reached mainstream fame as the slogan of the British pop-music group The Spice Girls; when they told us what they wanted—what they really, really wanted—in their 1996 song "Wannabe," they celebrated a girl's right to state a desire and have it fulfilled. In millennial fantasy tales, princesses and witches are also defined by strong desires; they really, really want specific goals. Success depends on the good or evil nature of their essential selves.

## The Power of the Self in Disney's Princess Tales

Fairy tales posit a world where good and evil are a simple binary, embodied in the hero/ine and an adversary. Disney's Princesses are inherently good, its witches inherently evil. Disney's highly traditional definition of feminine goodness mandates humility, sweetness, obedience, and altruistic desires (this definition widened somewhat after 1989, as I explain below). The qualities that mark "evil" are selfishness and a desire to dominate others, as we can see in the witches, stepmothers, and evil fairies of princess films. Whether good or bad, these characters' identities (and their fates) depend solely on qualities they were born with.

In Disney's earliest princess films (*Snow White and the Seven Dwarfs* [1937], *Cinderella* [1950], and *Sleeping Beauty* [1959]), the heroine's trials and triumphs alike spring from the identity she has at birth, not from her choices. It helps to have the right blood, as high birth has often been equated with high quality of character. Even our language associates wealth with goodness: "mean" is a synonym for lowly while "gentle" describes the gentry—people of high rank. To be born a fairy-tale princess is to be born doubly special, high both in character and social status. Neither of these traits comes from the princess's conscious choices.

Disney based *Snow White and the Seven Dwarfs* on the Brothers' Grimm version of this folktale, in which Snow White's rare beauty is determined by mystical forces before she is born:

> Once upon a time... a queen was sitting and sewing by a window with an ebony frame. While she was sewing, she looked out at the snow and pricked her finger with a needle. Three drops of blood fell onto the snow. The red looked so beautiful against

> the white snow that she thought: 'If only I had a child as white as snow, as red as blood, and as black as the wood of the window frame.' Not long after that, she gave birth to a little girl who was white as snow, red as blood, and black as ebony, and she was called Snow White. (Tatar 2004, 243–244)

The young queen soon dies; the king then marries a "domineering" beauty who is secretly a witch. When the new queen's magic mirror tells her that Snow White has surpassed her as "the fairest one of all," the queen brews the magical schemes that drive the story's conflict. "Fair" has three meanings: light-skinned, beautiful, and morally just. These qualities intertwine in Snow White, comprising her specialness. Her inborn, triple fairness inspires other people's actions and catalyzes the story's events.

We first see Disney's Snow White performing humble chores, surely inappropriate for a princess. The situation is unjust, forced upon her by the jealous queen. Despite her royalty, Snow White displays no arrogance; she works obediently and without complaint, pausing only to sing her wish that the man she's destined to love will find her. Her humility and patience prove her justice of spirit, which also informs the nature of her wish: she longs for true love, while her witchy stepmother longs only for superiority and sexual power. Although love is technically a selfish desire (it brings personal happiness), it functions in fairy tales as a sign of natural and correct femininity. Traditional views of gender see romance as the province of women and claim that a woman's essential nature makes her long for romantic love. Moreover, a good wife finds her happiness in serving her husband and children. Snow White's desire for love thus appears selfless, and her wishes come true, while the selfish queen/witch is doomed to failure and death.

All further important plot-points in the film result from the heroine's intrinsic specialness. When the queen orders a huntsman to cut out Snow White's heart, he finds himself unable to murder such innocent beauty, and tells Snow White to run away. As she flees through the forest, lost and terrified, animals sense her specialness: gentle creatures emerge from the dark to comfort her. Later, they help her clean the dwarfs' messy house.[4] So exceptional that even the beasts of nature respect it, Snow White's innate beauty has the same effect on the dwarfs; they take her in because she is lovely and has a spirit of humble "fairness" that makes her glad to do housework in exchange for a home. The story's climactic moment, in which Snow White accepts a poisoned apple from the disguised queen, also results from her fairness: guileless herself, she cannot perceive guile in others. Later, as her seemingly dead body lies in a glass coffin the bereaved dwarfs have built for her, Snow White's innate fairness continues to catalyze events: a passing prince is so struck by her beauty that he decides he must have her corpse for his own. In the Grimms' tale, Snow White resurrects rather comically: the prince's servants stumble while carrying her coffin, making the piece of apple "jolt" from her gullet. Disney has Snow White awaken more romantically, through the prince's kiss. At each turn the heroine's fate is shaped by qualities she was born with: royal blood and fairness of body and soul. While her words and deeds display no exceptional power, Snow White wields tremendous *symbolic* power as the apotheosis of goodness in her world.

A similar plot informs Disney's version of *Sleeping Beauty*, where the heroine is also long wished-for by her royal parents. When Princess Aurora finally arrives, the king and queen host a feast and invite all the land. As Disney's website says in the words cited earlier, girls feel "special" by dreaming of balls thrown in their honor. For Aurora, that event occurs merely because she is born. Good fairies enhance Aurora's specialness, bestowing gifts of beauty, sweetness, and talent upon her. Even the curse she suffers comes through no choice of her own: the evil fairy Maleficent casts the curse because she was insulted by the King's failure to invite her to the party (showing the same vindictive self-importance as *Snow White*'s wicked queen). The end of *Sleeping Beauty* mirrors the end of the earlier film: ultimate transformation comes not through the heroine's self-reflexive choices, but from a prince's choice to kiss her while she is inanimate—that is, while she is *least* able to demonstrate any powers of choice. No matter; a choice-making mind is not what attracts the prince. He is smitten by her natural beauty and the inner goodness it signals.

Maleficent, like the wicked queen in *Snow White*, proves that even the antagonists of Disney Princess films embody the idea that "specialness" is innate and determinant of one's fate. These villainesses are uniquely special in their worlds, and they do not self-reflexively construct their own identities. Untill Disney's 2014 live-action retelling of Sleeping Beauty's tale in *Maleficent*, we never saw them learning the dark arts they practice, or the events that turned them so cruel and bitter; magical powers and hatred are simply their birth rights and the guarantors of their deaths. Intrinsic nature determines desire, and desire, for good or ill, determines destiny.

It's easy to see why numerous feminist commentators have criticized Disney's fairy tales for their passive portrayal of approved femininity; powerful actions come only from male characters, or from the wrong kind of female. Over time, the rise of second-wave feminism made such passivity passé. Disney gradually responded to this cultural shift by altering its definition of goodness in latter-day princesses. Beginning with *The Little Mermaid* (1989), the studio began to portray princesses with greater measures of independence, choice, and agency, even while keeping the traditional virtues of sweetness, other-directedness, and a longing for true love. In a study of female characters in Disney's feature animation, Amy Davis describes the differences between earlier Disney princesses and those from 1989 to 2005:

> [T]he heroines of Disney's animated films of this period show their integrity through their actions, rather than through their inaction. Furthermore, the level of action and independence demonstrated by these heroines grew exponentially with each film, and could still readily be seen even when the main character of the film was male and the leading female character was in a more supporting role. (Davis 2007, 171)

Heroines like Ariel in *The Little Mermaid* and Jasmine in *Aladdin* (1992) have a feistier demeanor than Snow White, but the "independence" Davis names is rather questionable; these heroines' power has real limitations, and does not displace the inborn specialness that warrants their happy endings.

Disney portrays Ariel as a girl dissatisfied with the confines of her life as a mermaid, fascinated by the world of humans. Her father, King Triton, warns her against seeking human society, but she willfully disobeys: rising to the ocean's surface, she sees Prince Eric and falls in love with him. The prince nearly drowns when his boat capsizes, but Ariel saves his life, carrying him to shore. Proving natural nobility through this selfless action, she then shows humility by disappearing before he can see or thank her. To win Eric's love, Ariel strikes a deal with the sea-witch Ursula to trade her voice for a pair of human legs. Ursula transforms Ariel, and dictates the conditions of the deal: if Ariel cannot secure the prince's love for her in return, without her voice, she will meet a terrible fate.

Disney erases the darkness and complexity of Hans Christian Andersen's original story, in which the mermaid is a poignant figure who fails and dies. Her only recompense is that she becomes a benevolent spirit, one of the "children of the air" who will someday be able to enter heaven (Andersen 2007). Disney's version supplies a happier ending and simpler morals. Ariel's loveable nature overcomes the obstacle of her silence, and Prince Eric begins to love her—until Ursula, a more prominent and evil character in Disney's film than in Andersen's story, sabotages Ariel's efforts. Ursula disguises herself to vie for Prince Eric's affections, echoing the sexual jealousy of *Snow White*'s wicked queen. She further plots to seize control of the ocean from King Triton, displaying her gross power-hunger. At the film's climax, as Ursula swells to monstrous proportions (literal self-aggrandizement), Prince Eric kills her. In gratitude, King Triton consents to let Ariel marry the human prince; he uses his own magic to transform his daughter permanently into a human. Ariel's agency may catalyze the film's plot, but it is Ursula, Eric, and Triton whose *actions* cause Ariel's transformations and the film's happy ending. The only real power Ariel wields is her innate qualities of selflessness and sweetness, which Eric can sense even when she is mute.

Similarly, Princess Jasmine (*Aladdin*) expresses dissatisfaction with her confined life in the palace of her father, the Sultan. She rejects the suitors the Sultan presents to her, insisting that she will only marry for love—if at all. This reveals her independent spirit and the moral worthiness of her desires. In a daring act, Jasmine escapes the Sultan's palace and runs away. But her agency quickly proves unwise: because she has never seen, let alone functioned in, the outside world, she runs afoul of reality. Jasmine kindly helps a beggar-boy by giving him food from a street-vendor's cart—not realizing that she must purchase the food first, with money she doesn't have. The outraged vendor is about to have Jasmine arrested when Aladdin, who watches the scene from afar and falls in love (at first sight) with Jasmine's beauty and kindness, rushes in to rescue her. Thus, the girl's agency is good only for instigating her adventure. Subsequent success depends on the superior savvy of her man.

Most of the film's action centers on Aladdin; the scenes including Jasmine show a highly traditional vision of gender roles. She is the sheltered, wealthy innocent; he, the street-wise commoner who takes pride in initiating her. This formula is at least as old as the classic 1934 film *It Happened One Night*, in which a tough newspaperman rescues a runaway heiress, taking her on a memorably sexy road-trip. In *Aladdin*, the hero uses a magic carpet to show his runaway princess "A Whole New World," the duet they sing. One cannot help remembering Steppenwolf's seductive rock song, "Magic Carpet Ride" (1968), especially as some of Aladdin's lyrics have a vaguely suggestive undertone: he promises to "take [her] wonder by wonder / Over, sideways and under." Jasmine's only role is to be suitably awed.

Although more active and adventurous than earlier princesses, Ariel and Jasmine are similarly motivated by a dream of romantic love, and they achieve it through the specialness of their internal and external beauty. Like *The Little Mermaid*, *Aladdin* suggests that the ultimate adventure is traditional romance, and that marriage equals freedom (an equation far less reliable in real life than in fairy tales). Indeed, the general concept of "family" is never subverted in a Disney film; even daughters' rebellions against parents are ultimately negated and resolved. Through young men's brave deeds, royal fathers finally approve their daughters' previously forbidden romances. This obliterates each princess's need to subvert paternal authority; she can achieve her goal and still be an obedient daughter, without having to choose one over the other.

These patterns make it difficult to categorize Disney Princesses of the 1990s as exemplars of self-determination. Even the heroine of *Pocahontas* (1995) is motivated by her love for Captain Smith and by her bond with her father, Chief Powhatan. Romantic love is least apparent (but not wholly absent) in *Mulan* (1998), whose heroine frustrates her family by lacking the poise to make a good traditional wife. She is, however, a perfectly devoted daughter: sacrificing her own safety, she disguises herself as a man to take her elderly father's place in a war. Mulan fights nobly and emerges triumphant. In the film's final moments she is embraced by her proud father, and the hint of a future romance arrives in the form of a suitor who had previously fought beside Mulan on the battlefield.

Surveying the post-1989 princess films, we can see that Disney expanded its traditional definition of feminine "goodness" to include new qualities, while not jettisoning the older ones. No longer patient, meek, or obedient, latter-day princesses have strong desires and act upon them. But they still display traditional feminine goodness: selflessness, loyalty to parents, and a desire—or at least a willingness—to find true love with a man. Moreover, it is seldom the princess's conscious decisions or actions that secure her final outcome. Ultimately, a Disney princess's ability to "transform" relies on her essential goodness, which motivates the more potent actions and choices of others.

In later years, Disney departed further from traditions with *Tangled* (2010), *Brave* (2012), and *Frozen* (2013), which feature highly assertive princesses. Princess Merida of *Brave* is especially refreshing as a high-tempered and competitive archer who is rude to her mother, and determined to avoid an arranged marriage. After a hot family quarrel, Merida uses the services of a witch to turn her infuriating mother into a bear. Ultimately, Merida finds her happy ending through reconciliation with her re-humanized mother. Female bonds and independence, not romance, were the ultimate messages of *Brave*.

But Disney deserves scant credit for this Merida, who was created by the artists at Pixar Animation Studios, a subsidiary of Disney with their own roster of non-princessy heroines in such films as *Toy Story* (1995) and *The Incredibles* (2004). When Merida officially joined the stable of Disney Princesses in 2013, her image was changed to match Disney's Princess template: all the signifiers of female independence and fighting-spirit that had made *Brave* a success were softened or erased, replaced with a more sexualized image. No longer holding her bow and arrow, the Disney Princess Merida also sports an hourglass-figure (smaller waist, larger breasts), tamer hair, eye-makeup, and a "come hither" expression. This Merida raised ire and eyebrows among American consumers, who launched a petition at Change.org that garnered over 200,000 signatures. Disney refused to discard its sexed-up Merida, instead assuring the public that some of their Merida merchandise would continue to use her original image (Blake 2013).

Indeed, merchandising reveals what matters most in the "Disney Princess" lifestyle-brand: a glance at Disney's online store shows that the least sexualized and least romantically oriented princesses, Mulan and Pocahontas, have the fewest products in their likeness. Even the few that exist are not widely distributed; the websites of

Target and Walmart, two of America's largest national retailers, offer broad arrays of Disney Princess trinkets but virtually none with a Mulan or Pocahontas theme. At the other end of the spectrum, the princess with the greatest amount of widely available merchandise is—not surprisingly—the one who most iconically represents fairy-tale romance: Cinderella. More than fifty years after its release as a Disney film, *Cinderella* remains the most resonant and widely recognized package of "princess" signifiers in the world. The story of Cinderella (which has hundreds of variants in the folklores of numerous countries) has been adapted to more films, stage productions, and television movies than any other fairy tale, appearing in silent films as early as 1898 (Internet Movie Database), long before the creation of Walt Disney Studios. In the public imagination, Cinderella represents the definitive princess tale.

The most famous version of Cinderella, and the one upon which Disney based its film, was written by Charles Perrault, a seventeenth-century French courtier. His heroine, unlike that of the Brothers Grimm (and other versions), does nothing to choose her own transformation; her happy ending is guaranteed entirely by intrinsic specialness. Not royal by birth, she nonetheless comes from a distinguished family; her father is "a gentleman" (Perrault, 534). She thus has the benefit of high birth that marks her as special. Perrault enhances the importance of bloodline by describing Cinderella as having "rare goodness and sweetness of temper, which she took from her mother, who was the best creature in the world" (534). When Cinderella is left behind while her cruel, ugly stepsisters go to the royal ball, a Fairy Godmother appears out of thin air to provide Cinderella's transformation. All Cinderella needs to do is follow orders and pick a pumpkin from the garden.

At the ball, Cinderella turns heads and mesmerizes the Prince with her beauty. Encountering her stepsisters, who do not recognize her, Cinderella shows her *internal* beauty—her inherited "sweetness of temper"—by treating them kindly. The delicious possibilities of tormenting these mean girls do not cross Cinderella's sweet mind; she does not need to make a choice. At the tale's climax, when the prince seeks the girl who fits the glass slipper, the most important signifier of Cinderella's identity becomes the shape of her foot—something she did not choose. Thus, the most iconic fairy-tale princess of all deserves and receives her glorious transformation simply by being her natural self. Identity need not be laboriously built with our bare hands; it's guaranteed by our bare foot. It is Destiny.

## The Power of the Self in Teen-Witch Tales

The power of the essential self is equally central in stories of young witches, although teen-witch tales place a slightly greater emphasis on the importance of choice. Their heroines sometimes must choose between moral rights and wrongs, giving self-reflexivity and consciousness a role in determining the girls' outcomes. But the thing that fundamentally makes teen witches special, their magical power, is not the result of choice; like the princesses' specialness, it is inborn.

In genre, *Sabrina the Teenage Witch* is closer to princess-tales than to other teen-witch tales. True to its origins as a member of the Archie Comics family, the *Sabrina* series traffics in goofy humor rather than horror. It is a "family show," intended for audiences that include the consumers of Disney Princess media. Its protagonist, Sabrina Spellman, is a sunny-natured girl who lives with her father's sisters. On her sixteenth birthday, Sabrina's aunts watch with sentimental joy as their sleeping niece levitates off the bed; this is the mark of initiation, the moment that happens to all witches on their sixteenth birthdays. Like puberty, sleeping levitation is an uncontrollable biological event that marks a girl's passage from child to young woman/witch. As with Sleeping Beauty and Snow White, Sabrina's transformation occurs while she lies in a physical state that precludes conscious will or choice.

The following morning the Spellman aunts have "the talk" with Sabrina, telling her that she, and all her father's side of the family, are witches. Sabrina now has new powers and responsibilities, and she will have to study hard to earn her witch's license. Throughout the series, Sabrina's efforts often lead to foolish mistakes (as in the pilot episode, where she accidentally turns a mean girl into a pineapple). The consequences of these errors teach Sabrina valuable lessons and, because the Spellman family is cheerful and morally good, Sabrina learns her lessons with grace, becoming more adept and mature as the series continues. But although her journey includes choice-making and self-discipline, Sabrina's magic itself is a genetic trait shared by the close-knit Spellman family. In an interview with *The New York Times*, actress Melissa Joan Hart, who played Sabrina, said that the series' ultimate message is to "be yourself" (Gerston 1996). As with Disney's Princesses, the natural self is powerful and good.

In the film *The Craft*, nature is also the key to goodness. Its heroine, Sarah, is a lonely girl who moves to Los Angeles with her father and stepmother (her mother died in childbirth). As "the new girl" at her Catholic school, Sarah is soon noticed by a trio of girls who are also outsiders: Bonnie, whose back is covered with scars from an unnamed accident; Rochelle, an African-American taunted by racists; and Nancy, who lives in poverty with a "white trash" family, as Rochelle calls them. Victimized by popular kids, these three misfits embrace witchcraft to gain power. But their coven is incomplete; to do the biggest spells, they need a fourth witch. They bring Sarah into their group, discovering that she—who never studied "the craft" before—seems to have more skill than they. "A natural witch," Bonnie beams, thrilled that their protégé is such a prodigy. The group takes her to a local magic shop where Lirio, the wise proprietress, explains that magic is neither white nor black; good or evil exists only in the witch, herself.

Soon the young witches are powerful enough to effect their wills. At first, the film offers a fantasy of exhilarating "girl power" as they make their dreams come true, exacting some revenge in the process. Sarah turns a boy who mistreated her into a love-stricken fool. Rochelle makes a racist blonde classmate lose her hair. Bonnie makes her scars disappear. Nancy, the angriest and most intense of the group, casts a more ambitious spell: wanting to erase her lowly, "white trash" status, Nancy causes a fire to consume the hovel where she lives with her constantly fighting mother and stepfather. The brutish stepfather dies, leaving Nancy and her mother a life-insurance policy that lets them live in luxury. Because Nancy is rageful and has "trashy" genes, her spell manifests through horror. Lirio was right: the true self will out.

As Nancy casts larger and more dangerous spells, it is Sarah—the only "natural witch," and the only one with a Biblical name—who rejects the mounting violence. She leaves the coven, drawing the other girls' wrath. Turning to Lirio for counsel, Sarah discovers that her own dead mother had also been a witch. Armed with the knowledge that her magic is a birthright from a good woman, and is therefore stronger, Sarah faces her enemies for the film's climactic fight. When Sarah is injured and lies near death, the spirit of her dead mother whispers that Sarah must reach inside herself to find her power. Sarah then rallies and ultimately beats her foes, proving that the best power is wielded only by she who always already had it.

The girls who *acquire* magic have less positive outcomes. Bonnie and Rochelle lose their powers as a consequence of abusing them, and return to their humdrum lives. But Nancy, consumed by a level of fury that is truly "special," goes insane. The final scene shows her in a mental institution, screaming and struggling against a straitjacket. The morals of the story are clear: in order to be good, magical power must be inborn. Like Snow White, special by virtue of the fairness her mother wished for her, and like Cinderella, whose "rare sweetness" comes from her mother, Sarah's specialness is a maternal legacy.

The link between power and heredity appears most distinctly in the series *Charmed.* Sisters Prudence, Piper, and Phoebe Halliwell suddenly learn that they are witches who descend from a long line of magical women extending back to seventeenth-century Salem, Massachusetts. In the series' pilot episode, "Something Wicca This Way Comes," Phoebe researches the family history and explains:

> One of our ancestors was a witch named Melinda Warren. [...] Before Melinda was burned at the stake, she vowed that each generation of Warren witches would become

> stronger and stronger, culminating in the arrival of three sisters. These sisters would be the most powerful witches the world has ever known. They're good witches, and I think we're those sisters. We're the protectors of the innocent. We're known as The Charmed Ones. (Burge 1998)

As the fruition of a prophecy or wish, and as the inheritors of maternal gifts, the Halliwell sisters resemble Disney's classic princesses. By virtue of their matriarch's spell, they are special not only *as* witches, but *among* witches; they alone have the power to protect innocents and vanquish demons.

Phoebe's speech blithely ignores historical facts, for the women (and men) who were hanged (not burned) at Salem were not actually witches. But the erroneous stereotype serves to strengthen the dramatic goal of the *Charmed* pilot, providing a genetic origin for the girls' powers and establishing the centrality of female inheritance to the series' themes. The importance of bloodline remains prominent throughout the series' eight-season run; on several occasions the Halliwells are visited by the spirits of their dead mother, grandmother, and other female relatives from past generations. The three sisters make many decisions over the years about their jobs and their relationships, two of the choices named by David Gauntlett, quoted earlier, that construct our identities in late modernity. But neither the girls' careers nor their relationships, while important as sub-plots, form the center of their lives. That center lies in their genetic bonds to each other and to their maternal ancestry.

Among the teen-witch media characters of the 1990s, the only exception to the message of heredity is Willow Rosenberg in *Buffy the Vampire Slayer*. She begins to study witchcraft in the second season, gradually becoming more adept over time. Although naturally sweet, Willow has realistic weaknesses that negatively affect her use of magic. In the series' sixth season, Willow becomes addicted to magic as if to a drug; like all addicts, she alienates her loved ones and must undergo a process of withdrawal and recovery. But she relapses at the end of that season, when her lover is accidentally killed by a stray bullet. Shattered by grief and rage, Willow takes destructive powers from the darkest books of magic. After wreaking bloody vengeance on her lover's killer, Willow attempts to destroy the world. Then once again, more painfully than before, she must endure the harrowing toil of rehabilitation. Through this ordeal, Willow transforms herself back into a loving, healthy being.

More than other teen-witch tales, and far more than any Disney film, *Buffy* gives self-reflexive choice a major role in the construction of the self as "good." But even here, some forces beyond choice are at work. Although the series separates magic from DNA, it still requires an innate talent that not everyone has. In the episode "I Robot, You Jane," a woman who knows something about magic is asked if she's a witch; she demurs, saying "I don't have that kind of power. 'Technopagan' is the term" (Gable and Swyden 1997). Thus, although witchcraft can be studied like any craft, Willow's ability to excel at what she studies depends on an inborn gift. Moreover, the series' main protagonist, Buffy Summers, has super-human powers as The Slayer through mystical forces beyond her control. The Slayer is known as "The Chosen One"—not the one who chooses. Choice affects only how a girl uses her specialness, not the existence of the specialness itself.

## Identity: Fantasy vs. Reality

The power of fantasy lies in its ability to ignite the desire of consumers to identify with, to *be like,* princess and witch heroines. The previously quoted lines from Disney Consumer Products sum it up, noting that "feeling special" is the commodity they sell through their Princess lifestyle brand. In a late-modern world where we have taught children that they are special, and have infinite potential to be anything they want to be, the line between fantasy and reality is already blurred. Why not "become" a princess or a witch, those paragons of specialness?

Particularly in the case of millennial teen-witches, fantasy and reality had a widely discussed mutual impact on each other. Upon its release, *The Craft* launched a wave of interest in the Wiccan religion among teenagers (despite the fact that the film's special-effects "magic" bears scant resemblance to what actual Wiccans do). As Berger and Ezzy note (2007), Wicca had already been on the rise in the US since the post-WWII years, attractive especially to younger adults as a less judgmental, less rigid belief-system than traditional Christianity. As the twentieth century drew to a close, Wicca and Paganism drew more interest from teenagers. The teen-witch trend in popular media added fuel to this religious trend, launching a spate of mass-market books catering to the aspiring teenage witch. Numerous websites sprang up enabling global connections between far-flung practitioners.

Some observers found media-witches irksome in their impact on real-life Wiccan communities. Wiccan writer Peg Aloi notes that the narratives' emphasis on genealogy had an unfortunate effect on the identity-constructions of newcomers to Wicca:

> [*Charmed*] posits a heredity-based witchcraft that only encourages naïve viewers and witch wannabes to fabricate their own dubious claims to non-existent lineage. The three Charmed Ones are 'natural witches' (a term also used in *The Craft* to denote innate psychic ability—the term soon became popular among teen-aged seekers, too, and was found through web discussion groups and teen witchcraft pages at the time) who are connected to witchcraft through their matriarchal line. (Aloi, 62)

Christians, meanwhile, found their own cause for concern in the teen witches' influence on young consumers' identities. Disturbed by late modernity's assaults on tradition, Fundamentalist and Evangelical Christians became socially vocal and politically powerful after the 1970s; in the 1990s, numerous Christian groups produced books, websites, and activist campaigns to protect Christian values against the rising tide of threats in American culture. Simultaneously, the secular news media of the 1980s–1990s began increasingly to report a supposed rise of Satanism among American youth. Termed "the Satanic Panic" by sociologists, this fear far outstripped reality, as all moral panics do.[5] The Satanic Panic found new fuel in the rise of teen-witch media. Christian critics lambasted *The Craft*, *Buffy*, *Charmed*, and even the fluffy *Sabrina* for suggesting that any kind of witch can be "good." To this day, long after those texts have left our screens, one can still find critiques of their ungodly messages on several websites.[6]

While conservative Americans worried about the influence of witch-fantasies on teenagers' identities, only feminists seemed worried about what children learned from princess-fantasies.[7] Witch-fearing conservatives often championed the wholesome "family entertainment" of Disney as better fare for young minds. It's no surprise that conservatives did not share feminists' concerns; more surprising was their failure to note that the logics of Disney Princess tales actually refute some of the right-wing's other beloved values, like a traditional work-ethic. Only a thin line separates "specialness" from entitlement; in fairy tales, one always leads to the other. As we saw earlier, the message of intrinsic specialness in princess tales was simultaneously echoed in the educational philosophies that shaped today's young adults when they were children. As the millennial generation (born in the '80s and '90s) came of age, observers began to decry their attitudes of entitlement and their obsession with themselves. Writing for *TIME* magazine about "The ME ME ME Generation," Joel Stein reports:

> The incidence of narcissistic personality disorder is nearly three times as high for people in their 20s as for the generation that's now 65 or older, according to the National Institutes of Health; 58% more college students scored higher on a narcissism scale in 2009 than in 1982. Millennials got so many participation trophies growing up that a recent study showed that 40% believe they should be promoted every two years, regardless of performance. [...] They're so convinced of their own greatness that the National Study of Youth and Religion found the guiding morality of 60% of millennials in any situation is that they'll just be able to feel what's right. (Stein 2013, 28)

That last point should make any conservative Christian nervous; God has been replaced by personal hunches, which apparently are never wrong. (How could they be, when the inner self is always omnipotent, as fantasy tales tell us?) Stein's comment about "participation trophies" points to the movement in American schools toward hollow self-esteem boosting. Perhaps twenty years of teaching children songs like "I Am Special" might not have been such a great idea.[8]

Academic achievement and job performance are not the only realms to reveal flaws in the messages of intrinsic specialness; consumer debt has become a problem for many millennials as well, showing a link to the Disney fantasy of wealth ("clothes spun of silk and gold") as the marker of specialness. A Canadian reality-TV program, *Princess* (2010–2012), shows what can happen when real women adopt the princess fantasy for their identities.[9] In each episode, financial consultant Gail Vaz-Oxlade helps families driven to the edge of bankruptcy by their resident "princess"—a young woman who spends outrageously on luxuries, using her beleaguered loved-ones' money to support this "royal" lifestyle. Some of these young women freely admit that they feel entitled to be supported by others, past the age of legal adulthood, because they're so innately special and lovable. In every episode, the hardest lesson for these women to grasp is that they must abandon, once and for all, the unsustainable project of living in a fantasy world. Undoing years of conditioning is no easy task.

In one episode, "Princess Daniela" is so identified with Disney princesses that she expects her humbly middle-class parents to spend $34,000 on her princess-themed wedding, complete with a horse-drawn "Cinderella coach." But Vaz-Oxlade treats her subjects more like Sleeping Beauties than Cinderellas, giving each the harsh awakening of a crash-course in financial responsibility. Like most of Vaz-Oxlade's princesses, Daniela comes to realize that fleeting luxuries are not worth a lifetime of debt; she "transforms" into a higher state of being by the end of the process. Unlike Disney's fictional heroines, whose transformations usually come through the agency of others, Vaz-Oxlade's princesses must transform *themselves* through personal effort and difficult choices.

That this show has a ready supply of participants, and drew a sufficient audience to warrant multiple seasons, suggests that the princess syndrome is widely enacted and widely irritating. The economic crisis of the late 2000s surely helped sour people's taste for materialistic post-adolescents who use fantasy logic in real life. But it doesn't take a global disaster to make the princess "lifestyle brand" an illegitimate lifestyle for most women. Ironically, it might have been better if the spoiled brats of *Princess* had studied Disney's films more closely: for all their reliance on traditional gender codes, the saving grace of Disney princesses is that none of them is spoiled or narcissistic. Their stories construct them as special and entitled, but the princesses never see themselves that way. Each of them—even the fractious Merida of *Brave*—can, when necessary, put others' well-being ahead of her own desires. But a young woman who is entranced with the trappings of "specialness" sold through Disney's merchandising, and with the further messages of girl power (getting what you really, really want), can become a monster. A girl who demands her way, regardless of the consequences for others, is more like a Disney witch than a princess. Indeed, narcissism is the fatal flaw of the wicked queen in *Snow White*, who gazes into her magic mirror every day to confirm her superiority—and who becomes murderous when it's threatened.

Of course, not all girls who identify with princesses turn into such witchy creatures. Plenty of princess-loving girls grew up to be responsible, hard-working, and considerate of others. And, as ample evidence has shown, consumers can and do selectively subvert the messages of the texts they consume. By the same token, many teens who identified with media-witches did not attempt to master any dark arts; most did not even become life-long committed Wiccans. Contrary to popular fears, the media do not "make" children be anything, because people do not uniformly take the same inspirations from the same texts. The wide array of interpretive options inherent in any story precludes our assuming that fictional figures will affect viewers in any fixed way.

It is, however, useful to study which story elements are repeated most consistently and most frequently across a genre. In the case of girls' millennial fantasy tales, the most consistent theme is one of intrinsic specialness, and the inevitable success to which the morally good, "natural" self is entitled. Because the effects of princess/witch tales are variable, my purpose here is not to claim that one figure is necessarily superior to the other (though I admit a personal preference for those hard-working witches). Rather, my point lies in the paradox of how such figures function. As commodities that exemplify "girl power," the princesses and witches of popular culture are offered as choices for identification and inspiration, in a cultural context where one can choose to be anything she wants. Yet at the same time, the appeal of these fantasies lies in their tropes of an inborn, pre-conscious specialness that erases a heroine's need to choose her identity at all. In a postmodern world where identity is a social construct, Essentialism has become our favorite fantasy for the young.

## Endnotes

1. The series moved to the WB network in 2000 and ultimately ran for seven seasons.
2. I omit Hermione Granger, of the *Harry Potter* series, because her character is less developed than the others included here, most of whom (unlike Hermione) are the lead protagonists of their narratives. The only secondary character considered here is Willow Rosenberg, from the *Buffy* series, who is portrayed with more personal development than is Hermione.

3. For an analysis of this phenomenon, see Rebecca Hains, *Growing Up with Girl Power* (New York: Peter Lang Publishing, 2012).
4. The Brothers Grimm kept it simpler: "Wild beasts hovered around her at times, but they did her no harm" (Tatar, 245).
5. See especially Jeffrey S. Victor, *Satanic Panic: The Creation of a Contemporary Legend* (Chicago: Open Court Publishing, 1993).
6. See, for example, the television and film reviews at the Christian Answers Network (http://www.christiananswers.net).
7. One notable example is Peggy Orenstein's humorous and thoughtful critique, *Cinderella Ate My Daughter* (2011).
8. Even educators have begun to notice the problem. A headline in the *Washington Post* tells us that "In schools, self-esteem boosting is losing favor to rigor" (Chandler 2012).
9. *Princess* airs in the US on the CNBC cable channel.

## Bibliography

Aloi, Peg. 2005. "Enchanté…Not." In *Totally Charmed,* ed. Jennifer Crusie. Dallas [TX]: BenBella Books, Inc., 2005.

Berger, Helen A., and Douglas Ezzy. 2007. *Teenage Witches: Magical Youth and the Search for the Self.* New Brunswick [NJ]: Rutgers University Press.

Blake, Meredith. 2013. "Jon Stewart slams Disney's makeover of 'Brave' heroine Merida." *Los Angeles Times,* May 17.

Burge, Constance M. 1998. "Something Wicca This Way Comes." *Charmed.* WB Network, October 7.

Chandler, Michael Alison. 2012. "In schools, self-esteem boosting loses favor to rigor, finer-tuned praise." *Washington Post,* January 15.

Child Care Lounge. 2010. "I Am Special Themes and Activities." http://www.childcarelounge.com/general-themes/i-am-.php

Clark, Lynn Schofield. 2003. *From Angels to Aliens: Teenagers, the Media, and the Supernatural.* New York: Oxford University Press.

Davis, Amy M. 2006. *Good Girls and Wicked Witches: Women in Disney's Feature Animation.* New Barnet, Hertfordshire [UK]: John Libbey Publishing, Ltd.

Disney Consumer Products. 2008. "Disney Princess." https://www.disneyconsumerproducts.com/Home/display.jsp?contentId=dcp_home_ourfranchises_disney_princess_uk&forPrint=false&language=en&preview=false&imageShow=0&pressRoom=UK&translationOf=®ion=0

Gable, Ashley and Thomas A. Swyden. 1997. "I, Robot…You, Jane." *Buffy the Vampire Slayer.* WB Network, April 28.

Gauntlett, David. 2008. *Media, Gender and Identity,* 2nd edition. Abingdon, Oxon [UK]: Routledge.

Gerston, Jill. 1996. "A Normal Kid with Magical Powers." *The New York Times,* October 6.

Ghirardelli, Paolo. 2000. "Educational Theory: Herbart, Dewey, Freire and Postmodernists." *The Encyclopaedia of Educational Philosophy*, eds. Michael A. Peters, Paolo Ghirardelli, Berislav Žarnić, and Andrew Gibbons. http://www.ffst.hr/ENCYCLOPAEDIA/doku.php?id=educational_theory

Hains, Rebecca C. 2012.*Growing Up with Girl Power*. New York: Peter Lang Publishing.

The Internet Movie Database. http://www.imdb.com.

Orenstein, Peggy. 2011. *Cinderella Ate My Daughter: Dispatches from the Front Lines of the New Girlie-Girl Culture.* New York: HarperCollins Publishers.

Perrault, Charles. 2007. "Cinderella." (C. Welsh, Trans.) In *Crosscurrents of Children's Literature*, eds. J. D. Stahl, T. L. Hanlon, & E. L. Keyser, 534–537. New York: Oxford University Press.

Stein, Joel. 2013. "The ME ME ME Generation." *TIME*. May 20, 26–34.

Tatar, Maria (ed.). 2004. *The Annotated Brothers Grimm*. New York: W. W. Norton & Co.

Victor, Jeffrey S. 1993. *Satanic Panic: The Creation of a Contemporary Legend.* Chicago: Open Court Publishing.

Zipes, Jack. 1999. "Breaking the Disney Spell." In *Classic Fairy Tales,* ed. Maria Tatar, *332–352.* New York: W. W. Norton & Company.

CHAPTER TWO

# Applying for the Position of Princess: Race, Labor, and the Privileging of Whiteness in the Disney Princess Line

MEGAN CONDIS

Princesses have become ubiquitous in popular culture products aimed at girls. And while it is true that princesses have always had a place in the medium of animation (according to Amy Davis [2007], the first woman ever to be featured in an animated cartoon was the Princess of Slumberland in the animated adaptation of Windsor McKay's popular comic strip, *Little Nemo in Dreamland*), the new millennium finds audiences drowning in tulle and tiaras. Thrones and scepters are being added to nearly every girl-friendly franchise on the toy store shelves, from Barbie to Dora the Explorer, the formerly "intrepid, dirty-kneed adventurer" who now occasionally sports a "satin gown" and "hair that grows or shortens when her crown is touched" (Orenstein 2006, para. 8). And, of course, there is the fairest franchise of them all: the Disney Princess line, whose more than 40,000 pink and purple products (Giroux and Pollock 2010) earn billions for the Disney corporation. In the wake of this royal blitz it is important for media scholars to examine the ways in which animated princesses help to shape (and are shaped by) discourses of gender and race. After all, these products market princesshood as the ultimate distillation of perfect femininity that good girls dream about. Therefore, it is important to consider whether or not all little girls can access that dream in the same way. In the case of the Disney Princess line, the machine is designed to sell the princess lifestyle (and the toys, Halloween costumes, ice show tickets, and DVDs that attend it) to young girls. This chapter seeks to answer the following:

How is that lifestyle imagined differently for white girls and for little princesses of color? How does the Disney Princess line teach audiences about what it is that their gendered, racialized bodies are capable of achieving within the princessly framework of desirable femininity? I contend that, in keeping with historical patterns of gendered, racialized, and classed divisions of labor in which upper-class white women were expected to refrain from working while poor women of color were often forced to work outside the home to ensure their family's survival (Glenn 1985), the Disney Princess line presents two mirror images of the ideal imagined relationship between women and work. White princesses are seen to have fulfilled the requirements of attaining a perfect, princessly femininity when they are *relieved* of the need to work while princesses of color are portrayed as being glad to continue working even after they've reached their happy ending.

I contend that the assembly of these separate figures into a single franchise encourages consumers to compare each vision of princesshood with the others, to "shop around" for a princess they like, or perhaps for a princess *like them*. The Disney Princess product line (literally) draws together eleven racially and culturally diverse princesses (Snow White, Cinderella, Aurora, Ariel, Belle, Jasmine, Pocahontas, Mulan, Tiana, Rapunzel, and Merida; Elsa and Anna are also expected to join the official line-up) into one franchise that seems, at first glance, to embody the progressive notion that *any* little girl, regardless of her race or class, can dream of someday becoming a princess (Disney 2013). But not all princesses are created equal, and "the mere presence of any group or person" at the princesses' table "does not mean that a group or person participates equally, enjoys the same privileges, or exercises the same degree of power" (Breaux 2010, 400). A comparative close reading of the Princess films that focuses on labor and racial representation reveals the limitations that are placed upon the destinies of princesses of color. The Disney Princess films create two contrasting images of femininity: White princesshood can only be obtained/maintained through the labor of others. Princesses of color are self-made, simultaneously empowered by their own competence and ambition even as they are kept from experiencing the upper-class luxuries and privileges that come when one is wealthy enough to stop working. While Disney's definition of princesshood initially seems to be welcoming to girls of all races, it actually sorts its aspirants into different categories. Thus, while the gestures toward diversification in the Disney Princess line seem designed to allow the Disney corporation to reassure its audience that the company philosophy is inclusive and progressive, the texts of the Disney Princess films continue to imagine what it means to be a "good girl" differently, depending on the racial identity of the girl.

## Introduction: The Disney Princess Line

The Disney Princesses first appeared together in 2000 after Andy Mooney was hired to reverse the, at the time, steadily dropping sales of the Disney Consumer Products division. Peggy Orenstein (2006) describes Mooney's pixie-dust-filled moment of inspiration as follows:

> It was about a month after Mooney's arrival that the magic struck. That's when he flew to Phoenix to check out his first "Disney on Ice" show. "Standing in line in the arena, I was surrounded by little girls dressed head to toe as princesses," he told me last summer in his palatial office, then located in Burbank, and speaking in a rolling Scottish burr. "They weren't even Disney products. They were generic princess products they'd appended to a Halloween costume. And the light bulb went off. Clearly there was latent demand here. So the next morning I said to my team, 'O.K., let's establish standards and a color palette and talk to licensees and get as much product out there as we possibly can that allows these girls to do what they're doing anyway: projecting themselves into the characters from the classic movies."

Mooney eventually selected eight representatives from Disney's large stable of female characters to serve as the first Disney Princesses: Snow White, Cinderella, Aurora, Ariel, Belle, Jasmine, Pocahontas (who is the daughter of a Native American chief, but not a "princess"; see Orin [2007] for more on the problematic nature of the term "Indian princess"), and Mulan (who was not born a princess and who never married a prince but who, apparently, has been given an honorary royal title for the purpose of increasing the diversity of the franchise). The eight became nine in 2010 when Tiana was inducted (Verrill 2010) following the release of *The Princess and the Frog* (2009) on DVD. Mooney's line represented "the first time Disney marketed characters separately from a film's release, let alone lumped together those from different stories," although "to ensure the sanctity of what Mooney called their individual 'mythologies,' the princesses never make eye contact when they're grouped: each stares off in a slightly different direction as if unaware of the others' presence" (Orenstein 2006). This unprecedented decision to group the princesses together did more than breathe new life into Disney's merchandising division. It also encouraged audiences to engage with the Disney Princesses in a new way: as a *class* of related characters (to which little girls were encouraged to aspire to join through role play and the purchasing power of their parents) rather than as individual role models.

However, while membership in the Disney Princess franchise has its perks, those perks are not the same for all members. On the contrary, the diversity of the line is the mechanism that allows for the differentiation of a white model of princesshood from a racialized model. In this case, the standards that define white femininity are crystallized through the presence of non-white princesses like Jasmine, Pocahontas, Mulan, and Tiana, whose violations of the principles of the behavior models of their predecessors articulate a boundary between traditional (white) princesshood and "alternative" (non-white) models. Rather than expanding a single, inclusive image of princesshood, the newer princesses mark the boundary line that defines the idealized cultural image of the white woman.

## Snow White, Cinderella, and Sleeping Beauty: Setting the Standards for White Women's Relationships to Labor

Snow White, Cinderella, and Princess Aurora (otherwise known as Sleeping Beauty) are the three oldest characters in the Disney Princess line. The films introducing these princesses to the public were all released during Walt Disney's lifetime, and so can be thought of as representative of the "classic" definition of princesshood within the Disney universe. This definition of princessly femininity is fairly narrow: Princesses must be beautiful, young, white women. In fact, their beauty must be so legendary that it inspires love and devotion from all good-hearted people and kindly animals who behold them. And they are not to sully that beauty by stooping to perform labor.

At first glance, my claim that princesses and labor do not mix might seem quixotic. After all, some of the most famous sequences from *Snow White and the Seven Dwarfs* (1937) and *Cinderella* (1950) feature the title characters scrubbing floors and cleaning house. However, a closer look at these two films reveals that labor is coded as a great injustice that must be endured by princesses because it has been thrust upon them by an evil villain. This injustice must ultimately be overcome through the actions of a prince who saves them from drudgery and restores their rightful place within a version of femininity defined through romance, leisure, and privilege.

During *Cinderella*'s introductory sequence, a song describes our heroine and her "proper place" in the world: a throne. The song implies that a princess belongs in a position of rest and leisure. Just by looking at her we should be able to see that she wasn't made to slave away at common household chores. To be fair, at the beginning of her story, Cinderella is not yet a princess. She is merely the daughter of a (deceased) nobleman. However, the song suggests that Cinderella's great beauty marks her as having a princessly destiny awaiting her. And yet, just like Snow White, she is afflicted by an evil stepmother, Lady Tremaine, who reduces her to rags and denies her the status that she is owed by virtue of her beauty. The narrator tells us that, after her father's death, "Cinderella was abused, humiliated, and finally forced to become a servant in her own house." The voiceover emphasizes this last as if to imply that this servitude (and not the abuse or humiliation) is the worst, most unjust development of them all.

The final princess from Walt Disney's lifetime takes this narrative (that labor is an evil that is inflicted upon a princess and that leisure is her rightful destiny) to an even further extreme. Princess Aurora of *Sleeping Beauty* (1959) spends the last third of her own movie in a catatonic state awaiting rescue from her prince. Before that, her story mirrors that of Snow White and Cinderella. She, too, is forced to adopt a peasant's life because of the unjust interference of an evil antagonist. The bad fairy Maleficent curses the newborn Princess Aurora with a terrible fate: At some time before her sixteenth birthday, Aurora will prick her finger on an instrument of labor, a spinning wheel, and die. Luckily for the royal family, three good fairies offer to work together to protect the princess from this awful fate. They use their magic to soften the effects of the curse, replacing instant death with an endless sleep from which the princess will awaken when she receives true love's kiss. They then volunteer to hide Aurora from Maleficent, whisking her away to the forest to live a peasant's life until she turns sixteen. Afraid that their nemesis will discover the ruse if she detects the use of good magic, the three good fairies forswear their wands and decide to raise Aurora as mortals would. This means that someone will actually have to do all of the physical labor required to run the household (childcare, cooking, cleaning, the procuring of food and water, etc.).

That someone is not Aurora, however. Although *Sleeping Beauty* follows *Snow White* and *Cinderella* in establishing the prospect of labor as an injustice that must be endured by a princess, Aurora is never actually shown performing any of the labor that Flora, Fauna, and Merryweather are so worried about in the absence of their magic wands. Instead, she spends her days strolling through the forest and regaling the local wildlife with her songs. She is never even depicted completing a lone chore that she is given by her caretakers in her sixteen years (Davis 2007). Indeed, as the title of her theme song, "Once Upon a Dream," suggests, Aurora is defined by rest and leisure.

Rebecca-Anne C. Do Rozario sums up the attitude taken by these early princess characters toward labor thusly: "Walt's princesses scrubbed and waited with boundless cheerful energy, knowing that these chores of their peasant past would be taken from them and they would again waltz into a regal future" (2004, 57). When considered together, Snow White, Cinderella, and Sleeping Beauty paint a fairly consistent picture of princessly femininity, one that wouldn't be challenged until long after Walt Disney's death in 1966, the end of the "classic" era of Disney animation, and the introduction of a new face in the Disney boardroom: that of Michael Eisner.

## Ariel and Belle: Adding Feminist Flavor to the Classic Recipe

When Michael Eisner became the new Chairman and Chief Executive Officer at Disney in 1984 (Davis 2007) he introduced some changes to the standard model of the Disney Princess. Luckily for the Mouse House, those changes would prove wildly popular. However, these changes did little to alter the established pattern that had grown up around labor, whiteness, and femininity in the classic Disney films. Janet Wasko writes that "especially for popular culture production, economic factors set limitations and exert pressures on the commodities that are produced (and influence what is not produced)" (2001, 29), and this is just as true of the Disney corporation as it is of any other producer of mass media. As Michael Eisner put it in a memo to his employees, "We have no obligation to make art. We have no obligation to make a statement. To make money is our only objective" (as quoted in Wasko 2001, 28). This means that although media corporations are able to powerfully influence public opinion, they must be flexible enough to adapt in the face of political upheavals in order to ensure that their products continue to hold mass appeal. In Disney's case, the need to appear "apolitical" by reflecting broadly popular, "all-American" political sentiments in its films is paramount to ensuring that it continues to reign supreme as the source of what it markets as wholesome, innocent family entertainments. At the same time, its new films must retain some continuity with the classic Disney films of the past, both to ensure continued brand recognition over time and to evoke nostalgia in purchasing parents who grew up watching films from Uncle Walt and want to give their own children a moviegoing experience that mimics those from their own youth. The Disney corporation had a fine line to walk. It needed to "trace" over the popular template of the past, the classic Disney Princess, retaining its familiar contours (both in terms of the physical appearance of new characters and in terms of the shape of their stories) while simultaneously downplaying the aspects of those texts that had drawn criticism for being antiquated or politically incorrect. As Elizabeth Bell argues, even Disney's first animated women were already

> pentimentos, paintings layered upon paintings, images drawn on images, in a cultural accumulation of representations of good girls, bad women, and doting servants. The first layer of the pentimento, the folktale templates of Perrault, the Grimms, and Andersen, can be punned and dismissed as painted cyphers ... but as the painting accrues, with layers of contemporaneous film and popular images of women, live-action models for the characters, and cinematic conventions for representing women, the levels become increasingly coded and complex. (1995, 108–109)

Eisner's princesses, Ariel from *The Little Mermaid* (1989) and Belle from *Beauty and the Beast* (1991), merely added yet another layer, building upon the models of princesshood that came before while simultaneously obscuring some obsolete ideas about gender roles with a fresh coat of post-feminist pop culture paint.

Feminist critics had derided Walt's princesses for their passivity, arguing that *Snow White*, *Cinderella*, and *Sleeping Beauty* taught little girls to wait patiently for a prince to rescue them from their problems rather than going out and finding happiness themselves (see, as an example, Stone 1975). So, when Disney's first new princess of the Eisner era, Ariel from *The Little Mermaid*, was introduced in 1989, she was given a much more active persona and featured a personality that was "less prim, more democratic" (Do Rozario 2004, 45) and "more assertive," demonstrating "more agency" (King, Lugo-Lugo, and Bloodsworth-Lugo 2010, 95) than her predecessors. Shortly thereafter *Beauty and the Beast* (1991) gave us Belle, a "down to earth girl" (Craven 2002, 124) full of "feistiness" and "graceful, perky fighting spirit" (Craven 2002, 129) who could be perceived as "a bit of a feminist" (Craven 2002, 124) owing to her rejection of her forthrightly sexist suitor, Gaston. Marina Warner writes that the bookish Belle seemed purposefully "developed … for an audience of mothers who grew up with Betty Friedan and Gloria Steinem" (1994, 313). Unfortunately, much of this praise is, upon reflection, overwrought. Spunky though they might be, Ariel and Belle are quite similar to Snow White, Cinderella, and Princess Aurora.

For example, in *The Little Mermaid*, as in *Snow White*, *Cinderella*, and *Sleeping Beauty*, the idea that Ariel might have to perform labor is rejected as unfair and unjust. In a new twist, it is Ariel herself who complains that this is so, as she rebels against her father by skipping out on her job as a singer in a royal concert. Ariel rejects this labor to seek out her own leisurely pastimes, collecting the objects discarded by landlubbers and dreaming about someday living up on the land with her prince, Eric. Her rebellious attitude toward her father is a new development for a princess character, but the outcome of that rebellion puts her squarely into the slippers of previous princesses. She uses her considerable spunk to reject labor and to assert her right to pursue a hobby instead. And of course, at the end of the film, her father learns that he was wrong to expect her to work as a representative of the merfolk government, and he sets her free to follow her heart's desire: a leisurely life of romance on the land.

In *Beauty and the Beast*, Belle's relationship to labor is also reminiscent of the classic princesses, despite the fact that she begins the story as a mere peasant girl. Eleanor Bryne and Martin McQuillan are correct when they write that *Beauty and the Beast* revolves around the issue of domestic labor. They argue that it is "a film 'about' an economy of hospitality and hospitality as an economy" (Bryne and McQuillan 1999, 95). But Belle's place in that economy is not clear-cut. For a member of a family that is supposed to be struggling financially, Belle does very little to contribute to the survival of her household. Her father, Maurice, works to maintain their standard of living with his inventions, despite the acrimony of the townsfolk. But Belle does little more than swan around reading her beloved books (the ones feminist critics were so happy to see her reading) and complaining that the boring provincial life of the locals is beneath her. Even her righteous rejection of the noxious Gaston is couched as a rejection of the domestic labor that a marriage to him would foist on her.

As with her predecessors, Belle's initiation into labor is perceived as an injustice that has been thrust on her. When her father is captured by the imposing Beast, Belle bravely sacrifices her own freedom to take his place. While trapped in his castle, Belle becomes familiar with the curse that has condemned all of its residents to be trapped in inhuman bodies. Her job is to tame the Beast, turning him into an object worthy of love and therefore enabling the breaking of the curse. However, Belle's highly praised feminist feistiness enables her to reject that job at first. It is only after an organic, unforced (read: unlabored) relationship has begun to blossom between the two of them that Belle begins to teach the Beast civilized behavior via polite dinners and ballroom dancing. In other words, according to the romantic logic of the film, it is only once their relationship ceases to require work on the part of its participants (sustained as it is by the magic of True Love) that Belle will participate.

## Jasmine: A Liminal Case

In 1992, Disney's *Aladdin* continued and extended the feminist reframing begun in *The Little Mermaid* and *Beauty and the Beast*. *Aladdin*'s Princess Jasmine is also the first of several princess vehicles to feature a woman of color. This newfound commitment to diversity was triggered by the same types of market forces that encouraged the company to embrace pop feminism in the late 1980s. By adding diversity to its stable of animated characters, Disney simultaneously deflected criticism from liberals and activists by "drawing over" the racist mistakes of its past, replacing racist caricatures in films like *Song of the South* (1946) and *Fantasia* (1940) with what it believed were positive role models for young girls of color (see Terry 2010 and Breaux 2010), and opened up new markets for Disney merchandise:

> As Disney brought white American children (and their parents) to the movie theaters to see its various appropriations of nineteenth-century European folktales ... it uses a similar strategy to effect a multicultural, even multinational, appeal. Disney's appropriations

> in the 1990s were especially daring and controversial; the cultural territories of Arab folklore in *Aladdin* (1992), . . . have been reconstituted and sanitized to draw in a much larger portion of the children's market. Disney's move in the right direction might at first seem a worthy, even admirable, endeavor, no matter what the motivation (i.e., that a multicultural agenda is just good business). (Hines and Ayers 2003, 4)

At first glance, Princess Jasmine seems to confound the logic of racialized gender roles inscribed by the previous five Disney Princess films. Jasmine lives a life of leisure unmatched by that of previous princesses. She never faces a villain who unjustly thrusts her into the labor pool. In fact, she complains that her life behind the palace walls is so peaceful and stress free that it has become boring. She escapes into the local market disguised as a commoner to seek some excitement, and her naïve behavior on the city streets and her complete lack of familiarity with the basics of commerce (she is unaware that she has to produce a coin for the apple that she takes from a vendor's stall and gives to a local street urchin) prove that she has never before had to contemplate life without the privileges of princesshood. If *Aladdin* could be said to have successfully extended that privileged state to a body of color, then we could consider the "spell" that heretofore limited princesshood to white women to finally be broken. Unfortunately, however, the way in which the bodies of Jasmine and her prince are drawn "allow[s] audiences to forget her ethnicity" (Staninger 2003, 66), causing us to read them as de facto white folks who are raised above their darker, racialized countryfolk ("diamonds in the rough," if you will).

*Aladdin* is set in the fictional Middle Eastern city of Agraba, a city that was designed to showcase the seriousness with which Disney was taking its first attempt at a non-European fairy tale. Designers went to great lengths to ensure that Agraba would look believable:

> Buena Vista took painstaking measures to present a somewhat authentic Arab town. The animation was influenced by Arab calligraphy, primarily the S-curves, and by Persian miniature paintings from A.D. 1000 to 1500, from which the authentic shades of colors were taken. Artistic supervisor Rasoul Azadani, a native Iranian, flew to his hometown of Isfahan in 1991 to photograph buildings and interiors in order to authentically capture the Islamic world of the fifteenth century. (Staninger 2003, 69–70)

The text of the film itself, however, undercuts attempts by the animators to accurately portray Islamic culture by re-inscribing a number of virulent stereotypes about a supposedly "barbaric" place, as Agraba was described in the original recording of the film's opening song (Wise 2003). As Christopher Wise writes, the plot of the movie "vilifies Islamic law, or *sharia* (law that is based upon the Qur'an), promoting instead a largely Western notion of 'freedom'" (2003, 106). Perhaps this is unsurprising given that *Aladdin* was released shortly after the first Gulf War (Bryne and McQuillan 1999). One of the "Western notions of freedom" being promoted by *Aladdin* is the idea that women should be allowed to pursue a life outside of the household if they so desire. And while this lesson may not be harmful in and of itself, the fact that it is taught via the vilification of the backward racialized Other who threatens to curtail women's freedom is troubling. According to *Aladdin*, it is the backward priorities of Middle Eastern peoples that stifle women's self-actualization:

> Jasmine is a victim of the [*sharia*] Law, or tradition, which callously dictates that she must marry a wealthy, foreign prince, regardless of her personal desires. When Jasmine's father reminds her that "the law says [she] must be married to a prince," Jasmine simply replies, "The law is wrong!" Nothing more need be said because, by this point, it is quite clear to everyone that the Law is the real problem or issue. (Wise 2003, 107)

In other words, "[Jasmine's] values are the ones of a Western young woman. Nowhere is her faith addressed. She wants independence, rejects the suitors who approach her—and does so for reasons of personal dislikes—and runs away from home and its boredom" (Staninger 2003, 67). Politically, Jasmine is aligned with (white) Western feminism against a stereotypical depiction of Islam as an anti-feminist, anti-woman religion.

This ideological alignment is underlined by the style in which Jasmine is drawn. Although "her skin tone is appropriately darker [than that of the previous Disney Princesses] for the Middle Eastern setting of the story," she "retains many White features, such as a delicate nose and a small mouth" (Lacroix 2004, 220) thus causing her to be read as less racially marked than the residents of Agraba that can be seen in the background.

> Jasmine is a typical [again, read: white American] teenager in the trappings of an Arab princess, beginning with her clothing. The similarity between her garb and see-through dresses, baggy pants, halter tops, and long hair held in "scrunchies," part of the year's Southern California dress code at the time the film was released, is staggering. (Staninger 2003, 67)

Our hero, Aladdin, is also whitewashed. According to Disney animator Glen Keane, Aladdin was designed to embody "the confidence, likeability, and physical traits of Tom Cruise" and "certain personality elements of Michael J. Fox" (Staninger 2003, 67).

Conversely, the antagonists of the film including the burly, bullying palace guards and the nefarious Jafar (and the various unnamed characters who populate the Agraba market who are not characterized as good or evil but are merely there to flesh out the mise-en-scène) are explicitly and exaggeratedly racialized. As one Arabic activist put it,

> All the bad guys have beards and large, bulbous noses, sinister eyes ... and they're wielding swords constantly. Aladdin doesn't have a big nose; he has a small nose. He doesn't have a beard or a turban. ...What makes him nice is they've given him this American character. They've done everything but put him in a suit and a tie. (Macleod 2003, 183)

The evil Jafar is "a cross between the Ayatollah and Saddam Hussein. He is encoded by the familiar marks of Western racism, wearing black clerical robes and a 'sinister' Islamic moustache and goatee" (Staninger 2003, 76). Christiane Staninger writes,

> If one wants to insist that [*Aladdin*] features "people of color," then it is painfully obvious that the protagonists ... are not. Their features are decidedly white/European. The others have large noses, sinister eyes, and violence on the mind. Aladdin and Jasmine have none of these. They are dark-haired Ken and Barbie. While common stereotypes force images of Middle Eastern violence, harems for polygamist husbands, and bearded terrorists, Aladdin and Jasmine break that stereotype, it is true, but in a distinctly Western, not Middle Eastern, fashion. (2003, 68)

Jasmine is not useful in altering the racialized logic of labor in the Disney Princess line because, although she *is* afforded a leisurely life, she hews closely to a white Westernized feminine ideal, thereby robbing the image of a princess of color of much of its revolutionary potential.

## Pocahontas, Mulan, and Tiana: Non-White Femininity as Defined by Labor

The more explicitly racialized heroines in the Disney Princess line, Pocahontas, Mulan, and Tiana, unlike Jasmine, must bear the burdens of labor that earlier princesses were able to avoid. When these new characters are compared with the classic characters, an alarming pattern becomes evident. In the world defined by Disney, women of color (except those, like Jasmine, who can pass as white) will always be workers, even if they make it all the way to the throne room.

Readers might be forgiven for not knowing that Pocahontas and Mulan are even a part of the Disney Princess line. As Peggy Orenstein points out, they are often excluded from products that feature the entire lineup posing together:

> Mulan and Pocahontas, arguably the most resourceful of the bunch, are rarely depicted on Princess merchandise, though for a different reason. Their rustic garb has less bling potential than that of old-school heroines like Sleeping Beauty. (2006)

Nevertheless, the Disney Princess website (Disney 2013) lists Pocahontas and Mulan as official members of the royal club despite the fact that neither one of them is technically royalty. So why did Disney draft these women into the Princess line?

By including Pocahontas and Mulan in the Princess franchise (despite their seeming lack of royal qualifications), Disney continued the work begun with Princess Jasmine and extended through the introduction of Princess Tiana of diversifying the Princess model to simultaneously "draw over" unsavory depictions of racialized characters from the company's past. The corporation hoped to "signal that bad old Disney would be purged and a new agenda for approaching race and national identity might emerge" (Bryne and McQuillan 1999, 101). For example, with *Pocahontas*, Disney went to great lengths to be seen as culturally sensitive, as "the filmmakers responsible ... explained that they consciously intended to respond to the criticism that other Disney films had attracted because of racial stereotypes" (Wasko 2001, 141) of Native Americans, such the "red men" of *Peter Pan* (1953). Disney enlisted Native voice actors including Irene Bedard as Pocahontas and Native activist Russell Means as her father, Chief Powhatan, and attempted to "appl[y] a historically enlightened perspective" by suggesting "that the colonists are the villains" (Ward 2002, 39):

> In acknowledging the economic motivations of the early Jamestown settlers, *Pocahontas* attempts to face up to the debt that founded modern America. It does this both through the depiction of greed that motivates the white settlers, but also through its new-found "respect" for cultural and racial difference. (Bryne and McQuillan 1999, 108)

Of course, many critics have pointed out that Disney's attempt to use *Pocahontas* to right the wrongs contained in its previous depictions of Native Americans was hardly an unequivocal success (see Buescher and Ono 1996; Lacroix 2004; Strong 1998). But even if we were to accept Disney's flawed retelling of the tale of Pocahontas as a genuine effort to make amends for the company's negative depictions of Native characters, the film's contribution to the racialized, gendered divisions of labor crystallized within the Disney Princess line would remain troubling. Pocahontas might be an "Indian princess," but her non-white skin marks her as a laboring subject and therefore prevents her from performing princessliness in precisely the same way that the white princesses do.

Our introduction to Pocahontas's world is the song "Steady as the Beating Drum," which is accompanied by images depicting her people working to harvest crops, fishing, cooking, and even conducting a war. Pocahontas herself models the athleticism of a powerful body that has presumably been sculpted by her participation in that labor.

> The Disney animators … wanted to emphasize Pocahontas' athleticism, and certainly the character is shot in far more active scenes than any of her … predecessors. She is seen running, moving always nimbly through the forest, and, in one scene, diving from a cliff in perfect form. In many ways, particularly when compared to Ariel and Belle, Pocahontas appears to be almost an Amazon. She is tall, has long, strong legs, and a developed bust. (Lacroix 2004, 220)

Furthermore, her father's position of leadership in the tribe does not exempt her from performing the same tasks performed by all the other young men and women (for example, she is shown in one scene helping to pick ears of corn from the rows grown by her village with her friend, Nakoma). On the contrary, as the daughter of the tribe's chief, Pocahontas has *extra* work to do. At several points in the film, she discusses her need to prepare to work in the role previously occupied by her mother as the person the "people look to for wisdom and strength." Pocahontas fully enters into this role during the film's tragic conclusion, when she decides that she must remain behind to help mediate between her people and the remaining English colonists at Jamestown while her love interest, John Smith, sails back home. And in the sequel, *Pocahontas II: Journey to a New World*, her position as a diplomat is made official when she travels to England to act as an ambassador for her people to the King of England. This labor is presented as a consequence of her hereditary identity and a duty that she owes to her people. In other words, this labor is part and parcel of what makes her a leader of her people: She must sacrifice her happily-ever-after to stay and *govern*. Disney might have granted her the title of "princess," but the film withholds the leisurely respite that accompanies that title when it is conferred on white women.

Like *Pocahontas*, *Mulan* was also tailor-made to fix Disney's past mistakes while simultaneously positioning the company for a favorable entrance into a new market in China. Mulan (voiced by Cantonese American actress Ming-Na Wen) is one of Disney's first non-stereotyped depictions of an Asian woman, drawing over and replacing Disney "'orientals' like the Siamese cats in *Lady and the Tramp* (1955) and *The Aristocats* (1970)" (Ma 2003, 150). And yet, when compared with the other princesses in the Disney Princess line, Mulan, like Pocahontas, is still noteworthy for practicing a different, more labor-intensive version of princesshood. Work is a central motif of the film. All of the main characters have a work-related problem to solve. Mulan wants to be free to choose work that is fulfilling to her. She rejects the feminine labor of the "proper wife" in favor of the masculine labor of the soldier. Captain Shang, Mulan's love interest, to successfully manage and train his troops to ensure the successful completion of their work protecting the Emperor. Even the most popular song on the film's sound track, "I'll Make a Man Out of You," begins with a line about "getting down to business."

The same can be said of Princess Tiana from Disney's *The Princess and the Frog*. Like *Pocahontas* and *Mulan, The Princess and the Frog* was specially designed to open up the Disney Princess line to new markets by addressing criticisms that have been aimed at the Disney corporation. Richard M. Breaux writes that "Disney and Pixar studio executives and animators attempted to use *The Princess and the Frog* to respond to its critics' claims about the perpetuation of sexism and racism in its animated features" (Breaux 2010, 398) by taking "pre-emptive actions" like consulting with Oprah Winfrey (and enlisting her to serve as the voice of Eudora, Tiana's mother) and with members of the NAACP about the content of the movie (Breaux 2010). Animators also attempted to short-circuit criticism of the film by emphasizing their dedication to reverse the stereotyping and caricaturing of African Americans that abounds in the history of American animation and specifically in Disney's back catalog, inserting "Africanisms and verbal and visual references to African American expressive culture" (Breaux 2010, 401) and committing to a production process that takes real African American bodies (and not the stereotyped bodies imaginatively produced by white actors in blackface minstrel shows, who were often the models for animated black bodies in the early days of American animation) (Barker 2010, 485) as its models. The film also directly addresses feminist criticisms of the Disney Princess that she "put[s] getting her man before [her] own interests" and that she is a "passive victim awaiting rescue"(Breaux 2010, 403) by creating in Tiana a character who never gives up on her dream to one day own her own restaurant.

However, as Sarita McCoy Gregory (2010) points out, despite all the fanfare about the progressive move to extend the title of "Disney Princess" to an African American girl, the film reassuringly depicts black women as domestic laborers and not as upper-class nobility. She might technically be a Disney Princess, but Tiana is unable to entirely escape the specter of the "mammy, maid, auntie, washerwoman, [or] pickaninny" (Breaux 2010, 407) that looms over animation history. It is Tiana's dream to open up a restaurant that will serve food so good it will bring the community together (Parasecoli 2010, 452), and to achieve her goal, Tiana works two jobs at the beginning of the film, saving up all of her money in the hopes of buying a dilapidated warehouse that she wants to convert into "Tiana's Place." She would rather pick up an extra shift than go out dancing, an attitude that prompts her friends to complain, "All you ever do is work." In comparison to the princesses of previous Disney films, Tiana's dreams are small and humble and require quite a bit of elbow grease to get them off the ground. For example, when she imagines her life as a restaurateur in the musical number "I'm Almost There," she still performs the menial tasks of a line cook: "despite her role as patronne, in the fantasy Tiana is stirring a pot, chopping vegetables, whipping cream and putting it on desserts, as though even in her wildest dreams it was impossible for her to abandon completely a manual, hands-on role" (Parasecoli 2010, 462).

This obsessive focus on Tiana's relationship to the world of work undermines the inclusive spirit that motivated her induction into the Princess canon in the first place by relegating her to a separate plane of existence from the one occupied by Snow White, Cinderella, Aurora, Ariel, Belle, and even Jasmine. In fact, Tiana's exclusion from the type of princesshood available to white girls is made explicit in the way that the film compares her life to that of Charlotte, the daughter of her mother's employer. As Richard M. Breaux points out, Charlotte is played for a bit of a joke at the classic Disney Princesses' expense:

> In *The Princess and the Frog*, Charlotte "Lottie" La Bouff (voiced by European American actress Jennifer Cody) represents Disney's acknowledgement of its prince doting, slightly sexualized, single-parented, animated women characters. She is Disney's self-deprecating presentation of womanhood juxtaposed to the more modest, self-reliant Tiana. From the opening scene when Charlotte and Tiana are playing together as children and Eudora (voiced by Oprah Winfrey) reads "The Frog Prince" to the girls, the audience learns that Charlotte is prince-obsessed. While we hear Tiana declare: "There is no way in this whole wide world I would ever, ever, ever … I mean never kiss a frog," even if he's a prince; Charlotte can think of nothing better and would do anything, including "kiss 100 frogs" if it means life happily ever after as a princess with her prince. Years later, at the La Bouffs' masquerade ball, when Charlotte freshens up and Tiana changes into an evening gown that includes a tiara, Charlotte's desperation to woo Prince Naveen (voiced by Brazilian actor Bruno Campos) is most evident as she humorously over-applies her makeup and adjusts her ball gown to emphasize her cleavage. The once desperate-to-the-point-of-comedic little girl in an oversized pink princess gown has become an equally desperate and comedic adult in pink costume ball gown complete with a faux beauty mark. (Breaux 2010, 403)

And yet, this humorous portrayal masks a bit of pain in that such frivolity is not available to Tiana. On the contrary, it is Tiana's labor and that of her family that makes Charlotte's princess fantasies possible. When Charlotte is a child, Tiana's mother, Eudora, is the seamstress who sews all of her over-the-top princess dresses, and as an adult, she depends on Tiana's cooking at her masquerade ball in her attempt to win her the heart of Prince Naveen. It is Charlotte who "receive[s] the valorization of womanhood, dancing the princess dance, while Tiana remained firmly attached to work" (Gregory 2010, 446), an arrangement which admittedly reflects poorly on the spoiled Charlotte but which none of the film's characters ever question as the natural order of the world, the way things are supposed to be. The privilege of leisure is apparently "naturally" reserved for white folk.

Fabio Parasecoli writes that the film works to defuse the potential threat posed by its black female protagonist to race privilege and to confirm familiar power dynamics, thus reassuring mainstream audiences. Tiana is presented as a strong and motivated character, fighting to achieve her professional goals. Nonetheless, her dreams are framed within an occupation that has been historically connected with black women. Tiana's family, the neighborhood where she grows up, her cultural environment, and her jobs clearly represent her as working class. (2010, 452)

This stratification carries over from the movie into its related lines of toys and costumes, as "among the merchandise inspired by the movie is a cooking set complete with a corresponding recipe book for children named after the main character" with a cover depicting "Princess Tiana stirring batter" as well as a doll that comes with a "waitress outfit" (Parasecoli 2010, 453). As Sarita McCoy Gregory puts it, "Again, Disney ... ask[s] its audience to 'dig a little deeper' and try to move beyond race by accepting Tiana into its family of princesses" even as "it consoles the audience—through its visual text and cultural sentimentality—that social reality would not be changing too much" (Gregory 2010, 439). In other words, should little girls want to act out their princess fantasies through Tiana's black subjectivity, they are encouraged to imagine themselves as laborers, mixing up beignets and serving them to customers and not as ladies of leisure lounging on a throne beside their Prince Charming. In fact, at the conclusion of the film, Tiana has drawn her prince, Naveen, *into* the laboring life, teaching him a sense of responsibility and putting him to work as a waiter in her restaurant.

## Conclusion

The deliberately diverse Disney Princess line purports to encourage little princesses of all races and creeds to indulge in fairy-tale dreams. But as my analysis has shown, the diverse representations of princesshood found within the franchise actually work to erect a barrier (or rather, use the labor of princesses of color to build and maintain a barrier) that separates white women from women of color, thereby strengthening racialized, gendered divisions instead of breaking them down. The drawn bodies of Jasmine, Pocahontas, Mulan, and Tiana perform the work of serving as a foil to the traditional, white princesshood of Snow White, Cinderella, Aurora, Ariel, and Belle. The franchise invites girls of color to try their luck at adopting a princessly role only to insist that *their* princesshood be different from (and more difficult than) the one experienced by white girls.

## Brief Notes on Disney's Rapunzel and Merida

In the years since this chapter was first composed, two additional princesses, the first white princesses to make the cut since *Beauty and the Beast*'s Belle, were added to the line: Rapunzel from the 2010 film *Tangled* and Merida from the 2012 joint Disney-Pixar production *Brave* (Brigante 2011 and 2013). (Note that Elsa and Anna from *Frozen* have not yet, as of May 2015, joined the official Disney Princess brand.) Although these figures deserve more space than I can give them here, I do think it is important to situate them briefly in terms of the structures of race, labor, and femininity outlined above.

Rapunzel's princessly trajectory combines some of the tropes of the classic Disney princesses with those of the feisty Disney heroines of the 1990s: Like Snow White, Cinderella, and Sleeping Beauty, she was unfairly snatched away from a royal life of luxury to live the life of a laboring peasant, and yet, like Ariel and Belle, she shows a great deal of plucky determination when she is presented the opportunity to escape from her tower and see the world. However, the film allows her to re-enter her royal position only *after* her hair, the tool that allowed her so much mobility and resourcefulness during her journey, was drained of its magic. It is implied that she will no longer need this tool once she has attained her happily-ever-after because she will never again have to perform either the menial household tasks or the daring feats of escape that marked her peasant life.

Merida, the first princess to have been produced by the Disney-Pixar partnership, is a more complex case. Unlike the other white Disney Princesses, Merida both revels in work and resists the idea of marriage to a prince. And yet, the tribal Scottish setting of *Brave* suggests that to read Merida as "white" is not necessarily historically accurate; the colonial British likened the Scottish tribes to Native American peoples (Calloway 2010). The marketing of Merida outside of her film as a part of the Disney Princess family further complicates this picture, as her official induction into the Princess line apparently required a makeover "redesigning the character as thinner with a bigger bust, more revealing dress, a face full of makeup, less wild hair, and replacing her signature bow and arrows with a sassy sash" (Morrissey 2013), though to be fair, Disney did eventually pull this more feminine image of Merida and replace it with Pixar's original design after a sustained public campaign lobbied against the decision to "pretty up" the new princess. This suggests that, in order to make Merida "fit in" with the product line, Disney executives thought that many of the qualities that differentiated her from the other (white) princesses needed to be toned down. Thus, Pixar's first princess bucks some of Disney's racialized and gendered tropes while upholding others.

## References

*Aladdin*. 1992. Directed by Ron Clements and John Musker. Burbank, CA: Walt Disney Pictures. DVD.

*The Aristocats*. 1970. Directed by Wolfgang Reitherman. Burbank, CA: Walt Disney Productions. DVD.

Barker, Jennifer L. 2010. "Hollywood, Black Animation, and the Problem of Representation in *Little Ol' Bosko* and *The Princess and the Frog*." *Journal of African American Studies, 14*: 482–498.

*Beauty and the Beast*. 1991. Directed by Gary Trousdale and Kirk Wise. Burbank, CA: Walt Disney Pictures. DVD.

Bell, Elizabeth. 1995. "Somatexts at the Disney Shop: Constructing the Pentimentos of Women's Animated Bodies." In *From Mouse to Mermaid: The Politics of Film, Gender, and Culture*, ed. Elizabeth Bell, Lynda Haas, and Laura Sells, 107–124. Bloomington: Indiana University Press.

*Brave*. 2012. Directed by Mark Andrews and Brenda Chapman. Burbank, CA: Walt Disney Pictures and Pixar Studios. DVD.

Breaux, Richard M. 2010. "After 75 Years of Magic: Disney Answers Its Critics. Rewrites African American History, and Cashes in on Its Racist Past." *Journal of African American Studies, 14*, 398–416.

Brigante, Ricky. 2011. "Rapunzel Becomes 10th Disney Princess with Procession and Coronation Ceremony in London Palace." *Inside the Magic*. Accessed October 22, 2013. http://www.insidethemagic.net/2011/10/rapunzel-becomes-10th-disney-princess-with-procession-and-coronation-ceremony-in-london-palace/

Brigante, Ricky. 2013. "Merida to Become 11th Disney Princess in Royal Coronation Ceremony at Walt Disney World on May 11." *Inside the Magic*. Accessed October 22, 2013. http://www.insidethemagic.net/2013/04/merida-to-become-11th-disney-princess-with-new-look-for-royal-coronation-ceremony-at-walt-disney-world-on-may-11/

Bryne, Eleanor, and Martin McQuillan. 1999. *Deconstructing Disney*. London: Pluto Press.

Buescher, Derek T., and Kent A. Ono. 1996. "Civilized Colonialism: *Pocahontas* as Neocolonial Rhetoric." *Women's Studies in Communication, 19*(2): 127–153.

Calloway, Colin G. 2010. *White People, Indians, and Highlanders: Tribal People and Colonial Encounters in Scotland and America*. New York: Oxford University Press.

*Cinderella*. 1950. Directed by Clyde Geronimi, Hamilton Luske, and Wilfred Jackson. Burbank, CA: Walt Disney Productions. DVD.

Craven, Allison. 2002. "Beauty and the Belles: Discourses of Feminism and Femininity in Disneyland." *European Journal of Women's Studies, 9*: 12–142.

Davis, Amy M. 2007. *Good Girls and Wicked Witches: Women in Disney's Feature Animation 1937–2001*. Bloomington: Indiana University Press.

Disney. 2013. *Disney Princess: The Official Princess Website*. Accessed October 22, 2013. http://princess.disney.com

Do Rozario, Rebecca-Anne C. 2004. "The Princess and the Magic Kingdom: Beyond Nostalgia, the Function of the Disney Princess." *Women's Studies in Communication, 27*(1): 34–59.

*Fantasia*. 1940. Produced by Walt Disney. Burbank, CA: Walt Disney Productions. DVD.

Giroux, Henry A., and Grace Pollock. 2010. *The Mouse That Roared: Disney and the End of Innocence* (updated and expanded ed.). Lanham, MD: Rowman & Littlefield.

Glenn, Evelyn Nakano. 1985. "Racial Ethnic Women's Labor: The Intersection of Race, Gender, and Class Oppression." *Review of Radical Political Economics, 17*(3): 86–108.

Gregory, Sarita McCoy. 2010. "Disney's Second Line: New Orleans, Racial Masquerade, and the Reproduction of Whiteness in *The Princess and the Frog*." *Journal of African American Studies* 14, 432–449.

Hines, Susan, and Brenda Ayers. 2003. "Introduction: (He)gemony Cricket! Why in the World Are We Still Watching Disney?" In *The Emperor's Old Groove: Decolonizing Disney's Magic Kingdom*, ed. Brenda Ayers, 1–14. New York: Peter Lang.

King, C. Richard, Carmen R. Lugo-Lugo, and Mary K. Bloodsworth-Lugo. 2010. *Animating Difference: Race, Gender, and Sexuality in Contemporary Films for Children*. Lanham, MD: Rowman & Littlefield.

Lacroix, Celeste. 2004. "Images of Animated Others: The Orientalization of Disney's Cartoon Heroines from *The Little Mermaid* to *The Hunchback of Notre Dame*." *Popular Communication, 2*(4): 213–229.

*Lady and the Tramp*. 1955. Directed by Clyde Geronimi, Wilfred Jackson, and Hamilton Luske. Burbank, CA: Walt Disney Productions. DVD.

*The Little Mermaid*. 1989. Directed by Ron Clements and John Musker. Burbank, CA: Walt Disney Pictures. DVD.

Ma, Sheng-mei. 2003. "Mulan Disney, It's Like, Re-Orients: Consuming China and Animating Teen Dreams." In *The Emperor's Old Groove: Decolonizing Disney's Magic Kingdom*, edited by Brenda Ayers, 1–14. New York: Peter Lang.

Macleod, Dianne Sachko. 2003. "The Politics of Vision: Disney, *Aladdin*, and the Gulf War." In *The Emperor's Old Groove: Decolonizing Disney's Magic Kingdom*, ed. Brenda Ayers. New York: Peter Lang.

Morrissey, Tracie Egan. 2013. "Disney Pulls Sexy Merida Makeover after Public Backlash." *Jezebel*. Accessed October 23, 2013. http://jezebel.com/disney-pulls-sexy-merida-makeover-after-public-backlash-494274022

*Mulan*. 1998. Directed by Tony Bancroft and Barry Cook. Burbank, CA: Walt Disney Pictures. DVD.

Orin. 2013. "Why Your Great-Grandmother Wasn't an Indian Princess." *Native Languages of the Americas: Preserving and Promoting American Indian Languages*. Accessed February 24, 2013. http://www.nativelanguages.org/princess.htm

Orenstein, Peggy. 2006. "What's Wrong with Cinderella?" *The New York Times Magazine*, December 24. http://www.nytimes.com/2006/12/24/magazine/24princess.t.html

Parasecoli, Fabio. 2010. "A Taste of Louisiana: Mainstreaming Blackness through Food in *The Princess and the Frog*." *Journal of African American Studies, 14*: 450–468.

*Peter Pan*. 1953. Directed by Clyde Geronimi, Wilfred Jackson, and Hamilton Luske. Burbank, CA: Walt Disney Productions. DVD.

*Pocahontas*. 1995. Directed by Mike Gabriel and Eric Goldberg. Burbank, CA: Walt Disney Pictures. DVD.

*Pocahontas II: Journey to a New World*. Directed by Tom Ellery and Bradley Raymond. Burbank, CA: Walt Disney Pictures. DVD.

*The Princess and the Frog*. 2009. Directed by Ron Clements and John Musker. Burbank, CA: Walt Disney Pictures. DVD.

*Sleeping Beauty*. 1959. Directed by Clyde Geronimi, Les Clark, Eric Larson, and Wolfgang Reitherman. Burbank, CA: Walt Disney Productions. DVD.

*Snow White and the Seven Dwarfs*. 1937. Directed by David Hand. Burbank, CA: Walt Disney Productions. DVD.

*Song of the South*. 1946. Directed by Harve Foster and Wilfred Jackson. Burbank, CA: Walt Disney Productions.

Staninger, Christiane. 2003. "Disney's Magic Carpet Ride: *Aladdin* and Women in Islam." In *The Emperor's Old Groove: Decolonizing Disney's Magic Kingdom*, ed. Brenda Ayers, 179–192. New York: Peter Lang.

Stone, Kay. 1975. "Things Walt Never Told Us." *Journal of American Folklore, 88*(347): 42–50.

Strong, Pauline Turner. 1998. "Playing Indian in the 1990s: *Pocahontas* and *The Indian in the Cupboard*." In *Hollywood's Indian: The Portrayal of the Native American in Film* (expanded ed.), ed. Peter Rollins and John E. O'Connor, 187–205. Lexington: University Press of Kentucky.

*Tangled*. 2010. Directed by Nathan Greno and Byron Howard. Burbank, CA: Walt Disney Pictures. DVD.

Terry, Esther J. 2010. "Rural as Racialized Plantation vs Rural as Modern Reconnection: Blackness and Agency in Disney's *Song of the South* and *The Princess and the Frog*." *Journal of African American Studies, 14*, 469–481.

Verrill, Morgan. 2010. "Princess Tiana Inducted into Disney Princess Royal Court." *Yahoo! Voices*. Accessed October 22, 2013. http://voices.yahoo.com/princess-tiana-inducted-into-disney-princess-royal-6051664.html

Ward, Anne R. 2002. *Mouse Morality: The Rhetoric of Disney Animated Films*. Austin: University of Texas Press.

Warner, Marina. 1994. *From the Beast to the Blonde: On Fairy Tales and Their Tellers*. London: Chatto & Windus.

Wasko, Janet. 2001. *Understanding Disney* (3rd ed.). Cambridge: Polity Press.

Wise, Christopher. 2003. "Notes from the *Aladdin* Industry; or, Middle Eastern Folklore in the Era of Multinational Capitalism." In *The Emperor's Old Groove: Decolonizing Disney's Magic Kingdom*, ed. Brenda Ayers, 105–116. New York: Peter Lang.

CHAPTER THREE

# Ghetto Princes, Pretty Boys, and Handsome Slackers: Masculinity, Race and the Disney Princes

GUILLERMO AVILA-SAAVEDRA

According to a content analysis of the official Disney Princess films, Aladdin from *Aladdin* (1992) and Naveen from *The Princess and the Frog* (2009) are the only male protagonists that exhibit more feminine than masculine characteristics. Li Shang from *Mulan* (1998), although more masculine than feminine overall, exhibits fewer masculine characteristics than all the other Disney princes except for the ones in *Snow White* (1937) and *Cinderella* (1950) who have remarkably little screen time (England, Descartes and Collier-Meek 2011). What Aladdin, Naveen and Li Shang share is the distinction of being the only non-White princes or romantic interests in Disney Princess films. Based on that evidence, this chapter aims to explore the symbolic interconnections of race and gender and contributes to the conversation through qualitative discourse analysis of the construction of masculinities in the three films. The analysis exposes the performance of gender roles by the male protagonists in the context of their race and class as established by the narrative and their interactions with the female protagonists. A discursive analysis of these popular movies reveals the mediated construction of multiple forms of masculinities informed by race and class as well by changing notions of masculinity and femininity.

The representation of gender roles, class and race in children's media is an important area of study. Because of their cultural ubiquity, Disney films constitute a key site providing rich opportunities to examine the representation of gender identities.

Much attention has been placed on the construction of femininity in the official Princess films (England, Descartes and Collier-Meek 2011,Wohlwend 2011, Zafranz 2007). Similarly, scholars have explored the intersection of racial and gender identities in non-White princess characters such as Jasmine, Pocahontas, Tiana and Mulan (Breaux 2010; Lacroix 2004). In a lively scholarly debate, many researchers have argued that despite some superficial changes the archetype of the submissive female persists along with the exoticization of non-White female characters (Craven 2002; Lester 2010; Whelan 2012). Other scholars find progress and evolution in Disney's representations of gender. In an extensive content analysis of nine Disney Princess films, England, Descartes and Collier-Meek (2011) concluded that both princess and prince characters increasingly exhibited more androgynous, less rigid gender identities. Similarly, Gillam and Wooden (2008, 3) argue that while princess figures remain "thin, beautiful, kind, obedient or punished for disobedience, and headed for the altar," recent Disney-Pixar films provide a model of the "new male" that represents progress in the portrayal of masculinity.

However useful these studies are, none considers the interconnections of gender—especially masculinities—with race and class. This is a remarkable absence since we know the role the media play in reproducing hegemonic ideologies of gender directed at girls from a very young age (Currie 1999; Driscoll 2002; Kearney 2006; Mitchell and Reid-Walsh 2005; Zaslow 2009). Boys' ideas of masculinity must be shaped by media representations as well. Furthermore, the role of media is potentially stronger when representations of certain identities, such as working-class or racial minority characters, are scarce. The following section begins with a discussion of hegemony, the theoretical formulation that informs the analysis, in order to understand how hegemonic cultural norms may influence the mediated construction of gender, race and class identities.

## Hegemony, Culture and Representation

The concept of hegemony addresses the limitations of Marxism in seeing economic structures as the only source of social change. The notion of hegemony incorporates culture in the process of class struggle and social domination. Gramsci (1973) questioned why the working classes were not necessarily revolutionary and concluded that there must be a tacit consensus between the ruling and working classes based on culture and ideologies. He argued that a social class is successful in maintaining hegemony over society through economic domination but also through leadership based on intellectual and moral factors. Social institutions and cultural production disseminate such moral elements.

Strinati (1995) notes that in the concept of hegemony the working class is not ideologically indoctrinated or physically forced to accept the values and ideas of the dominant classes, but rather has its own reasons to accept their leadership. Strinati (1995, 165) defines hegemony as a dynamic process in which "dominant groups in society maintain their dominance by securing the 'spontaneous consent' of subordinated groups, including the working class, through the negotiated construction of a political and ideological consensus, which incorporates both dominant and dominated groups." Such consensual control occurs when individuals assimilate the views and leadership of the dominant groups as part of their notion of common sense.

Hegemony, therefore, can be understood as the set of values and ideas that dominant groups want subordinate groups to accept in order to secure their leadership. This set of values is then enforced as common sense, which organizes ideology and culture. Gramsci (1973) expands the notion of culture to include the distributions of power and influence in the social process wherein individuals organize their lives. Ideology is defined as the interest of a dominant class reflected in universally accepted social values. Hall (1999, 271) defines ideology as the "images, concepts, and premises which provide the frameworks through which we represent, interpret, understand, and 'make sense' of some aspect of social existence." As long as the concept of hegemony discusses the operation of social power ideologies, its reach is not limited to issues of economy and class but can be expanded to other instances of daily life that are shaped by social culture.

Sullivan (2003) expands on this idea to argue that race, sex and gender issues coincide in an ideology of social domination and control. Discussing racism in media representations, Hall (1999, 272) invokes hegemony when he argues that ideologies are most effective when "we are not aware how we formulate and construct statements about the world, when our formations seem to be simply descriptive statements about how things are, or what we can take for granted." His notion of a "grammar of race" (1981, 39) as an unconsciously learned ideology that influences cultural production can be understood as part of the hegemonic process of racism. The same thinking can be applied to other kinds of symbolic articulations of social power, such as mediated representations of gender, race and class.

## Hegemony, Masculinity and Race

Patriarchy, defined as a system in which men hold more social power than women, is the critical application of the hegemonic model to the study of gender roles and gender relations. Feminist theory argues that social institutions and cultural production often sustain or promote a model of gender relations wherein men are dominant and women are subservient. Connell (1992) challenges a purely patriarchal approach for its inability to explain all the dynamics of social power between the sexes, such as race and class, and develops a social theory of gender in which the concept of hegemonic masculinity occupies a central position. He defines external hegemonic masculinity as the strategy that maintains the patriarchal system in which men dominate women, and internal hegemonic masculinity as the domination of White heterosexual men over other men. This kind of hegemonic domination can be articulated in all kinds of social discourses and cultural practices. According to Wohlwend (2011, 7), "a hegemonic masculinity discourse in sports fandom achieves dominance over femininities and other masculinities through power relations based upon primarily male physical competitions and displays of strength or skill." In Connell's view, homosexual men and/or minority men are not necessarily active participants or beneficiaries of hegemonic masculinity. Demetriou (2001) challenges Connell's definitions and argues that hegemony is not the privilege of White heterosexual men but rather manifests itself through different kinds of masculinities in order to assure the survival of the patriarchal system. The interconnections between gender, race and class are fundamental to assess shares of social power. For example, Johnson (2003) explores how patriarchal notions of masculinity influence media representations of authentic male "Blackness." Qualitative analyses of mediated images of gender and sexuality need to consider how the hegemonic role of White masculinity affects different subjects' experience of oppression.

Hall notes that a hegemonic ideology or "grammar of race" (1981, 39) influences media products that are inferentially racist because their notions are perceived as normal. hooks (1993) places the commitment to end sexism and systems of class exploitation at the same level as the struggle to fight racism. She identifies a unified conservative discourse that groups all these systems of oppression under the umbrella of family traditions and social stability. hooks blames the mass media for suggesting that racism does not exist, that the feminist movement successfully eliminated patriarchal organizations and that poverty is a personal choice. She sees the mass media as part of "this collective cultural consumption and attachment to misinformation" (1993, 237). Jhally and Lewis (1992) examine the interrelation of race and class as represented on television and find that media narratives mostly ignore issues of racial inequality and attribute lack of financial success to other causes. They identify the American dream as hegemonic, a taken-for-granted notion of high social mobility in America.

The same hegemonic construct of individual responsibility that diminishes the role of race may affect the way gender identities are represented in cultural products and perceived by audiences. For example, traditional gender roles are often explained as necessary to sustain the family as the perfect social unit. Foucault (1978) argues that the enforcement of the family as the only valid structure is also a hegemonic paradigm since it responded to the need to ensure a labor force that could sustain the system of capitalist production. Essentially, the family is conceived as an agency of reproduction and control of other sexual behaviors perceived as unproductive. Foucault further notes that the family was regarded as the ideal means for political control and economic subjugation of the masses and initiated a campaign for the "moralization of the poorer classes" (1978, 122). Clearly, hegemony must be understood as an intersection of gender, race and class. Films constitute a key site to investigate since the ubiquity of media makes them a main site for the discursive articulation of social and cultural power. Films aimed at children are particularly relevant since their lighthearted tone along with the animation and musical elements may help disguise the pervasiveness of the hegemonic constructs.

## Method

In discourse analysis language is analyzed in light of the social positions of the speakers and the relationship of power between them. According to van Dijk (2001, 301) the fundamental nature of discourse analysis is "understanding the nature of power and dominance and how discourse contributes to their production." Therefore, discourse analysis is useful in exposing the power dynamics of gender and race relations in general, and within hegemonic masculinity in particular. Because masculinity cannot be understood in isolation but must be examined also in relation to femininity, the analysis also pays attention to the female protagonists of the films as they develop their gender identities. Discussion of masculinity/femininity constructions in both male and female characters provides a more nuanced and complex understanding of masculinity since, according to Wohlwend (2011, 7), "a view of gender as binary categories with inequitable power relations does not capture the dynamic and interconnected subjectivities within discourse: a discourse upholds power relations between its supporting subject positions but also produces the possibility of counter subject positions."

Because these films are produced in the context of other Disney films and media products, as well as within cultural and media references to princes and princesses, the analysis considers the intertextuality of media representations. Fiske (1987) identifies genre as the most influential form of horizontal intertextuality. The Disney Princess is in itself a media genre. Chandler (1997) emphasizes the idea of genre as an intertextual concept, because each text is defined by the conventions of the genre where it is situated, while at the same time, each new text serves to reinforce those conventions. Genre allows individual texts to be seen in relation to each other. In addition to the princess genre, intertextuality assumes that these films are interpreted within a larger cultural environment full of gender, race and class meanings.

Multiple in-depth readings of the text, identification of themes and categories and the relationship between themes and the broader conditions and contexts reveal how media language legitimates social control and allocates cultural power (MacMillan, 2006). In this chapter, the focus of analysis is the performance of gender roles by the films' protagonists as informed by their racial and class statuses established by the narrative. In order to identify gender performance, the analysis relies on the set of masculine characteristics (assertive, physically strong, unemotional, etc.) and feminine characteristics (submissive, nurturing, fearful, etc.) identified by England, Descartes and Collier-Meek (2001, 558–560) in their content analysis of Disney films, particularly as they develop through specific plot elements such as rescue, fighting and romantic encounter scenes. Finally, the analysis also focuses on the songs performed by the films' characters. Songs may be particularly deceptive since the hegemonic message can be disguised by a well-crafted and cheery melody. In addition, the rhymes make lyrics memorable and therefore the message is more influential.

## Aladdin, or the Ghetto Prince

*Aladdin* (1992) is an animated Disney film loosely based on the classic tale *Aladdin and the Enchanted Lamp* from *The Book of One Thousand and One Nights*. In the Disney adaptation, Aladdin is a young male, visibly orphaned, who survives by stealing food in the streets of the city of Agrabah. After falling in love with Princess Jasmine, he is deceived and betrayed by the evil royal vizier Jafar, who tries to use Aladdin to get the magic lamp. When Aladdin escapes Jafar and ends up in possession of the lamp, he orders the genie to transform him into a prince. As Prince Ali, Aladdin courts Princess Jasmine until Jafar steals the lamp, enslaves Jasmine and her father and exiles Aladdin. In the end Aladdin reveals his true identity, defeats Jafar and saves the princess, the sultan and the city.

The construction of the character of Princess Jasmine has been critically examined in its intersection of gender and race. Lacroix (2004) conducts an analysis of Princess Jasmine as part of her examination of other non-White Disney female characters. She argues that although Jasmine is less passive and more action-oriented than other Disney princesses, her physical portrayal corresponds to traditional Western ideals of female beauty such as fine facial features with a small nose and delicate eyes, and a slight frame and small waist. The only feature that establishes Jasmine as Middle Eastern is her dark complexion. In her analysis, Lacroix (2004) discusses the exoticization and orientalization of minority women in Disney films and explains how in the case of Jasmine, costuming and setting are used to establish a difference from previous Disney princesses:

> Jasmine's costuming emphasizes the Middle Eastern influence of the setting of *Aladdin* and depicts Jasmine in a more sexualized light. Although Jasmine's physique and physical activity work less to promote an overt eroticization of the character, the costuming accentuates the physical far more than does the costuming of the two White characters and plays into Western cultural notions of the Orient through the referencing of the imagery of the harem and the associated exotic, sexual stereotypes. (221)

The same analysis, even if not based on costuming and setting alone, can be applied to the character of Aladdin. If Jasmine is subtly sexualized in order to distance her from other Disney princesses, what strategies are used to distance Aladdin from the more traditional Prince archetype? Aladdin is portrayed with dark skin, hair and eyes. However, he is also portrayed as small-framed and delicate, which stands in opposition to the princely ideals of strength and imposing physique. According to Gillam and Wooden (2008, 3) a stereotypically patriarchal "alpha male" model with "unquestioned authority, physical power and social dominance, competitiveness for positions of status and leadership, lack of visible or shared emotion, social isolation" has worked as the Prince archetype for Disney for decades.

A more critical reading of Aladdin that goes beyond and beneath stereotypes reveals a more complex construction of masculinity at work. *Aladdin* is set in the fictional Middle Eastern city of Agrabah, easily recognizable as such by its architecture as well as by the clothing worn by locals. However, the setting may also draw parallels with American inner-city neighborhoods, ghettoes and urban denizens of color. Agrabah appears loud, crowded and a bit run down and dangerous, like the imagery of the American ghetto that is prevalent in the media. Furthermore, the facts that people of color populate Agrabah and that men vastly outnumber women in public spaces, although historically and culturally accurate, may reinforce the perception of the city as an American urban neighborhood. The song "One Jump Ahead" (Menken and Rice 1992) introduces Aladdin and defines his character. In this scene Aladdin gets in trouble for stealing a loaf of bread and is chased by guards wielding swords. The lyrics that efficiently establish Aladdin's character also connote a contemporary picture of a street-smart kid "hustlin' in the hood." Aladdin swiftly evades the law while singing:

> One jump ahead of the breadline
> One swing ahead of the sword
> I steal only what I can't afford
> That's everything!

During the song, while trying to escape the guards Aladdin breaks into a room full of women. While the young women appear attracted to Aladdin, a matronly character communicates that Aladdin does not have parents. The "broken home" analogy, the references to city blocks and Aladdin's wit all draw parallels between Aladdin and American inner-city minority youth. Even when his talents are appreciated, Aladdin is somewhat dismissively described as a "diamond in the rough."

Aladdin is not the only Disney prince to be portrayed as a petty criminal. In *Tangled*, the 2010 Disney version of the classic tale *Rapunzel*, Flynn Rider, the male protagonist, is also a thief. However, Flynn Rider is afforded the prince-like trappings of a horse, a sword and regal clothing. Other princes are also afforded regal horses and swords and sometimes even trustworthy sidekicks and companions, like the candelabra/butler in *Beauty and the Beast* (1991). By contrast, Aladdin has only his wit and the help of his pet monkey, Abu. Indeed, Abu could be interpreted as a more racialized version of a peer, particularly since Aladdin does not have any other network of personal relations. Again and again, Aladdin displays not the traditional masculine characteristics of courage and strength, but a more manipulative approach to problem solving. He rescues Jasmine in the market by pretending she is his insane sister and then explains, "You're only in trouble if you get caught." The scene reveals not only his shrewdness but also his dubious ethical and moral values. In the final scene, when Aladdin faces Jafar, the genie warns Aladdin that he cannot help him, to which he replies, "Hey, I'm a street rat remember? I'll improvise." Clearly, the emphasis on Aladdin's craftiness and ability to improvise are intended to establish the character's working-class ethos. Aladdin lacks formal instruction, adult support and resources, but he survives because he is street smart. In the end, Aladdin succeeds by outsmarting Jafar. Appealing to Jafar's desire for grandeur, Aladdin encourages him to wish to be a genie, thus entrapping him in the magic lamp.

A more transparent intertextual reference between the construction of masculinity in *Aladdin* and popular notions about inner-city male youth in America takes place when Aladdin commands the genie to transform him into Prince Ali in order to get the attention of Princess Jasmine. The song "Prince Ali" (Ashman and Menken 1992), a long musical sequence during which Aladdin, in the character of Prince Ali Ababwa, makes his grand entrance into Agrabah, is awe-inspiring in its excessive display. The song's lyrics construct Prince Ali's masculinity by emphasizing his remarkable strength and control over less able men:

Strong as ten regular men, definitely!
He faced the galloping hordes
A hundred bad guys with swords

The song goes on to describe amazing feats of bravery. Even if lightened up by the comedic tone of the animation, the focus on violence could arguably reference gangsta rap, a subgenre of hip hop music notorious for its hypermasculinity, misogyny and homophobia and the glorification of violence among urban youths (Oware 2011).

In a further gesture to the present, the genie "pimps" Aladdin into a "bling-bling" Prince Ali. The ostentatious and exaggerated claims of wealth in the lyrics of "Prince Ali" draw parallels with contemporary "bling-bling" culture, a term popular in hip hop that makes reference to a style of fashion and jewelry intended for ostentatious displays of wealth (Rehn and Sköld 2005). The lyrics describe Prince Ali's impressive collection of exotic animals in incredible numbers as well as his many loyal servants and slaves. This section of the song's lyrics is clear in its intertextual references to reversed racial roles. Prince Ali not only has monkeys, but white monkeys, in addition to slaves and flunkies who perform submission to him. Finally, and again not unlike contemporary inner-city youth culture and its media portrayal, the song makes exaggerated claims about Prince Ali's attractiveness and amorous abilities. The lyrics celebrate his physique, his command of women's attention and even his sense of style. It is interesting to note how the very same attributes traditionally used to describe Disney leading men, such as courage, strength, handsomeness and wealth, when taken to an extreme, actually discredit Aladdin's princely potential. Also, the lyrics emphasize how Prince Ali dresses, which is not traditionally a masculine concern.

There are redeeming qualities to Aladdin, however. His intentions are never in question even if his methods do not conform to dominant cultural practices and principles. At the film's end he does reveal his true identity to Jasmine and also sets the genie free. However, even these developments take place in less than heroic or prince-like circumstances. In one of the last scenes, still in disguise as Prince Ali, Aladdin realizes that he will become sultan:

Sultan: And you'll be happy and prosperous and then you, my boy, will become sultan.
Aladdin: Sultan?
Sultan: Yes! A fine upstanding youth such as yourself, a person of your impeachable moral character is exactly what this kingdom needs.

Aladdin is clearly troubled by this possibility. Arguably, it is the fear of responsibility that finally sets Aladdin free from his prince pantomime. The sequence infantilizes Aladdin by portraying the character with a childlike aversion to responsibility and commitment. This portrayal echoes in contemporary American media and the representation of minority youth as "refusing to grow up" and embrace adult manhood.

## The Warrior Princess and the Pretty Boy

*Mulan* (1998) is the animated Disney adaptation of the ancient Chinese tale of the female warrior Hua Mulan. In the animated film, the title character Mulan is the only daughter of the Fa family. After dishonoring her family by refusing to cooperate with the local matchmaker, Mulan takes the place of her aging father when the Emperor demands new recruits to fight a Hun invasion. Disguised as a male soldier, Mulan ends up in the recruitment camp commanded by dashing Captain Li Shang. After saving Li Shang's life during battle, however, Mulan's identity is revealed and she is expelled from the army. She eventually rejoins Li Shang to help him save the city and the Emperor and be declared a hero of China. Although *Mulan* features a heroine, the text sheds light on the articulation of masculinity in Disney films. Li Shang is a complex male protagonist with a developed personal story and considerable screen time. Additionally, Mulan adopts a male identity for part of the film, which may help uncover the more salient discourses of "how to be a man" embedded in the narrative, particularly in contrast to the rigidity of female roles enforced by traditional Chinese culture as represented in *Mulan* as well *Mulan II*, the direct-to-video sequel produced in 2004.

According to England, Descartes and Collier-Meek (2011), Mulan is one of three Disney princesses along with Pocahontas and Tiana from *The Princess and the Frog* who exhibit more masculine than feminine qualities, even if they are more feminine than masculine overall. Similarly, Li Shang displays only masculine characteristics (strong, assertive and athletic) as his three most common characteristics. At the same time, Li Shang manifests the third-lowest number of coded masculine characteristics (49) of all Disney princes. This section approaches the androgynous construction of the characters of Mulan and Li Shang by exploring both the context of race and class as provided by the film's narrative, as well as the larger cultural context of the moment when the film was produced and consumed.

A common theme of the Disney Princess films is that their narratives are in essence always love stories. Traditionally, Disney princesses have eagerly embraced the ideal of romantic love; in other words, they all want a Prince Charming. An interesting angle from which to examine the androgyny of Mulan and Li Shang is to explore the role of romantic love in the story. Even if not challenging the notion of romantic love, the film uses Mulan's uninterest in marriage to efficiently construct the character's non-traditional version of femininity early on. In the opening scene, as Mulan is getting ready to visit the local matchmaker, her family and entourage perform the song "Honor to Us All" (Wilder and Zippel 1998a), establishing the traditional roles:

> Men want girls with good taste
> Calm, obedient
> Who work fast-paced
> With good breeding
> And a tiny waist
> You'll bring honor to us all

The traditional narrative is somewhat disrupted by Mulan's not being feminine enough and failing to meet the expectations of her family. After being deemed an unsuitable bride by the matchmaker, Mulan sings, "Look at me / I will never pass for a perfect bride / When will my reflection show who I am inside?" Mulan is a Disney Princess who cannot find a prince; however, she is far from inadequate. The narrative quickly redeems Mulan when she displays her horse-riding skills and by her willingness to take her father's place in battle. This construction of Mulan's empowered femininity is consistent with notions of Girl Power, or the strong female character that became the dominant form of womanhood in popular media in the mid to late 1990s (Hains 2009). Mulan's temporary embracing of a male identity and Li Shang's construction of masculinity must be examined in the context of Girl Power.

Because Mulan's empowerment clearly comes from within, her adoption of male clothing and posturing can be seen as accessory and performative. She needs the trappings to pass as a man but not as a source of strength. After cutting her hair short and abandoning the family home, Mulan prepares to join the male recruits. Mushu, a dragon-guardian sent by Mulan's ancestors to protect her, teaches her how to behave like a man: "Okay this is it. Time to show'em your man walk. Shoulders back, chest high, feet apart, head up and strut. Two, three—Break it down. Hup, two, three. And work it!" In a comedic sequence, "manly" is defined as lacking in hygiene and punching men as a form of greeting. Because Mulan's attempt at manliness is clearly a temporary performance, the film can safely mock the most stereotypical aspects of masculinity and the fact that she can pass as a man at all also reveals masculinity as mere performance.

Mulan's sincere empowered femininity and mocking of stereotypical manhood complicates the construction of Li Shang's masculinity. He is introduced as the captain in charge of training the recruits, including the passing Mulan. The film adds complexity to Li Shang's character by revealing that he achieved his position in the army because he is a powerful general's son. When he starts the training by taking his shirt off and revealing his stunning physique, the recruits secretly mock him as a "pretty boy." Neither physical attractiveness nor nepotism (a prince is after all the son of a king) is traditionally used in Disney films to undermine the status of a male protagonist. This fragile construction of Li Shang's masculinity is consistent with cultural debates at the time of the film's production when the concept of Girl Power was quickly confronted with concerns of a crisis in boyhood. Stories of female empowerment, whether told symbolically in the media or in real life, were not met by celebrations of gender equality but rather by a newfound concern for the role of men in society (Pomerantz and Raby 2011; Ringrose 2007). Similarly, the film seems to imply that for every gain of social power Mulan makes there is a loss of masculine dignity Li Shang has to concede.

This crisis of masculinity is exemplified by Li Shang's emphasizing physical and stereotypical traits of manhood. In the musical sequence "I'll Make a Man Out of You" (Wilder and Zippel 1998b), edited to represent the passing of several days of hard training, Li Shang outlines the elements of manhood:

> We must be swift as the coursing river
> With all the force of a great typhoon
> With all the strength of a raging fire
> Mysterious as the dark side of the moon

All the archetypal characteristics of masculinity are present; men are strong, active, balanced, unemotional and restrained. Yet the only recruit capable of performing the ultimate task of manliness—retrieving an arrow from a tall pole while carrying weights—is Mulan. Her version of Girl Power does not allow Li Shang even the benefit of physical superiority. This portrayal of feminine dominance is further bolstered when Mulan saves Li Shang's life during a battle with the Huns. Even after being exposed as a female and expelled from the army, it is Mulan who becomes aware of the Huns' intentions to attack. In the film's final scenes, Mulan and Li Shang work together to save the city and the Emperor, and it is she who is acclaimed as a hero. Li Shang could be the only Disney prince who does not execute a rescue mission all by himself.

Presumably responding to the masculinity-in-crisis debates, early in *Mulan II* (2004) any disruptive notions of gender are tempered by Mulan herself. In the opening scene, a group of village girls ask Mulan to teach them how to fight. As one explains, "Mulan is going to teach us how to kick butt!" To their initial disappointment Mulan responds, "Calm down, that's lesson number two. The first and most important lesson is to be gentle at the same time we're being tough. But the world is full of opposites and so are you. To be a good warrior, you must bring it all into balance." Highlighting the instructive qualities of song and the memorability of rhymes, "Lesson Number One" (Junge and Tesori 2004) imparts a lesson on balance:

> Like a rock, you must be hard!
> Like an oak, you must be firm!
> Like a cloud, you are soft.
> Like bamboo, you bend in the wind.

The seemingly contradictory lyrics instruct girls to be quick and unafraid while remaining creepily slow since "It's okay to be afraid." The important lesson imparted is that all extremes are wrong, specifically that an aggressive assertion of female power needs to be balanced out by feminine softness. Just as a response to the crisis of masculinity is the emergence of a less aggressive, gentler male ideal, *Mulan II* seems to endorse a revised version of Girl Power that is willing to embrace and celebrate traditional femininity. Applying a vaguely defined but visually reinforced concept of yin and yang, the narrative brings "balance" to the construction of gender identities. Taken together, the performances of femininity in *Mulan* and *Mulan II* achieve a kind of compromise: It is acceptable to adopt a limited set of masculine traits as long as one preserves all the important feminine ones. The construction of masculinity in Li Shang is uncertain, as he is not allowed to embrace any positive feminine characteristics while remaining one of the least stereotypically masculine Disney princes. Li Shang's masculinity is ambiguously constructed in opposition to Mulan's assertive articulation of an androgynous gender identity. Arguably, in the spectrum of masculinities of color, Asian (and Asian American) masculinities are the most threatened by empowered femininities. Li Shang has something to prove, but he cannot fully embrace a gentler version of masculinity, and prevailing cultural norms prevent him from displaying overtly aggressive behaviors. In the end he is just a pretty boy, albeit an athletic and courageous one.

## The Princess and the Handsome Slacker

*The Princess and the Frog* (2009) is the first animated Disney film to feature a Black princess character. According to Breaux (2010), the film is Disney's attempt to both redeem itself of its racist past and cash in on the growing economic power of

Black households. Breaux (2010) describes how the studio was quick to respond to criticisms, even as the movie was being made, eventually rewriting the protagonist from a maid named Maddie into an entrepreneurial waitress, Tiana. The movie, set in 1920s New Orleans, tells the story of Tiana and her dream of opening a restaurant and fulfilling her deceased father's dream. To achieve her goal she works tirelessly and saves every penny. The city is excited about the arrival of Naveen, Prince of Maldonia, who is expected to marry Charlotte, a rich White girl and Tiana's friend. At a party, tempted by the offer of money to open her restaurant, Tiana kisses Naveen, previously transformed into a frog by a voodoo magician, Dr. Facilier. Instead of making Naveen human again, Tiana is transformed into a frog herself. Tiana and Naveen depart in search of Mama Odie, a voodoo priestess in the Louisiana bayou with the power to transform them back into humans. Their trip becomes a journey of self-discovery.

Breaux (2010) argues that on the one hand *The Princess and the Frog* presents a romanticized version of African American life in the 1920s, yet one that conveniently ignores all the historical struggles and limitations that Blacks faced. On the other hand, the inclusion of a Black female in the pantheon of Disney princesses at the very least addresses a shortage of symbolic representations. The contribution of Tiana's male protagonist, Naveen, is less evident. As Prince of Maldonia his royal credentials and clothing style suggest a European background, but his dark skin and his accent (the character is voiced by Brazilian-born actor Bruno Campos) indicate otherwise. Naveen is essentially a racially ambiguous prince. While his portrayal does not contribute to the symbolic representation of any specific ethnic group, he can easily be identified as non-White.

According to England, Descartes and Collier-Meek (2011) Naveen from *The Princess and the Frog* is portrayed as inept, with child-like innocence and without the means to support himself. Besides his athleticism, which could be conceived of as a more masculine trait, Naveen's most common characteristics are displaying emotion and being affectionate, which are traditionally feminine behaviors. By contrast assertiveness, a traditional masculine characteristic, is one of the most typical traits exhibited by Tiana. *The Princess and the Frog* portrays androgynous prince and princess characters even if the story ends with a traditional romantic union.

More so than in *Mulan*, where Li Shang's masculinity was undermined by Mulan's assertiveness and heroism, the contrast between Naveen's version of masculinity and his female protagonist is even starker. For every flaw in Naveen's character there is a positive quality in Tiana's. When the film introduces Naveen, audiences meet a handsome and athletic young man. It is also made immediately clear that he does not have money, that his parents cut him off, that he is a *bon vivant* who likes to party all the time but has not worked a day in his life and that he is ready and willing to marry for money and not for love. None of the strength and courage traditionally attributed to the prince archetype is present here. We are in the presence of a handsome slacker who just happens to be a prince. By contrast, Tiana is introduced early on as hard working and focused. She works double shifts in order to save money and fulfill her dream of owning a restaurant. When her friends and her mother suggest that she slow down, have some fun and find love, Tiana protests that she is "Almost There" (Newman 2009a):

> Mama! I don't have time for dancin'
> That's just gonna have to wait a while
> Ain't got time for messin' around
> And it's not my style

The lyrics elaborate on Tiana's ambition and perseverance, as well as on her defiance of traditional norms and expectations. Perhaps unwittingly so, the film adopts an accepted social narrative that proposes that women of color are more responsible than men of color. The narrative certainly fits within a larger social preoccupation with girl empowerment and boy crisis. The film reproduces discourses that present women's progress in education and employment as necessarily balanced by diminished opportunities for men (Pomerantz and Raby 2011; Ringrose 2007). This symbolic articulation of the notion that Black women bring their communities forward in spite of or in the absence of men may be empowering for Black girls but is certainly problematic for Black boys. There is no African American prince in Disney's world, and Tiana's racially ambiguous male protagonist is no match for her work ethic.

The notion of male obliviousness, positioned in contrast to female initiative, is not challenged even in the presence of a major crisis. Even after being transformed into a frog, Naveen has a difficult time assessing his priorities. While traveling down the bayou rivers looking for Mama Odie, Naveen and Tiana sing about what they will do once they become humans again. The song "When We're Human" (Newman 2009b) illustrates the differences in character between Naveen and Tiana. He sings that when he is a human again he wants "a great big party every night" and describes all the women he will have fun with because "life is short." This particular version of masculinity—the party animal—is generally problematic for patriarchy and particularly so for minorities. Data suggest that Black and Hispanic women intermarry with Whites at a significantly higher rate than their male counterparts. For women of color intermarriage usually translates into upward social mobility. Breaux (2010) highlights the importance of interracial marriage in *The Princess and the Frog* by noting:

> Some critics quickly pointed out that Tiana had no black prince and that this jaded the positive impact *The Princess and the Frog* would have on African American girls. Others argue that a racial double standard exists between the media's representations of white women, who are able to pine for and marry a white prince, while Tiana must fend for herself and marry a racially ambiguous prince. (411)

Naveen's racial ambiguity is no guarantee of increased social status for Tiana. His assertion of idle masculinity typically translates into stagnation or downward social mobility for young men of color. Tiana's portion of "When We're Human" (Newman 2009b), in contrast, is a model of Black female responsibility. She sings that she will go back to working hard because "If you do your best each and every day / Good things are sure to come your way," which is a lesson she learned from her father. Interestingly, Tiana quotes her father and not her mother as a role model. In fact, her dead father is the only male character of significant moral stature. The implication is that men used to be dependable and responsible. Men today only want to enjoy life and women have to empower themselves in order to provide for their families. This masculine/feminine binary mirrored in the work hard/enjoy life binary remains powerful even when Tiana reassesses her priorities and realizes that she needs love as well. In the end, Tiana and Naveen marry each other and, after being transformed back into humans, Tiana uses her life's savings to open her restaurant. One reading of the story is that the first Black princess got her racially ambiguous prince and her entrepreneurial dream. Even if Naveen is a less-than-perfect prince, Breaux (2010) argues there are other positive Black male role models in the film, like Tiana's father, James, who is portrayed as a hardworking and loving father and war hero. However, it is indisputable that the discursive weight of the narrative and symbolic power of representation falls with the figures of the prince and princess. In the closing scenes, Tiana is shown managing her restaurant while Naveen is depicted dancing and playing with the orchestra. An alternative reading of the story is that the first Black princess saved her handsome slacker from himself and ended up supporting him as well.

## Discussion

England, Descartes and Collier-Meek (2011) have demonstrated that Aladdin and Naveen are the only Disney princes to exhibit more feminine than masculine characteristics. Their content analysis shows that while Li Shang is manlier, he nevertheless exhibits fewer masculine characteristics than all other Disney princes except for those in *Snow White* (1937) and *Cinderella* (1950). What these researchers failed to consider is the role of race in the construction of the masculinity whereby the least masculine and most feminine Disney princes also happen to be of color. Race also influences how femininity is constructed in other Disney films. Lacroix argues that for White princesses such as Ariel from *The Little Mermaid* (1989) and Belle from *Beauty and the Beast* (1991), "their race is not connected to their choices in the narrative" but rather "attributed to their personal idiosyncrasies" (2004, 224), while for princesses and female protagonists of color such as *Pocahontas* (1995) and Esmeralda from *The Hunchback of Notre Dame* (1996), their personality traits were explained as related to their exoticism and race, such as Pocahontas's communion with nature or Esmeralda's gypsy ways. Following the same logic, one could argue that the more androgynous, less stereotypically masculine portrayals of Aladdin, Li Shang and Naveen are also related to their race.

This chapter is not lamenting the lack of normative masculine traits in characters of color. Arguably, it is a source of celebration if boys and girls in the audience are exposed to more emotional and less physically aggressive versions of manhood in Disney films. As Gillam and Wooden state, "The post-feminist world is a different place for men, and the post-princess Pixar is a different place for male protagonists" (2008, 3). Yet a big portion of Disney's undeniable cultural influence remains non-Pixar princesses and princes. What this chapter has attempted to demonstrate is that in the spectrum of masculinities of Disney's Princes, the three princes of color occupy a distinct place where the construction of their masculinities is informed by their race and by evolving discourses of gender that position female empowerment in opposition to a perceived crisis of manhood. Therefore, the masculinities of Aladdin, Li Shang and Naveen are hegemonically constructed since the empowerment of princes of color is not conducive to the survival of White patriarchy. In this context it is important to highlight the intertextuality of media interpretations in which each prince is evaluated not only in the context of each individual film, but also in contrast to all the other princes, from Snow White's savior Prince to Rapunzel's Flynn Rider. It is in the broader context of the archetypal ideal of the prince that the three non-White characters occupy a distinctly diminished place in the masculine hierarchy.

## References

*Aladdin*. 1992. Directed by Ron Clemens and John Musker. Walt Disney Pictures.

Ashman, Howard, and Alan Menken. 1992. "Prince Ali." Buena Vista Pictures Distribution Inc.

*Beauty and the Beast*. 1991. Directed by Gary Trousdale and Kirk Wise. Walt Disney Pictures.

Breaux, Richard M. 2010. "After 75 Years of Magic: Disney Answers Its Critics, Rewrites African American History, and Cashes In on Its Racist Past." *Journal of African American Studies, 14*, 389–416.

Chandler, Daniel. 1997. *An Introduction to Genre Theory.* Accessed September 10, 2004. http://users.aber.ac.uk/dgc/Documents/intgenre/

*Cinderella.* 1950. Directed by Clyde Geronimi, Wilfred Jackson, and Hamilton Luske. Walt Disney Productions.

Connell, R. W. 1992. "A Very Straight Gay: Masculinity, Homosexual Experience, and the Dynamics of Gender." *American Sociological Review, 57*(6): 735–751.

Craven, Allison. 2002. "Beauty and the Belles: Discourses of Feminism and Femininity in Disneyland." *European Journal of Women's Studies, 9*(2): 123–132.

Currie, Dawn. 1999. *Girl Talk: Adolescent Magazines and Their Readers.* Toronto, Ontario, Canada: University of Toronto Press.

Demetriou, Demetrakis Z. 2001. "Connell's Concept of Hegemonic Masculinity: A Critique." *Theory & Society, 30*(3): 337–361.

Driscoll, Catherine. 2002. *Girls: Feminine Adolescence in Popular Culture and Cultural Theory.* New York: Columbia University Press.

England, Dawn E., Lara Descartes, and Melissa A. Collier-Meek. 2011. "Gender Role Portrayal and the Disney Princesses." *Sex Roles, 64*, 555–567.

Fiske, John. 1987. *Television Culture.* London: Routledge.

Foucault, Michel. 1978. *The History of Sexuality* (Vol. 1). New York: Pantheon Books.

Gillam, Ken, and Shannon R. Wooden. 2008. "Post-Princess Models of Gender: The New Man in Disney/Pixar." *Journal of Popular Film & Television, 36*(1): 2–8.

Gramsci, Antonio. 1973. *Letters from the Prison.* New York: Harper & Row.

Hains, Rebecca. 2009. "Power Feminism, Mediated: Girl Power and the Commercial Politics of Change." *Women's Studies in Communication, 32*(1): 89–113.

Hall, Stuart. 1981. "The Whites of Their Eyes: Racist Ideologies and the Media." In *Silver Linings*, ed. G. Bridges and R. Brunt, 28–52. London: Lawrence & Wishart.

Hall, Stuart. 1999. "Racist Ideologies and the Media." In *Media Studies* (2nd ed.), ed. P. Marris and S. Thornham, 271–282. New York: NYU Press.

hooks, bell. 1993. "A Revolution of Values: The Promise of Multicultural Change." In *The Cultural Studies Reader*, ed. S. During, 233–240. New York: Routledge.

*The Hunchback of Notre Dame.* 1996. Directed by Gary Trousdale and Kirk Wise. Walt Disney Pictures.

Jhally, Sut, and Justin Lewis. 1992. *Enlightened Racism: "The Cosby Show," Audiences, and the Myth of the American Dream.* Boulder, CO: Westview Press.

Junge, Alexa, and Jeanine Tesori. 2004. "Lesson Number One." Walt Disney Records.

Johnson, E. Patrick. 2003. "The Specter of the Black Fag: Parody, Blackness, and Hetero/Homosexual B(r)others." *Journal of Homosexuality, 45*(2–4): 217–234.

Kearney, Mary Celeste. 2006. *Girls Make Media.* New York: Routledge.

Lacroix, Celeste. 2004. "Images of Animated Others: The Orientalization of Disney's Cartoon Heroines from *The Little Mermaid* to *The Hunchback of Notre Dame.*" *Popular Communication, 2*(4): 213–329.

Lester, Neal A. 2010. "Disney's *The Princess and the Frog*: The Pride, the Pressure, and the Politics of Being a First." *Journal of American Culture, 33*(4): 294–308.

*The Little Mermaid.* 1989. Directed by Ron Clements and John Musker. Walt Disney Pictures.

MacMillan, Katie. 2006. *Discourse Analysis—a Primer.* Loughborough University. Accessed March 25, 2006. http://www.lboro.ac.uk/research/mmethods/resources/links/da_primer.html

Menken, Alan, and Tim Rice. 1992. "One Jump Ahead." Buena Vista Pictures Distribution Inc.

Mitchell, Claudia, and Jacqueline Reid-Walsh. 2002. *Researching Children's Popular Culture: The Cultural Spaces of Childhood.* New York: Routledge.

*Mulan.* 1998. Directed by Tony Bancroft and Barry Cook. Walt Disney Pictures.

*Mulan II.* 2004. Directed by Darrel Rooney and Lynne Southerland. Walt Disney Pictures.

Newman, Randy. 2009a. "Almost There." Walt Disney Records.

Newman, Randy. 2009b. "When We're Human." Walt Disney Records.

Oware, Matthew. 2011. "Brotherly Love: Homosociality and Black Masculinity in Gangsta Rap Music." *Journal of African American Studies, 15*(1): 22–39.

*Pocahontas.* 1995. Directed by Mike Gabriel and Eric Goldberg. Walt Disney Pictures.

Pomerantz, Shauna, and Rebecca Raby. 2011. "'Oh, She's So Smart': Girls' Complex Engagements with Post/Feminist Narratives of Academic Success." *Gender & Education, 23*(5): 549–564.

*The Princess and the Frog.* 2009. Directed by Ron Clements and John Musker. Walt Disney Pictures.

Rehn, Alf, and David Sköld. 2005. "'I Love the Dough': Rap Lyrics as a Minor Economic Literature." *Culture & Organization, 11*(1): 17–31.

Ringrose, Jessica. 2011. "Gendered Risks and Opportunities? Exploring Teen Girls' Digitized Sexual Identities in Postfeminist Media Contexts." *International Journal of Media & Cultural Politics,* 7(2): 121–138.

*Snow White.* 1937. Directed by David Hand. Walt Disney Productions.

Strinati, Dominic. 1995. *An Introduction to Theories of Popular Culture.* New York: Routledge.

Sullivan, Nikki. 2003. *A Critical Introduction to Queer Theory.* New York: NYU Press.

*Tangled.* 2010. Directed by Nathan Greno and Byron Howard. Walt Disney Pictures.

van Dijk, Teun Adrianus. 2001. "Principles of Critical Discourse Analysis." In *Discourse Theory and Practice: A Reader*, ed. S. Taylor and S. J. Yates. London: Sage.

Whelan, Bridget. 2012. "Power to the Princess: Disney and the Creation of the 20th Century Princess Narrative." *Interdisciplinary Humanities, 29*(1): 21–34.

Wilder, Matthew, and David Zippel. 1998a. "Honor to Us All." Walt Disney Records.

Wilder, Matthew, and David Zippel. 1998b. "I'll Make a Man Out of You." Walt Disney Records.

Wohlwend, Karen E. 2011. "'Are You Guys *Girls*?': Boys, Identity Texts, and Disney Princess Play." *Journal of Early Childhood Literacy, 12*(1): 3–23.

Youngs, Gillian. 1999. "The Ghost of *Snow White.*" *International Feminist Journal of Politics, 1*(2).

Zarranz, Libe G. 2007. "Diswomen Strike Back? The Evolution of Disney Femmes in the 1990s." *Atenea, 27*(2): 55–67.

Zaslow, Emilie. 2009. *Feminism, Inc.: Coming of Age in Girl Power Media Culture.* New York: Palgrave Macmillan.

CHAPTER FOUR

# Rescue the Princess: The Videogame Princess as Prize, Parody, and Protagonist

SARA M. GRIMES

## Introduction

In November 2012, a number of news outlets covered the story of one father's heart-warming efforts to make videogames more gender-inclusive for his three-year-old daughter, Maya. According to the reports, Mike Hoye spent several weeks hacking the underlying software code of *The Legend of Zelda: The Wind Waker* (Nintendo 2003) in order to re-write the game's text to allow for a female version of the male avatar/main character, Link (McWhertor 2012; Narcisse 2012). As reported by Johnston (2012), Hoye had been playing the game with his daughter, and was bothered by the fact that while the game allowed players to rename Link with a female name if so desired, the character was nonetheless addressed as male both during game play and within the larger storyline. Hoye replaced "My lad" with "Milady," "young boy" with "young girl," and Maya was arguably able to see herself represented within the game's narrative. When asked why he felt altering the game text was important, Hoye was quoted saying, "I'm not having my daughter growing up thinking girls don't get to be the hero" (Johnston 2012).

The Hoye story is significant for a number of reasons. It unfolded during a year that was particularly notable for both the resurgence of longstanding debates around gender representation within digital game contents, development and advertising, as well as a number of disturbing, high-profile examples of misogyny within the gamer community (Consalvo 2012; Salter and Blodgett 2012). Both trends highlight the need for further discussion, research and action around gender and games. In addition, the particular game that Hoye elected to modify, *The Legend of Zelda: The Wind Waker*, happens to belong to an enormously successful digital game series that has played a key role in both (re)producing and reflecting evolving trends in the role and function of female characters within digital game narratives.

The series' namesake, Zelda, is in many ways a quintessential female videogame character. She is rarely the protagonist, but instead frequently serves as *objet petit a* to the game's (until Hoye's intervention, at least) male hero, Link. Across all eight of the official *Legend of Zelda* sequels (as well as many of the dozens of re-releases, spin-offs and adaptations)[1] that have appeared since the first installment was published in 1986, Zelda[2] most often appears as a non-playable secondary character—either as a 'damsel in distress' or as an intermittent, magical helper. This 'rescue the princess' storyline, wherein a male hero is called upon to search out and eventually rescue a kidnapped, imprisoned or otherwise incapacitated princess, reproduces a highly typical version of the hero's quest that continues to feature prominently throughout Western literature and media (de Lauretis 1984; Haase 2004; Propp 1968). Concurrently, as various digital game scholars have observed, the 'rescue the princess' plot device has become a common, even clichéd, way of structuring and directing action within digital games (Dietz 1998).

On the other hand, in two spin-off games, *Zelda: Legend of Ganon* (Philips Media 1993) and *Zelda's Adventure* (Philips Media 1994) (both of which were licensed games produced by third parties and released on the short-lived Philips CD-I [Warner 2006]), the roles are reversed as Zelda serves as the player-controlled protagonist who must rescue Link. Even more recently, grown-up versions of Zelda have appeared in the cross-branded Nintendo fighting games *Super Smash Bros. Melee* (HAL Laboratory 2001) and *Super Smash Bros. Brawl* (Nintendo 2008), as a playable 'warrior princess' character who can fight and jump with the best of them. Here too, Princess Zelda can be understood as reflective of broader trends, namely, those found within the numerous games that seek to engage more deeply with the princess archetype by mobilizing, subverting, transgressing and at times deconstructing her role and symbolic power (or lack thereof).

This chapter seeks to examine the multiple functions of the princess within console-based videogame narratives and mechanics. Rather than reexamine issues raised in previous works on the topic, many of which have focused on visual representations of female characters within games and associated marketing, the current discussion focuses instead on the various ways in which the princess has come to provide a diverse set of intertextual cultural meanings within videogame narratives, culture and lore. Special attention will be placed on the use of parody and transgression within digital game depictions of princess characters, as well as the ways in which some games have engaged with the 'rescue the princess' trope as a key entry point for highlighting and opening up a space for critical discussion about the conservative gender politics that continue to prevail within much of mainstream gamer culture.

## The Many Perils of the Videogame Princess

Unlike many of the princesses explored elsewhere in this book, videogame princesses are not always, or even particularly closely, linked to girl culture.[3] Videogames, the game industry and the broader gamer culture have historically been heavily male-centric. For one, the digital game industry is disproportionately male—according to Williams et al. (2009), only 11.5% of gamemakers are female. Meanwhile, videogame advertisements, promotional events and conventions and many design features (of both games and game-related media) appear to assume a predominantly male audience. This continues to be the case despite the fact that a large percentage of girls and women play digital games. According to the 2012 annual report produced by the industry-based Entertainment Software Association, 47% of all gamers are female. Meanwhile, studies by Rideout et al. (2010; see also Roberts et al. 2005) and Lenhart et al. (2008) have found that engagement in some form of digital gaming is nearly ubiquitous among both girls and boys.

However, such statistics often merge all forms of digital gaming together—from online, casual games played through Facebook, to the technologically sophisticated 'triple A' titles that are heavily promoted by the mainstream game industry. They therefore do not necessarily describe participation rates when it comes to the titles and technologies most strongly associated with mainstream 'gamer' culture, such as console games, where a significant amount of the videogame market is both focused and generated. For instance, a recent study by market research firm M2 Research estimated that among the 45 million players in the United States who 'game' primarily on a console system, only 26% are female. The company furthermore reported that the majority of female console players use the family-friendly Wii (80%), while only 11% play primarily on an Xbox 360, and only 9% play on a PlayStation 3 (cited in Ohannessian 2010).

Participation rates relate in complex ways to how and for whom games are designed and targeted (advertised to certain players and not others), and to the underlying assumptions the games' designers bring to the design process (Chess 2011; Fullerton et al. 2004; Salter and Blodgett 2012; Schott and Thomas 2008).

They are also implicated in many of the efforts that have been made over the past two decades to expand videogames into new and/or broader markets, for instance, through the numerous attempts to establish a separate but concurrent "girls' games" market (Cassell and Jenkins 2000). While these relationships are in no way deterministic, they are nonetheless important factors to consider when thinking about the roles and functions of princess characters within videogames, as well as the broader gender politics of digital gaming. For instance, many of the most popular videogame princesses—from Zelda and *Super Mario Bros.*'s (Nintendo 1985) Princess Peach, to *Mortal Kombat II*'s (Midway 1993) Princess Kitana—first appeared in titles designed and marketed with a predominantly male audience in mind. While significant headway has been made over the past thirty years to introduce more gender balance into videogame development, content and advertising, the game industry remains dominated by men (Williams et al. 2009), while the gaming culture is still largely framed in male-centric terms (Taylor et al. 2009).

Feminist analyses of gender representation within game narratives, imagery and marketing have thus far tended to focus on two key issues: the continued underrepresentation of female characters within popular videogames (Provenzo 1991; Williams et al. 2009), as well as the specific way in which female characters are depicted and treated when they *are* present (Dietz 1998; Graner Ray 2004). In both cases, these issues have remained pertinent despite the massive growth and diversification that has unfolded within both game genres and markets over the past twenty years. This is particularly the case within the most 'popular' mainstream console games.[4] While in 1991 Provenzo (1991) calculated that only 8% of popular videogames contained female characters, more recent studies have discovered only a slight increase. For instance, as Williams et al. (2009, 824) describe, "Male characters are vastly more likely to appear than female character [*sic*] in general." Only 10.45% of the 150 most popular games released between March 2005 and February 2006 featured female primary characters, and only 14.65% featured female secondary characters. In comparing the contents of games sold to the total games released during that same time period, Williams et al. found only a small difference in the male to female character ratio (which was 81.24/18.76 male/female among all games made, compared to 85.23/14.77 male/female among the games that sold the most units).

Kuchera (2012) describes that industry-based research on gender in games suggests that "the very idea of a female-led game seems so toxic to publishers and marketing that there is [*sic*] barely enough examples from which to draw conclusions" (n.p.). In a recent study of 669 games that featured protagonists with discernible gender, market researchers Electronic Entertainment Design and Research (EEDAR) found that while nearly half ("a little under 300") provided the option of playing as a female,[5] only 24 (under 4%) featured an exclusively female protagonist. In response to oft-cited statistics that games with female-only leads do not sell as well as games with female-optional or male-only protagonists, Zatkin (EEDAR's Chief Operating Officer) points to the likely influence of marketing in skewing the figures. For example, the EEDAR study also found that "games with a female only protagonist, got half the [advertising] spending of female optional [*sic*], and [less than] 40% of the marketing budget of male-led games" (as cited in Kuchera 2012).

In terms of how this relates to the aforementioned second issue—the way in which female characters are portrayed in games and advertisements—the research to date has largely focused on the predominance of highly idealized 'bodies' and beauty ideals, as well as evidence of mechanical (e.g., through the inclusion of "male gaze" inspired camera angles) and aesthetic sexualization (e.g., skimpy attire, objectified poses) (Dietz 1998; Miller and Summers 2007). For instance, according to a widely cited study conducted by Children Now in the late 1990s (2000, 4), 85% of female characters had "large breasts, unusually small waists or very thin bodies," while 38% "displayed significant body exposure." A more recent analysis of videogame covers by Burgess et al. (2007, 427) similarly discovered that "the relatively rare cases where women were portrayed as central ... almost always came with an exaggerated sexuality."

Significantly less attention has been given to the specific roles that these female videogame characters are engaged in (e.g., their back story, the actions they perform in the game) or to the functions that they fill within the games' narratives. At least some of this resistance to delving into character types and histories likely stems from the longstanding debates about the role and relevance of narrative to games that unfolded in the early years of digital game studies. As King and Krzywinska (2006, 39) describe, "counter-arguments" to the idea of analyzing narrative in games have emerged "on at least two levels: that narrative is not central to games or that it exists essentially in opposition to gameplay." Game scholars such as Juul (1998) have argued that because narrative theories are inadequate for accounting for the player's agency and role in 'co-authoring' the gameplay experience, analysis of game contents should stay away from stories and focus instead on mechanics, spatial elements or temporal elements. Indeed, players do bring an enormous amount of interpretation and subjectivity to their gameplay, as well as to their virtual embodiment of the main protagonist/avatar. This is a core dimension of the experience, and is not adequately accounted for by narrative theory or textual analysis.

Nonetheless, there remain several digital game scholars who defend the importance of taking game narratives, and narrative elements, seriously (Bizzocchi

2007; Fuller and Jenkins 1995; Goetz 2012; Ip 2001a, 2001b). In most games, fictional elements are not disconnected from the rules of play or underlying mechanics privileged by Juul (1998) and others. In addition to providing intertextual cues and other cultural signifiers, narrative elements and "fictional world-building" provide context and rationale for action, as well as contribute significantly to (at least some) videogame designs and player enjoyment (Wilson 2007, 24). Furthermore, while they may not hold any real textual authority, they nonetheless often contribute to various facets of the player's experience and interpretation. As Pohl (2008, 101) argues, "It makes a difference if we have to arrange blocks in an optimal position or if we have to save the princess from the jaws of a monkey."

Others point to the players themselves as evidence of the significance of narrative, as found in the many examples of player-produced fan fiction and artwork that revolve around games' embedded plotlines, character back stories and other game lore (Newman 2005). A key example of this approach can be found in the work of Consalvo (2003, 325), who argues, "I think it is premature to give up on the idea of narrative in games and its place in helping us understand games and gamers. This view is based on evidence that some gamers' understandings or use of narrative may differ from these theoretical understandings [such as Juul's], and it is important to take them into account."

There are many reasons a deeper analysis of videogame princesses and other female characters is important. Previous investigations on this topic have emphasized the links between gender representation and worldview (e.g., cultivation theory), self-esteem and identity (as well as perception of others), social power relations and issues of inclusion/exclusion (Bryce and Rutter 2003; Dietz 1998; Fullerton et al. 2008; Graner Ray 2005; Martins et al. 2009; Williams et al. 2009). The research also indicates that gender representations in games, and players' relationships to them, are extremely complex and often rife with contradiction (Jenson and de Castell 2008; Kennedy 2002; Schleiner 2001; Taylor 2006; Walkerdine 2007). These findings reflect those found throughout the literature on gender, media and audience studies. For instance, in their analysis of princess characters (found across literary and popular media forms) and women's recollections of childhood play practices, Forman-Brunell and Eaton (2009, 338) found that "what explains the princess' power is girls' identification with the mixed messages embodied in the figure whose identity has been broadly constructed beyond a single conventional standard." Close readings of these characters can thus provide an important stepping-stone into developing a fuller, more holistic understanding of some of the cultural 'messages' that digital gamers are engaged with.

Similarly, numerous game creators have engaged with the princess archetype in diverse and significant ways. Just as traditional fairy tales have been appropriated, deconstructed and subverted by various authors across a wide range of media, there are numerous examples of videogame princesses that defy, transgress, parody or subvert the established tropes and clichés. The remainder of this chapter will explore both the dominant and some of the key alternative functions that the 'princess' has performed within a number of popular console videogames that have appeared over the past three decades.

## The Princess as MacGuffin

*Thank you Mario! But our Princess is in another castle!*

– Mushroom Retainer, *Super Mario Bros.* (Nintendo 1985)

While Princess Zelda and Princess Peach are arguably the most well-known objects of the 'rescue the princesses' plot device, they are not the only examples that emerged during the early years of home console videogames. In one of the earliest investigations of gender in games, Provenzo (1991) found that many of the female characters featured on the covers of the 47 most popular console games of 1990 essentially functioned as "damsels in distress"—the objects of desire driving the male heroes' actions, the prizes to be won at the end of the game. Subsequent research by Dietz (1998, 434–435) confirmed that "the second most common portrayal of women in [a subsequent] sample of games was the woman as the victim or as the proverbial 'Damsel in Distress.' Women were portrayed in this manner 21% of the time (N=7)." While in Dietz's sample only three of the characters were specifically designated as princesses (including Princess Zelda), both studies point to the early emergence of the 'rescue the princess' trope within videogame narratives and designs.

Sherman's (1997) "Perils of the Princess"[6] was the first and remains one of the only academic studies to specifically examine the role of the princess within videogames. Rather than focus on statistical or visual representations, Sherman's analysis applies theories and concepts drawn from the field of folklore studies to unpack a seminal videogame princess, Princess Peach of the Super Mario series. She (1997, 244) says, "Computer games, like *Mario*, fit within the study of both narrative and game, albeit a genre constructed not to be folk narrative but to model it." Like Zelda, Princess Peach[7] first appeared as the 'damsel in distress' that the Super Mario brothers (Mario and Luigi) must set out to rescue from Bowser, the evil King of the Koopas.

Sherman analyzes Princess Peach using Propp's (1968) system for identifying common structural elements in Western folklore, as well as Jung's (1968) primary archetypes. She describes that videogame princesses most often (but not always) occupy passive and or non-playable roles, and are frequently featured as the call to action for the (male) hero's journey (Campbell 1949). She (1997, 253) argues, "The princess may be seen as the female counterpart of the hero," but that "for males, she is that which the hero lacks in all of the games; ... this lack of a princess sets the plot in motion." Notably, this is a position not only often occupied by princesses in a hero's quest and other fairy tales, but by monsters as well. As de Lauretis (1984, 109) describes it, such characters are "inscribed in hero narratives, in someone else's story, not their own; so they are figures or markers of positions—places and topoi—through which the hero and his story move to their destination and accomplish meaning."

As many of the above-mentioned scholars suggest, the 'rescue the princess' plot device is consistent with larger heteronormative gender discourses. In many ways, the recurring subordination of the (oftentimes sole) female lead into a largely passive, objectified role as prize and locus of the hero's desire contributes to an ongoing gendering of the hero's quest (and arguably of the game itself) as a male-centric narrative structure. The princess can thus be understood as serving first and foremost as a 'MacGuffin'—the term screenwriters use to describe the arbitrary object or goal that the hero and/or villain are in pursuit of (J. Williams, personal communication, April 5, 2013).

Of course, players themselves may very well subvert the gender roles implied within such storylines—for instance, if the player is female, or if the storyline is ignored, or if it is substituted for the player's own motivations and interpretations. Nonetheless, the emergence of this particular discourse as an early and pervasive narrative staple served to align videogames—a relatively new media form—with established, hegemonic discourses. In so doing, however, it also established a norm and provided a 'shorthand' through which other possibilities could (and eventually would) be explored.

## Warrior Princesses

Videogame princesses did not all remain in distress for very long. In fact, the very first sequel to *Super Mario Bros.* (Nintendo 1985) (*Super Mario Bros. 2* [Nintendo 1988]) featured a landmark divergence from the 'rescue the princess' trope established in the first installment of the series. In this game, Princess Peach is featured as one of four playable protagonist characters that players can select in their quest to save "the people" of Mushroom Kingdom. The title was also the focus of Sherman's (1997) interviews with child players. She describes that the girls and boys she interviewed all expressed a profound awareness of the traditional messages and roles assigned to women in games and other media, and had a range of reactions to the role reversal found in *Super Mario Bros 2*. Sherman (1997, 253–254) writes, "Every girl I asked responded instantly that she played the princess," while "boys see the option of playing the princess in *Mario 2* as strange because 'she's the one you're trying to save.'"

Since the mid-1980s, both Princess Peach and Princess Zelda have periodically (but not frequently) appeared as playable characters within their respective series. Each has also served as the lead character in self-contained, spin-off titles, which recast the princesses as heroes/protagonists on a quest to save their former rescuers. Their traditional function as 'damsels in distress' is perhaps most overtly contradicted, however, in *Super Smash Bros. Melee* (HAL Laboratory 2001) and *Super Smash Bros. Brawl* (Nintendo 2008). As mentioned above, this cross-title series pits popular characters from different Nintendo console games against each other in slapstick fighting competitions. Here, the princesses are featured alongside a range of other playable characters as formidable fighters with their own special skills, a context in juxtaposition with their traditional attire of full-length ball gowns and tiaras.

Theirs are not the only or even earliest examples of warrior princess protagonists. For instance, the popular and controversial *Mortal Kombat* fighting (or combat) game series introduced the iconic Princess Kitana to its roster of playable characters in its first sequel, *Mortal Kombat II* (Midway 1993). More recently, Princess Hildegard von Krone was added to the fourth installment of the *Soulcalibur* series (Project Soul 2008). In *Code of Princess* (Agatsuma Entertainment 2012), a Japanese action–role playing game for the Nintendo DS handheld console, players can play as protagonist Princess Solange Blanchefleur de Lux, slaying monsters or fighting other players in online competitive combat matches. In each of these cases, the princesses appear alongside other playable character options, including other female characters (e.g., *Mortal Kombat* also features U.S. Army Special Forces officer Sonya Blade). They are presented as able warriors and formidable opponents.

Such characters engage with and in some ways invert the stereotypical notions and associations surrounding the princess's function within action and adventure narratives, particularly her traditional role as the passive victim in need of rescuing. The warrior princess "inverts stereotypical gender expectations and provides entertainment through deviation from the norm" (Hutchinson 2007, 288). While inversion alone is not necessarily transformative, or even critical, such characters nonetheless have the *potential* to act as entry points for subverting the conservative gender politics established in early videogames and across various segments of mainstream gamer culture. They can serve as a type of "symbolic inversion," which as Babcock (1978) argues can be found in "any act of expressive behavior which inverts, contradicts, abrogates, or in some fashion presents an alternative to commonly held cultural codes, values and norms be they linguistic, literary or artistic, religious, social and political" (as cited in Stallybrass and White 1986, 17).

In terms of her role and function, on the one hand, the active, powerful warrior princess certainly seems to present an antipodal alternative to the passive, objectified 'damsel in distress.' On the other hand, as a genre, fighting games have also contributed to the very gender norms that they symbolically invert. Cassell and Jenkins (1998, 9) point out that "in some fighting games, the overarching goal of the game is to rescue 'helpless damsels.'" Other scholars emphasize that fighting games frequently feature hyper-sexualized depictions of female characters. Hutchinson, on the other hand, highlights that in this particular context, even stereotypes and hegemonic aesthetic approaches can function in multiple and complex ways. Dietz (1998, 288) proposes that sexually provocative depictions of warrior princesses and other female fighters can be read as both challenging the norm and "strengthening the norm that is challenged." This duality is reminiscent of numerous other female protagonists found across popular media, which are presented as heroic and active on the one hand, yet compliant to traditional beauty and gender norms on the other (Inness 1999; Jones 2002).

Figure 1. © 2011 NetherRealm Studios: Screenshot of *Mortal Kombat*'s Princess Kitana.

As Kennedy (2002) argues, when dealing with videogame characters, questions of gender are never straightforward, as the "complex relationship between subject and object" that unfolds between the player and her/his avatar blurs and at times challenges established notions of representation. In keeping with Kennedy's approach, since videogame princesses exist concurrently as both character and proxy for the (oftentimes male) player, as both subject and object, it should not be assumed that they function as "feminine subject[s] in any real sense" (n.p.). The fact that the "femininity" of these otherwise highly masculine avatars is largely established through the very same "key exaggerated signifiers" most often identified as evidence of sexualization, such as attire and physique, further complexifies matters (Kennedy 2002, n.p.).

Hutchinson (2007) suggests that there are elements of spectacle and of the carnivalesque within the hyper-sexualized, hyper-feminine portrayals of female characters in fighting games. She notes that fighting games are also notorious for their depictions of gore and hyper-violence, for featuring grotesque and monstrous characters and for their heavy reliance on ethnic stereotypes and hyper-masculine signifiers. Hutchinson describes that since the format of the fighting game is a binary—with one winner and one loser—these elements are mobilized in both reinforcing and subversive ways, depending on which character the player chooses to play as, as well as which player/character ultimately wins. As every character option available is technically capable of winning, the games afford the possibility that the grotesque mutant will vanquish the handsome hero, and that the petite princess will overpower a hyper-muscular male thug twice her size. This potential subversion is only partial, however, and leaves many hegemonic norms intact. These games, Hutchinson (2007, 288) explains, "[do] not deviate from gender norms to an uncomfortable extent, providing reasons for perceived deviance beyond the expected gender roles."

## Princess as Parody

The videogame princess appears in other forms, including games that make the very notion of a 'damsel in distress' the subject of parody. Reflexive and transgressive engagements with the conventions first established in early titles such as *Super Mario Bros.* (Nintendo 1985), as well as across Western media forms, highlight the centrality and increasingly clichéd status of the 'rescue the princess' plot device within videogames. Examples include the over-the-top depictions of kidnapped princesses in *Castle Crashers* (The Behemoth 2008), the tongue-in-cheek use of the trope in *Catch the Princess* (Robots and Pencils Inc. 2012) and *Monsters*

*(Probably) Stole My Princess* (Mediatonic 2010), and the multitude of princesses the player amasses—and must subsequently contend with—in *Little King's Story* (Cing 2009).

Figure 2. ©2000 Square: Screenshot of Princess Garnet asking Zidane to "kidnap" her in *Final Fantasy IX.*

Parodic interpretations of the 'damsel in distress' often appear as one among many plot devices mobilized in a game's narrative structure, rather than as the central motif. In these cases, the princess often essentially fills the same function she does in traditional hero's quest narratives—as the 'MacGuffin' or driver of the action. For instance, *Final Fantasy IX* (Square 2000) begins with the main protagonist, Zidane, setting out with his posse of thieves to kidnap Princess Garnet in order to hold her for ransom. Upon arriving at the castle, however, Zidane finds out the princess is in fact trying to escape. Unaware of his original intentions, Garnet enlists Zidane's help by asking him and the other thieves (who are all disguised as an acting troupe) to "kidnap" her. These exchanges unfold in a comedic fashion, with Zidane displaying humorous slapstick reactions, and funny music playing in the background. While Garnet eventually becomes a playable character and ally to Zidane, her role as 'damsel in distress' is repeatedly re-established: A monster imprisons her in the forest, and Zidane and friends must rescue her; the evil Queen spends much of the game trying to retrieve the Princess in order to drain her magical powers and execute her for treason. In *Final Fantasy IX*, the 'rescue the princess' plot device is thus parodied as a cliché in one moment, and faithfully reproduced in the next.

Other examples use parody in ways that overtly disrupt the narrative and aesthetic conventions of the 'rescue the princess' trope, including the standard representation of the princess as a young, demure and petite beauty. In *Fat Princess* (Titan Studios 2009), a capture-the-flag meets 'tower defense' game, the player controls an army tasked with rescuing its own abducted princess, while simultaneously trying to retain possession of the opposing army's princess (or vice versa). Captured princesses can be rescued, but rescues can also be impeded by feeding the princess multiple slices of cake. The cake is enchanted, the game's accompanying storybook explains, and both princesses are addicted to it (and incessantly demand "cake please"). The more cake the princess eats, the larger and heavier she becomes. This in turn makes both rescuing *and* kidnapping her more difficult, as additional knights are needed to bear the extra weight.

Long before its release, *Fat Princess* became the subject of heated debate and controversy online. The game's title, its depiction of the princesses and its apparent irreverence toward what is for many a highly sensitive and serious issue were critiqued at length (Eisen 2008; Nelson 2008). Others praised the title for its originality, highlighting the fact that the game contains and in many ways celebrates non-stereotypical physiques, in that princesses remain desirable and sought after even after attaining their heftier size (Benedetti 2009). The game's inclusion of non-thin princesses places it in stark contrast with the vast majority of video games, which systematically present "female body shapes that conform to the thin-ideal observed with other mainstream media" (Martins et al. 2009).

The cake-loving princesses of *Fat Princess* may be positioned in compelling juxtaposition with other videogame princesses, such as *Mortal Kombat*'s Kitana, whose conformity to traditional beauty ideals is argued by some to undermine her potential to challenge gender stereotypes. On the other hand, in *Fat Princess*, the deviation from gender norms is largely aesthetic: The princesses are non-playable and almost entirely passive, with the exception of their wanting and eating cake. They are the objects of repeated rescues and abductions, as the two opposing armies manically engage in fleeting renditions of the hero's quest in their attempt to accrue points. Nonetheless, the princesses' limited circle of agency is a symbolically meaningful one—the more their armies obey their demands for cake, the more they come to corporealize trangression and defy hegemonic beauty ideals.

Moreover, such literal interpretations run the risk of obscuring the other ways in which *Fat Princess* contains a potential for subversion and critique. The game's frequent use of tongue-in-cheek humor and the frenetic pace at which the players' armies must capture-rescue-recapture-protect their princesses challenge the very structure and validity of the hero's quest. Schwartzman (1978) suggests that satire, parody, caricature and burlesque are all forms of play that can work to subvert the existing social order. Much like Bakhtin's carnivale, Schwartzman argues, such games can act as an arena for criticism of the status quo. By inviting players to endlessly rescue and capture princesses, the epic quest once symbolized by the 'damsel in distress' plot device is made both ridiculous and mundane. The princesses' shared dual role as objects of desire and evidence of victory is amplified (in multiple ways), but also defetishized in the process. These facets not only draw attention to the stereotypical function of the princess within videogames, but also invite players to engage in nuanced forms of reflexivity and critique.

## Deconstructing the Princess

In addition to using parody and role reversal, game designers have found a multitude of other ways to engage with the 'rescue the princess' trope in non-traditional, and oftentimes thought-provoking, ways. Arguably two of the most palpable and sophisticated examples that have emerged to date are *Ico* (Team Ico 2001) and *Braid* (Number None, Inc. 2008). While very distinct in terms of their content and genre, both titles contain elements that draw reflexively on core facets of the archetypical hero's quest and the princess's role within it. Furthermore, both titles have been widely celebrated by critics and players alike for their creativity, design innovations and advanced approach to videogame narrative.

*Ico* begins with the imprisonment of the main protagonist (intended as human sacrifice) amid the ruins of a seemingly abandoned castle. In contrast to most male videogame heroes, Ico (the game's namesake and sole playable character)[8] is depicted as a very small, young boy who is physically quite average apart from the two horns that are growing out of his head. Within the first few minutes of gameplay, the player stumbles upon a fellow prisoner, Princess Yorda—a young girl who speaks a language the player cannot understand, and who emits a luminescent glow. The princess is soon 'rescued,' or at least freed from her cage, but the game is far from over. From this point forward, gameplay revolves around keeping Yorda safe, helping Yorda traverse the various rooms of the castle (each one a puzzle that the player must solve by manipulating objects) and fighting off the shadowy enemies that repeatedly come to reclaim her. As Herold (2009) describes, "Once Yorda appears, she becomes the game's entire focus .... [She] requires constant attention. Leave for more than a moment and she will be attacked by shadow demons; fail to rescue her in time and the game ends." Although she yields a mysterious power (with which she can open many of the magical doors that bar the way out of the castle), Yorda is otherwise fragile, easily frightened and utterly dependent on Ico.

As examined above, in videogames and other media, rescuing the princess is often presented as the overarching goal or the driver of the action. As such, it most often unfolds as the denouement or resolution at the end of the hero's epic adventure. According to Propp (1968, 84), the standard form is for the princess to appear only twice during a quest narrative: once when she is "introduced into the initial situation," and then again when she is presented "as a personage who has been sought out." This is certainly reflected in early videogames like *The Legend of Zelda* (Nintendo 1986) and *Super Mario Bros.* (Nintendo 1985), where the princess primarily serves as a symbolic prize for completing the quest. In these games, once all the monsters have been vanquished, and the hero's skills have been adequately tested, the princess simply *is* rescued. She is intact and eager for the 'happily-ever-after' to commence, thereby symbolizing the hero's multifaceted achievement of riches, social standing and romantic success.

In *Ico*, rescuing the princess is a prolonged, tense and eventually emotionally painful process. The rescue itself spans nearly the entirety of the game. Perhaps more important, however, is that no matter how carefully the player leads Yorda through the castle, no matter how diligently she is protected from the shadow demons, she is not ultimately rescued at all. Ico is destined to fail, just as Yorda is destined to be recaptured in order to be transformed into a host for her evil Queen mother's shadow demon soul. As the game nears its end, Ico defeats the Queen but is knocked unconscious, as the earth begins to tremble and the castle starts crumbling to the ground. Yorda uses her new demon strength to carry Ico from the wreckage and place him in a rowboat, in which he floats away to safety down an underground stream. In the end, despite Yorda's vulnerability and obvious distress, and perhaps because of Ico's loyalty and patience, the game resolves with the princess rescuing the hero.

The second example, *Braid*, engages with the 'rescue the princess' narrative on the literal and the meta levels. Early on, the player is told that the main protagonist, Tim, is "off on a search to rescue the Princess. She has been snatched by a horrible and evil monster. This happened because Tim made a mistake." References to the original *Super Mario Bros.* also abound, as when the player encounters a diminutive dragon that states, "I'm sorry, but the Princess is in another castle." Initially, through these overt references to established 'rescue the princess' narrative conventions, as well as the cryptic entries contained in a series of tomes the player gains access to by completing the game's increasingly complex puzzle levels, the Princess is presented as a lost love.

As the player moves through the game, however, new pages describe a troubled romantic relationship that gradually dissolved for relatively mundane reasons. Each new piece of the story muddies the seemingly straightforward object of the quest. Couched in themes of nostalgia and regret, the story of what happened between Tim and the unnamed Princess becomes contradictory and questionable. Later in the game, the player reads of Tim's quest for self-improvement, which, "day, by day, takes him ever-closer to finding the Princess. If she exists—she must!—she will transform him, and everyone." As the game reaches its murky conclusion, it is revealed that Tim is in fact the monster that drove the Princess away. An additional meta-level critique is introduced, moreover, as the final scenes and story entries suggest that both the quest and the Princess are actually metaphors for some larger (the race to build the first atomic bomb? [Clark 2012]), or deeper (Oedipal complex?) or simply more obscure meaning. The game's ambiguous treatment of these core narrative conventions opens up a space for further reflection on the relevance and, ultimately, the futility of the 'rescue the princess' plot device.

## Conclusion

In the early 1990s, Provenzo (1991) argued that the majority of female characters in videogames functioned as mere 'damsels in distress' waiting to be saved. These characters represented a digitized version of the princess "dramatis personae," identified by Propp (1968) and others as a character that served a key, yet also secondary and largely passive, function within traditional hero's quest folktales. Since the time of Provenzo's study, however, videogames have expanded and evolved considerably. Today, female videogame characters come in many forms: from relic-hunting archeologists to S.W.A.T. team leaders, from geneticists to ninjas, from bounty hunters to psychotic artificial intelligence computer systems. While there are clearly still a fair number of princesses around, female characters (including some of the princesses themselves) now appear in a range of active, main protagonist roles, as well as in a multitude of supporting, secondary and non-playable characters in videogames.

On the other hand, female characters within both console games (where gender is more often assigned by the game's design) (Williams et al. 2009) and massively multiplayer online games (where all players select their own avatar's gender) (Yee 2005) remain notably underrepresented. It is within this context that the longevity of the 'rescue the princess' plot device and the 'damsel in distress' archetype become particularly significant. While alternatives do indeed exist, it is unclear how prevalent they may actually be. In gathering the data for the current analysis, finding examples of princesses was extremely easy. As a core component of one of the most clichéd narrative frames in videogames, they resurface again and again, in various forms, genres and platforms. However, in using a convenience sampling method, this study not only fails to provide generalizable data, but also falls short of providing a complete picture of the fuller gender-in-games landscape. In short, a key limitation of the current study is that it does not describe just how prevalent the 'rescue the princess' trope is among the hundreds or thousands of new videogame titles released every year. Unfortunately, there is also a lack of existing, up-to-date, large-scale empirical data on the roles and functions of female videogame characters upon which such comparisons might otherwise be drawn.

Nonetheless, in focusing on an unrepresentative handful of some of the princess characters that have appeared in popular console videogames over the past thirty years, an indication of their broader significance within videogame narrative and culture has arguably emerged. The 'rescue the princess' plot device appears in some of the most foundational and influential titles in videogame history, and is still commonly used. The importance and longevity of this particular narrative trope are furthermore apparent in the growing number of games that mobilize and engage with it in unconventional or transgressive ways: from the symbolic inversion of the fighting princesses in the *Super Smash Bros.* and *Mortal Kombat* series, to parodic iterations found in *Final Fantasy IX* and *Fat Princess*, to the reflexive meditations provided in *Ico* and *Braid*. In each of these cases, the 'rescue the princess' narrative conventions are central—providing the materials and cultural signifiers out of which reinvention, deconstruction and critique are made possible.

Future research in this area should pay greater attention to the ways in which such clichés and conventions also circulate among players and throughout gamer culture(s). As described at the start of this chapter, previous studies have identified numerous reasons gender portrayals in videogames are important—including their potential to inform players' worldviews, contribute to evolving notions of identity as well as reinforce existing power relations (Bryce and Rutter 2003; Dietz 1998; Fullerton et al. 2008; Martins et al. 2009; Williams et al. 2009). There is much to suggest that these issues may be particularly relevant to female players, who are generally more likely to play as female characters when the option is available (Yee 2005). Scholars such as Graner Ray (2004, 95) suggest, "If there is no ability to choose a female avatar, or if the female selection is limited or poor in quality, the game will be less attractive to the average female." Within the context of the current discussion, such arguments beg the question of how players interpret and in turn contribute to the evolving notions and uses of the princess archetype and 'rescue the princess' plot device identified herein.

At the same time, there is compelling evidence that both male and female players develop complex relationships with the gender ideals, representations and archetypes found in and around videogames. These relationships warrant further attention, beyond merely inferring consumer satisfaction and preference based on which games sell the most. For example, there are currently a wide variety of cultural artifacts suggesting re-appropriation or reclamation of the princess as a figure of empowerment and role reversal. A "This Princess Saves Herself" meme has been circulating within 'girl gamer' culture for several years, a sort of Girl Power–esque slogan that can be found emblazoned on T-shirts, laptop decals, weblogs and fan art. Yet the meme, and the many girls and women who mobilize it, have not yet garnered much, if any, attention within the broader gender-in-games debates. Reflective of the Third Wave feminist perspective, the slogan communicates a desire to re-position the princess as the active hero(ine) of her own story, rather than serve as an object in someone else's (de Lauretis 1984).

Much like the princess characters examined herein, the political potential of such memes may appear partial and compromising, at once a rejection of and identification with the princess/damsel stereotype. As in other areas of media culture, the videogame princess appears to embody a "range of contradictory notions about what it mean[s] to be a girl," and a girl gamer in particular (Forman-Brunell and Eaton 2009, 358). While she may have started life as a one-dimensional 'MacGuffin,' she has clearly come to serve as the basis for a range of innovative interpretations and playful engagements. These in turn have much broader implications, not only for videogames and game players, but also in terms of what such developments reveal about shifting social norms and expectations about the role and function of the hero, the princess and the quest itself.

## Endnotes

1. This figure includes both original titles, as well as adapted and re-release versions for new console systems. In total, the industry market measurement site VGChartz estimates that the franchise for console has sold nearly 39 million units as of June 2012 (d'Angelo 2012).
2. It should be noted that Princess Zelda is not actually just one character. It is a name given to different princesses of the Hyrule family. As this particular game series spans across time and multiple generations, each of the Zeldas might be seen as a descendent of the prior versions. The character of Link has a similar back story.
3. There are, however, a number of licensed and cross-branded games targeted primarily at girls that feature princess characters based on existing media brands—such as *Barbie as the Island Princess* (Ivolgamus 2007), and multiple titles based on the Disney Princess franchise. The current analysis and discussion focus exclusively on characters originally developed for console-based videogames.

4. As determined by sales figures—a problematic way to measure popularity, but one that is used quite frequently in the academic literature in this area.
5. Although there are many more games today that allow players to select the gender of their avatar, cultural critics and scholars have indicated that even in games in which protagonists of either gender are available, there is a tendency to market the games featuring the male option (Near 2013).
6. The title of Sherman's article likely makes reference to *The Perils of Pauline*, an early twentieth-century film serial that revolved around 'damsel in distress' scenarios.
7. An earlier iteration of this character, perhaps Pauline, served as a 'damsel in distress' in the pre-NES arcade game featuring Mario, *Donkey Kong*.
8. According to Davidson (2011), there are "versions" of *Ico* in which both Ico and Yorda are playable in a two-player co-op mode. However, in both the original and in the version reviewed for this chapter (the recent, remastered in high definition North American re-release [Team Ico 2011]) this does not become available as an option until the player has successfully completed the game.

## References

Agatsuma Entertainment. 2012. *Code of Princess*. Art by Kinu Nishimura. Japan: Agatsuma Entertainment, Videogame.

The Behemoth. 2008. *Castle Crashers*. Designed by Dan Paladin and Tom Fulp. San Diego, CA: The Behemoth/Microsoft Game Studios, Videogame.

Benedetti, Winda. 2009. "Controversial *Fat Princess* Game Is Big Fun." *NBCNews.com*, August 10. Accessed April 1, 2013. http://www.nbcnews.com/id/32316148/ns/technology_and_science-games/

Bizzocchi, Jim. 2007. "Games and Narrative: An Analytical Framework." *Loading … Journal of the Canadian Gaming Studies Organization, 1*(1). Accessed November 3, 2013. http://journals.sfu.ca/loading/index.php/loading/article/view/1/1

Bryce, Jo, and Jason Rutter. 2003. "Gender Dynamics and the Social and Spatial Organization of Computer Gaming." *Leisure Studies, 22*, 1–15.

Burgess, Melinda C. R., Steven Paul Stermer, and Stephen R. Burgess. 2007. "Sex, Lies, and Video Games: The Portrayal of Male and Female Characters on Video Game Covers." *Sex Roles, 57*, 419–433.

Campbell, Joseph. 1949. *The Hero with a Thousand Faces*. New York: Pantheon Books.

Cassell, Justine, and Henry Jenkins. 1998. "Chess for Girls? Feminism and Computer Games. In *From Barbie to Mortal Kombat: Gender and Computer Games*, ed. Justine Cassell and Henry Jenkins, 2–45. Cambridge: MIT Press.

Chess, Shira. 2011. "A 36-24-36 Cerebrum: Productivity, Gender and Video Game Advertising." *Critical Studies in Media Communication, 28*(3): 230–252.

Children Now. 2000. *Girls and Gaming: A Console Video Game Content Analysis* [Report]. Oakland, CA: Children Now.

Cing. 2009. *Little King's Story.* Designed by Yasuhiro Wada, Yoshiro Kimura, and Tomohiro Misei. Torrance, CA: Xseed Games.

Clark, Taylor. 2012. "The Most Dangerous Game." *The Atlantic, 309*(4): 40.

Consalvo, Mia. 2003. "*Zelda 64* and Video Game Fans: A Walkthrough of Games, Intertextuality and Narrative." *Television and New Media, 4*(3): 321–334.

Consalvo, Mia. 2012. "Confronting Toxic Gamer Culture: A Challenge for Feminist Game Studies Scholars." *Ada: A Journal of Gender, New Media, and Technology, 1*(1). Accessed April 1, 2013. http://adanewmedia.org/2012/11/issue1-consalvo/

d'Angelo, William. 2012. "The Legend of Zelda: A Sales History." *VGChartz*, June 19. Accessed May 25, 2013. http://www.vgchartz.com/article/250202/the-legend-of-zelda-a-sales-history/

de Lauretis, Teresa. 1984. *Alice Doesn't: Feminism, Semiotics, Cinema.* Bloomington: Indiana University Press.

Davidson, Drew. 2011. "Playing Ico: From Involvement through Immersion to Investment." In *Well Played 3.0: Video Game, Value and Meaning*, ed. Drew Davidson, 273–288. Pittsburgh, PA: Carnegie Mellon University/ETC Press.

Dietz, Tracy L. 1998. "An Examination of Violence and Gender Role Portrayals in Video Games: Implications for Gender Socialization and Aggressive Behavior." *Sex Roles, 38*(5–6): 425–442.

Eisen, Andrew. 2008. "Sony's *Fat Princess* Causing Controversy." *Game Politics*, July 24. Accessed November 6, 2013. http://www.gamepolitics.com/2008/07/24/sony039s-fat-princess-causing-controversy

Forman-Brunell, Miriam, and Julie Eaton. 2009. "The Graceful and Gritty Princess: Managing Notions of Girlhood from the New Nation to the New Millennium." *American Journal of Play, 1*(3): 338–364.

Fuller, Mary, and Henry Jenkins. 1995. "Nintendo and New World Travel Writing: A Dialogue." In *Cybersociety: Computer-Mediated Communication and Community*, ed. Steve G. Jones, 57–72. Thousand Oaks, CA: Sage.

Fullerton, Tracy, Jacquelyn Ford Morie, and Celia Pearce. 2008. "A Game of One's Own: Toward a New Gendered Poetics of Digital Space." *The Fibreculture Journal, 11.* Accessed May 2, 2013. http://eleven.fibreculturejournal.org/fcj-074-a-game-of-one%e2%80%99s-own-towards-a-new-gendered-poetics-of-digital-space/

Graner Ray, Sheri. 2004. *Gender Inclusive Game Design: Expanding the Market.* Hingham, MA: Charles River Media.

Goetz, Christopher. 2012. "Tether and Accretions: Fantasy as Form in Videogames." *Games and Culture, 7*(6): 419–440.

Haase, Donald. (ed.). 2004. *Fairy Tales and Feminism: New Approaches.* Detroit, MI: Wayne State University Press.

HAL Laboratory. 2001. *Super Smash Bros. Melee.* Directed by Masahiro Sakurai. Kyoto, Japan: Nintendo, Videogame.

Herold (2009) Yorda/Ico Herold, Charles (2009). "Ico: Creating an Emotional Connection with a Pixelated Damsel." In *Well Played 1.0: Video Game, Value and Meaning*, ed. Drew Davidson, 3–12. Pittsburgh, PA: Carnegie Mellon University/ETC Press.

Hutchinson, Rachael. 2007. "Performing the Self: Subverting the Binary in Combat Games." *Games and Culture, 2*(4): 283–299.

Inness, Sherrie A. 1999. *Tough Girls: Women Warriors and Wonder Women in Popular Culture.* Philadelphia, PA: University of Pennsylvania Press.

Ip, Barry. 2011a. "Narrative Structures in Computer and Video Games: Part I: Context, Definitions, and Initial Findings." *Games and Culture, 6*(2): 103–134.

Ip, Barry. 2011b. "Narrative Structures in Computer and Video Games: Part 2: Emotions, Structures and Archetypes." *Games and Culture, 6*(3): 203–244.

Ivolgamus. 2007. *Barbie as the Island Princess.* Santa Monica, CA: Activision and Fox Interactive, Videogame.

Jenson, Jennifer, and Suzanne de Castell. 2008. "Theorizing Gender and Digital Gameplay: Oversights, Accidents and Surprises." *Eludamos: Journal for Computer Game Culture, 2*(1): 15–25.

Johnston, Casey. 2012. "'I Am No Man': For Zelda-Playing Daughter, Dad Gives Link a Sex Change." *Ars Technica,* November 8. Accessed May 14, 2013. http://arstechnica.com/gaming/2012/11/i-am-no-man-for-zelda-playing-daughter-dad-gives-link-a-sex-change/

Jones, Gerard. 2002. *Killing Monsters: Why Children Need Fantasy, Super Heroes and Make Believe Violence.* NY: Basic Books.

Jung, Carl. 1968. *The Archetypes and the Collective Unconscious* (2nd ed.), trans. R. F. C. Hull. Princeton, NJ: Princeton University Press.

Juul, Jesper. 1998. "A Clash between Game and Narrative: Interactive Fiction. (Why Computer Games Do Not Tell Good Stories and Why This is Not a Problem)." Paper presented at Digital Arts and Culture 1998. Accessed February 7, 2014. http://cmc.uib.no/dac98/papers/juul.html

Kennedy, Helen W. 2002. "Lara Croft: Feminist Icon or Cyberbimbo? On the Limits of Textual Analysis." *Game Studies: The International Journal of Computer Game Research, 2*(2). Accessed May 24, 2013. http://www.gamestudies.org/0202/kennedy/

King, Geoff, and Tanya Krzywinska. 2006. *Tomb Raiders and Space Invaders: Videogame Forms and Contexts.* London: I. B. Taurus.

Krotoski, Aleks. 2004. *Chicks and Joysticks: The Exploration of Women and Gaming* [White Paper]. London: Entertainment and Leisure Software.

Kuchera, Ben. 2012. "Games with Exclusively Female Heroes Don't Sell (Because Publishers Don't Support Them)." *Penny Arcade Report,* November 21. Accessed May 16, 2013. http://penny-arcade.com/report/article/games-with-female-heroes-dont-sell-because-publishers-dont-support-them

Lenhart, Amand, Joseph Kahne, Ellen Middaugh, Alexandra Rankin Macgill, Chris Evans, and Jessica Vitak. 2008. *Teens, Video Games, and Civics.* Washington, DC: Pew Internet and American Life Project.

Martins, Nicole, Dmitri C. Williams, Kristen Harrison, and Rabindra A. Ratan. 2009. "A Content Analysis of Female Body Imagery in Video Games." *Sex Roles, 61*(11–12): 824–836.

McWhertor, Michael. 2012. "Father Hacks *The Legend of Zelda: The Wind Waker* for His Young Daughter, Making Link a Girl." *Polygon,* November 9. Accessed April 12, 2013.http://

www.polygon.com/2012/11/9/3623358/father-hacks-the-legend-of-zelda-the-wind-waker-for-his-young

Mediatonic. 2010. *Monsters (Probably) Stole My Princess.* London: Mediatonic, Videogame.

Midway. 1993. *Mortal Kombat II.* Designed by Ed Boon and John Tobias. Chicago: Midway, Videogame.

Miller, Monica K., and Alicia Summers. 2007. "Gender Differences in Video Game Characters' Roles, Appearances, and Attire as Portrayed in Video Game Magazines." *Sex Roles, 57*(9–10): 733–42.

Narcisse, Evan. 2012. "Father Hacks *Zelda* for His Daughter, Makes Link a Girl." *Kotaku,* November 8. Accessed April 12, 2013. http://kotaku.com/5958918/father-hacks-zelda-for-his-daughter-makes-link-a-girl

Near, Christopher E. 2013. "Selling Gender: Associations of Box Art Representation of Female Characters with Sales for Teen- and Mature-Rated Video Games." *Sex Roles, 68*(3–4): 252–269.

Nelson, Randy. 2008. "So It Begins: Feminist Gamers Decry Sony's *Fat Princess.*" *Joystiq,* July 22. Accessed April 12, 2013. http://www.joystiq.com/2008/07/22/so-it-begins-feminist-gamers-decry-sonys-fat-princess/

Nether-Realm Studios. 2011. *Mortal Kombat.* Directed by Ed Boon, Steve Beran, and Alan Villani. Burbank, CA: Warner Bros. Interactive Entertainment, Videogame.

Newman, James. 2005. "Playing (with) Videogames." *Convergence, 11*(1): 48–67.

Nintendo. 1985. *Super Mario Bros.* Directed by Shigeru Miyamoto. Kyoto, Japan: Nintendo, Videogame.

Nintendo. 1986. *The Legend of Zelda.* Created by Shigeru Miyamoto, Takashi Tezuka, and Eiji Aonuma. Kyoto, Japan: Nintendo, Videogame.

Nintendo. 1988. *Super Mario Bros. 2.* Directed by Kensuke Tanabe. Kyoto, Japan: Nintendo, Videogame.

Nintendo. 2003. *The Legend of Zelda: The Wind Waker.* Written by Mitsuhiro Takano, Hajime Takahashi, and Eiji Aonuma. Directed by Eiji Aonuma. Kyoto, Japan: Nintendo, Videogame.

Nintendo. 2008. *Super Smash Bros. Brawl.* Directed by Masahiro Sakurai. Kyoto, Japan: Nintendo, Videogame.

Number None, Inc. 2008. *Braid.* Designed by Jonathan Blow. Redmond, WA: Microsoft Game Studios (XBLA), Videogame.

Ohannessian, Kevin. 2010. "Women in Gaming: Female PC Players Will Soon Pwn You." *Fast Company,* March 9. Accessed April 12, 2013. http://www.fastcompany.com/1576744/women-gaming-female-pc-players-will-soon-pwn-you

Philips Media. 1993. *Zelda: Legend of Ganon.* Amsterdam, The Netherlands: Philips Media, Videogame.

Philips Media. 1994. *Zelda's Adventure.* Amsterdam, The Netherlands: Philips Media, Videogame.

Pohl, Kristen. 2008. "Ethical Reflection and Involvement in Computer Games." In *Conference Proceedings of the Philosophy of Computer Games 2008,* ed. Stephan Günzel, Michael Liebe, and Dieter Mersch, 92–107. Potsdam, Germany: Potsdam University Press.

Project Soul. 2008. *Soulcaliber IV.* Montreuil, France/Tokyo Japan: Ubisoft/Namco Bandai, Videogame.

Propp, Vladimir. 1968. *Morphology of the Folktale.* Austin: University of Texas Press.

Provenzo, Eugene F. 1991. *Video Kids: Making Sense of Nintendo.* Cambridge, MA: Harvard University Press.

Rideout, Victoria J., Ulla G. Foehr, and Donald F. Roberts. 2010. *Generation M2: Media in the Lives of 8- to 18-Year-Olds* [Report]. Washington, DC: Kaiser Family Foundation.

Roberts, Donald F., Ulla G. Foehr, and Victoria J. Rideout. 2005. *Generation M: Media in the Lives of 8- to 18-Year-Olds* [Report]. Washington, DC: Kaiser Family Foundation.

Robots and Pencils Inc. 2012. *Catch the Princess.* Calgary, AB: Robots and Pencils, iOS application.

Salter, Anastasia, and Bridget Blodgett. 2012. "Hypermasculinity and Dickwolves: The Contentious Role of Women in the New Gaming Public." *Journal of Broadcasting and Electronic Media, 56*(3): 401–416.

Schleiner, Anne-Marie. 2001. "Does Lara Croft Wear Fake Polygons? Gender and Gender-Role Subversion in Computer Adventure Games." *Leonardo, 34*(3): 221–226.

Schott, Gareth, and Siobhan Thomas. 2008. "The Impact of Nintendo's 'For Men' Advertising Campaign on a Potential Female Market." *Eludamos: Journal of Computer Game Culture, 2*(1). Accessed May 12, 2013. http://www.eludamos.org/index.php/eludamos/article/view/vol2no1-6

Schwartzman, Helen B. 1978. *Transformations: The Anthropology of Children's Play.* New York: Plenum Press.

Sherman, Sharon R. 1997. "Perils of the Princess: Gender and Genre in Video Games." *Western Folklore, 56*(3–4): 243–258.

Square. 2000. *Final Fantasy IX.* Directed by Hiroyuki Ito. Tokyo, Japan: Square, Videogame.

Stallybrass, Peter and Allon White. 1986. *The Politics and Poetics of Transgression.* London: Methuen.

Taylor, Nicholas, Jen Jenson, and Suzanne de Castell. 2009. "Cheerleaders/Booth Babes/*Halo* Hoes: Pro-Gaming, Gender and Jobs for the Boys." *Digital Creativity, 20*(4): 239–252.

Taylor, T. L. 2006. *Play between Worlds: Exploring Online Game Culture.* Cambridge, MA: MIT Press.

Team Ico. 2001. *Ico.* Directed by Fumito Ueda. Tokyo, Japan: Sony Computer Entertainment, Videogame.

Team Ico. 2011. *Ico* [Remastered]. Directed by Fumito Ueda. Tokyo, Japan: Sony Computer Entertainment, Videogame.

Titan Studios. 2009. *Fat Princess.* Tokyo, Japan: Sony Computer Entertainment, Videogame.

Walkerdine, Valerie. 2007. *Children, Gender, Video Games: Towards a Relational Approach to Multimedia.* New York: Palgrave Macmillan.

Warner, S. 2006. "Philips CD-i." *Retro Gamer, 32*(December): 40–45.

Williams, Dmitri, Nicole Martins, Mia Consalvo, and James D. Ivory. 2009. "The Virtual Census: Representations of Gender, Race and Age in Video Games." *New Media and Society, 11*(5): 815–834.

Wilson, Jason A. 2007. *Gameplay and the Aesthetics of Intimacy* (Unpublished doctoral dissertation). Nathan, Australia: Griffith University. Accessed April 2, 2013. http://spooner.beds.ac.uk/nmrg/wp-content/uploads/2008/04/jason-wilson-phd.pdf

Yee, Nick. 2006. "WoW Gender-Bending." *The Daedalus Project: The Psychology of MMORGs*. Accessed May 27, 2013. http://www.nickyee.com/daedalus/archives/001369.php

CHAPTER FIVE

# Playing to Belong: Princesses and Peer Cultures in Preschool

KAREN WOHLWEND

Children's extensive engagements with princess culture have sparked controversy over the potential identity-shaping effects of popular media on young girls, evident in high levels of public debate in social media spheres around recent mass-market books, including, *My Princess Boy* (Kilodavis and DeSimone 2010) *Cinderella Ate My Daughter: Dispatches from the Front Lines of the New Girlie-Girl Culture* (Orenstein 2011) and *The Princess Problem: Guiding Our Girls Through the Princess-Obsessed Years* (Hains 2014). Educational research in the past decade shows benefits to literacy learning when teachers build upon young children's diverse strengths and popular media interests that show up so often in their play (Dyson 2003; Marsh et al. 2005). For young preschool girls today, these literary repertoires often connect to their deep knowledge of princess characters and stories in popular culture (Sekeres 2009; Wohlwend 2009). At the same time, literacy studies have alerted us to the gendered and consumerist ideological messages in these identity-shaping princess texts (Mackey 2010; Marshall and Sensoy 2011; Saltmarsh 2009). Yet we know little about the ways that the target consumers—very young girls—actually enact princess media messages during play. What happens when girls play together in classrooms where teachers provide princess dolls and encourage children to remake the princess stories into versions of their own? In this chapter, I share findings from a year-long study of critical media literacy in preschool and primary classrooms that suggest when children collaborate during play, storytelling, and media production at school, they work out issues of belonging in friendships, brand affiliations, and classroom routines in ways that open opportunities for remaking princess texts and mediate children's cultures.

Using mediated discourse theory (Scollon 2001; Wertsch 1991), I examine princess play as a site of engagement: a social space where everyday practices, artifacts (e.g., dolls), and player identities come together as social actors perform naturalized ways of belonging that are expected in each culture (Bourdieu 1977; Scollon and Scollon 2004). During princess play in early childhood classrooms, these ways of being and belonging—in other words, a *nexus of practice* (Scollon 2001)—collide and resonate across the multiple cultures that converge in classrooms (Wohlwend 2009, 2011, 2012). In my studies of sites of engagement, I look closely at pretend play to see how young children use dolls and toys to influence who can participate in local play groups in ways that align with and transgress global gender discourses. In preschool, very young children are just learning how to belong: how to play together rather than playing next to others, how to equitably take turns with scarce classroom materials, how to negotiate who plays which role, and so on. They are also learning tacit gender expectations in these practices of belonging: who can play a princess, whose ideas for princess narratives are followed, who gets access to a treasured doll, or how a favorite princess character might be revised. Further, it is important to recognize the developmental influences in preschool sites of engagement where children are not only learning to belong but also learning to communicate and cooperate through language, literacy, and play. For example, our notions of criticality may need to be retooled for early childhood settings: the verbal critique of princess stereotypes expected in a primary school critical literacy lesson is not well-suited to a 3-year-old child's developing language or passionate attachment to media characters. However, exploratory play is the young child's strength, making doll play a promising site for productive critique that positions the young child as an inventive maker of new play scenarios and materials and invites re-imaginings and alternate identities and ways of belonging.

Elsewhere, I have examined Disney Princess dolls to uncover the expected identities for child fans, consumers, producers, and players that the toys evoke (Wohlwend 2012). In this view, Disney Princess dolls are not just playthings but cultural artifacts that represent sedimented histories of practices (Rowsell and Pahl 2007) as well as anticipated identities that designers and marketers have layered into products (Wohlwend 2009, 2012). For example, Disney Princess dolls come pre-packaged with memorized film scripts, mingled with expectations for who should play with the toys and how they should be used. When children play with princess toys at school, the mix of expectations for belonging expands to include children's histories of friendships in peer cultures and rules and routines in school cultures. According to my previous analysis (Wohlwend 2012), these ways of belonging include:

- Models of hyperfeminine characters, "damsel-in-distress" fairy tale narratives, and "girly-girl" fans in princess culture
- Embodied responses (unspoken, emotional, sensory/modal, gendered) to meanings fabricated into the pastel colors, vinyl bodies, and silky, sparkly fabrics of the dolls through production processes
- Target demographics in brand identity marketing production and marketing histories in consumer culture
- Negotiated play narratives in children's collectively imagined play worlds (Medina and Wohlwend 2014)
- Expected friendship relations in play groups in social histories in peer cultures (Madrid and Katz 2011)
- Classroom roles, relationships, and rules that enact student responsibilities in school cultures

How are preschool children learning and remaking ways of belonging through princess doll play within the nexus of overlapping princess, consumer, peer, and school cultures? In this chapter, I argue that as children pretend together, they also mediate these ways of belonging through artifacts that pivot (Vygotsky 1935/1978) among princess, consumer, and classroom cultures to access more identities and practices. As we shall see, children renamed characters and reimagined restrictive commercial narratives by turning princesses into mothers and sisters to make roles for friends or by making their own materials by turning clumps of tape into princess shoes. The productive power of these remakings derives in part from girls' shared understandings of the Disney Princess franchise and expected practices across cultural contexts.

## Ways of Belonging in a Princess Play Site of Engagement

### Doll Players in Princess Culture

Belonging is at the heart of children's play. When children pretend, they use toys to mediate and participate in their immediate and imagined worlds (Göncü 1999). During doll play, children produce shared pretense with fluid meanings that must be continually negotiated with other players. When they play with princess dolls, the fluidity of these shared meanings moves beyond passive reproduction of commercial narratives and allows children to come up with alternative ideas that can mediate princess culture—at least in the immediate setting—by revising characters and stories (Wohlwend 2009). At the same time, children are also learning how to share toys, to be friends, and to belong in the surrounding peer culture (Pugh 2009). In this way, princess doll play brings together ways of belonging in both princess culture and peer culture, opening a space to mediate both worlds.

Gendered ways of belonging in princess culture are molded into dolls through commercial designs and children's play histories. Disney Princess dolls trigger more than verbal parroting of film narratives; they also send nonverbal messages through their material designs for their intended uses. Dolls are designed to clearly communicate a player/doll relationship so that children can easily use them for play (Brougère 2006). Dolls elicit performances of imagined characters for doll players in relation to the doll (e.g., baby dolls elicit pretend mothers). But dolls can also be proxies that allow children to pretend an imagined self through the doll (e.g., Disney Princess dolls elicit portrayals of players as princess characters). Dolls are identity texts that communicate a gendered play role and anticipate particular identities for children as doll players (Carrington 2003). For example, a snippet of dialog enacted from a movie script as a child plays with a princess doll materializes the fairy tale character as well as an intended player forecasted by marketing teams. The films circulate anticipated identity texts of "girly-girls" in an emphasized femininity discourse (Blaise 2005) in princess culture that is amplified across films' scripts in the animated fairy tales and drawn into the princess body images during media production processes (Haas, Bell, and Sells 1995).

## Child Consumers in Consumer Culture

The identity texts in Disney Princess dolls are not limited to characters and players, but also include expectations for consumers, manufactured into product designs and circulated through international marketing strategies in a multi-billion dollar flow of goods that seep into all aspects of children's lives. Children's play worlds are furnished with *transmedia* (Kinder 1991), glocalizing franchises that connect princess narratives from television programs, films, video games, and websites to everyday consumer goods such as dolls, toys, collectibles, apparel, beauty products, food, and school supplies (Medina and Wohlwend 2014). Bringing in $4 billion in annual global retail sales, this highly profitable "lifestyle brand" (Giroux and Pollock 2010) targets 3- to 5-year-old girls as its primary market (Disney Consumer Products 2011), allowing children to live in character from breakfast to bedtime.

Children participate in consumer cultures through purchases but also through interactions with a brand identity or "brand as person" that marketers develop to establish an aspirational and emotional bond with target consumers, inviting consumers to transact with an imagined person rather than a functional product. The princess characters provide the foundational personalities for the franchise's brand identity, merged into one persona and distilled into its primary identity text. Although the princesses in these films enact individual variations in personality traits that range from demure (Snow White, Cinderella, Sleeping Beauty) to curious (Ariel) to plucky (Belle from *Beauty and the Beast*, Mulan, Tiana from *The Princess and the Frog*), the brand identity plays up the glitter and glamour of royal status, reducing differences to color variations in the characters' hair and dress styles (Wohlwend 2009). The *Disney Princess* brand persona is a friendly, always-beautiful, self-sacrificing ingénue on her way to a happily-ever-after with an attractive hero (Orenstein 2011). In the brand-consumer relationship, the Disney Princess offers a lovely loving friend and role model that positions young girls as adoring fans and wannabes, and of course princess product buyers. Children are anticipated as particular kinds of consumers by producers and marketers, so that at birth children already belong, fully immersed in products and their expected brand relationships (Cook 2008). However, it is equally important to recognize the potential for creative production and the agency that children exercise in their relationships with popular transmedia (Buckingham 2007).

## Friends and Students in Peer and School Cultures

When Disney Princesses arrive at school, the ways of belonging in princess culture mingle with expected practices in classroom cultures. Dolls become capital that children can wield in their power relations with other children during play as they strategically play in and out of gendered identity texts in ways that affect their status as students in school culture but also their friendships in peer culture (Dyson 2003; Marsh 2000; Wohlwend 2011). *School culture* is the set of official goals, rules, values, curriculum, and teacher-sanctioned activities that organize the classroom. *Peer culture* is the set of "common activities, routines, artifacts, values, concerns, and attitudes" (Corsaro 1985, 171) developed by children for children, further bounded by their play patterns and friendship groups, by school rules and routines, and by gendered expectations of how people interact in everyday life (Kantor and Fernie 2003). The current study examines how children learn from and with each other through their play interactions as they collectively imagine other cultures into the classroom space and negotiate pretended identities with other players (Kendrick 2005; Schwartzman 1976). Children's play narratives are collaborative but also full of contradictions that must be negotiated as children sort out who-is-being-what in both the imagined and the here-and-now contexts. To stabilize their shared pretense, young children use toys as tools to anchor their pretend roles; they also use access to toys to open and restrict group play, so that a doll stands not only for a particular character but also has a role and the right to participate in the play group. As conflicts arise over who plays what, children spend much time negotiating and protecting their fragile play frames built upon hard-fought investments of cultural capital. Sociologist and play theorist William Corsaro (2003) views these conflicts as productive catalysts for meaningful negotiations that allow children to preserve their pretense while they work out social relationships in a multiparty space. Young children negotiate who gets which materials as well as who plays which roles as they try to reconcile their individual, often contradicting, meanings within a collectively imagined play frame and in the peer culture (Corsaro 2003). Galbraith (2011) found that as preschool children took up superhero roles in play, they assumed leadership positions in peer culture, changing the superhero media narratives to allow friends to participate in ways that strengthened the children's friendships, supported by negotiations mediated by their teachers. When teachers acknowledge and engage peer cultures, they "take play seriously" as an important resource for developing curriculum that matters to children (Kontovourki and Siegel 2009, 37). In this way, princess play practices offer children opportunities for pleasure and cooperation, a means of transforming social relationships, and a source of empowerment in peer culture. Of course, play is never innocent; it is also a site of tears and contestation as children struggle over highly valued toys, vie for coveted roles, or insist upon portrayals of dominant stereotypes (Davies 2003).

## Studying Princess Doll Play in a Preschool Classroom

### Classroom Context

This chapter reports findings from ethnographic research conducted in classroom *literacy playshops*, emergent critical media literacy curricula that we developed with teachers (Wohlwend, Buchholz, Wessel-Powell, Coggin, and Husbye 2013), designed to help children engage popular media as producers and not just consumers. In these playshops, young children collaborated within and around a played text, that is, as they played together with popular media dolls and action figures, they recorded their own stories with simple handheld digital cameras. The data presented in this chapter are excerpted from a larger study in a U.S.

midwestern community that took place during one school year with six early childhood teachers in three preschool and K–1 classrooms as teachers developed and implemented play-based literacy curriculum using popular media and filmmaking. The study was conducted at two sites: a K–1 classroom in a public charter elementary school and a university childcare center. This chapter focuses on several weeks of princess play in one preschool classroom with two teachers and twenty-three 3- to 5-year-old children during the spring semester of the project; the children also played Dora the Explorer, Transformers, Star Wars, pirates, and others as they created their own films with popular media toys. The classroom, situated in a university childcare center, served families of faculty, graduate students, and community members.

During the fall semester, the teachers worked together to develop a curriculum called Literacy Playshop (Wohlwend et al. 2013), an early childhood approach to critical literacy using play, filmmaking, and popular media. The curriculum aimed to:

1) Draw upon children's media expertise and utilize peer culture interests to enrich students' reading and writing and expand their participation in classroom literacy activities (Dyson 2003; Fernie, Madrid, and Kantor 2011)
2) Encourage critical awareness of commercial product messages and help children see popular media (films, video games, toys) as pliable texts that can be revised through playful production to create their own storylines and character identities (Wohlwend 2011)
3) Incorporate filmmaking as a key literacy activity for producing action texts that integrate play and drama

Teacher study groups met regularly about every other week to read early childhood research on critical literacy (Vasquez 2004) and technology (Vasquez and Felderman 2012), play and popular media (Marsh 2005), and media production (Bazalgette 2010; Nixon and Comber 2005; Riddle 2009). Teachers also used this time to analyze samples of children's media, learn filmmaking technologies, talk through issues, and plan classroom activities. For example the teachers worked together to analyze fast-food media toy commercials for film conventions and composition. The teachers then developed activities that supported children's collaborations to write scripts, draw storyboards, animate media toys and handmade puppets as main characters, and produce their own films with popular media themes. The teachers set up a "moviemaking" center with popular media toys and two Flip video cameras to allow children to independently explore and produce their own films during pretend play. I focus here on the negotiations in children's play with eight princess dolls; the children's films of princess play and filmmaking explorations are beyond the scope of this chapter.

## Method

I was assisted in this research by a team of university graduate students who video-recorded classroom activity, visiting each classroom two to four days a week during the spring semester. During classroom visits, the research team observed and talked with teachers and children, photographed storyboards and writing samples, and videotaped children during dramatic play, storying, and filmmaking activities. The research team videotaped classroom activity as teachers tried out their planned media engagements with their students. Children's activity during play, writing, and filming with media toys was analyzed for mediation levels (teacher-led, tools, and child-led) and processes (playing, storying, collaboration, and media production). Finally, the research team analyzed three sets of video data (child-produced films, classroom play and filmmaking activities, and teacher study group discussions) to identify and compare patterns across levels and processes. The vignettes in this chapter are excerpted from classroom activity video data as some children played with dolls and others engaged in making shoes as part of costume- and set-making for filmmaking.

Mediated discourse analysis (Scollon 2001; Scollon and Scollon 2004) makes expected ways of belonging visible and identifies how belonging is mediated through artifacts such as dolls, including the making and remaking of artifacts (Norris and Jones 2005). Close analysis of video data located princess play practices in which children used dolls in ways that affected their shared meanings and their social positioning in the play group. Interaction segments of social conflict and meaning negotiation were chosen for close analysis to identify how children enacted valued ways of belonging in particular cultures and how these overlapped and interacted across cultures. For example, during conflicts, teachers and children explicitly referred to rules and routines, making these normally tacit valued practices of belonging visible and available for analysis. (See Table 1 for an example of close analysis.)

Table 1: Sample of Close Analysis of Ways of Belonging and Mediation of Cultures

| | Actor | Mediated Action with Doll | Talk | Enacted Ways of Belonging | Using Tensions/Openings/Bridges in Belonging to Mediate Culture |
|---|---|---|---|---|---|
| 1 | Teacher: | [Stacy notices that Chloe has two dolls] | Chloe, you may take one and take it back to the table. | Comply with teacher directive Follow school rule: Take turns with toys | *Tensions as Openings*<br>School Culture: Compliance with turn-taking rule to teach equitable sharing and belonging |
| | Chloe: | [Chloe clutches both dolls to her chest] | No! I want to take two. | Holding Jasmine and Tiana<br>Holding two dolls<br>Holding more dolls than peers | Princess Culture: Passionate emotional connection to princess dolls<br>Consumer Culture: Possession of new dolls<br>Peer Culture: Status of holding two markers of highly valued commodity among children |
| 2 | Teacher: | | The purple girl [Jasmine] or the green girl [Tiana]? | Offers choice but repeats directive for turn-taking rule<br>Princess identities unnamed and reduced to dress color | *Enforcing Ways of Belonging*:<br>School Culture Imposition of Turn-Taking Rule Upheld<br>Consumer Culture: Emphasis on color variation of dolls and devaluing of individuality of princess characters: consistent with franchise brand identity |
| | Chloe: | [Chloe holds up Jasmine and waggles the doll, considering with lips pursed, frowning.] | | Nonverbal signaling with doll to indicate compliance with turn-taking rule; retains one doll | School Culture: Concedes; will comply with turn-taking, unhappily |
| 3 | Chloe:<br>Megan: | [Chloe approaches Megan and hands her Tiana in a trade for Snow White. Chloe picks up Snow White.] | | Complies with teacher demand to give up one doll but also retains two through friendly trading with another child | *Mediate Culture through Bridging:*<br>School Culture: Literal compliance<br>Princess Culture: Third princess held<br>Consumer Culture: Material possession<br>Peer Culture: Friendly trading, Retains commodities and greater status |

Mediated discourse analysis of physical actions with a doll within play events linked doll handling to practices of belonging to answer the following questions:

- Who gets access? How?
- Which practices seem routine (natural, expected) and necessary for participation in the princess play group?
- Which princess identities are expected and which alternate identities are imagined? For dolls and for players?
- How are artifacts used for making and remakings of imagined and immediate identity texts such as princess characters, player roles, cooperating friends?

The data vignettes in the following sections are excerpted from one event in which children's play with Disney Princess dolls prompted moments of conflict or negotiation that made visible how children engaged ways of belonging in the intersecting cultures in the classroom. Pseudonyms are used for all participants.

## Showing and Sharing Princess Dolls: Making Belonging Visible

On an afternoon in early spring, the preschool teachers decided to add eight Disney Princess dolls to the moviemaking center: the heroines from *Snow White* (1937), *Cinderella* (1950), *Sleeping Beauty* (1959), *The Little Mermaid* (1989), *Beauty and the Beast* (1991), *Aladdin* (1992), *The Princess and the Frog* (2009), and *Tangled* (2010).[1] The teachers had conducted an informal transmedia audit, noting which popular media characters decorated children's backpacks, clothing, and school supplies (Galbraith 2011). After their audit identified Disney Princess as a common media interest among the girls in the preschool class, the teachers provided a set of dolls to ensure that all children would have equal access, whether or not they personally owned a princess doll. Stacie, one of the preschool teachers, stationed herself at this center on the first day that the dolls were introduced, anticipating that many children would be interested in playing with the dolls. Twelve girls in the class immediately clustered around the table, their attention consumed by the dolls. Grace picked up Ariel, the princess from the *Little Mermaid*, and began talking with her teacher. Grace preferred talking with the teachers and rarely played with other children, a matter of concern to the teachers who actively looked for ways to involve her in social activities. Today, Grace talked about bringing her own doll—Sleeping Beauty—to school for Sharing Time: a period when preschoolers held up favorite toys in front of the class and answered the teachers' questions about their "treasures." A surprising plan emerged: Grace decided, better still, she would bring the entire class to her house to see her doll *and* her room.

| | |
|---|---|
| Grace: | Stacie, I'm gonna bring *my* doll. |
| Teacher: | Your doll? What is your doll? |
| Grace: | My doll is ... I'm gonna bring Sleeping Beauty. Her have a skirt. I'm gonna bring her. [Twirling doll as she speaks.] |
| Teacher: | You're gonna *share* her? |
| Grace: | Yeah. |
| Teacher: | On Monday? |
| Grace: | Yeah. ... [Head down, looking at doll.] I think I'm gonna take her. I want you to go to my house. |
| Teacher: | You want me to go to your house? |
| Grace: | You need to, you need, you didn't see my room. |
| Teacher: | I haven't seen your room yet. You're right. |
| Grace: | On [Monday], you might go to my house. |
| Teacher: | Maybe you can take pictures and show us pictures. |
| Grace: | Okay. I'm gonna take the whole class there! |
| Teacher: | Oh, wow. The whole class. |

As in many early childhood classrooms, regular "Show and Tell" sessions allowed children to bring possessions from home to "share," that is, to stand in front of the class, show the featured object, and talk about it. Beyond the obvious attraction of displaying valued capital to admiring peers, this activity is often the site of identity-building as teachers shape children's narratives to fit gendered discourse expectations (Gee 1996). For example, Kamler (1999) critically analyzed a kindergarten Show-and-Tell session for gender, demonstrating how a teacher's prompts, "Look at this lovely doll who's come to school," limited a preschool girl's talk to description of the doll's hair and clothing, instantiating teacher assumptions about displays of appropriate femininities, or ways of belonging in local communities of feminine practice (Paechter 2006).

Grace's desire to take her teacher and, moreover, the entire class to her house to see her princess doll demonstrates the attraction of the practices of "sharing"—or more accurately *showing*—among the preschoolers as a way of belonging, valued within both peer culture and school culture. Grace's expressed desire to have her class come to her house to see her princess collection was remarkable as Grace seldom showed any interest in playing with other children, despite the teachers' efforts to encourage her to join in. Additionally, the practice of showing and talking about toys was valued in peer culture as well as school culture, with social positioning that extended beyond the official class sharing time. The teachers reported that during lunch, many girls invited one another over to their houses to see their princess dolls.

The practice of showing dolls demonstrates belonging in another sense: Dolls belong to their owners as material possessions and purchases. In this way, the routine of Show and Tell is an intersection of consumer culture and school culture that enables problematic "showing off" or displays of consumer wealth that emphasize children's relative socioeconomic status. The preschool teachers actively worked against inequitable displays in the classroom: by limiting the number of "home toys" children could bring for sharing time and by supplying a set of classroom princess dolls for play and media production so that all children could have equal access whether they personally owned a princess doll or not.

Despite the teachers' efforts, claims of doll ownership abounded and access to the classroom set of dolls caused disputes and intense negotiations, apparent in the following vignette. While Grace talked with the teacher, the rest of the children tried several strategies for solving the problem of sharing eight highly coveted princess dolls among twelve girls. Some tried to physically wrench dolls away from other girls; in these cases, Stacie intervened immediately to encourage children to ask for a turn.

[Melanie tries to get one of Chloe's dolls; both girls hold tightly to one of the dolls.]

| | |
|---|---|
| Teacher: | Girls, if you pull on them, they will break [falling pitch, sorrowfully]. |
| Teacher: | Melanie, did you ask anyone? Or did you just try pulling? |
| Melanie: | I didn't puuuull. |

[Olivia silently hands the Cinderella doll to Melanie.]

| | |
|---|---|
| Teacher: | Oh look at that! Thank you [talking to Olivia but modeling an appropriate verbal response for Melanie]. You can ASK someone for a turn [talking to Melanie]. |

However, the school culture rule of "asking for a turn" did not work in actual toy-sharing conflicts in the peer culture. Children found that a verbal request for a doll was often no more successful than a physical attempt to simply take it, unless enforced by a teacher. The expected sharing practice as an appropriate way of belonging in school culture required children to take turns with popular materials, that is, to give up a doll when a player was "done" playing or to play with only one doll rather than two so others could have a doll.

| | |
|---|---|
| Teacher [noticing that Chloe has two dolls]: | Chloe, you may take one and take it back to the table. |
| Chloe: | No! I want to take two [clutching both dolls to her chest]. |
| Teacher: | Pick one. |
| Chloe: | No! |

| | |
|---|---|
| Teacher [firmly]: | One girl [doll]. Because we have a lot of people wanting to use them. Which one would you like? [Chloe continues to look down at the two dolls.] |

[Chloe holds up Jasmine and waggles the doll, considers with lips pursed, frowning.]

| | |
|---|---|
| Teacher: | The purple girl [Jasmine doll] or the green girl [Tiana doll]? [Chloe waggles the Jasmine doll again.] The purple girl. OK. Put that [Tiana doll] back on the table. I think Victoria wanted one. Where did she go? [Stacie, the teacher, leaves to find Victoria but in the meantime Chloe approaches Megan and hands her Tiana in a trade for Snow White. Chloe picks up the Snow White doll and is now holding both Jasmine and Snow White (Fig. 1).] |
| Teacher: | Victoria, Victoria? We have a girl [doll]. Oh! [Stacie, the teacher, looks down and sees that Chloe's dolls have changed; she seems momentarily puzzled but restates the directive to Chloe.] Never—yeah, pick ONE, Chloe, and give Victoria one. |

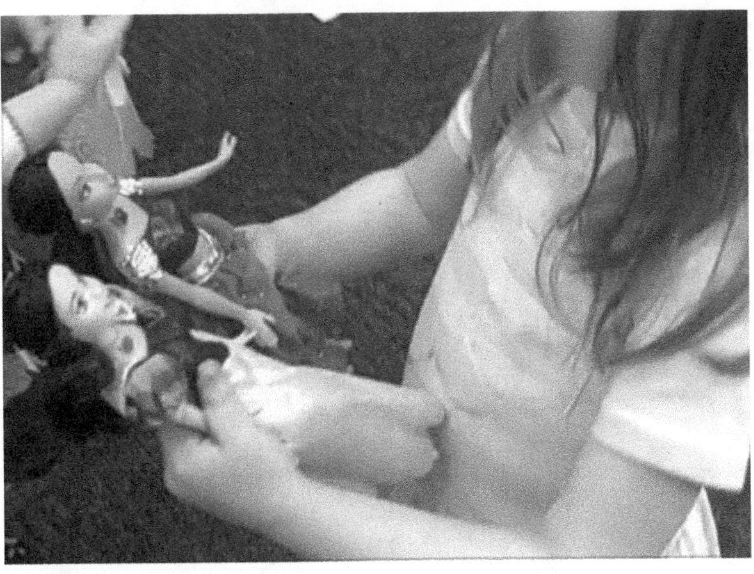

Figure 1. Choosing between Snow White and Jasmine

A closer look at the interaction in this doll-sharing conflict makes visible the overlapping desires and identities that Chloe engaged in as she juggled the rules of school culture with princess and consumer culture (see Table 1). In this interaction, Chloe is caught between conflicting ways of belonging: giving up one doll to obey the teacher as a good student in school culture and keeping two dolls and satisfying consumer culture desires. In consumer culture, she enjoyed multiple satisfactions of possession: 1) having two (new) material toys, 2) wielding the power of possessing two objects that others wanted, and 3) the sensory pleasure of holding princess dolls with long shiny curls and silky dresses. These desires conflicted with school culture expectations for participation, circulated through the practice of sharing (both showing dolls and taking turns with dolls) and in the practice of complying with teacher directions or at least voicing compliance. In interaction 2, school culture dominates and Chloe agrees to comply and give up one doll while Stacie de-emphasizes the individuality of the dolls by ignoring their meanings in princess culture by referring to the dolls only by their dress colors: "the purple one" or "the green one." In interaction 3, Chloe strategically resolved the conflict in a way that allowed her to comply with expectations across cultures: She actively resisted giving up one of the dolls, complying at a literal level by giving away one of her dolls but only in a trade that replaced it with another doll. This kind of friendly trading among children was a valued practice in peer culture as a way of avoiding conflicts. Interestingly, children rarely objected if one child had more toys than others, and appeared only concerned when they did not have a toy of their own.

Gendered expectations in school culture prohibitions against physically taking materials caused Victoria to stand by Chloe patiently and quietly asking, then passively waiting for a turn. By contrast, Carter, a 3-year-old boy, asked for a toy immediately when he approached the table, evoking immediate teacher assistance. Tacit gender-differentiated teaching practices make boys more likely to receive teacher attention, assistance, and turns in classroom interactions (Grumet 1988). Stacie's references to the dolls as "girls" further foregrounds gender differentiation as a primary concern of the doll play.

| | |
|---|---|
| Carter: | I want one. |
| Teacher: | You want a girl [doll] too? Well, Victoria is next. You can ask someone for a turn, Carter. |
| Teacher [noticing that Chloe has two dolls … again]: | Chloe. Which one are you using? |

A few minutes later, Isabel who had been more interested in a spin-off project (making shoes for the dolls) than in playing with the dolls, stepped in with an undisputed and unsubstantiated claim of prior ownership of the Snow White doll that Chloe was holding. Isabel largely ignored the teacher's attempt to have children resolve the conflict verbally and enforce the toy-sharing routine in the school culture. Instead, Isabel solved the problem physically and quickly by handing the doll to Victoria. This decisive physical action—sanctioned by the teacher and contradicting the earlier prohibition—was a far more powerful means of ending the dispute. By sidestepping the school culture turn-taking procedures with its verbal requests, Isabel's silent trade enacted the typical trading practices valued in peer culture, including Victoria in the play with no objection from Chloe.

Isabel [comes in from the art center, holding paper and scissors]: This one is mine [pointing to Snow White].
Teacher: Oh, that's where the extra one came from.
Isabel: Okay, give it up. [Isabel drags the Snow White doll away from Chloe and hands it to Victoria.]
Teacher: Thanks, Isabel.

## Mediating Cultures through Making and Remaking Artifacts

Meanwhile across the room, several girls, including Isabel, had decided that the barefoot princess dolls needed shoes and Stacie suggested that they could make some.

Olivia: How do you make shoes, Stacie? [Olivia is holding the Belle doll.]
Teacher: I don't know. How could you make shoes?

[Olivia shrugs.]

Teacher: I've never made shoes before.
Olivia: I never either.
Isabel: Can I make shoes for this princess? [to Olivia, indicating the Belle doll]
Teacher: You can make shoes if you would like.
Girl, off camera: I want to make shoes. How to make shoes?
Teacher: I don't know. You'll have to come up with something. What could you use for shoes?

A few minutes later, Isabel returned to the table to invite Melanie to join the shoe-making activity, which required Melanie to leave the princess doll play, and the doll.

Isabel [to Melanie]: Okay, come and make shoes now?
Teacher: Oh, you're making shoes!

| | |
|---|---|
| Isabel: | Yeah, we're making shoes. |
| Teacher: | Did you come up with an idea? |
| Isabel: | Come and make shoes now. [Melanie runs across room with Cinderella to make shoes with Isabel.] |
| Teacher: | Melanie! The girl [doll] has to stay at the table. |

[Melanie returns, handing Cinderella to Victoria.]

| | |
|---|---|
| Melanie [to Victoria]: | Can you save this for me? Can you save this? |
| Teacher [to Melanie]: | You can't save it but you can come back later. |
| Melanie [to Victoria]: | I'm gonna get some paper. [Melanie leaves with Isabel to get more paper.] |
| Teacher [to Victoria]: | Keep the girl [doll] at this table and they're going to make shoes. |

Making props and costumes constituted an important way of recording story meanings by creating anchors that held roles and story actions, providing bookmarks that allowed children to pick up where they left off when they returned the next day (Wohlwend 2011). Making things is also a key way of demonstrating in a tangible way to children that commercial media products and their messages are open and available for children to revise by adding additional content.

In this preschool, doll play narratives were simple, often limited to naming the dolls or their relationships to each other or changing doll clothing or placing the dolls in various locations. Two girls spent the rest of the play period absorbed in making shoes for the dolls using pieces of multi-colored masking tape. Making shoes constituted a way of mediating the dolls so they would fit to the models and belong in princess culture. Each packaged Mattel doll included shoes, tiara, and combs, but these small accessories had not been placed in the play center as they could be so easily lost in the preschool classroom. In this case, the girls' spontaneous shoemaking reinscribed the hyperfeminine discourse and fashion focus of princess culture.

## Remaking Meanings and Ways of Belonging

Among a number of goals, teachers aimed to help children critique and produce alternatives to stereotypes in the commercial culture. Toward this end, the teachers encouraged children to create their own products as in the shoemaking project, but they also modeled this by helping children to produce their own movie sets as alternate contexts for doll play scenarios. For example, Stacie modeled playing with the princess doll using the commercial dollhouse but found that the children were not very interested in doing more than putting the dolls in and out of the front door.

| | |
|---|---|
| Carter: | I need to fit in the house. |
| Teacher: | Oh, she's going in the house? |
| Carter: | Yeah, she can't fit [vertically]. [Then Carter tries pushing the doll's head into the closed door of the small dollhouse.] |
| Teacher: | Oh, no. She's a mighty tall girl. |
| Carter: | Ee-yah! [Carter opens the door and puts dolls in sideways.] |
| Victoria: | That's because she's tall, that's because she's a big girl. |

When teachers invited children to create three-dimensional scenes, several girls built a "swamp" with small pebbles, clay, plastic grass, and craft materials and studded it with twigs and pipe cleaner trees (see Fig. 2). The scenes inspired new play narratives such as princesses who wandered through the swamp and met new characters such as a "swamp monster."

Figure 2. Princesses in the Swamp

| | |
|---|---|
| Allison: | Don't touch that [monster] because you die really quickly. |
| Teacher: | Be careful of the [intoning slowly] Swamp Monster, or what's his name. |
| Allison: | Um, Delicate. |
| Teacher: | Delicate! And what is he again? |
| Allison: | A creature, a swamp creature who eats people. |

When teachers entered directly into children's play as co-players, they could inspire remakings in productive and collaborative ways by modeling and supporting changes in the commercially given storylines within the imaginary context, in this case princesses wandering in a swamp and, later, fighting a swamp monster—which Stacie made male and Allison remade as weak through the name Delicate. These remakings of commercial narratives created ruptures with expected characterizations, mediating princess culture by opening up possibilities for less stereotypical roles in children's storying.

Similar verbal remakings through renaming of the princess dolls combined with revised roles in which players turned princesses into mothers or villains. But this met resistance when other players upheld the "real" or authorized names of characters they knew, sparking renegotiations as children worked through their conflicting ideas. These negotiations allowed children to demonstrate their affiliation with princess culture as they upheld the proper names of the princesses. Grace, Melanie, and Allison challenged the renamings and upheld commercial princess culture.

| | |
|---|---|
| Grace [holding Ariel doll]: | And I'm Ariel. |
| Allison [holding Sleeping Beauty doll]: | And mine is Minishawn [inventing a new name for Sleeping Beauty]. |
| Grace [picking up a second doll, Snow White, rejects Allison's renaming of Sleeping Beauty]: | No, her name is Cinderella. |
| Melanie [holding Cinderella doll]: | *My* name is Cinderella! |
| Allison: | This is Sleeping Beauty! |
| Grace [higher pitch, shifting into character to voice Snow White and affirming Allison's claim]: | "And this is my friend Sleeping Beauty. Hello!" |

[Allison bounces Sleeping Beauty across the tabletop to meet Grace's Snow White doll.]

| | |
|---|---|
| Grace: | "And this is your friend Snow White." |

By including Allison and reinstating the commercial names of all the dolls, Grace resolved the conflict and upheld princess culture. However, she also assumed a leadership role in the play group in peer culture by bringing all players back into the scenario and moving the play forward. For Grace, this collaboration with other girls was a key moment in mediating the peer and school cultures and to participate more actively.

At other times, renamings enabled more children to play as children altered the commercial narratives and character relationships among the dolls to make room for meaningful roles for friends. For example, in one scenario, the Belle doll became Sleeping Beauty's mother so that the girls could enact a familiar domestic storyline. In this case, friendship bonds and play goals in peer culture supported and strengthened children's remediations of princess culture. In these remakings, children imported familiar contexts and cultural resources. Like other play groups I have studied, children played the stories they knew best, drawing upon scenes and scripts from family life for collaborative play. In preschool, the typically brief stories involved lots of physical movement of toys, simple greetings and labeling, and extended physical manipulation and exploration of the dolls, dresses, and materials.

Remakings were physical as well as narrative. Melanie spent twenty minutes intently tugging and stretching Belle's yellow dress onto the Cinderella doll's body, working the sleeves over the doll's arms and struggling with the fasteners. Melanie's re-costuming of the doll successfully ruptured the princess culture color scheme that Stacie unknowingly reinscribed when she described the "purple girl" or "green girl." Melanie focused on the doll's sensory aspects as she concentrated on the task of pulling a tight satin sleeve over the stubborn stickiness of the soft vinyl of the doll's arm. Interestingly, a child could almost always be found sitting and stroking the silky hair of one of the dolls; this accounted for the popularity of the Rapunzel doll, with smooth, straight hair longer than its body. The sensory pleasure of handling the doll's materials made it more difficult for children to relinquish a doll or to forgo the satisfaction of clutching a doll and wielding social capital in the classroom.

Importantly, another aspect of remaking or revising the standard story was the repositioning of 1) children as experts in relation to teachers and 2) girls as experts in relation to Carter and other boys who were also interested in playing with the dolls.

| | |
|---|---|
| Teacher: | Oh, Carter, you found one. [Carter is holding Tiana.] Who did you find? |
| Carter [looking down at his doll, puzzled]: | Ahhh, Cinderella. |
| Teacher: | Cinderella? |
| Megan: | No that's Tiana. |
| Teacher: | Who? |
| Megan: | That's Tiana. |
| Teacher: | Who's Tiana? |
| Megan: | Tiana has a green—green dress on. |
| Teacher: | Does she always wear a green dress? |
| Megan: | No. Because my, my Tiana at my house what has a blue dress. |

The teachers noticed that, like Carter, boys were interested in playing with the Disney Princess dolls but did not know the characters. This created slippages that enabled girls to display media knowledge and wield this expertise in renaming and remaking doll identities and storylines.

The ability to draw on girls' shared princess attachments and expertise had transformative effects on peer culture participation, particularly for Grace. Throughout the school year, the teachers had repeatedly and unsuccessfully attempted to involve her in a play group. However when Grace began regularly playing princesses, she joined easily in collaborative play with other girls through the princess dolls. Both teachers felt that Grace's combined passion for princesses and shared media knowledge motivated her play with other girls. It is important to acknowledge the emergent nature of preschool children's social friendships, which often needed teacher support, as did their collaborative play and storytelling. It was not uncommon for children to play alone but side-by-side with the dolls; this parallel play—a sort of separate togetherness—is also a valid way of belonging in peer culture at the preschool level.

These excerpts show that princess media are undeniably major resources of pleasure, shared understandings, and social status for young girls—in short, the stuff of belonging in children's play worlds and peer cultures. All too often, peer and school cultures do not mesh comfortably and children's outside interests in princess culture and consumer culture are not recognized at school. In some classrooms, children's media knowledge and peer culture purposes are devalued and supplanted by a school culture constrained by "the basics" (Dyson 2006, 2008), overriding attention to mastering a set of simplistic skills in math and reading (Paris 2005). However, in order to help children critically and productively engage the ubiquitous transmedia that they read, play, and live in, we also need to thoughtfully consider peer culture and school culture issues to effectively help young children navigate the conflicts, social relationships, and emotional attachments that constitute belonging within complex mixtures of childhood cultures.

In this chapter, the focus has been on princess play rather than on other aspects of a critical media literacy curriculum, such as critique, collaboration, storying, or children's media production. All these components must be closely examined and reinterpreted to fit the emergent understandings, strengths, and needs of early childhood learners; this work is ongoing (Vasquez and Felderman 2012; Wohlwend et al. 2013). However, an existing and growing body of research on play in preschool classrooms shows that children draw upon their knowledge of popular media in their literacy practices in school culture and to participate and even assume leadership positions in peer culture (Dyson 2003; Wohlwend 2011). For example, one study found that children invented new superhero narratives that allowed more players or honored peers' contributions in ways that strengthened children's friendships, with the support of thoughtful negotiations by teachers (Galbraith 2011). It is important to recognize the productive opportunities in what appears at first blush to be a conflict between children's popular media passions and school culture concerns for appropriate content, as these can lead to innovative practices (Sanderson 2011). If teachers acknowledge and engage peer culture interests in princess culture and consumer culture, cultures can converge "in ways that create a very mutually supportive intersection …" (Fernie, Madrid, and Kantor 2011, xii). [If] teachers take play seriously, that is, as a way to learn more about children and their literacies, they may come to treat it as a valuable resource for child and teacher learning" (Kontovourki and Siegel 2009, 37). In this way, princess play, despite its problematic portrayals of gender, can offer a source of pleasure and a resource for critical spaces that enable children to make and remake media texts and transform social relationships in classroom cultures.

## References

Bazalgette, Cary. 2010. *Teaching Media in Primary Schools*. London: Sage.

Blaise, Mindy. 2005. *Playing It Straight: Uncovering Gender Discourses in the Early Childhood Classroom*. New York: Routledge.

Bourdieu, Pierre. 1977. *Outline of a Theory of Practice*. Cambridge: Cambridge University Press.

Brougère, Gilles. 2006. "Toy Houses: A Socio-Anthropological Approach to Analysing Objects." *Visual Communication, 5*(1): 5–24.

Buckingham, David. 2007. "Selling Childhood? Children and Consumer Culture." *Journal of Children and Media, 1*(1): 15–24.

Carrington, Victoria. 2003. "'I'm in a Bad Mood. Let's Go Shopping': Interactive Dolls, Consumer Culture and a 'Glocalized' Model of Literacy." *Journal of Early Childhood Literacy, 3*(1): 83–98.

Cook, Daniel Thomas. 2008. "The Missing Child in Consumption Theory." *Journal of Consumer Culture, 8*(2): 219–243.

Corsaro, William A. 1985. *Friendship and Peer Culture in the Early Years*. Norwood, NJ: Ablex.

Corsaro, William A. 2003. *We're Friends Right? Inside Kids' Culture*. Washington, DC: Joseph Henry Press.

Davies, Bronwyn. 2003. *Frogs and Snails and Feminist Tales. Preschool Children and Gender* (rev. ed.). Cresskill, NJ: Hampton Press.

Disney Consumer Products. 2011. "Disney Princess." Disney, https://www.disneyconsumerproducts.com/Home/display.jsp?contentId=dcp_home_ourfranchises_disney_princess_us&forPrint=false&language=en&preview=false&imageShow=0&pressRoom=US&translationOf=null®ion=0

Dyson, Anne Haas. 2003. *The Brothers and Sisters Learn to Write: Popular Literacies in Childhood and School Cultures*. New York: Teachers College Press.

Dyson, Anne Haas. 2006. "On Saying It Right (Write): 'Fix-Its' in the Foundations of Learning to Write." *Research in the Teaching of English, 41*(1): 8–42.

Dyson, Anne Haas. 2008. "Staying in the (Curricular) Lines: Practice Constraints and Possibilities in Childhood Writing." *Written Communication, 25*(1): 119–159.

Fernie, David, Samara Madrid, and Rebecca Kantor. (Eds.). 2011. *Educating Toddlers to Teachers: Learning to See and Influence the School and Peer Cultures of Classrooms*. New York: Hampton Press.

Galbraith, Jeanne. 2011. "'Welcome to Our Team, Shark Boy': Making Superhero Play Visible." In *Educating Toddlers to Teachers: Learning to See and Influence the School and Peer Cultures of Classrooms*, ed. David Fernie, Samara Madrid, and Rebecca Kantor, 37–62. New York: Hampton Press.

Gee, James Paul. 1996. *Social Linguistics and Literacies: Ideology in Discourses. Critical Perspectives on Literacy and Education* (2nd ed.), ed. Allan Luke. London: RoutledgeFalmer.

Giroux, Henry A., and Grace Pollock. 2010. *The Mouse That Roared: Disney and the End of Innocence*. Lanham, MD: Rowman & Littlefield.

Göncü, Artin. (Ed.). 1999. *Children's Engagement in the World: Sociocultural Perspectives*. Cambridge: Cambridge University Press.

Grumet, Madeleine R. 1998. *Bitter Milk: Women and Teaching*. Amherst: University of Massachusetts Press.

Haas, Lynda, Elizabeth Bell, and Laura Sells. (Eds.). 1995. *From Mouse to Mermaid: The Politics of Film, Gender, and Culture*. Bloomington: Indiana University Press.

Hains, Rebecca. 2014. *The Princess Problem: Guiding Our Girls Through the Princess-Obsessed Years*. Naperville, IL: Sourcebooks.

Kamler, Barbara. 1999. "This Lovely Doll Who's Come to School: Morning Talk as Gendered Language Practice." In *Constructing Gender and Difference: Critical Research Perspectives on Early Childhood*, ed. Barbara Kamler, 191–214. Cresskill, NJ: Hampton Press.

Kantor, Rebecca, and David Fernie. (Eds.). 2003. *Early Childhood Classroom Processes*. Cresskill, NJ: Hampton Press.

Kendrick, Maureen. 2005. "Playing House: A 'Sideways' Glance at Literacy and Identity in Early Childhood." *Journal of Early Childhood Literacy, 5*(1): 1–28.

Kilodavis, Cheryl, and Suzanne DeSimone. 2010. *My Princess Boy*. New York: Aladdin.

Kinder, Marsha. 1991. *Playing with Power in Movies, Television, and Video Games: From Muppet Babies to Teenage Mutant Ninja Turtles*. Berkeley: University of California Press.

Kontovourki, Stavroula, and Marjorie Siegel. 2009. "Discipline and Play with/in a Mandated Literacy Curriculum." *Language Arts, 87*(1): 30–38.

Mackey, Margaret. 2010. "Spinning Off: Toys, Television, Tie-Ins, and Technology." In *Handbook of Research in Children's and Young Adults' Literature*, ed. Shelby Wolf, Karen Coats, Patricia Enciso, and Christine A. Jenkins, 495–507. New York: Taylor & Francis.

Madrid, Samara, and Laurie Katz. 2011. "Young Children's Gendered Positioning and Emotional Scenarios in Play Narratives." In *Gender and Early Learning Environments*, ed. Beverly J. Irbe and Genevieve Brown. Charlotte, NC: Information Age.

Marsh, Jackie. 2000. "'But I Want to Fly Too'! Girls and Superhero Play in the Infant Classroom." *Gender and Education, 10*(2): 209–220.

Marsh, Jackie. (Ed.). 2005. *Popular Culture, New Media and Digital Literacy in Early Childhood.* New York: RoutledgeFalmer.

Marsh, Jackie, Greg Brooks, Jane Hughes, Louise Ritchie, Samuel Roberts, and Katy Wright. 2005. *Digital Beginnings: Young Children's Use of Popular Culture, Media and New Technologies*. Sheffield, UK: University of Sheffield.

Marshall, Elizabeth, and Özlem Sensoy. (Eds.). 2011. *Rethinking Popular Culture and Media.* Milwaukee, WI: Rethinking Schools.

Medina, Carmen L., and Karen E. Wohlwend. 2014. *Literacy, Play, and Globalization: Converging Imaginaries in Children's Critical and Cultural Performances*. New York: Routledge.

Nixon, Helen, and Barbara Comber. 2005. "Behind the Scenes: Making Movies in Early Years Classrooms." In *Popular Culture, New Media and Digital Literacy in Early Childhood*, ed. Jackie Marsh, 219–236. New York: RoutledgeFalmer.

Norris, S., & Jones, R. H. (2005). *Discourse in Action: Introducing Mediated Discourse Analysis.* London: Routledge.

Orenstein, Peggy. 2011. *Cinderella Ate My Daughter: Dispatches from the Front Lines of the New Girlie-Girl Culture.* New York: HarperCollins.

Paechter, Carrie. 2006. "Constructing Femininity, Constructing Femininities." In *The Sage Handbook of Gender and Education* [Electronic version], ed. Christine Skelton, Becky Francis, and Lisa Smulyan. London: Sage.

Paris, Scott G. 2005. "Reinterpreting the Development of Reading Skills." *Reading Research Quarterly, 40*(2): 184–202.

Pugh, Allison J. 2009. *Longing and Belonging: Parents, Children, and Consumer Culture*. Berkeley: University of California Press.

Riddle, Johanna. 2009. *Engaging the Eye Generation: Visual Literacy Strategies for the K–5 Classroom*. Portland, ME: Stenhouse.

Rowsell, Jennifer, and Kate Pahl. 2007. "Sedimented Identities in Texts: Instances of Practice." *Reading Research Quarterly, 42*(3): 388–404.

Saltmarsh, Sue. 2009. "Becoming Economic Subjects: Agency, Consumption and Popular Culture in Early Childhood." *Discourse, 30*(1): 47–59.

Sanderson, Michelle. 2011. "'Do You Want to Rough and Tumble?' Toddler Project Work as an Intersection of School Culture and Nascent Peer Culture." In *Educating Toddlers to Teachers: Learning to See and Influence the School and Peer Cultures of Classrooms*, ed. David Fernie, Rebecca Kantor, and Samara Madrid, 15–30. New York: Hampton Press.

Scollon, Ron. 2001. *Mediated Discourse: The Nexus of Practice*. London: Routledge.

Scollon, Ron, and Suzanne Wong Scollon. 2004. *Nexus Analysis: Discourse and the Emerging Internet*. New York: Routledge.

Sekeres, Diane Carver. 2009. "The Market Child and Branded Fiction: A Synergism of Children's Literature, Consumer Culture, and New Literacies." *Reading Research Quarterly, 44*(4): 399–414.

Schwartzman, H. B. (1976). The anthropological study of children's play. *Annual Review of Anthropology, 5*(289–328).

Vasquez, Vivian Maria. 2004. *Negotiating Critical Literacies with Young Children.* Mahwah, NJ: Lawrence Erlbaum.

Vasquez, Vivian Maria, and Carol Branigan Felderman. 2012. *Technology and Critical Literacy in Early Childhood.* New York: Routledge.

Vygotsky, Lev. 1935/1978. *Mind in Society,* trans. Alexander Luria, Martin Lopez-Morillas, and Michael Cole. Cambridge, MA: Harvard University Press.

Wertsch, James V. 1991. *Voices of the Mind: A Sociocultural Approach to Mediated Action.* Cambridge, MA: Harvard University Press.

Wohlwend, Karen E. 2009. "Damsels in Discourse: Girls Consuming and Producing Gendered Identity Texts through Disney Princess Play." *Reading Research Quarterly, 44*(1): 57–83.

Wohlwend, Karen E. 2011. *Playing Their Way into Literacies: Reading, Writing, and Belonging in the Early Childhood Classroom.* New York: Teachers College Press.

Wohlwend, Karen E. 2012. "The Boys Who Would Be Princesses: Playing with Gender Identity Intertexts in Disney Princess Transmedia." *Gender and Education, 24*(6): 593–610.

Wohlwend, Karen E., Beth A. Buchholz, Christy Wessel-Powell, Linda Skidmore Coggin, and Nicholas E. Husbye. 2013. *Literacy Playshop: Playing with New Literacies and Popular Media in the Early Childhood Classroom.* New York: Teachers College Press.

# Part II
# Princess Cultures Beyond Western Cultures

CHAPTER SIX

# Mono- or Multi-Culturalism: Girls around the World Interpret Non-Western Disney Princesses

BY DIANA NATASIA AND CHARU UPPAL

Disney Princesses have shaped children's and adults' imaginations around the world for generations. As the ubiquity of U.S. media internationally and the paucity of domestic media in many countries narrow what is available to youth and adult audiences alike, and as mass media increasingly replace local storytelling, girls across the globe may learn more about Disney Princesses than about the princesses existing in their own cultures. The Disney industry has even begun narrating stories about non-Western princesses, and in so doing it takes pride in positioning itself as a multicultural brand. However, girls in international settings are rarely asked to provide opinions of these princesses' representations. The main purpose of our project is to give voice to such girls regarding Disney's depictions of several princesses with non-Western heritage.

Despite her status as a perennial staple, the Disney Princess has undergone numerous changes since the premiere of *Snow White and the Seven Dwarfs*, the first animated film produced by the Disney studios in 1937. Bolstering Disney's plausibility as a multicultural brand, Disney Princesses are no longer solely of European descent; in the past quarter of a century, there have been Disney Princesses of Asian, Native American, and African American descent. Additionally, Disney target audiences are no longer restricted to Caucasian children; today, youth everywhere can get access to Disney Princess animated films and merchandise. Disney

Princess clothing, home furnishings, dolls, and party items are particularly popular internationally.

These multicultural shifts in the Disney Princess brand have been of interest to us on both personal and professional levels. Diana was raised in a country in Eastern Europe, where the communist totalitarian regime in power at that time banned most U.S. media programming. She is currently raising two daughters in the United States, where Disney Princesses are ever-present across media channels. Charu has navigated various media systems and forms of popular culture: Raised in India, which has its own rich tradition of media production in rivalry with U.S. media production, she later taught in Africa, pursued graduate education in the United States, and has worked as a university faculty member in Fiji and Sweden.

Drawing on our own diverse backgrounds, we noted the multicultural shifts in the Disney Princess brand, and asked ourselves: Have Disney Princesses surpassed monoculturalism? To what extent are girls learning about multiculturalism from the Disney princesses? In 2009, supported by a grant from Internationales Zentralinstitut für das Jugend- und Bildungsfernsehen (Izi) in Munich, we sought answers to these questions by studying 120 girls of various ethnicities from four countries (the United States, India, Fiji, and China) within three age categories (8–10, 11–12, and 13–15). We aimed to investigate what these Western and non-Western girls were learning from Jasmine, Pocahontas, and Mulan, the only three Disney Princesses with non-Western heritage at the time of our study. (Disney's African American princess, Tiana, had not yet made her debut in the animated film *The Princess and the Frog*, which was released at the end of 2009.) As we thought that multiculturalism in the Disney Princess world would be particularly located in the realms of the Disney Princesses with non-Western heritage, we became interested in finding out how the research participants would respond to these characters. We provided them with clips from the three Disney Princess movies, *Aladdin*, *Pocahontas*, and *Mulan*, prompted them to talk individually and in groups, and asked them to draw pictures. This chapter is based on our analysis of what they said and drew.

After surveying the ever-expanding presence of the Disney industry around the world, our chapter provides an overview of scholarship on Disney animated films positioning this research at the intersection of Neo-Marxist, critical race, and feminist critiques of Disney and its princesses. Our chapter then offers an outline of our research methods, explaining how we adjusted data collection and analysis to address the international nature and age cohorts of the study's subjects. Our findings, grounded in a comparative consideration of themes emerging from the data, indicate several areas of consensus among our research participants, and several areas of disagreement between girls in Western settings and girls in non-Western settings. Many girls in all the countries included in the study defined princesses, including Disney ones, by reference to an appealing physical presence, and described the Disney Princesses with non-Western heritage as not much different from other princesses in Disney animated films. However, most girls in the United States regardless of ethnicity characterized Disney Princesses as wealthy and free, expressed a strong desire to be like them, and felt a strong identification with them; yet most girls in India, Fiji, and China characterized Disney Princesses as having numerous duties but not being free, lacked the desire to be like them, and did not identify even with the Disney Princesses with non-Western heritage. Our conclusion aims to contribute to a more complete understanding of how girls from diverse backgrounds formulate, interpret, and perform gendered identities by emulating media content situated at the intersection of the local and the global.

## Literature Review: Scholarly Critiques of Disney's Kingdom

Disney animated films have received critiques from three different but converging scholarly perspectives: Neo-Marxism, critical race theories, and feminism. These critiques have provided much insight into the construction of the Disney realm, but have many times been quickly invalidated by the Disney industry. Our study situates itself at the intersection of these three scholarly perspectives, and also attempts to give a new impetus to critical studies of the Disney world by paying close attention to Disney's adjustments following various critiques.

In the pioneering study *The Disney Version*, Schickel (1968) critiqued Disney animated films for constructing a universe in which characters are positioned in dichotomous pairs of heroes who are always victorious and villains who are constantly defeated. Schickel viewed this binary version of reality proposed by the Walt Disney Company as overly tamed and highly sanitized, suiting the interests of commercial enterprises and promoting the values of the Western world's upper class. Neo-Marxist scholars elaborated on Schickel's early observations (Brockway 1986; Croce 1991; Dorfman and Mattelart 1975; Giroux 1999; Hansen 1993; Hiassen 1998; Wasko 2000). They have discussed how such an approach encourages the compliance with the current societal order and discourages dissent. Several Neo-Marxist scholars have specifically focused on what is placed in the Disney world at the margin or even outside of the admissible margins. In *How to Read Donald Duck: Imperialist Ideology in the Disney Comic*, Dorfman and Mattelart (1975) took such an approach while comparing the order of the magical realm with that of capitalism. They argued that in the Disney world, just like under capitalism, insignificance attributed to certain issues is represented through silence; labor is one of them. Although capitalism would be impossible without the efforts of the working classes, these efforts are overall missing from capitalist mainstream discourses (such as policy, public, and media discourses). Labor is also "hidden or banished" in Disney fantasies, in which "necessities of life," such as food, drink, household-related items, and means of transportation, "appear suddenly and then disappear magically" (Dorfman and Mattelart 1975, 68). By ignoring and hiding work, these narratives inherently glorify the lives of the rich and the vision of the corporate capitalists (70). In *Understanding Disney: The Manufacture of Fantasy*, Wasko (2000) highlighted that the Walt Disney Company continues to disregard what is associated with the ways of living of those who are not in the most privileged positions in the Western world.

Critical race and feminist scholars have uncovered in the Disney world other hierarchical patterns: positioning whiteness and masculinity as central and positive and conversely positioning non-whiteness and femininity as marginal and negative. Lawrence (1989) evidenced how whiteness is privileged in Disney animated films by analyzing the construction of Disney characters in terms of their physical characteristics. Lawrence stated that in films from the 1937 *Snow White and the Seven Dwarfs* to the 1989 *Little Mermaid* positive characters were represented as having features usually associated with Caucasians, whereas negative characters were represented with features typically linked to African Americans, in terms of the shapes and configurations of the eyes, nose, cheeks, bones, and body. According to Lawrence and others (Benton 1995; Smoodin 1994; Ward 1996), racism is detectable in Disney animated films in the recurring connection of villains with people of color. Moreover, according to several scholars (Ayers 2003; Brode 2005; Cheu 2013), racism is discernible in Disney animated films when looking at their ideological tendencies, namely, those of glorifying Euro-American myths such as individualism and freedom and contesting other traditions focusing on community and duty. Privileging a particular type of outlook and a particular set of beliefs, an aspect of "the pervasive racist value system that children have been exposed to and internalize—a system that is reinforced to a large extent by the culture industry …, and in particular through such devices as that of the Disneyfied princess," affects positively the self-image of Western children and negatively that of non-Western children (Hurley 2005, 223).

A 1995 book by Bell, Haas, and Sells and a 1996 special issue of *Women's Studies in Communication* (Bell 1996; Downey 1996; Henke, Umble Zimmerman, and Smith 1996; Hoerner 1996; O'Brien 1996) documented how masculinity is privileged and femininity is subdued in Disney animated films by examining the construction of Disney characters in terms of their psychological and physical characteristics. These scholars discussed the prevalence in Disney animated films of strong, determined male characters and of frail, shy female characters. Moreover, these scholars affirmed that in Disney Princess animated films from the 1930s to the 1990s conformity with the naturalized patriarchal gender order was unequivocally rewarded, as the positive female character was granted physical beauty and was the one who always got the love of the positive male character at the end of the story. Conversely, defiance of the reified traditional gender roles was attributed to ugly and unpleasant female characters, and was penalized with misery and eternal unmarried status. Paralleling critiques by critical race scholars, feminist scholars of the 1990s and later (Do Rozario 2004; Klein, Shiffman, and Welka 2000; Li-Vollmer and LaPointe 2003) claimed that sexist stereotypes, including those related to oppressive standards dictating what constitutes appropriate feminine behavior and what counts as women's beauty, have a powerful sway on children worldwide by means of their occurrence in the Disney animated films, particularly the Disney Princess ones.

Neo-Marxist, critical race, and feminist studies have revealed how Disney animated films help universalize the values of the rich and those of upper-class Euro-American elites and help privilege whiteness and patriarchy. However, the representatives of the Disney industry seem to have been highly cognizant of scholarly critiques of their products (or perhaps they have learned about objections to their stories and characters from their own research involving parents and children), as they have made changes that address such critiques. In its collaboration with and subsequent incorporation of the Pixar Animation Studios, the Walt Disney Company de-sanitized its narratives, showing less dichotomous characters (by not always equating beauty with goodness) and situations (by including references to labor), in animated films such as *Monsters, Inc.* (2001), *The Incredibles* (2004), and *Ratatouille* (2007). The corporation also integrated main characters from different cultures around the world, and positive female characters who can be strong and determined, and who could even choose to be warriors or not to marry, in animated films such as *Aladdin* (1992), *Pocahontas* (1995), *Mulan* (1998), *The Emperor's New Groove* (2000), and *The Princess and the Frog* (2009). Despite these changes within the Disney franchise, we argue that Neo-Marxist, critical race, and feminist critiques of Disney still remain relevant, because Disney's de-sanitization, ethnic diversity, and gender liberation are rather superficial. Situated at the intersection of these types of scholarship, our study seeks to uncover how the slightly cosmeticized "Emperor's old groove" (Ayers 2003) is assiduously passed off as a new, multicultural groove.

## Methods: Asking Girls about Disney Princesses

The central purpose of this project has been to offer girls in international settings, who often consume Disney products but are rarely asked to express their thoughts about them, an opportunity to assess several Disney Princesses with non-Western heritage (specifically Jasmine, Pocahontas, and Mulan). To that end, we combined an array of age-appropriate (suited for subjects who are children) and culturally appropriate (suited for subjects of various ethnicities residing in different countries) reception-oriented research methods.

Our study sampled girls from eight different ethno-cultural groups in four countries, and in three different age subgroups within each ethno-cultural group. The reason for our sample selection was to ensure the inclusion of a diverse set of participants, allowing for a wide range of perspectives. The research participants included girls of Indian descent in India; girls of Indian and Fijian descent in Fiji; girls of Chinese descent in China; and girls of Indian, Chinese, Native American, and European descent in the United States. We chose these types of participants based on a loose association of their groups' cultural heritage with Disney Princesses' cultural heritage (Jasmine is featured by Disney creators generically as a South Asian princess, Mulan as a Chinese princess, and Pocahontas as a Native American one; all other princesses in Disney animated films at the time of our research were of European descent). By including girls in Western and non-Western settings, we were able to critically consider the intricate connections between geographic location, exposure to Western media sources, and interpretation of Western media materials. Additionally, by including girls of Indian descent in India, Fiji, and the United States, as well as girls of Chinese descent in China and the United States, we could examine the role migration plays in the interpretation of media materials. We added a further dimension to our study by including within each ethno-cultural category three subgroups: pre-teens (8- to 10-year-old girls), tweens (11- to 12-year-old girls), and teens (13- to 15-year-old girls). Each age subgroup was formed of five girls. Overall, 120 girls participated in the research.

All study participants belonged to the middle class of their respective countries, living in urban areas and in families with stable incomes. The parents of most of the U.S. girls of Indian and Chinese descent, either first or second generation in that country, held higher education degrees. The families of all of the U.S. girls of Native American descent resided and went to school in a city in the Upper Midwest region, not on a reservation. This socio-economic uniformity was a relative one, as being middle class in the United States is different from being middle class in India, Fiji, or China. However, the socio-economic uniformity ensured to some extent that regardless of the country the research participants were able to access and to consume audio-visual and material products bearing the Disney brand. The girls growing up in India and China were exposed to Disney animated cartoons both in English and in versions that were somehow indigenized by means of voice-over. Fiji was the only one of the three non-Western countries in which our study participants resided where Disney animated films were not dubbed, and as such they were unavailable in Hindi or Fijian, the two languages other than English that are widely spoken in the country.

After obtaining Institutional Review Board approval, we proceeded with our data collection. Diana was responsible for the data collection in the United States, with the aid of four paid research assistants, and Charu was responsible for the data collection in India and Fiji, with the aid of two paid research assistants per country. In China, we hired a research associate, a university faculty member with research experience, who collected the data and translated the participants' statements from Chinese into English. Five participants at a time were gathered in one location, all belonging to a specific age subgroup within one of the ethno-cultural groups. Participants were recruited either through local schools or personal contacts, and prior to meeting with researchers the girls and their legal guardians were informed about the scope and the procedures of the study and were invited to sign the assent and, respectively, the consent forms. After all participants in a group arrived at the designated location, they were briefed about our research. Then, a series of clips, arranged from the Disney animated films featuring the three Disney Princesses with non-Western heritage, were screened for the respective group. We showed the clips to ensure that all study participants had fresh memories of the three Disney Princesses with non-Western heritage and the main storylines in the animated films. Next, all participants in the group received paper, pencils, and crayons and were asked to draw their own versions of princesses. During this drawing period, girls were pulled out one at a time for individual interviews held in a separate room. There, each girl had a 10- to 20-minute conversation with a researcher. Finally, all five participants in each group were invited to join a focus group discussion lasting 20 to 30 minutes facilitated by a researcher.

In the process of data collection, we elicited information from our participants about how they viewed Disney Princesses in general and Disney Princesses with non-Western heritage in particular. During the individual interviews, girls were invited to share their ideas about what a princess is, how a Disney Princess looks and acts, and whether a Disney Princess with non-Western heritage looks and acts differently from other Disney Princesses. During these interviews, each girl was also invited to state whether she ever wanted to be a princess, whether she could be a princess, and whether she felt that she looked and acted like a Disney Princess, especially like Jasmine, Pocahontas, and Mulan. In the course of the focus group discussion, girls were prompted to talk about their favorite Disney Princesses and compare notes in this respect. In these focus groups, girls were also prompted to consider similarities and differences among Jasmine, Pocahontas, and Mulan and other princesses in Disney animated films.

What the girls said individually or in groups was recorded, transcribed, translated where necessary, and analyzed thematically. Thematic analysis is "a way for researchers to gather information about how other human beings make sense of the world" not only by examining "specific words" in their utterances but "more so the meanings hidden within them" (Merskin 2011, 131). Each researcher separately reread the transcribed materials looking for recurring expressions and ideas. Together, we evaluated these by paying close attention to their contexts and meanings. This examination led us to the identification of patterns and themes, which helped us to gain insight into the research participants' identities and the lasting impact of Disney Princesses on their identities.

## Research Results: Girls' Interpretations of Disney Princesses

Individual interviews, focus group discussions, and drawing sessions provided the girls with opportunities to reflect on Disney characters, narratives, and imagery. Our findings are based on a thorough examination of the girls' reflections, with a view to showing in what ways there was mostly consensus and along what lines there were marked differences among the girls.

### A Consensus: Princesses Are Beautiful

"Princesses are beautiful" and "Disney princesses are beautiful" were sentences uttered by many research participants in our study in the United States, India, Fiji, and China, in all ethno-cultural groups and age subgroups included in our study.

We observed that study participants of various ethnicities and different ages residing in the United States mostly held in high regard the appealing physical presence of princesses in general and Disney Princesses specifically. Many preteen and tween girls said that one main reason they watched animated films with Disney Princesses was that they found beautiful princesses enchanting. Some teen girls said that they used to be charmed by the beautiful Disney Princesses, but had moved on to media products for older ages. Sample comments included:

- "All princesses I know from cartoons and movies are really nice. They have nice eyes and nice hair." (8-year-old girl, European descent, U.S.)
- "Princesses are pretty. ... Disney princesses watch themselves in the mirror to make sure they are still pretty. People like them because they are pretty. I like to watch them because they are pretty." (12-year-old girl, European descent, U.S.)
- "When I was little, I used to watch Disney princesses movies all the time. I was captivated because I thought they were pretty." (14-year-old girl, European descent, U.S.)
- "I like Disney princesses because they look good." (9-year-old girl, Native American descent, U.S.)
- "Princesses keep their hair straight. They have big, nice eyes." (12-year-old girl, Native American descent, U.S.)
- "Disney princesses are gorgeous, and all about them is like that." (14-year-old girl, Native American descent, U.S.)
- "I really, really like Disney princesses. They are the prettiest in the whole world." (8-year-old girl, Indian descent, U.S.)
- "I used to like the Disney princesses because they seemed always lovely." (14-year-old girl, Indian descent, U.S.)
- "A princess is pretty from head to toes." (12-year-old girl, Chinese descent, U.S.)

However, not all study participants from the United States appreciated the focus on physical appearance in Disney animated films. For example, an 11-year-old girl of Native American descent associated the Disney Princess with the obligation to always stay pretty. She said, "Princesses can't have bad hair days. They must look good all the time." A 15-year-old girl of Chinese descent associated the slimness of the Disney Princesses with anorexia. She said, "Princesses in Disney cartoons look good because they are very slim. Just like anorexic kids ... I know a few anorexic kids."

Similar to many girls in the United States, most girls in India, Fiji, and China said that princesses in Disney animated films were beautiful, and that the beauty of those princesses made the animated films appealing. Study participants in non-Western settings considered that beauty meant a pretty face, nice hair, and nice hands. Sample comments included:

- "Princesses are very beautiful, I like their style." (8-year-old girl, India)
- "A princess is a beautiful girl. ... She is tall. She is beautiful." (11-year-old girl, India)

- [Disney princesses] "are too beautiful but like not true." (14-year-old girl, India)
- "A princess is pretty … her face, her hands." (9-year-old girl, Indian descent, Fiji)
- "A princess is beautiful, and a prince loves her. Her skin is white or yellowish, her hair is golden and wavy." (12-year-old girl, Indian descent, Fiji)
- "A princess is pretty, she's confident because she's pretty." (14-year-old girl, Indian descent, Fiji)
- "I think a princess is beautiful because in all the cartoons that I've watched, all the princesses are beautiful." (8-year-old girl, Fijian descent, Fiji)
- "Their father is the king, his blood is in his children. … They are beautiful. They look good." (11-year-old girl, Fijian descent, Fiji)
- "She is beautiful, has long hair, she is quite short and she is skinny. She is fancy and glamorous." (14-year-old girl, Fijian descent, Fiji)
- "A princess should be beautiful, and good-hearted, and very hard-working. It seems to me all princesses are like that, aren't they?" (8-year-old girl, China)
- "A princess is beautiful. … All stories I read and cartoons I watched showed princesses like that." (11-year-old girl, China)
- "I used to dream to be a princess because they are always so beautiful and they are always adored and praised by a lot of people." (15-year-old girl, China)

As evidenced by these quotes, some contradictory meanings were found in the interpretations of Disney Princesses' physical appearances offered by study participants in India, Fiji, and China. An 11-year-old girl in India associated "tall" with "beautiful," whereas a 14-year-old girl of Fijian descent in Fiji associated "short" with "beautiful." The same Fijian girl mentioned that to be beautiful a princess has to be skinny. Apart from the 12-year-old girl of Indian descent in Fiji who specified a lighter shade of skin and hair as beauty attributes of princesses and Disney Princesses, no other girl mentioned hair or skin color when discussing definitions of princesses (although many non-Western girls brought up this aspect when discussing whether they could be princesses, as outlined later in this chapter). However, many research participants in India, Fiji, and China, as well as in the United States, drew princesses with white skin and fair hair even after they were showed clips with the princesses with non-Western heritage (see Figure 1). All girls in non-Western settings felt that princesses' beauty contributed to their self-confidence, helped them gain the love of a prince, and led to their adoration by many people—except the 14-year-old girl in India who thought that Disney Princesses were too beautiful to be true.

Drawn by 13-year-old girl, European descent, U.S.

Drawn by 12-year-old girl, India

Drawn by 11-year-old girl, Fijian descent, Fiji

Drawn by 8-year-old girl, China

Figure 1.

## Another Consensus: Disney Princesses Are All Alike

Many of our research participants in the United States and non-Western settings perceived the Disney Princesses of non-Western heritage as being similar to the Disney Princesses of Western heritage. When asked in individual interviews whether Jasmine, Pocahontas, and Mulan looked and acted differently from other Disney Princesses, 90% of the girls in our study answered "no."

Several research participants referenced physical beauty as a point of similarity between Western and non-Western Disney Princesses. Examples include:

- "Jasmine is beautiful, just like Snow White." (9-year-old girl, European descent, U.S.)
- "Jasmine, Pocahontas, and Mulan look like Disney princesses because they have grace." (12-year-old girl, China)

A few additional research participants found elegance of attire to be a point of similarity:

- "The princesses you showed us have nice dresses. ... I can tell they are Disney princesses by the nice dresses." (11-year-old girl, Native American descent, U.S.)
- "Jasmine and Mulan wear long gowns and shiny tiaras. Princess Aurora and Princess Belle wear those, too." (10-year-old girl, India)

Some research participants also considered the non-Western and Western princesses to be alike because their stories focused on the theme of love. For example:

- "These princesses appear in love stories. Disney cartoons are always love stories." (14-year-old girl, Indian descent, U.S.)

- "They are like all Disney princesses. They are not allowed but they fall in love. In the end, the prince loves them back. They like romance." (14-year-old girl, Fijian descent, Fiji)

Another point of similarity was related to the Disney Princesses' kind behavior. For example:

- "I think Mulan acts like other Disney princesses because she is good hearted." (9-year-old girl, Chinese descent, U.S.)
- "Most princesses in the Disney cartoons are gentle and kind. ... Mulan is kind to her people." (10-year-old girl, China)

Only a few research participants in Western and non-Western settings expressed the opinion that Jasmine, Pocahontas, and Mulan looked and acted differently from other Disney Princesses; yet these girls noted some important differences. A 12-year-old girl of European descent in the United States and a 14-year-old girl in China made the explicit statement that Pocahontas and Mulan are non-fictional characters, whereas other Disney princesses are fictional. A small number of girls made reference to ethnic heritage. A 10-year-old girl of European descent in the United States said that she thought Jasmine was Australian. Four girls of Native American descent in the United States (a 9-year-old, an 11-year-old, a 13-year-old, and a 14-year-old) focused on Pocahontas's Native American heritage and said they were proud of it; the 11-year-old thought Pocahontas looked like her mother. Two girls in China also tried to consider which Disney Princesses shared their heritage: A 9-year-old girl said, "Mulan, Jasmine, and Snow White are all Chinese because they are dark-haired. Belle and Cinderella are American. Again it's the hair." An 11-year-old girl stated, "Mulan is Chinese, she has many traditional Chinese virtues. She is good to her parents, especially to her father. And she is also good to her motherland. Jasmine is adventurous, and Jasmine is definitely a foreigner to me. And these Disney Princesses are from different countries and cultures." Additionally, several girls (an 11-year-old of Indian descent and a 12-year-old of Chinese descent in the United States, as well as a 10-year-old of Indian descent, a 9-year-old of Fijian descent, and a 13-year-old of Fijian descent in Fiji) stated that the Disney Princesses with non-Western heritage were more adventurous than other Disney Princesses, and were even involved in battles.

Additionally, when prompted in the focus group discussions to discuss the similarities and differences between Jasmine, Pocahontas, and Mulan and other Disney Princesses, most girls again focused on similarities, primarily beauty and kindness. A 13-year-old girl of Indian descent in India synthesized what most of the girls in her group believed about the Disney Princesses with non-Western heritage: "Pocahontas is American, … Jasmine is from India and Mulan is from China … but they look like Americans and behave like Americans." Of all focus group discussions, only one—the 8- to 10-year-old girls of Fijian descent in Fiji—focused on differences; these girls talked for a while about Jasmine, Pocahontas, and Mulan as being "louder" than other Disney Princesses. The girls in this group seemed to sympathize with the three princesses more than with other Disney Princesses because of this feature.

## A U.S. Perspective: Princesses Are Wealthy and Free

What particularly distinguished girls in the United States regardless of ethno-cultural background and age from girls in non-Western settings was their view of princesses in general and Disney Princesses in particular in terms of their material possessions and self-determination. In the interviews, girls in the United States declared that princesses would have lots of money, and would own castles or palaces as well as furniture, animals, jewelry, dresses, and shoes. Sample comments included:

- "A princess is someone who lives in a palace, has jewels, and has a lot of money." (9-year-old girl, European descent, U.S.)
- "They are very rich." (12-year-old girl, European descent, U.S.)
- "They have special things like dresses, animals." (13-year-old girl, European descent, U.S.)
- "Princesses have lots of money." (9-year-old girl, Native American descent, U.S.)
- "A princess has dresses, tiaras, glass slippers, beautiful jewels, anything she wants." (11-year-old girl, Native American descent, U.S.)
- "A princess has a big castle with many rooms. She has beautiful things, fancy dresses." (14-year-old girl, Native American descent, U.S.)
- "They have rich families, they have money" (9-year-old girl, Indian descent, U.S.)
- "Their families are like royal. … They have palaces and stuff. … They get spoiled." (11-year-old girl, Indian descent, U.S.)
- "A princess is someone with a castle, like all the stuff that they really have. … They are rich, their dads would have money." (14-year-old girl, Indian descent, U.S.)
- "They live in very nice palaces." (9-year-old girl, Chinese descent, U.S.)
- "Princesses wear pretty clothes." (12-year-old girl, Chinese descent, U.S.)
- "To be a princess you will have to be really rich, to have a rich family. … You will have many things." (15-year-old girl, Chinese descent, U.S.)

Two research participants in the United States linked power with wealth in their definitions of princesses. A 13-year-old girl of European descent said, "I think a princess has these people who are her servants. … She has servants and tells them what to do, and they do things for her, and they obey her." A 14-year-old girl of European descent stated, "A princess is rich, and she is famous, and people listen to her." Among research participants in the United States, only one (a 12-year-old girl of Indian descent) viewed princesses as having duties rather than possessions; she said that a princess is "nice and good to people" and "helps others," taking a similar stand to that of most of our research participants in non-Western settings.

In addition to material possessions, girls in the United States also mentioned individual liberty as a defining characteristic of princesses and Disney Princesses. Many of our research participants in the United States viewed princesses as determined to get their own way, even to the extent of being stubborn; they expressed their admiration for Disney Princesses for doing what they wanted, sometimes in spite of those around them. Sample comments included:

- "The princesses get to stick up for themselves." (10-year-old girl, European descent, U.S.)
- "They get to do whatever they want." (12-year-old girl, European descent, U.S.)
- "They can choose what to do." (15-year-old girl, European descent, U.S.)
- "A princess fights for what she believes in. Pocahontas goes against her father." (12-year-old girl, Native American descent, U.S.)
- "Some of the princesses even ran away from home when their father tried to marry them with someone they didn't love." (15-year-old girl, Native American descent, U.S.)
- "They don't do what they are told." (10-year-old girl, Indian descent, U.S.)
- "They are strong and brave. … They do dangerous things." (13-year-old girl, Indian descent, U.S.)
- "She says what she thinks and she does what she wants. She gets her way. I like that." (12-year-old girl, Chinese descent, U.S.)

By referring to wealth and freedom as the two main attributes of princesses and Disney Princesses, girls in the United States regardless of ethnicity and age seemed to uncritically adopt a set of Western, capitalist values often reified by the Disney corporation and other U.S. media conglomerates.

## A Non-Western Perspective: Princesses Have Many Duties but Are Not Free

Unlike girls in the United States who mainly focused on material wealth, girls in India, Fiji, and China often highlighted princesses' duties. Many of the girls in non-Western settings defined princesses by means of involvement in and assistance to families and communities. Several of the girls in India, Fiji, and China said that princesses have special connections with animals. For example:

- "Princesses help their fathers." (8-year-old girl, India)
- "They put their family and their friends first." (12-year-old girl, India)
- "A princess would take care of her mom, dad, and family. She would fight for the city." (14-year-old girl, India)
- "Princesses are respected because they take care of people." (8-year-old girl, Indian descent, Fiji)
- "Princesses respect others and are never unkind to people and animals. … Jasmine thought about the others, she helped the poor, she cared for the tiger." (11-year-old girl, Indian descent, Fiji)
- "Princesses do not commit murder." (15-year-old girl, Indian descent, Fiji)
- "I like Snow White and Cinderella. I like Snow White, she cooks soup for everyone." (9-year-old girl, Fijian descent, Fiji)
- "Princesses help their people." (12-year-old girl, Fijian descent, Fiji)
- "Princesses are good for service jobs." (13-year-old girl, Fijian descent, Fiji)
- "I don't remember which cartoon it is now, there is such a princess who was not careful enough when she tried to save some animal because in doing so she did a lot of damage to delicate flowers and worms. She should have been more careful." (8-year-old girl, China)
- "A princess keeps her people together. She fights for the truth. She is sympathetic to the poor and she treats other people as equals." (12-year-old girl, China)
- "She is very gentle and good to people and to small animals." (12-year-old girl, China)

Moreover, unlike girls in the United States who mostly viewed princesses as doing what they wanted, girls in India, Fiji, and China frequently perceived princesses as doing what was needed. Many of the girls in non-Western settings said that princesses had responsibilities related to their duties and limitations resulting from societal constraints. For example:

- "Mulan does what she needs to do. Her father was a warrior but his leg got injured. She had to fight for her country so she took his place." (9-year-old girl, India)
- "A princess cannot wear jeans or short skirts." (12-year-old girl, India)
- "They can't go out when they want." (14-year-old girl, India)
- "Princesses shouldn't shout at anybody so they keep quiet." (9-year-old girl, Indian descent, Fiji)
- "She has to be hard working. She has many things to do." (11-year-old girl, Indian descent, Fiji)
- "She respects the law and does everything by the law." (13-year-old girl, Indian descent, Fiji)
- "Princesses do what is proper for them." (9-year-old girl, Fijian descent, Fiji)
- "Princesses are not allowed to get out." (12-year-old girl, Fijian descent, Fiji)
- "A princess sacrifices for others, so she can't always be happy." (15-year-old girl, Fijian descent, Fiji)
- "They do not have much freedom." (10-year-old girl, China)
- "When you are a princess, you are not as free as other people." (12-year-old girl, China)
- "The life of a princess is not without worries. She has to follow rules but she also has to fight for justice." (15-year-old girl, China)

While girls in India and Fiji rarely mentioned material possessions in regard to princesses, 6 of the 15 girls in China talked about princesses' duties to their families and communities as well as princesses' possessions such as money and castles. For these girls in China, duty and wealth did not seem irreconcilable. Additionally, many girls in China, Fiji, and India considered that princesses had one important freedom: that of getting married to someone of their own choosing, rather than their families'. For a 12-year-old girl of Fijian descent in Fiji, a princess was someone "who can have a boyfriend if she wants to." For a 13-year-old girl of Indian descent in Fiji, "a princess has freedom and love." Many girls in India, Fiji, and China reported that they liked how princesses could get the boys they wanted and could get married to whomever they wanted.

We found non-Western girls' negotiations of the meanings of princesses particularly interesting. Their references to princesses' duties and responsibilities signaled their alignment with traditional Asian values, as well as their resistance to the globally dominant Western values. However, their references to princesses' freedom to marry for love suggested a departure from their societies' traditional values, and perhaps even a disagreement with the arranged marriages still encountered in these societies. Additionally, references to princesses helping others, in opposition to a materialistic trend linked to Western capitalism (and with connections with the Disney industry), are at least to some extent consonant with the sexist stereotype of women as nurturers—a mark of global patriarchy (frequently reinforced by Disney products).

## U.S. Girls Identify with Disney Princesses

The research participants' answers to the question "Can you be a princess?" provided the grounds for another sharp contrast between the girls in Western settings and the girls in non-Western settings: Most research participants in the United States had a sense of entitlement regarding the Disney Princesses, including the ones with non-Western heritage, whereas girls in India, Fiji, and China largely appeared disconnected from the Disney Princesses.

Girls in the United States, regardless of ethnicity and age, seemed to have appropriated Disney Princesses as part of their identities. Many girls expressed a belief that they were like princesses. Their arguments were that they owned many material goods, that their families and friends treated them like princesses and offered them support, that they often got their own way, and that their lives were worth living. For example:

- "I am a princess for my mom and dad." (9-year-old girl, European descent, U.S.)
- "I am pretty, my family and friends love me, I am a princess for them." (12-year-old girl, European descent, U.S.)
- "I am pretty cool, and I have a lot of friends, so I could be a princess." (15-year-old girl, European descent, U.S.)
- "I have a good house and nice toys. I am like a princess." (10-year-old girl, Native American descent, U.S.)
- "I do what I want like the Disney princesses. Like Jasmine or Pocahontas." (14-year-old girl, Native American descent, U.S.)
- "In my mind I am sometimes a princess." (9-year-old girl, Indian descent, U.S.)
- "I could be like a princess, though sometimes I could be better than a princess." (13-year-old girl, Indian descent, U.S.)
- "I feel that I can be a princess. I am pretty, I am thin. I have good things. My life is good." (12-year-old girl, Chinese descent, U.S.)

- "When I was little I dreamed of being a princess. I don't anymore because I grew up. … But I would do well as a princess." (14-year-old girl, Chinese descent, U.S.)

These girls put trust in themselves, their social groups, and their environment; this trust benefits them, but the question is: Does the typically Western self-assurance manifesting in our U.S. research participants hurt the identities of other people around the world? This is especially significant considering that U.S. girls' appropriation of Disney Princesses extended to those with non-Western heritage. Some examples include:

- "Mulan, Pocahontas, and Jasmine don't necessarily look like me but they behave like me. … Like me, they all have something good about them." (13-year-old girl, European descent, U.S.)
- "Jasmine, Mulan, and Pocahontas look and behave like me. Yet when they are trying to change the law they are not like me, I would not be able to do that." (15-year-old girl, European descent, U.S.)
- "They don't look like me, but they behave like me a little bit." (9-year-old girl, Indian descent, U.S.)
- "I am like Jasmine, Mulan, and Pocahontas. I know what I want. I try to be strong like them." (12-year-old girl, Indian descent, U.S.)
- "I have a pretty face like Mulan and Jasmine. I learned from these princesses how to enjoy myself and to be happy." (10-year-old girl, Chinese descent, U.S.)
- "I like these princesses. They are not afraid to do things. I am like that too." (14-year-old girl, Chinese descent, U.S.)

As outlined previously, several girls of Native American descent in the United States took pride in Pocahontas and considered her one of their own. This constituted a difference between girls of Native American descent and girls with other ethnic backgrounds in the United States. Yet this did not constitute a similarity between girls of Native American descent in the United States and girls in non-Western settings, because research participants in China, India, and Fiji did not identify with Disney Princesses, even with those with which they had common heritage. As for the other girls in the United States, to some extent they might have felt closely connected to the Disney Princesses, including those with non-Western heritage, owing to linguistic identification (as Jasmine, Pochantas, and Mulan all speak American English in the Disney animated films). However, these girls in the United States also expressed a strong cultural identification with the Disney Princesses when they stated that princesses are like them and they could be princesses.

## Non-Western Girls Do Not Identify with Disney Princesses

Unlike our U.S. research participants, most girls from China, India, and Fiji did not identify with the Disney Princesses and expressed little desire to be one. Some stated alternative occupations of interest to them. A 9-year-old girl from India thought for a few seconds before stating, "I am not a princess." An 8-year-old girl of Indian descent from Fiji said, "I want to be an artist. A princess cannot be an artist, because she is always in a palace. I want to become an artist." A 12-year-old girl of Fijian descent from Fiji affirmed, "I will become grown up and become a mother. No, I do not want to be a princess. My life is best if I grow up and be a mother."

Some non-Western girls seemed certain about their life's goals, and many girls in these settings considered princesses to be less free than they were. Yet the girls in India, Fiji, and China often felt they lacked the qualities required for being a princess, whereas the girls in the United States, regardless of ethnicity, believed they had the qualifications required for being a princess. Notably, the qualities that girls in non-Western settings believed they lacked and the qualities that girls in the United States thought they had regarding princesses only partially overlapped: on one hand, U.S. girls stated that they were similar to princesses in that they had beauty and support, and non-Western girls said that they were different from princesses in that they did not have enough beauty or support, and in these respects the qualities identified overlapped. On the other hand, U.S. girls stated that being wealthy and getting one's own way were princess qualities, whereas non-Western girls specified that being good and having Western-like features were princess qualities, and in these respects the qualities identified did not overlap.

Some girls in India, Fiji, and China said that they could not be princesses because they were not as pretty as princesses. For example:

- "I can't be a princess. I think [I] am pretty, but not pretty like a princess." (9-year-old girl, India)
- "Princesses are older than me. … Nicer than me." (11-year-old girl, Indian descent, Fiji)
- "Jasmine was very beautiful. I can't compare to her." (10-year-old girl, Fijian descent, Fiji)
- "I would have to change to be a princess, to be more careful about my looks." (13-year-old girl, China)

A few girls in non-Western settings suggested that they do not have the support needed to be a princess. For example:

- "My parents wouldn't let me act like a princess. They wouldn't want me to be a princess." (12-year-old girl, India)
- "She does good things because others join her, animals help her. I don't even have a pet." (14-year-old girl, India)
- "I wouldn't have the means to do what princesses do." (10-year-old girl, China)

Some girls in India, Fiji, and China asserted that Disney Princesses were good—too good—whereas they themselves were sometimes mean and did not always do the right thing. For example:

- "A princess behaves nicely, politely. I could never be a princess. … I am not like good. Not nice and polite. … Sometimes I don't talk politely to my brother." (10-year-old girl, India)
- "I could not be a princess. No Disney princess has bad behaviors … like shouting. I get bad sometimes. … I get angry with my brother and hit him." (13-year-old girl, Indian descent, Fiji)
- " I can't be a princess. I sometimes am naughty." (12-year-old girl, Fijian descent, Fiji)
- "Princesses are good. I am not always good." (12-year-old girl, China)

But most significantly, especially in light of our interest in Disney's efforts at multiculturalism, many girls in non-Western settings said that they would not qualify to be princesses because they lacked Western characteristics such as white skin or straight hair. Asked how Jasmine, Mulan, and Pocahontas looked, a 9-year-old girl from India affirmed, "beautiful, white"—but said she herself was not white. A 12-year-old girl from India said, "They were white and I want to be like them. But I am not really like them."Asked whether Jasmine, Mulan, and Pocahontas look like her, a 10-year-old girl of Indian descent in Fiji said, "They have a different skin color. … I play too much in the sun." Talking about Jasmine, Mulan, and Pocahontas, a 12-year-old girl of Fijian descent in Fiji said that one thing these princesses have in common is straight hair, and stated, "I don't have their straight hair." A 9-year-old girl in China said, "I am darker than most princesses I've seen. Some Disney princesses have dark hair, but they are not as dark as me." It was interesting for us to see that although several of the girls in India, Fiji, and China drew princesses with darker skin (see Figure 2), and even with marked non-Western features (see Figure 3), when they talked about princesses, they did not consider such features princess-like.

Drawn by 13-year-old girl, India

Drawn by 11-year-old girl, Indian descent, Fiji

Drawn by 10-year-old girl, China

Figure 2.

Drawn by 12-year-old girl, India

Drawn by 10-year-old girl, Indian descent, Fiji

Drawn by 9-year-old girl, China

Drawn by 15-year-old girl, China

Figure 3.

It is clear from these statements that while girls in the United States regardless of ethnicity identified with princesses and Disney Princesses, including the Disney Princesses with a non-Western heritage, girls in India, Fiji, and China did not. In contrast to the girls in Western settings, the girls in non-Western settings believed they were not beautiful enough, not supported enough, not good enough, and not white enough to be princesses. We view this as our study's most important contribution to the critical scholarly literature about Disney, with wide-ranging consequences regarding the multiculturalism claims of the Disney corporation and of the U.S.-based entertainment industry of which Disney is a major part.

## Discussion and Conclusion

The first two findings we reported on in this chapter pertain to the areas of consensus among the research participants. Among the 120 girls included in our study, across eight ethno-cultural groups and three age subgroups, many girls considered an appealing appearance to be the defining characteristic of any princess and of any Disney Princess. The research participants overwhelmingly agreed that princesses have to be beautiful, and that all Disney Princesses are indeed beautiful. This affirms the conclusions of other feminist critical scholars (Bell, Haas, and Sells 1995, Do Rozario 2004, England, Descartes, and Collier-Meek 2011) that gender stereotypes, widely disseminated by Western media conglomerates including the Walt Disney Company, have negative effects on children worldwide. Additionally, most girls sensed few differences between the princesses with non-Western heritage and the other princesses in Disney animated films. The perception among research participants that Jasmine, Pocahontas, and Mulan are similar to the princesses of European descent in the Disney world goes against Disney's claim of providing new representations suitable for an ethnically diverse and multicultural global society, supporting the arguments of critical race scholars that Disney hasn't truly changed (Ayers 2003; Brode 2005; Cheu 2013).

Two additional findings we reported on in this chapter pertain to the research participants' differing views on princess culture, specifically regarding the characteristics of princesses and girls' identification with princesses. Geographic location played a more significant role in girls' views of Disney princesses than did their ethnic heritage: Girls raised in the United States, regardless of their ethnicity, had similar ideas about princesses; and girls in India, Fiji, and China made comparable comments about Disney princesses, but their remarks were mostly incongruous with those of the research participants in the United States.

One finding highlighting the disagreement between girls raised in the Western world and girls raised in non-Western countries refers to the characteristics girls attributed to princesses. Most girls in the United States considered material wealth and individual freedom as the most important characteristics of princesses. In contrast, most girls in India, Fiji, and China focused on princesses' duties rather than their wealth, yet stated that because of such duties and because of societal constraints, princesses are not free. U.S. girls' focus on wealth and freedom led us to raise issues similar to those noted by Neo-Marxist scholars (Dorfman and Mattelart 1975; Wasko 2001) regarding the dominance of elites' values in Disney animated films as well as to those discussed by critical race scholars (Ayers 2003; Cheu 2013) regarding the privileging of Western ideals in these films. Yet non-Western girls' focus on duties and constraints led us to raise issues related to how these girls negotiate various sets of values through their alignment in some respects and resistance in other respects to Asian traditional values as well as to Western, capitalist, and patriarchal ideals.

Another finding highlighting the disagreement between girls raised in the Western world and girls raised in non-Western countries is their level of identification with Disney Princesses. Girls in the United States expressed a strong desire to be like Disney Princesses and a strong identification with them. In contrast, girls in India, Fiji, and China lacked the desire to be like Disney Princesses. The girls in non-Western settings did not even identify with the Princesses who had a non-Western heritage. Considering the U.S. girls' entitlement in regard to the Disney Princesses (including those with non-Western heritage) and non-Western girls' lack of identification with them, we agree with Hurley (2005): Children internalize a prejudicial system, reinforced by the culture industry and specifically by Disney's representation of princesses. This positively affects the self-image of Western children and negatively affects that of non-Western children.

The results of our research support a growing critical trend in Disney scholarship: Disney's attempts to embrace multiculturalism have not changed its socialization of children in the Western biases. For example, Disney still promotes Western beauty standards and cultural ideals. Our research also suggests that Disney's claims of multiculturalism neither prevented girls residing in the Western world from appropriating non-Western princesses, nor made girls in non-Western settings identify with princesses. Despite including Jasmine, Mulan, and Pocahontas in their lineup, the evidence from our international research is strong: In the lives of real girls around the world, the Disney Princess brand has failed to surpass monoculturalism.

## References


Ayers, Brenda. (Ed.). 2003. *The Emperor's Old Groove: Decolonizing Disney's Magic Kingdom.* New York: Peter Lang.

Bell, Elizabeth. 1996. "Do You Believe in Fairies? Peter Pan, Walt Disney, and Me." *Women's Studies in Communication, 19*(2): 103–126.

Bell, Elizabeth, Lynda Haas, Lynda, and Laura Sells. (Eds.). 1995. *From Mouse to Mermaid: The Politics of Film, Gender, and Culture.* Bloomington: Indiana University Press.

Benton, Sherrole. 1995. "Pocahontas as a Traitor." *Tribal College, 6*(4): 34–35.

Brockway, Robert. 1986. "The Masks of Mickey Mouse: Symbol of a Generation." *Journal of Popular Culture, 22*(4): 25–34.

Brode, Douglas. 2005. *Multiculturalism and the Mouse: Race and Sex in Disney Entertainment.* Austin: University of Texas Press.

Budd, Mike, and Max Kirsch. (Eds.). 2005. *Rethinking Disney: Private Control, Public Dimensions.* Middletown, CT: Wesleyan University Press.

Cheu, Johnson. 2013. *Diversity in Disney Films: Critical Essays on Race, Ethnicity, Gender, Sexuality, and Disability.* New York: McFarland.

Croce, Paul Jerome. 1991. "A Clean and Separate Space: Walt Disney in Person and Production." *Journal of Popular Culture, 23*(3): 91–103.

Dorfman, Ariel, and Armand Mattelart. 1975. *How to Read Donald Duck: Imperialist Ideology in the Disney Comic.* New York: International General.

Do Rozario, Rebecca-Anne C. 2004. "The Princess and the Magic Kingdom: Beyond Nostalgia, the Function of the Disney Princess." *Women's Studies in Communication, 27*(1): 35–58.

Downey, Sharon. 1996. "Feminine Empowerment in Disney's *Beauty and the Beast.*" *Women's Studies in Communication, 19*(2): 185–212.

England, Dawn Elizabeth, Descartes, Lara, & Collier-Meek, Melissa. 2011. "Gender Role Portrayal and the Disney Princesses." *Sex Roles, 64*: 555–567.

Giroux, Henry. 1999. *The Mouse That Roared: Disney and the End of Innocence.* Lanham, MD: Rowman & Littlefield.

Hansen, Miriam. 1993. "Of Mice and Ducks: Benjamin and Adorno on Disney." *South Atlantic Quarterly, 92*(1): 28–62.

Henke, Jill Birnie, Diane Umble Zimmerman, and Nancy Smith. 1996. "Construction of the Female Self: Feminist Readings of the Disney Heroine." *Women's Studies in Communication, 19*(2): 229–249.

Hiassen, Carl. 1998. *Team Rodent: How Disney Devours the World.* New York: Ballantine.

Hoerner, Keish. 1996. "Gender Roles in Disney Films: Analyzing Behaviors from Snow White to Simba." *Women's Studies in Communication, 19*(2): 213–228.

Hurley, Dorothy. 2005. "Seeing White: Children of Color and the Disney Fairy Tale Princess. *Journal of Negro Education, 74*(3): 221–232.

Klein, High, Kenneth Shiffman, and Denise Welka. 2000. "Gender-Related Content of Animated Cartoons, 1930 to the Present." *Advances in Gender Research, 4*, 291–317.

Lawrence, Elizabeth. 1989. "In the Mick of Time: Reflections on Disney's Ageless Mouse." *Journal of Popular Culture, 20*(2): 65–72.

Li-Vollmer, Meredith, and Mark LaPointe. 2003. "Gender Transgression and Villainy in Animated Films." *Popular Communication, 1*(2): 89–109.

Merskin, Debra. 2011. *Media, Minorities, and Meaning: A Critical Introduction.* New York: Peter Lang.

O'Brien, Pamela Colby. 1996. "The Happiest Films on Earth: A Textual and Contextual Analysis of Walt Disney's *Cinderella* and *The Little Mermaid.*" *Women's Studies in Communication, 19*(2): 155–183.

Schickel, Richard. 1968. *The Disney Version: The Life, Times, Art, and Commerce of Walt Disney.* New York: Simon & Schuster.

Smoodin, Eric. (Ed.). 1994. *Disney Discourse: Producing the Magic Kingdom.* New York: Routledge.

Ward, A. R. 1996. "*The Lion King*'s Mythic Narrative." *Journal of Popular Film and Television, 23*, 171–178.

Wasko, Janet. 2000. *Understanding Disney: The Manufacture of Fantasy.* Williston, VT: Blackwell.

CHAPTER SEVEN

# Princess Culture in Qatar: Exploring Princess Media Narratives in the Lives of Arab Female Youth

KIRSTEN PIKE

## Introduction

Although princesses have long been an important part of girls' culture, most academic research in this area has focused on Western princess narratives and their significance in the lives of American and/or European girls. But what role do princess media narratives (e.g., Western and non-Western movies and TV shows about princesses as well as princess stories made by girls) play in the lives of Arab female youth who grew up in the Middle East? Which characters and gendered themes do Arab girls value? Which do they reject? And why? In view of the heavy circulation and popularity of Disney media in the Middle East, how do Arab girls interact with and interpret Disney's representations of Arab and non-Arab princesses? And how have Arab girls' encounters with both commercial and independent princess media shaped their cultural experiences and gendered identities? These are some of the questions my chapter seeks to answer.

Considering Arab girls' marginalization in critical studies of media and youth, this chapter aims to bring Arab girls' voices and viewpoints about princess media to the fore. In so doing, the project takes up calls by feminist scholars, such as Mary Celeste Kearney (2006, 2011), Emilie Zaslow (2009), and Rebecca Hains (2012a, 2012b), to do more research *with* girls within the field of girls' media studies, while also following the lead of scholars such as Marwan Kraidy and Joe

Khalil (2008) to investigate youth media culture in the Middle East. Given the "Arab Spring" political uprisings and movements toward independence occurring in several countries in the Middle East and North Africa, the time seems particularly ripe to explore how themes of gendered independence in princess media exist within (and possibly contribute to) a broader climate of social change for female youth. Indeed, as we shall see, Arab girls in Qatar are taking the ideological lessons they've learned from commercial princess media and adapting and transforming them into powerful new stories more attuned to their gendered interests and identities.

## Study Overview: Interviewing Arab Girls in Doha, Qatar

My research with Arab female undergraduate students at Northwestern University in Qatar (NU-Q) was granted IRB approval by Northwestern University. I designed the study to gather in-depth information from a small number of Arab female youth about the role and significance of princess media in their lives. Fourteen girls volunteered to participate in the study following a recruitment email sent to all NU-Q students. I conducted and audio-recorded each interview, which took place in my office on campus in the spring of 2013. Each interview lasted between 60 and 90 minutes.

Several key question sets guided the study. The first group of questions investigated the appeal, form, and function of Western and non-Western princess media in the girls' childhoods and adulthoods. A second set of questions gauged the girls' perceptions about representations of gender, race, and class in Disney Princess media generally, and *Aladdin* specifically. A third set of questions explored the girls' experiences with and views about independent, girl-produced princess media (as opposed to commercial princess media made by adults). And a fourth set of questions collected demographic information about the girls.[1] All girls answered the same questions from a standardized interview script.

The interviews took place in Doha, Qatar, located on the Arabian Peninsula. With the third largest natural gas resources in the world, Qatar is one of the world's wealthiest countries. As of 2012, Qatar's population was around 1.7 million; approximately 225,000 were Qatari nationals—most of whom practice Sunni Islam—and the remaining 80%, expatriate workers from around the world (Fromherz 2012, 2–25). The Al Thani family rule Qatar. Although Sheikh Hamad bin Khalifa Al Thani was the Emir when I conducted the interviews, he abdicated the throne on June 25, 2013, and his son—Sheikh Tamim bin Hamad Al Thani—now rules Qatar.

While Qatari society is often considered to be conservative by Western standards, it is "much more flexible in certain family and social norms" than Saudi Arabia (Fromherz 2012, 27). As Allen J. Fromherz explains,

> Especially when compared with the situation of women in neighbouring Saudi Arabia, women in Qatar have a free and prominent role in society. The most prominent symbol of this is the stature of Sheikha Mozah bint Nasser Al-Misnad [*sic*],[2] the most public of Sheikh Hamad's wives, whose fame may surpass that of her husband ... in some international circles. (2012, 27)

Indeed, Sheikha Moza[3]—the mother of the current Emir—has been a driving force behind educational and social reforms in Qatar. She currently serves as the Chairperson of the Qatar Foundation—the organization that built Doha's "Education City," which houses branch campuses of international universities, including Northwestern. Many girls in Qatar greatly admire Sheikha Moza as her initiatives have enabled them to obtain college educations they otherwise wouldn't be able to receive. As Anne Sobel points out, Arab girls in Qatar are often "kept closer to home" while their brothers are allowed to attend university in the United States or the UK (2010).

While the girls in the study traced their roots to a variety of places in the Middle East, including Jordan, Egypt, Syria, Palestine, and Saudi Arabia, all but one grew up (and/or spent a significant portion of their youth) in Qatar. Nine of the 14 participants (64%) claimed Qatari citizenship. All described themselves as "Arab," though a few made a more specific ethnic identification (e.g., "Egyptian"). All reported that religion was a "moderate" or "major" part of their lives, and all but one identified as Muslim. The 12 girls who commented on their socio-economic background described it as either "middle" or "upper-middle" class. All of the girls were unmarried, fluent in Arabic and English, and ranged in age from 18 to 24 years old; two lived in campus housing, and the others lived at home with their families. While one participant had not decided on her future path after college, the others planned careers in such fields as filmmaking, communications, business, teaching, and/or international relations. Several said they hoped to attend graduate school, and all reported that their parents had encouraged them to attend college—details demonstrating both the importance of, and family/community support for, girls' higher education in Qatar.

Because the term "women" is typically reserved for females who are married, the study's participants referred to themselves as "girls." As Rodda Leage and Ivana Chalmers explain, "It is highly problematic in Middle-Eastern Arab countries to refer to unmarried females as 'women,' since the title signifies that the female has engaged in sexual intercourse" (2010, 29). In line with Leage and Chalmer's approach, then, I adopt the terminology used by the participants and refer to them throughout the chapter as Arab "girls."

## Princess Media Culture in the Lives of Arab Female Youth in Qatar

While all the girls reported that princess media appealed to them during their youth, the study revealed that media produced by the Walt Disney Company had a particularly strong presence in their lives. When explaining their childhood attraction to princess media, for instance, 13 out of 14 (93%) talked about pleasurable experiences with Disney Princess entertainment (without me asking them to comment specifically on this company's content). And when I asked which princess products they collected (if any), all gave examples of Disney media and merchandise, from magazines, books, music, and movies, to stickers and stationery, bags and lunch boxes, makeup and hair accessories, clothes and jewelry, toys and dolls, and bedding and furniture. While most of the girls had attended a princess-themed party during their youth, all reported owning Disney Princess costumes or apparel as well as Disney Princess movies (with a number owning complete collections). Additionally, more than half of the participants indicated they had visited a Disney theme park in the United States or France (including multiple visits for some); and three girls discussed plans to travel to Disney theme parks during their upcoming summer vacations—a detail that underscores Disney's ongoing attraction to some Arab girls as they grow up.

Perhaps the greatest indication of the degree to which Disney was woven into the cultural fabric of the girls' childhoods, however, was in their avid consumption and enjoyment of Disney Princess media. Animated feature films starring such princesses as Ariel, Belle, and Cinderella were especially popular among the participants, and many fondly recalled magazines, direct-to-video sequels, and television spin-offs featuring these (and other) Disney princesses. A few also pinpointed *The Princess Diaries* (2001) and *The Princess Diaries 2: Royal Engagement* (2004)—the live-action films starring Anne Hathaway as Princess Mia—as important and pleasurable when they were growing up. While one respondent estimated she had probably seen the Disney Princess films a relatively modest number of "two times each," others estimated their consumption at much higher levels. For example, several girls indicated they had watched the films between 25 and 50 times each, and three said they had watched certain favorite films "more than 100 times," including *Cinderella* (Gina), *Mulan* (Hasna), and *Beauty and the Beast* (Nora).[4] A participant named Muna offered the highest viewing estimate of her favorite Disney film when she guessed that she had seen *Beauty and the Beast* "like 1000 times." As she explained, "I've seen it so many times I can actually speak with them [the characters] while they're speaking. Like I know what they're gonna say before they say it."

All but one girl (93%) reported that princess media still appeals to them, although several qualified this point by explaining that they are also more critical of princess media now because they are older and/or because they have honed their analytical skills in college. Still, most described their adult, leisure-time experiences with princess media as pleasurable. A few, for instance, detailed their passion for Disney Princess "movie marathons"—the most zealous described watching five princess movies with her friends in a single day. Nostalgic memories appeared to drive many girls' continued consumption of princess media. As Leila noted of a recent purchase,

> I bought my sister shampoo and a mirror that looks like all the [Disney] princesses.... So we still do that, and we're in our twenties. It reminds us of, like, this bonding time that we had when we could spend hours and hours together as opposed to now [when] we're in university, or we're getting jobs, so we're not at home as much anymore. So it kind of reminds us of those days where we had, like, time for each other.

An anecdote shared by Eliza, though, reveals how girls who do not conform to the feminine ideals of the Disney Princess brand can feel excluded from participating in certain types of consumption.

> Looking back, it was such an idealized version of what a girl should look like. Like [the Disney Princesses] were all skinny; they were all white; and they were all so perfect.... I was a chubby kid growing up, so, like, I remember trying to get the [Disney Princess] dresses, but they were never in my size.... I think there should be more focus [in Disney Princess media] on, like, just girls being comfortable with who they are.

As Eliza's account powerfully conveys, not all encounters with Disney will "make dreams come true," as the company's marketing and promotions often suggest (Disney, "Dreams," 2013).

While Disney Princess media was by far the kind that participants interfaced with most regularly, some of the girls (43%) identified other Western and non-Western princess narratives that were important to them during their youth, including the American films *A Little Princess* (1995) and *Shrek* (2001), the British children's television series *Little Princess*, and Japanese anime TV shows dubbed into Arabic, including *Lady Lady*, *Remi*, and *Princess Sakura Cardcaptor*; while the youthful protagonists in *Lady Lady* (Leen) and *Remi* (Remi) were not princesses per se, the girls identified their attributes and behavior as princess-like nonetheless. Although none recalled watching princess-themed media produced in the Middle East, several enjoyed reading and/or hearing the stories from *One Thousand and One Nights*—a collection of Islamic fictional tales, including the adventures of Aladdin, translated into Western languages at the beginning of the eighteenth century (Felperin 1997, 139). Muna, in fact, identified the book's female narrator, Scheherazade (or Shahrazad, as Arabic speakers typically refer to her), as a role model for girls since her smarts and creativity helped save her life. In line with Muna's assessment, Suzanne Gauch (2007, ix) eloquently captures Shahrazad's "brilliance, daring initiative, and political acumen" when she explains in the opening of *Liberating Shahrazad*,

> She was that courageous woman who confronted a king so enraged by the infidelity of his first wife that he took to marrying a virgin every evening and putting her to death the following morning. Offering herself as the king's next victim, Shahrazad postpones her execution by telling him a lengthy and intricate story each night, leaving it unfinished as dawn breaks. Over the course of many nights, her stories divert the king from his obsession with women's infidelity, both entertaining him and altering the manner in which he looks on human behavior. Shahrazad, then, saves not only her own life but also the lives of countless other women, employing her narrative skills to alter those representations of women—as deceitful beauties dominated by physical desire—that the king had so cruelly acted on. (2007, ix–x)

Although technically a queen rather than a princess, Shahrazad stands out as an important and powerful representation of female royalty in Middle Eastern literature, despite the work of Western translators to marginalize and silence her (Gauch 2007, xi). If, as Gauch suggests, Shahrazad's voice has been transformed in troubling ways through Western colonial discourses, can the same be said of the youthful princesses featured in Disney's adaptations of her stories? And more important to the project at hand, what do Arab girls think about Disney's representation of the Aladdin story and characters, especially Princess Jasmine?

To explore these questions, the analysis that follows takes a closer look at girls' perceptions of *Aladdin*, the 1992 film produced by the Walt Disney Company—"one of the most powerful media conglomerates in the world" (Giroux and Pollock 2010, 208) and, arguably, the most influential global producer of children's media. While much has been written about *Aladdin*'s problematic identity politics and its controversial reception in the United States (Griffin 1994; Shaheen 2001), little has been said about how audiences in the Middle East generally, and girls specifically, have responded to this film.[5] To help address this gap, the analysis highlights Arab girls' views about Disney's representations of Arabs, but it also extends beyond this by exploring their perceptions of gender in Disney's broader body of princess entertainment. To better situate this discussion, let us begin with an overview of Disney's circulation and status in Doha, Qatar, where the interviews took place.

## Disney in Doha

As the girls' extensive viewing of Disney Princess movies no doubt suggests, the Disney brand is extremely popular in the Middle East generally, and Qatar specifically. It is not unusual, for instance, to see Arab children sporting Disney clothes, bags, and accessories, with female youth showing a particular fondness for Disney Princess items. As in American cities, supermarkets in Doha carry a dizzying array of products featuring Disney princesses—from perfume and toothpaste to cereal and canned spaghetti. Although Disney has not yet opened a store in Doha, the latest Disney Princess products are nevertheless available for purchase at numerous retail outlets. The Disney Princess movie, *Brave* (2012), enjoyed a successful run in local movie theaters in the fall of 2012. And in June 2013, several Disney princesses appeared in Doha as part of *Disney on Ice: 100 Years of Magic*—the first Disney ice show ever held in the Middle East (Salama 2013). So successful was the event that an extra performance was added to accommodate fans ("Disney on Ice" 2013). In all, 40,000 people attended eight sold-out shows, prompting the event's organizers to announce that they will return to Qatar with more "Disney Live!" productions ("Disney to Return" 2013). Taken together, these details suggest that young people in Qatar have contributed to the Disney Princess brand becoming in 2012 the "best-selling licensed entertainment character merchandise" with "1.6 billion in North American retail sales and 3 billion globally" (Goudreau 2012).

Disney's presence in the region solidified after the 1997 launch of the Disney Channel in 23 countries across the Middle East and North Africa ("Disney Channel" 1996). Indeed, several girls reported watching Disney TV programming while growing up in Qatar, including the animated TV series *Aladdin*, based on the 1992 film of the same name. During the 1990s and early 2000s, Disney films screened in movie theaters and/or sold in Qatar were typically dubbed into Egyptian Arabic—a process that, as Kirsten Drotner argues, helps "to enhance the 'naturalization' of Disney products" abroad (2001, 115). Indeed, many girls said their first encounters with Disney films and TV shows were with Arabic-dubbed versions. Jamilah, for instance, remembered watching *The Little Mermaid* in Arabic at a movie theater in Qatar when she was around 6 years old. As she explained, "For me, the Arabic [Disney Princess media] is the original because that's the first thing I saw." Other girls reported watching English-language versions of Disney

Princess movies more often, while still others indicated that they moved back and forth between English and Arabic versions—sometimes owning copies of each. Ten of the girls (71%) said they prefer to watch Disney Princess media in English, citing the importance of watching content in its "original" form, since meaning can be lost in translation. On the other hand, four girls (29%) said they prefer to watch Disney Princess media in Egyptian Arabic, finding the dialogue and cultural references funnier.

A corporate agreement struck in early 2013 between Disney and Al Jazeera Children's Channel (JCC)—the Doha-based, pan-Arab media organization that offers Arabic-language children's TV programming to millions of homes throughout the Middle East—will likely make Disney entertainment even more entrenched in the region. Despite grumblings from some members of the Qatari community, JCC acquired the rights to some of Disney's "most popular kids and family content, including Disney and Disney/Pixar movies as well as Disney Channel's live action and animated series" ("JCC to Offer" 2013). As part of the deal, Disney content aimed at children aged 2 to 6 (e.g., *Little Einsteins*) now airs on JCC's new channel for preschoolers, Baraem TV, and content aimed at children aged 7 to 12 (e.g., *Phineus and Ferb*) now appears on JCC's new channel for preteens, Jeem TV.

While Disney's global expansion undoubtedly raises concerns about American cultural imperialism in the region (Wasko and Meehan 2001), the circulation of Disney Princess media in Qatar also creates the opportunity to explore Arab girls' perceptions about "glocalization"—or, "the consumption of global products by locally contextualized audiences, who create their own meanings and process them to serve their own social and cultural needs" (Lemish et al. 1998, 540). One interesting aspect of the JCC/Disney agreement with regard to "glocalization" is that all Disney content aired by JCC will be dubbed into classical Arabic (as opposed to Egyptian Arabic). This decision upset some girls in the study, who felt that the "formal," "serious," and/or "educational" tone of classical Arabic would detract from their pleasure in watching Disney media. One participant, however, voiced support for JCC's decision, explaining that it could help young viewers learn "proper Arabic," thereby better preparing them for academic success.

The decision to dub Disney programming into classical Arabic, combined with JCC's plan to edit out parts of Disney films deemed unsuitable for consumption by Arab children, highlights how cultural authorities in Qatar are working to preserve, and reassert the primacy of, the country's language and social traditions against a backdrop of globalization and transnational media conglomeration. When the Disney Princess movie *Tangled* (2010) aired on Jeem TV in the spring of 2013, for instance, it had been dubbed and edited to eliminate the romance between Rapunzel and Flynn, including kisses and amorous looks. The sequence featuring the young lovers' romantic duet, "I See the Light," was deleted from the movie, as was the closing sequence detailing their marriage. (The film ends when Rapunzel is reunited with her parents.) As a result of these changes, Rapunzel and Flynn appear to have a brother-and-sister-type of relationship (I. Alhashmi, personal communication, July 25, 2013). Considering that dating is forbidden in Qatari society (unless a man and woman are formally engaged to be married) and themes of romance generally, and kissing specifically, are thought to be inappropriate for children, *Tangled*'s revised form on Jeem TV makes sense. Not only did it reflect the region's dominant gender customs and tenor, but it also accommodated JCC's regional goal of being "loved by children, trusted by parents" while operating within the logics of global capitalism (JCC, "JCC's Vision," 2013).

Of course, this practice of editing Disney content to better suit the social and cultural mores of Arab audiences is not new. In the 1990s and early 2000s, VHS and DVD box covers featuring scantily clad female characters, including Ariel from *The Little Mermaid* and Tinkerbell from *Return to Neverland*, were altered for Middle East distribution by the Saudi distributor, Stallions, to cover the girls' exposed upper bodies—a practice also identified by Jehan Zitawi (2008) in her research on the translation of Disney comic books into Arabic. Kissing scenes were also eliminated from Disney movies distributed by Stallions.[6] While JCC's revised version of *Tangled* can be situated within this broader history of English to Arabic translation and adaptation, it also raises new questions about what it means to be a Disney princess in the Arab world, particularly when changes to narratives fundamentally alter dominant gendered themes. Although eliminating romantic overtones from a Disney film might be seen as making it more wholesome and culturally appropriate for Arab children, an unintended (and possibly beneficial) outcome of this process is that it may be reaffirming themes of girlhood power and independence for young female viewers. Indeed, while Rapunzel in the original version of *Tangled* is subjected to the conventional Disney ending wherein the princess finds, falls in love with, and then marries her prince, JCC's version of *Tangled* arguably makes Rapunzel a much more autonomous and self-reliant heroine. Given that her adventurous ways are not domesticated via romance, marriage, and/or motherhood in the closing scene, JCC's Rapunzel may offer Arab children a more unrestricted and agential vision of youthful femininity, as her future endeavors are largely left up to children's imaginations. (Given that my interviews were completed prior to JCC's airing of *Tangled*, future research on Disney in the Middle East might compare young people's responses to censored and original versions of Disney films.)

Although some of the Arab girls voiced concerns about Disney's commercial dominance in the Middle East, most also regarded Disney as a quality provider of entertainment in a region where local production of children's media has, historically, been limited (especially in the pre-JCC 1990s and early 2000s when the girls were growing up). As Chanda declared, "If we didn't have an American company showing or selling films here, we wouldn't have anything because not many people were doing films or making [media]." Sabreena identified an additional benefit of Disney's regional circulation: watching the Disney Channel helped her learn English. Still others, such as Eliza, illuminated how competing social, cultural, and economic interests complicate Disney's circulation in the Middle East. As she noted of Disney's dominance in Qatar,

> It is problematic to a certain extent because like the culture here is different. So I feel like [local producers] should circulate, or like produce things, that are more specific to the culture here and not rely on Western films. But then again ... I'm just thinking about my cousin's daughters ... even if I show them something in Arabic, they'd still go like, "yeah, no, we wanna watch the Disney films."

Reina echoed this sentiment, indicating that her nephew prefers officially licensed Disney products to those from the Spacetoon store—the retail arm of the Dubai-based children's TV network. As she explained, "Disney remains on top because ... if you have Disney, or you like Disney, or you watch Disney, kids think that ... you're better." This pattern is consistent with Lemish et al.'s finding that young people "often identify imports with quality, innovation, and 'coolness,' particularly for products from the USA" (1998, 545), but tend to see local productions as "'old-fashioned' in style and substance" (1998, 553); it also highlights the challenges faced by local film and television producers in Qatar. How does a local producer create quality content that will appeal to Arab children (and satisfy parents and cultural authorities) while also competing with a powerhouse like Disney? As JCC's recent deal with Disney suggests, the answer seems to lie in striking a balance between local and global children's media forms while also using resources and technological expertise (e.g., translation and editing of Western narratives) to manage cultural meanings.

## Global and Local Visions of (and in) Arabia: Arab Girls Discuss *Aladdin* and Other Disney Tales

Of the 11 princesses who are currently part of the Disney Princess franchise, only one—Jasmine—is of Arab decent. Debuting in *Aladdin* (1992), Jasmine is the sixth animated Disney princess and first non-white Disney princess. Although Jasmine comes from a fictional Arabian town called Agrabah—a "backward mythical kingdom" populated by "thieves, harem maidens, and ugly vendors" (Shaheen 2001, 51)—she talks with an American accent, prompting one scholar to dub her "the Valley Girl in veils" (Staninger 2003, 65). Jasmine's adventure in *Aladdin* hinges on her culturally unconventional quest to find love on her own terms; at the end of the film, she achieves her goal by choosing to marry Aladdin (with her father's blessing). Although *Aladdin* debuted at roughly the same time that the girls in this study were born, all reported watching the film (sometimes dozens of times) during their youth. As is customary of Disney's corporate branding and synergistic practices, Jasmine's narrative universe has been extended to the present through a variety of media and merchandizing forms, including two direct-to-video *Aladdin* movie sequels and an animated *Aladdin* TV series as well as books, dolls, toys, videogames, and DVDs (e.g., *Disney Princess Enchanted Tales: Follow Your Dreams* [2007]).

Although not uncommon for girls to identify with characters with whom they share similar physical and/or cultural traits, none of the Arab girls in the study identified Jasmine as her "favorite" Disney princess. (However, one did name Jasmine from the Egyptian-dubbed *Aladdin* TV series as her "second favorite" princess after Ariel, primarily because this rendering of Jasmine/*Aladdin* reminded her of treasured tales from *One Thousand and One Nights.*) While several girls did discuss how their identification with a particular princess was related to their perceived physical resemblance to the character, they nevertheless felt stronger affinities with non-Arab Disney princesses and female characters. Chanda and Nasrine, for instance, both said they liked Snow White as a child because they "looked similar" to her. Likewise, Ariana was drawn to Pocahontas and Esmeralda and wore T-shirts emblazoned with their images because "they looked Arab."

So how do we account for the participants' overall tendency not to identify with Jasmine? Did Jasmine not look Arab? Interestingly, a majority of the girls did not think so, with nine of the 14 (64%) reporting that when they first saw *Aladdin*, they believed Jasmine was from India, not the Middle East. Of the five participants who indicated that they were not entirely certain where Jasmine was from, one guessed that she was a non-Arab from Persia, another remembered asking her father and being told that she was from Iraq, and two girls thought that she possibly lived in "old" Arabia, like "maybe … the Gulf before … oil," as Jamilah put it. Only one participant said that she "assumed" Jasmine was Arab. The girls who thought that Jasmine was Indian drew on a range of details from the film to support their assessment—from the palace resembling the Taj Mahal to Jasmine being "exposed," as Maryam put it, in a belly-baring ensemble complete with "Punjabi pants" (Muna) and a "top [that] basically looks like some sort of a bra" (Nora). Such "exotic" visual and iconographic details led many of the girls to feel distanced from *Aladdin*'s cultural milieu. As Leila explained, "When I was younger watching [*Aladdin*], I never perceived it as Arab … it never dawned on me 'cuz Jasmine, Aladdin, their features, I would say their dress, their palaces, their architecture … look more Indian. So I didn't relate to it at all."

Several participants who shared Leila's perspective also voiced frustration with Disney's seemingly inaccurate representation of the Arab world. As Muna explained with regard to Jasmine's construction, "We thought she was Indian. Like at least do it right. At least have the right portrayal so everyone will understand where she's from. Because before I found out she was Arab, I had no idea. … I kept asking myself, why don't they have an Arab princess? But then everyone said there was already one." In a similar vein, Nora felt that *Aladdin* circulated ill-informed representations of both India and the Middle East. As she explained:

> To be honest, I was really confused if *Aladdin* was supposed to be a representation of Arab culture because I see some aspects of the Indian culture there as well. … So I find it a bit problematic that the lines between both cultures were kind of blurred, in the sense that like … I don't want to say that it was racist, but a bit ignorant, I think, is the better way to describe it.

Although Nora was hesitant to call Disney's fantasy-oriented representations "racist," Muna offered this appraisal more freely, asserting that *Aladdin*'s original opening song lyrics were "offensive" and "racist" for constructing Arabs as ruthless barbarians.[7] While the girls' assessments suggest that Disney fell short in creating authentic representations of Arabs, the cultural ambiguity that characterizes *Aladdin* can also be seen as a pragmatic global marketing strategy, priming audiences from a range of different backgrounds and locales to potentially identify with the film.

The girls' responses to several open-ended questions about *Aladdin* highlight a keen ability to critique problematic representations while simultaneously mining the film for moments of gendered pleasure. For instance, all the girls indicated that *Aladdin* stereotyped Arabs in troubling ways—a finding that supports Jack Shaheen's assertion that in Hollywood films, "Arabs were and are Public Enemy #1" (2001, 29). While many girls found *Aladdin*'s villainous Jafar and Jasmine's inept father especially insulting, others were bothered by Aladdin's status as a thief and/or Jasmine's sexually provocative persona. Maryam also disliked how Jasmine was "always inside" and "had nothing to do"—details that point to her desire for a more active, independent, and publically engaged heroine. Yet alongside criticisms of

Jasmine, a majority of the girls (86%) praised her strength, intelligence, confidence, and/or determination—in other words, the more constructive aspects of what Erin Addison has referred to as Jasmine's "pseudo-feminist image in service of a deeply racist film" (1993, 19). Chanda, for example, appreciated Jasmine's resolve to leave the castle and mingle with Agrabah's citizens, while Eliza and Reina admired Jasmine's willingness to take a stand for what she believed in (i.e., marrying Aladdin instead of Jafar). That the girls were able to find pleasure in Jasmine's construction while also criticizing her less revered traits is consistent with contemporary feminist scholarship that sees girls as active negotiators of complex and often contradictory gendered meanings in popular culture (Forman-Brunell 2009; Hains 2012b; Pike 2011; Zaslow 2009).

Media scholars have commonly critiqued *Aladdin*'s brazen celebration of contemporary American values over traditional Middle Eastern ones—including the power of romance to "liberate" Jasmine from so-called restrictive Islamic gender codes (Addison 1993, 18). As Christiane Staninger suggests, "*Aladdin* could be called a propaganda movie for Western imperialism, because it shows the supposed unworkability of Middle Eastern traditions and the need for American intervention" (2003, 69). The Arab girls, however, did not discuss *Aladdin* in these terms. While there are likely many good reasons for this (e.g., it had been a while since some girls had seen the film; most did not read *Aladdin* as a film about Arab culture), the absence of commentary on *Aladdin*'s broader "West conquers East" ideology points to concerns about Disney's potential to naturalize and disseminate Western political agendas to vast global audiences through seemingly innocuous entertainment (Giroux and Pollock 2010).

Although none of the girls discussed Jasmine's representation in terms of Islamic traditions, their critiques of her persona nevertheless illuminate the cultural dissonance that some of them experienced when consuming Disney's anxious and titillating gendered vision of Arabia. For instance, many of the girls were put off by Jasmine's eroticized persona. As Leila explained, "She's hyper-sexualized. She's very seductive. … I think it is problematic." Leila, Nasrine, and Maryam all commented that they "didn't like [Jasmine's] outfit." While Ariana believed Jasmine looked "beautiful" in the film, she also noted that her revealing clothes and seductive behavior made her seem like a "hooker." Given that Qatari women and girls who are Muslim practice modesty (and reinforce their regional identity) by "covering"—or, more specifically, by wearing the "abaya" (traditional black robe) over their clothes and "shayla" (head scarf) over their hair—perhaps it makes sense that no participant selected Jasmine as her favorite princess. Jasmine's sultry appearance, which "plays into Western cultural notions of the Orient through the referencing of the imagery of the harem and the associated exotic, sexual stereotypes" (Lacroix 2004, 221), runs counter to notions of modesty, thereby inviting the male gaze in the film rather than deflecting it. Indeed, as Celeste Lacroix has demonstrated with regard to the costuming and physique of 1990s-era Disney princesses, depictions of non-white princesses such as Jasmine and Pocahontas reinforce their physicality and sexuality, while white princesses such as Belle and Ariel are delicate and demure, reflecting more conservative and romantic feminine ideals (2004, 221).

Looking more closely at whom the girls picked as their favorite Disney princess further reinforces this point. *Beauty and the Beast's* Belle ranked first among the girls with four votes (29%), while Cinderella came in second with three votes (22%). Snow White and Ariel each earned two votes (14%), and Mulan, Esmeralda, and Mia (the only live-action princess of the group) each earned one vote (7%). The girls offered various reasons for these selections. While some were captivated by the traditional, feminine ideals (e.g., kindness and beauty) embodied by princesses like Cinderella, others were drawn to princesses who pursued learning (Belle), adventure (Ariel), and/or unconventionally feminine activities (Mulan). As this tally reveals, 12 of the 14 participants (86%) identified a white Disney princess as their favorite. While this finding taps into concerns about Disney's role in promoting whiteness as a cultural ideal (Hurley 2005), it is important to consider it within its broader cultural and regional context. In so doing, we might read the majority's preference for Belle, Cinderella, Snow White, and Ariel as a sensible vote *against* Disney's problematic practice of eroticizing and exoticizing its non-white heroines, including Princess Jasmine.

In line with this point, some girls explained their fondness for a particular princess by making connections between the heroine's virtues and the values advocated in their Arab upbringing. As Saadiya said of her preference for Cinderella,

> It's part of Arab tradition, like the emphasis on patience and working hard. ... My mom used to be like, "Okay, if you wanna hang out with your friends ... you have to earn it. Like you have to finish your chores on time, you have to like behave, you have to finish your homework." So I think it's a resemblance of that ... like [Cinderella] earning what she gets. That's what made me think of [her] as a favorite.

Muna also connected her passion for Belle with childhood lessons she learned from her mother, including the importance of getting an education and choosing a romantic partner based on the quality of one's character. As she explained, Belle "didn't want the pretty guy, Gaston ... because he was like, mean. He was so stuck up, and he was arrogant. And she was smart enough to see through that. ... She read books. She was educated. She was intelligent. She was like something ... I wanted to become ... and my mom raised us to be."

Although this pattern of identification with culturally valued feminine traits was dominant among the participants, it was in no way absolute. Gender characteristics coded as "masculine," such as Merida's tomboyism in *Brave* and Mulan's ability to fight on equal footing with men in *Mulan*, appealed to some girls precisely because they fell outside the realm of normative traits traditionally promoted to Arab girls in Qatar. Hasna, for instance, appreciated Mulan's strength and independence as well as the freedom embodied by Kiara, the youthful lion princess in *The Lion King II: Simba's Pride* (1998). As she explained of her connection to the latter,

> I've always ... felt like independent, and I've wanted to do things that like, I wasn't allowed to do ... that weren't expected of a girl. Like to me, Kiara, like going ... wherever she wasn't allowed to go ... that to me is like basically representing travel. 'Cuz like, boys can go wherever they want, but like in our culture, girls can't travel alone. Like it's not allowed. ... Some parents allow it, but my dad doesn't, so like I've always wanted to travel and just like be more independent around the world, not just here [in Qatar].

In a similar vein, Disney's recent princess, Merida—who eschews traditional princess behavior (e.g., cultivating beauty and pursuing romance) in favor of archery, horseback riding, and outdoor adventures—resonated strongly with Nora. As she explained of Merida's story,

> I felt like I could relate to that a lot ... 'cuz she's portrayed as kind of more as a tomboy, and I've had like very similar fights, like with my mom especially, about like, a lot of the same things. ...What I loved about that story was, in the end she comes out of it ... [with] a new perspective. Like she understands where her mother's coming from. She was able to establish ... a connection with her mother. And in the end ... she kind of does get what she wants, which is a little bit more of her freedom to express herself.

Nora's account of *Brave*'s gendered appeal, including a more active and independent heroine (who doesn't marry in the end) and a more compassionate rendering of a mother/daughter relationship, is in line with popular commentary that sees *Brave* as a "refreshing" (Valenti 2012)—if not "radical" (Rosin 2012)—shift in the Disney Princess canon. Yet what is particularly compelling about Hasna's and Nora's insights is that they remind us there are productive aspects to girls' interactions with Disney Princess culture. With the ever-expanding body of popular and academic criticism that tends to see princess culture, generally, and Disney Princess media, specifically, as an insidious cultural force—from Peggy Orenstein's (2011) and Jennifer Hartstein's (2012) warnings about princess culture's potentially deleterious effects on girls to the myriad scholarly studies that find Disney Princess media perpetuating harmful stereotypes—it is crucial to consider how girls actually use this media to work through real-life problems, to contemplate traditional and alternative feminine pathways, and, ultimately, to navigate their own futures. This is not to suggest that scholars and critics shouldn't critique princess media's problematic commercial and cultural ideologies (of which there are many); rather, what Arab girls' viewpoints suggest is that princess media narratives are best understood when the pleasures and possibilities they offer to girls are considered alongside criticisms of their textual limitations.

Interestingly, the girls' complaints about Disney narratives did not appear to dramatically alter their pleasure in consuming them. As Leila confessed after carefully outlining *Aladdin*'s uneven gender politics, "But I enjoyed watching it. And probably, if you put it on right now, I would watch it still." Although this mixed response may seem somewhat contradictory, it is not uncommon within the existing body of scholarship on youth audiences and global media. Lemish and her co-researchers found that while children in Denmark, France, and Israel recognized the commercial nature of imported media products, "this in no way prevent[ed] their enjoyment" (1998, 545). And as part of the research undertaken for *Dazzled by Disney*—an impressive collection exploring audience responses to Disney in 18 countries (though none in the Middle East)—Mark Phillips found that young people often delivered harsh appraisals of Disney's commercial practices while concurrently reporting high levels of enjoyment with Disney products (2001, 47–48). Ultimately, these findings underscore the value of balancing close analysis of media texts, ideologies, and industries with young peoples' own assessments of media use and worth.

## Arab Girls as Cultural Producers: Perceptions and Practices

To this end, it is important to consider how Arab girls' interactions with princess media have shaped their cultural activities and gendered identities. Notably, more than half of the girls (57%) reported that their childhood experiences with princess media led them to engage in new forms of princess-themed cultural production—a finding that counters popular discourses that frame girls as victims and/or passive recipients of hegemonic media messages. Reina, for instance, wrote and illustrated princess stories and comics in her childhood free time, and she also composed, directed, and acted in princess-inspired videos and plays with her sisters. Likewise, Muna devised a new princess narrative for Disney's Belle as part of a fourth-grade school project. In her fairy tale, she constructed Belle as a beast instead of a human—a move that not only made her a stronger and more suitable match for her love interest, the Beast, but also challenged traditional ideas about how a princess should look and act. When the two characters eventually fell in love, they both became human. Although Muna's story adheres in some ways to romantic conventions, it also deconstructs Belle's customary beauty and femininity by reimaging the heroine in the realm of the abject; this, combined with the story's prescient foreshadowing of the princess-as-beast premise of the hit movie *Shrek*, which came out after Muna wrote her story, testifies to the narrative's captivating and innovative nature.

Some participants detailed more recent princess-themed creations. Ariana, for example, demonstrated how she uses Photoshop to construct whimsical, princess-themed visual media collages for family and friends. And Maryam offered a fascinating account of the princess-themed theatrical play that she wrote, produced, and starred in at her high school when she was 17 years old; the production featured approximately 25 female actors and four public performances for family and friends. Although she described the play as "an Arab version of Cinderella," the play countered traditional gendered outcomes in that the heroine—despite being sought after by the prince—"refused to become a princess in the end." The reason, Maryam explained, was that "she liked being herself. She liked being normal." Just as feminist critics heralded *Brave*'s Merida for "finally giv[ing] us the option of a princeless princess" (Valenti 2013), so too does Maryam's play—a point made even more persuasively, perhaps, by the fact that all roles in her production, including the prince, were performed by girls. Ultimately, by choosing to have her heroine forgo marriage to lead a more independent existence, Maryam's play boldly intervened in the traditional "happily-ever-after" ending of princess tales—and did so, significantly, ahead of Disney's *Brave*.

Interestingly, 64% of the participants reported that their childhood experiences with princess media had shaped their personal and/or professional goals, including, for several of the girls, their decision to pursue media studies at NU-Q. Sabreena, for instance, said watching Disney Princess movies had made her "want to write more stories about girls"—not only to counter representations of "passive" females that she had encountered in Disney films, but also to bolster her own agency within the landscape of girls' media production. In a similar vein, Leila relayed how her contradictory encounters with commercial media generally, and *Aladdin* specifically, had inspired her own filmmaking ambitions, including creating more authentic representations of Arabs. As she explained with regard to Jasmine's representation,

> It inspired me, like, now in my films … to always be like very hyper-aware when I'm representing an Arab, you know, character. Because now I feel like it's my responsibility to correct … the image that's been projected so far, and like make people aware that there is a difference. Like Indian culture, even religion, language, dress, it's all completely different than Arab. And perhaps to a Western audience that might not

> have ever traveled or been exposed to this side of the world, they might not understand the difference. But to me it's kind of offensive. … So … now I wanna change it.

Ultimately, the girls' creative projects and goals offer important evidence of how some Arab female youth are channeling and transforming commercial princess media's problematic identity politics into new and compelling forms of cultural production and social critique. This finding supports research by scholars such as Mary Celeste Kearney (2006) on the progressive potential of girl-made media to resist and subvert dominant race and gender ideologies while also reaffirming girls' cultural agency.

Although not all participants engaged in creating their own princess media narratives, 86% indicated that it would be "beneficial," "highly beneficial," or "extremely beneficial" for girls to create their own princess media narratives (such as stories, poems, videos, plays, and/or games) when they are growing up. More freedom for girls to tell their own stories, and more diversity in the kinds of stories that they might tell, were themes that emerged in many responses. As Nora observed, girls who craft their own stories do not "hav[e] to follow a certain set of rules or expectations," thus expanding the ways they might choose to express themselves; as she explained, "Maybe one girl wants to make her princess a ninja." Karen Wohlwend's valuable ethnographic work on "Disney Princess Play" among young girls offers support for this position; when girls were given the opportunity to animate Disney Princess dolls and/or write their own stories or plays about Disney Princesses, they empowered female characters in ways that challenged gender stereotypes (2009, 75–78). Whether constructing a more unconventional princess, or crafting a tale to "fulfill [one's] subconscious goals" (as Reina put it), the participants suggested that a primary benefit to female youth in creating their own stories is greater narrative control. Girls who produce princess stories, Nora surmised, "[wi]ll add what they think is important, not what other people are trying to tell them is important about princesses."

## Conclusion

Ultimately, the Arab girls' views on Disney Princess media highlight a complex negotiation of Western and non-Western ideologies about gender, sexuality, race, class, and national identity on the one hand, and the globalization and commercialization of children's media culture on the other. As their thoughts about *Aladdin* suggest, the gap between Disney's perception of the Arab world and the girls' own lived experience of it is wide indeed—leading many of the girls to feel not only distanced from, but also uneasy and/or angry about, the company's unenlightened representations of Arab people and places. Although Disney's Arab princess story mostly misses the mark with female youth in Qatar, this study also points to beneficial aspects of their experiences with commercial princess media; not only have Arab girls used Disney narratives, for instance, to help them navigate the politics and parameters of girlhood in the Middle East, but their consumption has also functioned as a springboard for new forms of cultural production more in line with their gendered identities and concerns. Despite the recent spate of popular discourses rebuking princess culture's numerous ideological problems and pitfalls, then, this study highlights how Arab girls are indeed consuming, yet also countering, dominant narratives with creative stories of their own.

This discovery brings to mind Naomi Wolf's recent recommendation that Disney Princesses, who "are busy being the heroines of their own lives," be read more productively by critics and parents. Citing the strength and capabilities of Mulan, Belle, and Mia, she coolly advises, "Don't worry if your 5-year-old girl insists on a pink frilly princess dress. It doesn't mean she wants to subside into froth; it just means, sensibly enough for her, that she wants to take over the world" (2011). Like other girls around the world, Arab female youth are imbricated in an ever-growing web of commercial princess media narratives—most of which circulate contradictory ideas about what it means to be a girl. Yet, in raising their voices through cultural criticism and powerfully recasting gendered norms in their own creative works, girls in Qatar demonstrate that they are active agents in the growing global march toward improving girls' media—and by extension, the cultural experiences of Arab female youth in the Middle East and beyond.

## Acknowledgments

I would like to thank Ibrahim Alhashmi for his invaluable research assistance as well as Miriam Forman-Brunell and Rebecca Hains for patiently supporting this project and for providing helpful comments. I would also like to thank the amazing girls who participated in this study.

## Endnotes

1. While a fifth set of questions gauged the girls' perceptions about media related to real-life princesses, these data fall outside the scope of the current chapter.
2. Her Highness's name should be spelled "Sheikha Moza bint Nasser Al-Missned."
3. Although the spelling of Her Highness's name varies across publications, I use "Skeikha Moza" here as this is the spelling endorsed on her website (Her Highness 2013).

4. All girls' names are pseudonyms.
5. My search revealed just one scholarly essay on *Aladdin*'s reception outside the United States; see White and Winn 1999.
6. In 2006, the entertainment company Rotana—owned by Saudi Prince Alwaleed Bin Talal—took over the distribution of Disney media in the Middle East ("Saudi's" 2006). Unlike Stallions, Rotana does not alter Disney's film content or box covers.
7. Following protests by Arab Americans, Disney altered the offending lyrics for *Aladdin*'s 1993 home video release as well as all subsequent releases of the film (Fox 1993).

## References


Addison, Erin. 1993. "Saving Other Women from Other Men: Disney's *Aladdin*." *Camera Obscura, 31*, 4–25.

"Disney Channel Added in the Middle East." 1996. *New York Times*, December 2.

Disney. "Dreams Come True at Magic Kingdom Park." 2013. Accessed August 8, 2013. http://www.disneyworld.disney.go.com/

"Disney on Ice Adds Extra Show." 2013. *Qatar Tribune*, June 5.

"Disney to Return to Qatar with More Live Shows." 2013. *Gulf Times*, June 18.

Drotner, Kirsten. 2001. "Denmark: 'Donald Seems So Danish': Disney and the Formation of Cultural Identity." In *Dazzled by Disney: The Global Disney Audiences Project*, ed. Janet Wasko, Mark Phillips, and Eileen Meehan, 102–120. London: Leicester University Press.

Felperin, Leslie. 1997. "The Thief of Buena Vista: Disney's *Aladdin* and Orientalism." In *A Reader in Animation Studies*, ed. Jayne Pilling, 137–142. Sydney, Australia: John Libbey.

Forman-Brunell, Miriam. 2009. *Babysitter: An American History*. New York: NYU Press.

Fox, David J. 1993. "Disney Will Alter Song in 'Aladdin' Movies." *Los Angeles Times*, July 10.

Fromherz, Allen J. 2012. *Qatar: A Modern History*. London: I. B. Tauris.

Gauch, Suzanne. 2007. *Liberating Shahrazad: Feminism, Postcolonialism, and Islam*. Minneapolis: University of Minnesota Press.

Giroux, Henry A., and Grace Pollock. 2010. *The Mouse That Roared: Disney and the End of Innocence* (2nd ed.). Lanham, MD: Rowman & Littlefield.

Goudreau, Jenna. 2012. "Disney Princess Tops List of the 20 Best-Selling Entertainment Products." *Forbes*, September 17. Accessed July 15, 2013. http://www.forbes.com/sites/jennagoudreau/2012/09/17/disney-princess-tops-list-of-the-20-best-selling-entertainment-products/

Griffin, Sean. 1994. "The Illusion of 'Identity': Gender and Racial Representation in *Aladdin*." *Animation Journal, 3*(1): 64–73.

Hains, Rebecca. 2012a. "An Afternoon of Productive Play with Problematic Dolls: The Importance of Foregrounding Children's Voices in Research." *Girlhood Studies, 5*(1): 121–140.

Hains, Rebecca. 2012b. *Growing Up with Girl Power: Girlhood on Screen and in Everyday Life*. New York: Peter Lang.

Hartstein, Jennifer L. 2012. *Princess Recovery: A How-To Guide to Raising Strong, Empowered Girls Who Can Create Their Own Happily Ever Afters.* Avon, MA: Adams Media.

Her Highness Sheikha Moza. 2013. "Biography." Accessed August 13, 2013. http://www.mozabintnasser.qa/en/Pages/MozabintNasser/Biography.aspx

Hurley, Dorothy L. 2005. "Children of Color and the Disney Fairytale Princess." *Journal of Negro Education, 74*(3): 221–232.

"JCC to Offer Selection of Disney Kids and Family Content in Middle East and North Africa." 2013. *Zawya*, March 11.

JCC. 2013. "JCC's Vision and Mission." Accessed July 24, 2013. http://www.jcctv.net/vision-and-mission/

Kearney, Mary Celeste. 2006. *Girls Make Media.* New York: Routledge.

Kearney, Mary Celeste. 2011. "Girls' Media Studies 2.0." In *Mediated Girlhoods: New Explorations of Girls' Media Culture*, ed. Mary Celeste Kearney, 1–14. New York: Peter Lang.

Kraidy, Marwan M., and Joe F. Khalil. 2008. "Youth, Media and Culture in the Arab World." In *The International Handbook of Children, Media and Culture*, ed. Sonia Livingstone and Kirsten Drotner, 336–350. Los Angeles: Sage.

Lacroix, Celeste. 2004. "Images of Animated Others: The Orientalization of Disney's Cartoon Heroines from *The Little Mermaid* to *The Hunchback of Notre Dame.*" *Popular Communication, 2*(4): 213–229.

Leage, Rodda, and Ivana Chalmers. 2010. "Degrees of Caution: Arab Girls Unveil on Facebook." In *Girl Wide Web 2.0: Revisiting Girls, the Internet, and the Negotiation of Identity*, ed. Sharon R. Mazzarella, 27–43. New York: Peter Lang.

Lemish, Dafna, Kirsten Drotner, Tamar Liebes, Eric Maigret, and Gitte Stald. 1998. "Global Culture in Practice: A Look at Children and Adolescents in Denmark, France and Israel." *European Journal of Communication, 13*(4): 539–556.

Orenstein, Peggy. 2011. *Cinderella Ate My Daughter: Dispatches from the Front Lines of the New Girlie-Girl Culture.* New York: HarperCollins.

Phillips, Mark. 2001. "The Global Disney Audiences Project: Disney across Cultures." In *Dazzled by Disney: The Global Disney Audiences Project*, ed. Janet Wasko, Mark Phillips, and Eileen Meehan, 31–61. London: Leicester University Press.

Pike, Kirsten. 2011. "'The New Activists': Girls and Discourses of Citizenship, Liberation, and Femininity in *Seventeen*, 1968–1977." In *Mediated Girlhoods: New Explorations of Girls' Media Culture,* ed. Mary Celeste Kearney, 55–73. New York: Peter Lang.

Rosin, Hanna. 2012. "Critics Are Missing What's Radical in *Brave*." *Slate*, June 20. Accessed August 10, 2013. http://www.slate.com/blogs/xx_factor/2012/06/20/pixar_s_brave_a_princess_with_raw_physical_power.html

Salama, Ramy. 2013. "*Disney on Ice* Shows for Doha Kids in June." *Qatar Tribune*, April 30.

"Saudi's Rotana to Bring Walt Disney to Middle East." 2006. Reuters, November 6. Accessed August 8, 2013. http://www.reuters.com/article/2006/11/07/industry-leisure-saudi-disney-dc-idUSL0638470520061107

Shaheen, Jack G. 2001. *Reel Bad Arabs: How Hollywood Vilifies a People.* New York: Olive Branch Press.

Sobel, Anne. 2010. "The Sheikha & I." *Huffington Post*, November 10. Accessed August 5, 2013. http://www.huffingtonpost.com/anne-peterson/the-sheikha-i_b_780477.html

Staninger, Christiane. 2003. "Disney's Magic Carpet Ride: *Aladdin* and Women in Islam." In *The Emperor's Old Groove: Decolonizing Disney's Magic Kingdom*, ed. Brenda Ayres, 65–77. New York: Peter Lang.

Valenti, Marinda. 2013. "Disney's Not-So-Brave Makeover." *Ms. Magazine Blog*, May 14. Accessed August 8, 2013. http://msmagazine.com/blog/2013/05/14/disneys-not-so-brave-makeover/

Wasko, Janet, and Eileen R. Meehan. 2001. "Dazzled by Disney? Ambiguity in Ubiquity." In *Dazzled by Disney: The Global Disney Audiences Project*, ed. Janet Wasko, Mark Phillips, and Eileen R. Meehan, 329–343. London: Leicester University Press.

White, Timothy R., and J. Emmett Winn. 1999. "Islam, Animation, and Money: The Reception of Disney's *Aladdin* in Southeast Asia." In *Themes and Issues in Asian Cartooning: Cute, Cheap, Mad, and Sexy*, ed. John A. Lent, 61–76. Bowling Green, KY: Bowling Green State University Popular Press.

Wohlwend, Karen E. 2009. "Damsels in Discourse: Girls Producing and Consuming Identity Texts through Disney Princess Play." *Reading Research Quarterly*, *44*(1): 57–83.

Wolf, Naomi. 2011. "Mommy, I Want to Be a Princess." *New York Times*, December 2.

Zaslow, Emilie. 2009. *Feminism, Inc.: Coming of Age in Girl Power Media Culture*. New York: Palgrave Macmillan.

Zitawi, Jehan. 2008. "Contextualizing Disney Comics within the Arab Culture." *Meta*, *53*(1): 139–153.

# Part III
# Princess and Performance Cultures

CHAPTER EIGHT

# Blue Bloods, Movie Queens, and Jane Does: Or How Princess Culture, American Film, and Girl Fandom Came Together in the 1910s

DIANA ANSELMO-SEQUEIRA

In the early 1910s, as the American film industry moved away from trick shorts and one-reelers, movie fan magazines began presenting adolescent actresses as real-life embodiments of fairy tale princesses. For instance, in September 1918, leading fan publication *Photoplay Magazine* introduced Paramount's youngest star, fourteen-year-old Lila Lee, not only as a magically precocious talent, but moreover as an everyday personification of the Cinderella myth.

> If you had grown up to be a great big girl of fifteen or sixteen, and had seen a lot of moving pictures, and thought they were wonderful, and you could do it too—if [a] man came along and said, "I wanna make you a star"—just like that—would you believe your good fairy was on the job again? [… After all] many a *Cinderella* has found her way to fame and fortune thus unexpectedly in the world of make-believe.[1]

Titled "Do You Believe in Fairies?" Joseph Shorey's article epitomizes the typical write-up released by the fan press in the mid-1910s, a decade when girl actors in their teens and early twenties emerged as the clear preference of American movie audiences. In fact, by 1915 teenage players such as Mary Pickford, Viola Dana, and Mary Miles Minter—curly-haired, rosy-cheeked, and famous for impersonating fairy princesses and "the doll baby character of the heroine"[2] on screen—often placed first in nationwide popularity contests published by film fan magazines. Simultaneously, the trade press appointed them as the most well-paid players in the motion picture business. In 1916, the *New York Dramatic Mirror* even remarked that "from the first day, the dramatic level of picture acting has hovered around a *pair of cupid lips*."[3]

Shorey's reading of Lila's professional success as a rags-to-riches Cinderella story actually undergirded many early actresses' publicized biographies. From emotive Mae Marsh to comedic Mabel Normand, and from teenage Mary Miles Minter to childlike Mary Pickford, most Thumbelina-sized female players were imagined as "Cinderella [...] girls who [...] became famous overnight when their good fairies led them into the magic light of the Kliegs."[4] A trade reviewer later reinforced this romanticized view of female stardom when he mused that box-office successes often hinged on a girl star's alchemistic ability to, "with her presence, [...] transform a strip of celluloid into a fairytale ribbon of spun gold."[5]

Forging a strong homology between fairy tale princesses and adolescent film actresses, while concurrently inviting female movie fans to identify with such fabricated "fairy" biographies, articles such as "Do You Believe in Fairies?" reveal how popular culture made sense of young femininity during a transitional decade. In fact, the years between 1910 and 1920 marked a time when narrative film, celebrity movie culture, and, more important, the new life-stage of adolescence first took root in popular culture. By 1910, pioneering American psychologist G. Stanley Hall had defined girlhood as a liminal phase between childhood and womanhood, deeply rooted in the make-believe world of nursery rhymes and in the romantic expectations of a fairy tale happy ending. "Just blossoming into beauty, enjoying for the first time that most exhilarating experience of being taken for a young lady," the adolescent girl, Stanley Hall noted, tended to revert to images of fairy tale royalty, fantasizing that "perhaps she is really destined to become a superior being, queening it through the world, "[6] or maybe one of the mystical "priestesses, pythonesses, [and] maenads" that populated her delirious subjectivity.[7]

At the same time that Stanley Hall defined female adolescents as excessively romantic, gullible, and imaginative, successful narrative films—such as *The Good Little Devil* (1914), *Cinderella* (1914), *The Fairy and the Waif* (1915), *Lady Little Eileen* (1916), *Snow White* (1916), and *The Princess of the Dark* (1917)—visualized adolescent heroines' interaction with fairies. In fact, eighteen-year-old Fay Herron—the sightless "Princess of the Dark"—and blind teen Juliet from *The Good Little Devil* both embodied Stanley Hall's typical delusional girl. Both fictional maidens imagined themselves as a monarch of fairy realms, "holding her lonely court, day by day" in an empty mountain grove, while "through her busy brain there passed a procession of princes and princesses, come to pay her homage."[8]

Many scholars have contributed enormously to our understanding of "women's" lives and cultures in the early 1900s. Film historians Miriam Hansen and Shelley Stamp[9] first suggested that the 1910s fostered the emergence of a visible female spectatorship. Cultural theorists Nan Enstad and Kathy Peiss importantly documented working girls' increased identification and consumption of narrative cinema at the dawn of the twentieth century.[10] However, none of these landmark studies considered silent movie stars and their audiences within the context of female adolescence. How did the creation of such an interim life-stage influence the emergence of a first generation of movie stars that were no longer children, and yet not quite women? Did this biological in-betweenness affect the presentation of young actresses as fairy tale royalty? How did adolescent female fans respond to the film industry's presentation of young movie actresses as everyday Cinderellas?

This chapter seeks to reexamine narrative film from the 1910s through the lens of fairy tale imagery and miraculous class ascendance, tropes that constructed female identity at a time the institutionalization of mass-marketed cinema coincided with psychology's seminal formulation of adolescence. I argue that contemporary understandings of the mythic fairy tale princess—invariably adolescent, beautiful, and transformative—originates from this particular historical confluence. During such a formative time, popular culture began filtering girls' identities—both as movie lovers and screen laborers—through well-established tropes of female adolescence, tropes rooted in Old World fairy tales of rags-to-riches transformation. In this chapter, I set out to explore how and why the liminal figure of the adolescent girl became a privileged site for negotiating American anxieties regarding social mobility, national identity, shifting gender roles, and industrial disenchantment, cultural issues greatly amplified by the outbreak of World War I.

## "Have You a Little Fairy in Your Play?": The Cult of Fairy Girls and Real-Life Princesses in Early-Twentieth-Century American Visual Culture

As many contemporary art historians and media theorists have remarked,[11] the turn of the twentieth century witnessed the birth of a highly industrialized visual culture. Mass-marketed illustrations, photo-postcards, color lithographs, and fashion plates all adorned theater playbills, movie ephemera, women's magazines, and children's books, thus signaling Western culture's burgeoning romance with reproducible technologies. In Great Britain and the United States, cheap mechanical modes of visual reproduction fostered a particular desire to render visible the fantastic creatures that inhabited the ethereal realm of childhood fairy tales, nursery rhymes, and Old World folktales. However, the most popular representations of such fantastic creatures often took the shape of diminutive, nubile fairies and transformative, young princesses—such as Cinderella, Snow White, and Donkeyskin—anachronistically covered in animal pelts, rags, and wild flowers. In their awkward cross between childish innocence and womanly sensuality, these figurations functioned as romanticized embodiments of the ambiguous psychophysiological transformations underpinning female adolescence. Simultaneously, their ubiquitous presence in early-twentieth-century visual culture articulated a cultural understanding of girlhood reflective of that seminally proposed by Stanley Hall: as a mysterious developmental phase defined by elusive, shape-shifting, liminal pliability, and uncanny "becomings."[12]

In addition, the germ of a fledgling "princess culture" emerged at the same time that a multimediated film industry began marketing individual players as deified "picture personalities."[13] Both these occurrences became linked by a popular desire to make visible the newly defined figure of the adolescent girl through already established, and thus legible, paradigms of femininity. Therefore, to understand why at the time of its inception the American star system promoted young film actresses as royalty—as fairy princesses on the screen, and as "movie princesses" in everyday life—one has to trace early-twentieth-century audiences' widespread fascination with the princess figure, a figure that pervaded mass-marketed illustrations, stage plays, and actual newspaper reports throughout the 1910s.

There is significant evidence attesting to British and American culture's tendency to render adolescent girlhood identifiable through the well-known figures of youthful fairies and fairy tale princesses. Notorious illustrators from both countries, including Arthur Rackham, Cicely M. Barker, Jessie Willcox Smith, and Elizabeth Shippen Green, spearheaded such mass-marketed "fairyland fever."[14] Throughout his long career, Rackham gave life to some of the most revered fairy princesses—from Undine (1909) to Catskin (1918), Cinderella (1919), and Sleeping Beauty (1920)—as well as to some of the most enchanted magical realms: from Alice's Wonderland (1907) to Peter Pan's Neverland (1906) and Titania's Fairyland (1908). In 1918, English artist Cicely M. Barker produced a popular postcard series depicting elves and fairies, the seed to her masterpiece *Flower Fairies of the Spring* (1923) and *Flower Fairies of the Summer* (1925). These colorfully illustrated books portrayed barefooted fairy-girls clad in petals, small elfin ears, and butterfly wings that rendered them incongruently humanoid. Such lovely crossings between human girlhood and animalistic flora visually represented what Stanley Hall influentially classified as "the budding girl's [...] real nature [...]: wild, with a charming, gamey flavor."[15] By 1920, two pubescent English girls, Elsie Wright and Frances Griffiths, captured the imagination of British and American audiences by taking photographs of themselves posing with alleged real-life fairies in the Cottingley woods. Sir Arthur Conan Doyle, the respected British author, wrote a corroborating eulogy to the girls' photographs, further reasserting prevalent cultural associations between young femininity, magical thinking, and fairylands.[16]

Dialoguing with these main themes founded by the golden age of British illustration, notable American artists Jessie Willcox Smith and Elizabeth Shippen Green drew dreamy images of bourgeois girls, fairy tale heroines, and regal maidens wrapped in diaphanous gowns. They placed them in sunny seasides, secret woods, groomed gardens, and well-to-do domestic scenarios, daydreaming, doll-playing, or being courted by princely men who emerged in scenarios of invariable royal opulence and atemporal magic.

The popular desire to visualize young femininity through the figures of fairy girls and fictional princesses further emerged hand-in-hand with a revived interest in the foundational fairy tales of the Brothers Grimm, Hans Christian Andersen, and Charles Perrault. These European compilations greatly influenced two coming-of-age novels that importantly impacted the American imagination: J. M. Barrie's *Peter Pan; or, The Boy Who Wouldn't Grow Up*, first published as a play in 1904 and then as a novel in 1911; and L. Frank Baum's *Oz* series, whose first volume, *The Wonderful Wizard of Oz*, came out in 1900, followed by thirteen other novels, the last one released posthumously in 1920. While Barrie's narrative centered on a prepubescent boy's refusal to mature and a girl's (Wendy) decision to embrace adulthood, the figure of the capricious fairy Tinkerbell was the one aptly embodying the emotional turmoil experienced by a teenage girl conflicted by the first pangs of sexual desire. Similarly, Baum's delirious world of Oz offers many possible readings of Dorothy's abandonment of girlhood and incipient trespassing over the threshold of adolescence. Such confusing developmental twilight is personified by several fantastic characters she encounters throughout her self-discovering journey into Oz's dystopian fairyland. These include two opposite figures of female power: Glinda, the Good Witch of the South, and the nameless Wicked Witch of the West, two magical figures who read in tandem present Dorothy with antithetical visions of womanhood.

Following in the footsteps of their predecessor, Lewis Carroll's *Alice's Adventures in Wonderland* (1865), both Barrie's and Baum's novels quickly became best-sellers in America, propelling an avalanche of similarly fairy-themed, coming-of-age works: Harley Granville-Barker and Laurence Housman's *Prunella; or, Love in a Dutch Garden* (1906); Grace Miller White's *Tess of the Storm Country* (1909); Austin Strong's best-selling Broadway version of Rosemonde Gérard and Maurice Rostand's stage play *A Good Little Devil* (1912); Owen Davis's *The Wishing Ring: An Idyll of Old England* (1914); Georgette Leblanc's novelization of Maurice

Maeterlinck's haunting fairy play *The Blue Bird* (1914); Betty T. Fitzgerald's "Little Lady Eileen" (1916); and Lanier Bartlett's "Princess of the Dark" (1917), to name only a few.[17] Tellingly, most of these texts focused on young girls' sexual awakening and its negotiation via direct (or imaginary) contact with fairies and other supernatural entities. The sheer volume of plays and novels featuring young princesses, rags-to-riches maidens, and girlish fairies evinces a pervasive, cultural preponderance to visualize girlhood via fairy tale tropes.

In America, such visual fascination with fairy girlhood found its most active and lasting shape on the theatrical stage. In March 1913, the weekly periodical *New York Dramatic Mirror* ran an article titled "Have You a Little Fairy in Your Play?" which, playing upon the then-popular commercial slogan "Have you a little fairy in your home?" confirmed the ubiquity of the "whimsical fairy play" on American stages.[18] The definition of "fairy play" as employed by journalist Fred J. Smith reveals how popular American culture came to understand the concept during the 1910s. Rather than as a strict genre, as later proposed by mid-twentieth-century literary luminaries Northrop Frye and Tzvetan Todorov,[19] the fairy play served as a label that described narratives in which fantastic motifs—namely, fairy intervention, magical turns of fate, contact with ghostly entities, talking animals, and feudalistic class asymmetries—framed a young girl's passage from adolescent daughterhood to wifely womanhood. As a case in point, many of the acclaimed "fairy plays" taking over Broadway in the 1910s—*A Good Little Devil*, *Poor Little Rich Girl*, *A Kiss for Cinderella*, *Alice in Wonderland*, and *Snow White*—focused on adolescent heroines' confrontation with the adult world by way of wondrous events. For example, in *A Good Little Devil*, lovelorn Juliet's friendship with fairies allows the girl to magically regain her sight and reunite with her childhood sweetheart; in *Snow White*, the budding princess's exile from her father's home, and magical resuscitation from slumberous death via a suitor's kiss, signified the girl's transformation from childlike daughter to sexually mature bride.

American audiences' fascination with fairy tale princesses quickly stretched from Broadway to Main Street. By 1916, local newspapers frequently reported on amateur productions of "fairy plays." Invariably, they emphasized the play's reliance on a strong female character and a young female player. In December 1916, the *New York Times* commented that a pubescent New York socialite, "Miss Tanis Guinness," turned her mother's Christmas party into a big success by playing "the title role" of Snow White.[20] By 1917, the *San Francisco Chronicle* commended the city's Girls' High School for its "scoring success" performing a revised version of the Grimms' "Snow White."[21]

The widespread cultural consumption of fairy tale narratives permeating local theatrical productions and large-scale stage shows participated in a specific spectatorial desire for escapism into an ahistorical time of myth and magic, inured to the ravages of urbanization, industrialization, and World War I. In 1915, a *Motion Picture Magazine* reader, Mary Carolyn Davis, submitted a poem ascribing to "dreamy" "Filmland" the "gift of forgetfulness": "Forgetfulness of our own cares and grief / From hard reality an hour's relief— / This is the gift that Filmland tenders free / To tired life-travelers—you and me."[22] The year before a *New York Dramatic Mirror* journalist had identified fairy films—"with [their] golden key of imagination," uplifting whimsicality, and old-fashion values of "courtliness and kindness"—as educational tools against an otherwise overly industrialized and alienated society. The reporter guaranteed that by "instilling poetry and beauty in the minds of children and driving hardness and hatred from the hearts of older players," fairy plays taught large audiences to "realize and fight modern evils."[23] By 1916, the film-fan magazine *Motion Picture Classic* introduced a new kind of female star, "the 'homey' girl," as the vessel through which such restorative effect reached movie audiences. The affective power of this female type originated from an "essentially feminine and adorable" old-fashionedness that harked back to the fairy tale imagery of Cinderella slippers and thumb-size fairies; with the "homey girl," the journalist guaranteed, "came memories of maids whose tiny feet have long since traveled their last, flower-strewn path."[24]

Ironically, this intense search for mass-marketed renditions of fairy girls, fantasy princesses, and romanticized Old World royalty occurred as centuries-old empires came crashing down. At their height of popularity during the war years, the machinations of European royal families—especially young, unmarried princesses—were splashed across the pages of popular periodicals for American audiences to devour. *The Day Book*, Chicago's daily, often presented European princesses' matchmaking dramas as war-riddled dilemmas. One sensationalistic article, "Pretty Princess Must Give Up Love to Bring Royal House Together," speculated that the teenage Princess Victoria Louise of Germany, known as "The Little Princess" and "the best catch of Europe," had to sacrifice "her heart [...] as a bridge over a chasm between hostile royal houses."[25] Years later, the same magazine positioned twenty-year-old Princess Margaret of Denmark's potential wedding to the Prince of Wales as a consequence of Europe's "war-torn" scarcity, which "left [her] the only girl eligible to become the fiancée of the heir to the British throne."[26] The headline "No 'War-Brides' in Royal Family, No Husbands for Royal Ladies" melodramatically addressed the dearth of suitable partners for young princesses, since "with all the eligible princes fighting on land or sea, it would be useless to arrange a marriage feast at which Death might preside."[27] The article included two photos of Princess Maud of Fife and Princess Mary of Britain, the two well-coiffed faces framing the drawing of a cupid crying over his broken bow.

Safely positioned as distant spectators of a war-torn Europe, in short, American audiences ambivalently reveled in European monarchies' domestic dramas, while still revering princesses and queens as compelling, superior beings, magnified by their ancestral sophistication and mythologized social status.

The publicized discourse on European princessdom also centered on issues of beauty. In 1912, the *Salt Lake Tribune* steadily reported on the serial love affairs of Prince Adalbert and Count Fugger of Germany. However, all these features focused not on the Don Juan duo, but on the physical gifts of the many princesses they deceived.[28] Throughout the war years, both *The Sun* and *The Day Book* similarly released images of the prettiest European princesses, as well as "the newest photographs of Europe's most beautiful royal family," a title conquered by Rumania because of the reputed facial perfection of Queen Marie and her two eldest daughters. Large photos of the three showed the queen in regal profile, while the two teenage girls appeared fresh-faced, well coiffed, and tastefully bejeweled.[29] Three years later, the *New York Tribune* gushed over the Rumanian princesses in a lavish, multi-photo article. This piece addressed the Parisian opening of a "fairy play" authored by the Queen herself, minutely describing the three princesses' luxurious attires and well-bred poise. The piece dubbed the blue bloods' "beauty an asset" that—similar to the rhetoric used to promote fairy tale princesses—allegedly functioned as a civilizing instrument. Presented as "an extraordinaryly beautiful woman," the Queen was said to "take extreme care of her appearance [...] because she feels that in this way she best helps represent her people before the civilized world."[30]

Although impossible to determine the veracity of readers' letters, those published in newspapers and movie fan magazines of the late 1910s suggest that, reflective of their cultural milieu, female audiences negotiated their identities through imaginary royal figures. In 1917, a Chicago moviegoer sent a query to *Photoplay* under the name "Princess Zim-Zam." In 1916, Lauren S. Hamilton, a *Motion Picture Magazine* reader, submitted a poem in which she imagined herself "a Moving Picture queen." In April 1917, a girl signed her letter "The Lonely Princess" and sent it to "The Cousins' Letters," a popular section of the *Washington Post* aimed at school-age youth.[31]

In fact, throughout the 1910s "The Cousins' Letters" invited young readers to write autobiographical letters and submit drawings in exchange for prizes. Most participants had to choose an alias by which they wanted to be known to "Dear Aunt Anna," the ringleader of the club. By 1917, at the apex of nationwide interest in fairy tale princesses, girls writing to "The Cousins' Letters" vied for the right to be known as "Snow White." In April, Margaret Kelley wrote asking whether the "Dear Aunt" "had room for one more cousin? [...] If you will accept me, I will choose Snow White for my pen name." The Aunt declined her request, claiming, "We already have a Snow White."[32] In fact, in January of that year the "original" Snow White had emerged after a long hiatus. She wrote apologetically, wondering whether "you have forgotten that you ever had a 'Snow White' in your club. But you had one and here she is [… and] don't think for a minute that I have forgotten you or 'our page.'" The girl further confessed that her prolonged silence resulted from her growth into adolescence: "I joined when I was in fourth grade [but] I am now in high school." However "grown up," the Eastern High School girl still identified her adolescent self with that of the fairy princess: She signed her letter "Snow White" in capital letters, and kept her given name, "E. Mogenweck," abridged, minimized, and bracketed under her fairy persona.[33] Thus, the fairy tale heroine's adolescent transformations from teen rags to womanly riches, or from princess-child to married queen, not only undergirded the successful stagings of many fairy plays, but moreover functioned as an identity lens through which everyday girls negotiated their own teenage growth.

In conclusion, American audiences' particular fascination with European, unmarried princesses focused on the girls' unparalleled physical beauty, expensive fashions, and exciting romantic engagements. However, these reports constantly bypassed princesses' relevance as political subjects, i.e., as potential heiresses to a country's throne. In fact, in the popular press, real-life princesses appeared as romanticized embodiments of antiquated mores and social etiquettes, and as legible effigies of enviable female refinement, established social ascendancy, and desired class status. In other words, unmarried princesses' cultural capital remained mainly superficial and ornamental. With this in mind, it can be suggested that during the 1910s, American popular culture positioned real-life princesses as servicing very much the same cultural functions as that of their fairy tale counterparts: (1) They reasserted deep-seated associations between girlhood, fantasy, frivolity, and mandatory romantic completion; (2) they stimulated female audiences' class fantasies of rags-to-riches transformation and absorbing self-identification with out-of-reach, imaginary identities; and (3) they exemplified ladylike and material opulence, while simultaneously promoting a conservatively disempowered image of femininity defined by fleeting youth and beauty, whose intrinsic value resided in premarital virginity.

It is curious that at the same time American audiences idolized European blue bloods, the 1910s witnessed an increased dissipation of the boundaries between actual princessdom and stage performance. In 1912, *The Day Book* reported on an inverted rags-to-riches story: Princess Ibrahim Hassan of Egypt—originally Ola Humphrys from Oakland, California—decided to trade "palaces for footlights." After pronouncing "Oriental men's […] age-old treatment of women […] intolerable," the young California actress decided to leave her royal husband,

and return to her home-country and theatrical trade.[34] Two years later, a similar princess-to-performer transformation made international news: The "nation-wide hunt for the Princess Metchersky of Russia," a girl "scarcely out of her teens," culminated when the princess was found "dancing on the sea shore of Nice, France." Reportedly, the girl "known as the 'dancing princess'" had escaped her home country "to satisfy a whim" of becoming a stage performer.[35]

Last, the article on the "fairy play" penned by the Queen of Rumania importantly articulated an elision of boundaries that in the mid-1910s became fundamental for the successful promotion of early movie actresses. The play visualized an imaginary princess who wandered through a fantastic land of mermaids and fairies in search of the magical "lily of life."[36] By describing the make-believe "princess" featured in Queen Marie's "fairy play" as the creation of an actual ex-princess, and moreover by casting such fantastic figuration as an accurate personification of the queen's autobiographical experiences of postwar bereavement, the *New York Tribune* collapsed the lines separating performed fantasy from lived identity, and imaginary fairy tale princessdom from actual real-life royalty. Such crucial erasure underpinned early-twentieth-century fascination with fairies, (living and fictional) princesses, and screen stars, figures presented in an increasingly multimediated film culture as larger-than-life personalities, self-made gods that belonged to a magnificent oligarchy positioned above anonymous mortals. In common, fairies, princesses, and female film stars shared their mythic narratives of origin; their uncanny status as flesh-and-blood wonders; and last, their feminine youth and compelling girlish beauty.

## "The Slipper Fits—You Are Cinderella, My Princess":[37] Movie Princesses, Fairy Films, and the Rags-to-Riches Ethos of Early Female Stardom

After the "fairyland fever had [held] the theatre within its grasp" for years,[38] contagion ensued, spreading to the silver screen. Stage adaptations of famous fairy plays created such large box-office revenues that film producers decided to bring fairyland to the movies. During the 1910s, substantial evolution in trick cinematography, editing technology, narrative storytelling, and reel length allowed movies to create complex visual spectacles that only a decade before had eluded the grasp of pioneer filmmakers Thomas Edison, Edwin S. Porter, and Georges Méliès. Thus, not only the fantastic transformations undergone by Cinderella (rags-to-riches), Snow White (teen corpse to queenly bride), and Alice (fairy-small to gargantuan giant to child-size again) could now be visualized in all their magical splendor but, moreover, these heroines' narratives of adolescent growth could now be fully articulated in multi-reel films.

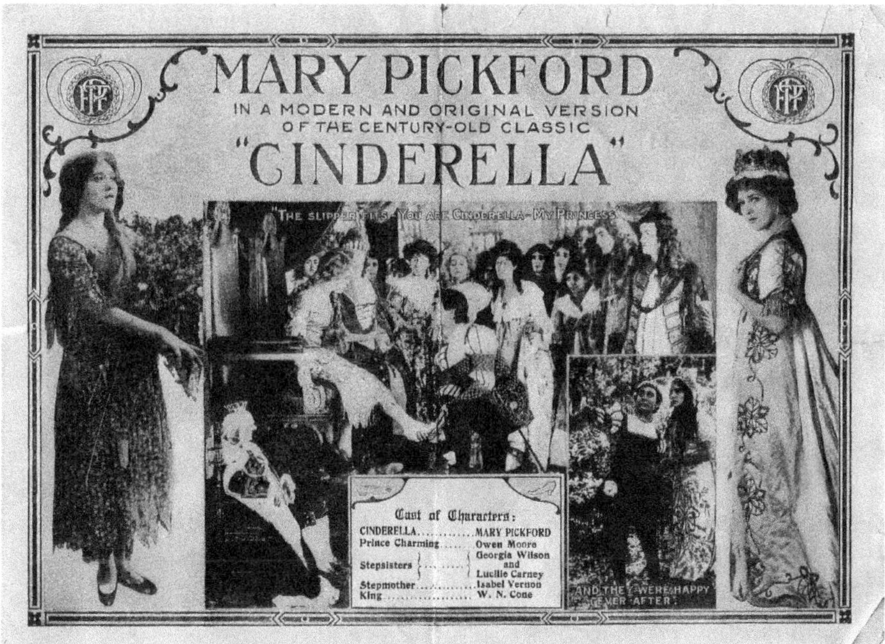


Famous Players's 'Cinderella,' *Exhibitor's Herald*, 1914.

We clearly see this shift from optical spectacle into subjective storytelling in the first narrative adaptation of Cinderella. Slotted to premier on Christmas week, Famous Players' 1914 *Cinderella* was marketed as a child-friendly fantasy for the whole family, whose cutting-edge cinematography would bring to life the popular fairy tale of rags-to-riches girlhood. *Cinderella* also functioned as a vehicle for rising star Mary Pickford. At this time, Pickford had already built a reputation playing ingénues at Biograph; however, only in 1913 did she cease starring in shorts and graduate to feature-length productions. Sorely disappointed with her first feature-length effort—a film adaptation of her latest stage success, the fairy play *A Good Little Devil*—Pickford wanted to prove her acting skills.[39] As a result, she portrayed Cinderella not as Perrault's flattened archetype, but as an everyday adolescent girl from the Progressive Era. Pickford humanized the imaginary figure with her trademark warmth and childlike mischief, characteristics clearly displayed in the scenes where a raggedy Cinderella interacts with her evil stepfamily.

Foremost, this five-reeler revealed an awareness of audiences' growing dissatisfaction with an overuse of gimmicky trick cinematography. For the sake of optical wonder, previous versions of *Cinderella*—such as Méliès's 1899 protean rendition—had reduced the tale of female transformation to its magical components, consequently evacuating the female protagonist of any psychological depth.

In James Kirkwood's five-reeler, however, trick cinematography made visible the adolescent girl's inner world: Split-screens show Cinderella wistfully remembering an earlier encounter with the Prince (Pickford's real-life husband, Owen Moore), while double-exposures visualize her horrible nightmare, conjured in the afterglow of the forbidden ball.[40]

Although the movie helped to cement Pickford's girlish stardom, in fact by 1914 Cinderella was already the most popular princess in American narrative cinema. Between 1910 and 1920, the number of known *Cinderella* renditions reached almost three dozens. A list of titles produced by top-tier companies—Edison, Vitagraph, Selig, Thanhouser, Famous Players, Universal, and Fox—includes *A Modern Cinderella* (1910), *Cinderella* (1911), *Lord Browning and Cinderella*, (1912), *Cinderella's Slippers* (1913), *An Awkward Cinderella,* (1914), *Cinderella* (1914), *The Vanishing Cinderella* (1915), *Kentucky Cinderella* (1917), *A Studio Cinderella* (1917), *The Princess of Patches* (1917), *A Modern Cinderella* (1917), *A Kitchen Cinderella* (1920), and *Cinderella's Twin* (1920). Not all of these films followed Perrault's fairy tale, instead using the legible trope of Cinderella as a way to encapsulate a girl's rags-to-riches story. However, a majority of such *Cinderella*-ish plots did function as vehicles for young actresses who, at that early point in their film careers, still vied for recognition and stardom. Marie Prevost, Ruth Clifford, June Caprice, Florence LaBadie, and Dorothy Davenport were some of the silent-screen girls who played Cinderella before rising to worldwide fame as Hollywood's leading ladies.

Silent cinema frequently adapted two other young female characters credited to the Grimm Brothers' and Perrault's fairy anthologies: Little Red Riding Hood and Snow White. The 1911 versions of *Little Red Riding Hood* included James Kirkwood's facetious adaptation starring a pre-stardom, nineteen-year-old Mary Pickford, and an Essanay short with twelve-year-old Eva Prout. By 1913, Selig released a two-reel fantasy starring child actress Baby Lillian Wade in *When Lillian Was Little Red Riding Hood.* At least two more adaptations appeared in 1917 and 1918, both sporting all-children casts.

In 1914, Thanhouser filmed *The Legend of Snow White*, America's first known narrative rendition of *Snow White.* The now-lost movie starred one of the notorious Thanhouser Twins, fourteen-year-old Marion Fairbanks, as the title "Fairy Child." Snow White's film adaptations appeared two more times in 1916: a less-known, extravagant seven-reel production made by Ohio's Regent Photo Play Company and released by the Educational Films Corporation of America, which starred "about 200 well-known Cleveland children,"[41] and an immensely successful Christmas release in which beloved film star Marguerite Clark "dusted off the darling little costumes she wore in [Winthrop Ames's applauded stage] play and donned them again for the Famous Players version of the story."[42]

A last adaptation from 1917, an obscure three-reeler produced by Rex/Universal, remained lost until a Dutch copy recently resurfaced at the UCLA Film and Television Archive. This film is particularly unusual in its visualization of female adolescent growth. It begins by employing an anonymous child actress who plays the scenes of domestic bliss predating the turning point at which Snow White's budding beauty threatens the evil stepmother's vanity. As the princess enters pubescence, her stepmother engages a henchman to kill her, thus hindering the girl's unavoidable transformation into superior womanhood. Once a childish Snow White is cast into the woods, finds refuge in the Seven Dwarfs' abode, and engages in new mature roles of housekeeper and motherly caregiver, the actress changes. Now Elsie Albert—a player who built her movie career impersonating fairy tale princesses—emerges as the adolescent Snow White.[43] Under the "grown-up" guise of the shapely actress, the princess metamorphoses into a full-fledged object of desire, concurrently spurring her evil stepmother's murderous jealousy and arousing the wandering Prince's marital lust.

In sum, if the transformative figure of the fairy tale princess once governed the American stage, by the late 1910s it ruled the American screen. There are two main reasons fairy tales about female metamorphosis embodied by adolescent princesses came to be favored by early film producers. First, as film scholar Tom Gunning has influentially argued, early film audiences enjoyed being astonished by mechanical wonder.[44] As film technology matured, so did the complexity of visual tricks displayed on screen. Reviews of Famous Players' *Cinderella* (1914) and *Snow White* (1916) invariably focused on the perfected quality of believable trick cinematography. *Motion Picture News* emphasized *Cinderella*'s "transformation of the pumpkin, rats and mice into the coach, and attendants [as] prettily effected," praising "the photography" for being "beautiful in all scenes, with some excellent light effects be[ing] obtained."[45] When advertising his *Snow White*, director J. Sealey Dawley similarly argued that,

> Of course there had to be a good deal of trick work in the telling of the tale because of the magic and witchcraft [...] but Broening did something in one scene which I do not believe any other photographer has accomplished. That was the crowning of Miss Clark at the end of the picture while she was surrounded by the whole throne room full of people. It is the first time, so far as I know, that this double exposure trick has been employed with a whole stage full of people.[46]

In its glowing review, *Motography* concurred with the director's claims of groundbreaking cinematography, stating that "in developing advance advertising on

'Snow White,' the exhibitor can hardly over-emphasize the exquisiteness of its staging, and the exceptional way in which trick photography was made to subserve the desired results."[47] Inherently magical and transformative, fairy tales held ideal components to test the advancements of film technology.

By 1917, blood-soaked reports on massive European casualties and distress over America's entrance in World War I had also altered the national mood. The eyes of American audiences—from "kiddies" to adults, and from non–English speaking immigrants to literate individuals—turned to fairy tales, not necessarily seeking the recreational astonishment of the early 1900s, but actively procuring respite rooted in the "clean" nostalgia of childhood tales. Reviewing *Snow White* in January of that same year, the *Chicago Daily Tribune* guaranteed that "the only difference between [...] the self-same fairy story you hung over and devoured in your childhood [...] and the picture is that [... the latter] brings fairyland to your vision. *With your own world tired eyes* you gaze rapturously over the vistas of the impossible."[48] As the decade came to an end, girlish "Cinderella and her magic slipper" also became heralded in popular press as the embodiment of childish wonder, "a story that clings to us, bathed in the romance of our youth [... even if] as we move along the years our faith in them tends to dim."[49] Young female stars personified such restorative "vistas of the impossible" and such unretrievable "romance of youth" through their screen impersonations of dispossessed orphans and fairy princesses who, faced with adversities, still managed to magically develop into perfectly hopeful, beloved, and kind-hearted queens. Case in point, when in the early 1920s a reporter commented on the rerelease of Mary Pickford's 1914 hit *Tess of the Storm Country*, he claimed that "if [Pickford] ever fails to touch us, we are going to feel that something vital—the slumbering embers of youthful illusions and dreams—had died within us. And we shall know that all that is lost."[50]

Further, as noted by Smith in his 1913 article, the majority of Broadway "fairy plays" producing handsome profits already starred

> youthful players who have [...] been trained in motion pictures. Mary Pickford, of *A Good Little Devil*, was one of the greatest favorites of all photoplay actresses and her playing in Biograph film plays is known everywhere; Viola Dana, of *A Poor Little Rich Girl* and known in pictures as Viola Flugrath, played child parts delightfully in Edison pictures. Gladys Hulette, whose Beth in *Little Women* was so appealing, was graduated from films. [... Finally] this season's *Snow White* [...] was vivified by Marguerite Clark's admirable and artistically delightful playing.[51]

Seeking to secure similarly generous box-office revenues, film producers often engaged the same female stars who had shined in theatrical fairy plays, asking them to replicate on screen the fairy roles that glorified them on the legitimate stage. In

1914 alone, Mary Pickford appeared in film adaptations of *A Good Little Devil* and *Cinderella*. Two years later, Pickford's direct contender for the title of "America's Sweetheart," diminutive Marguerite Clark, conquered picture audiences with her screen performances of *Prunella* and *Snow White*, roles that had catapulted Clark to stage stardom in 1913 and 1915, respectively. In fact, throughout the 1910s, the tiny actress would relive dozens of transformative fairy tale heroines: from destitute princess raised by gypsies in *The Goose Girl* (1915) to Pierrot's heartbroken bride in *Prunella* (1918); from feral daughter of the woods turned society lady in *Wildflower* (1914) to fairy-loving Irish lass in *Little Lady Eileen* (1916).[52]

Established leading girls Viola Dana and Gladys Hulette, as well as rising stars Mary Miles Minter and Lila Lee, also performed their biological adolescence through screen representations of fairy girls and transformable princesses. Eighteen-year-old Dana starred as the fairy queen in *The Blind Fiddler* (1915), and as a scullery maid turned belle of the ball in *Cinderella's Twin* (1920). At thirteen, Hulette played the pliable heroine in Edwin S. Porter's *Alice's Adventures in Wonderland* (1910), and a fairy princess who precociously smokes and flirts with an older gentleman in Vitagraph's one-reeler *The Princess Nicotine; or, The Smoke Fairy* (1909). Similarly, in her screen debut *The Fairy and the Waif* (1915), fourteen-year-old Minter appeared as a girl who converses with fairies; fourteen-year-old Lila Lee's first role was that of "a poor little girl who rigs up a 'boat' in her tenement back-yard, and [...] sends her imagination roving over the seven seas."[53] A year after playing the lead in this "mild little fantasy" appropriately titled *The Cruise of the Make-Believe* (1918), Lila impersonated another dreamful little heroine, Mary Lennox, in the first film adaptation of Frances Hodgson Burnett's 1911 children's classic *The Secret Garden*.

So often American cinema cast the first generation of young female stars in the roles of fairy girls and rags-to-riches princesses that their imaginary screen personas quickly became melded with their perceived lived identities. As noted by film scholar Richard deCordova, throughout the 1910s the star system promoted complete homogeneity between a player's screen characters and off-screen identity.[54] To achieve such fabricated illusion of consistency, the star system repackaged their most girlish stars as real-life princesses, everyday Cinderellas, or ugly-ducklings-turned-ruling-swans when placed under the all-powerful tutelage of the motion picture kingdom. As early as 1913, the *Washington Times* promoted "charming Mary Pickford" as a magical performer who possesses "a budding girlish figure," and, at the same time, "although she is almost twenty, still believes in fairies, and especially the good fairy who has presided over her destiny since the time she made her first appearance in the 'movies.'"[55] Six years later, Mary Pickford's star text had evolved from Cinderella-ish fairy-believer into blue-blooded royalty: In 1919, the actress confessed to *The Tattler* "how tickled she has been at the reports that she is the daughter of a duchess."[56]

A year before, touting the "astound-new" debut of their first "made-for-order" star Lila Lee, Paramount press agents built up the hype surrounding the unseen prodigy's first production by releasing a manufactured account of "the young girl's extraordinary [... and] exotic antecedents":

> No living woman has emerged from such strange circumstances of life and [royal] parentage. Her father, a follower of Rasputin and an adherent of the old Russian regime, was sent by the Czar into exile. Her mother, a princess who was also a revolutionist, died a heroine of the Battalion of Death on the Western front. The child herself was captured and taken to Germany, and after appalling adventures escaped to Sweden and made her way to America a stowaway.[57]

Although it was clearly fictional (in fact, Lila was a New Jersey girl, born Augusta Appel to a middle-class German American family), *Photoplay* guaranteed that this account was "truthful publicity," further quipping that "what a sad, dull pass the movies are coming to when managers and press-agents spring on a new star on nothing but the truth."[58] At the same time Lila emerged as a Russian princess turned American "movie queen," *Photoplay* presented Mae Marsh's linear trajectory from child movie fan to adolescent film star as an actual embodiment of fairy tale transformation: "Without going further into the details of the early ambitions of this Ugly Duckling, this Cinderella, let us pause to observe the essential truth of the fairy stories as here exemplified. Just as the Ugly Duckling became a wonderful Swan, just as Cinderella alone could wear the Golden Slippers, so Mary is now Mae Marsh."[59]

The rags-to-riches Cinderella figure appears as much on the screen as it does in connection with early young actresses' narratives of "discovery" and stardom. Recurrently, film critics described barely-of-age stars, such as "Mae Marsh, Mabel Normand, Norma Talmadge, Mary Pickford," as part of a growing group of inexperienced "Cinderellas [who] found [their] way to fame and fortune thus unexpectedly in the world of make-believe: girls who were never, or hardly ever, heard of became famous overnight when their good fairies led them into the magic light of the Kliegs."[60] By 1916, fourteen-year-old Mary Miles Minter was being heralded as "The Fairy of Filmdom," her fabricated biography promoted by the fan press as an actual fairy tale of magical metamorphosis: "No story ever written by Grimm, the necromancer of the nineteenth century, or related by the doomed Scheherazade," mused *Motion Picture Magazine*, "could contain more of the elements of romance than the real story of the little fourteen-year-old Southern girl now playing in the movies [...] and drawing a salary more than that of a United States senator."[61]

The idea that everyday, untried girls became movie stars because of a male producer's transformative action participated in the rags-to-riches myth of female stardom created by the star system in the mid-1910s. Mary Pickford's "good fairy of male persuasion [was] David Belasco [who] happened to hear of her [...] and transplanted her to Broadway where she became a star overnight."[62] Similarly, Lila Lee metamorphosed from street urchin to Paramount's youngest star owing to the intervention of "her good fairies:" stage producer Gus Edwards and film producer Jesse L. Lasky. Such manufactured texts of female "discovery" further underscored the biographies of many of D. W. Griffith's young leading ladies, including Bessie Love, Mae Marsh, and Miriam Cooper. Press agents assigned them fairy tale narratives by alleging that the three teenagers had been transformed from untrained extra girls into Griffith's screen muses overnight. According to *Photoplay*, all Bessie Love had to do to be "discovered" was timidly rap at Griffith's office door: "Griffith looked up and saw the girl's face framed in the door way, [...and] two minutes later Bessie Love was on the Fine Arts payroll. She was a star almost from the start."[63] Cooper's "discovery" followed a similar pattern: One day Griffith happened to notice "a quiet, sad-eyed little girl" skulking around the studio. After speaking to her roughly, Griffith was so struck by "the little trembling figure, [...] hurt pride, fear, humiliation, all expressed in her wonderful dark eyes" that he decided to replace a "famous actress" for the unknown girl.[64]

In conjunction with their fictional inexperience, Pickford (who had actually been on stage since childhood), Marsh, and Talmadge also became known as fatherless waifs, the breadwinners of broken families often composed of a managerial materfamilias and another sister who was also an actress.[65] In turn-of-the-century theatrical lore it was said that "it makes no difference who your mother is, but your father must be a glamorous and romantic figure—if you have a father. If you cannot invent a fascinating devil of a sire, kill him in your infancy—and kill him with dramatic suddenness."[66] The lack of a supportive father figure reinforced the image of feminine fragility and emotional vulnerability that many girl stars embodied onscreen; it also made them more readily pliable to a director's demands.

The romanticization of young actresses' fatherlessness also aligned their star texts with two of the most famous fairy tale heroines of the 1910s: Cinderella and Snow White, two fatherless adolescent girls turned ruling queens. However, it must be noted that not only press agents but also the actresses themselves magnified the absence of father figures in their publicized biographies. For example, underprivileged actress Jeanne Eagels openly admitted that, by eighteen, she had transformed her father "from a failure, a poor, meek ambitious" Midwestern carpenter, into "a gay and reckless, ne'er do well artist from Spain" that resembled actor Antonio Moreno.[67] Stories of Mae Marsh's early loss of two father figures—first her biological father in a train accident, and then her stepfather in San Francisco's 1906 earthquake—seemed to have been disseminated by Marsh herself in an attempt to romanticize her screen persona, as well as to mitigate her father's chronic alcoholism. The same can be said of the Talmadge sisters' sentimental reworking of their father's early abandonment.

Clearly, these manufactured biographies aimed to mythologize female stardom. Relentlessly, they introduced young actresses as real-life personifications of well-known and well-beloved fictional figures: the blue-blooded princess demoted to a lower station—"a stowaway"—as a child, only to be restored to rightful queenliness in her adolescent years; the plain little Duckling transformed into a "wonderful Swan" as childhood wore off; and the talented, but dispossessed Cinderella, swept away from poverty and insecurity by a larger-than-life, magical happenstance. Ripening into adolescence under the "the magic light of the Kliegs," in short, allowed ragged Cinderellas like Lee to return to their original riches; spurred "Ugly Ducklings" like Marsh to metamorphose into beautiful creatures; and offered Little Orphan Annies, such as Eagels and Talmadge, the opportunity to live a life of luxury and love their humble origins otherwise denied them. After all, like the life of fictional Cinderella, the careers of these young actresses also underwent a vital transformation from anonymous menial workers to affluent belles of the ball at the cusp of adulthood. Mass-marketed as figures of magical transformation, girl stars thus led a fairylike life of romance and adventure in the wonderful land of make-believe that was early Hollywood. The only difference between both narratives, however, is that in fabricated star texts film producers and directors acted as a girl's fairy godfather, while the institutionalized film industry stood as the magical power enabling the actresses' life-altering, rags-to-riches metamorphoses.

In sum, young actresses' star texts functioned as stories of multifarious transformation: of class ascendance paralleling a girl's biological evolution from childish larva to ladylike butterfly; and of adolescence marking the threshold to an enchanted life of economical affluence, physical perfection, and romantic completion as embodied by the real-life European princesses then gracing the stories in America's popular newspapers. In fact, the press drew that parallel often. Articles in fan and trade magazines recurrently referred to young female stars as "princesses" and "queens," and equated their mass popularity, lavish lifestyle, coiffed beauty, and professional status with that of blue-blooded royalty. In 1914, *The Day Book* claimed that the Thanhouser studio "created the Princess films especially for Miss [Muriel] Ostriche," a fifteen-year-old actress "whose girlish beauty and peculiar talents inspired the title of Princess."[68] The following year, *Motion Picture*

*Magazine* announced that Billie Burke's "highest salary ever paid to a Motion Picture artist" made her equitable to a veritable "queen."[69] Two years later, the same magazine introduced twenty-something Beverly Bayne as "Princess Beverly of Metro."[70] In 1916, *Picture Progress* crowned the most well-paid actress in motion pictures, Mary Pickford, as "the little blonde-haired Princess of Photoplays,"[71] while in 1918, *Motion Picture Magazine* praised Norma Talmadge for achieving "phenomenal success with her own company" and described "the dainty and wise little woman" as a "peerless queen."[72]

Although America lacked monarchic bloodlines or princely fountainheads, the plethora of articles published in the popular press proves that American audiences followed with fascination the activities of European royals. The edification of a film industry built on an aloof pantheon of stars fostered a unique opportunity to manufacture a mythology of superior creatures supposedly chosen not by lineage but by innate talent. This pervasive mythologizing of film actors as professional deities—exclusive laborers organized in aristocratic hierarchies—participated in a larger cultural shift toward what historian Warren Susman diagnosed as the early-twentieth-century "cult of personality."[73] Endowed with regal characteristics—such as good looks, determination, and charisma—but also equipped with edifying biographies of economical struggle, class metamorphoses, and world conquest, film personalities, by the mid-1910s, had their manufactured texts serve as testimonies to an individual's superhuman abilities. These texts also served as collective lessons to the transformative power of perseverance and ambition, characteristics that always undergirded the protean narrative of a self-reliant and self-made young civilization such as America.

Furthermore, American cinema's eager absorption of aristocratic titles and hierarchies, as well as the highly publicized myth of the rags-to-riches screen queen, participated in a cultural moment that historians Nan Enstad and Kathy Peiss have noted spoke to the growing influx of young girls joining the urban workforce. As a result of increased paid labor, a higher number of underage females now enjoyed economical independence and personal leisure time without being prematurely impaired by the constraints of wifehood, housekeeping, and maternity. This change in female lifestyle significantly altered movie-going constituency. Film scholars Miriam Hansen and Shelley Stamp have influentially remarked that, by the mid-1910s, women and teenage girls emerged as important movie patrons, visible to film producers and exhibitors who increasingly attempted to lure working females' patronage with beauty competitions, discounted admission prices, star-endorsed cosmetics, and glossy giveaways. By the late 1910s, Goldwyn Productions' ads addressed working girls directly, promising them escapist respite "whenever you are tired of yourself and your work-a-day life—when you wish to be whisked away to other worlds—go to a Goldwyn picture. Gone are your troubles. You are the heroine—you can lead a thousand lives. [...] Tonight the daughter of an earl—tomorrow you marry a cowboy."[74] Dreamful, romantic, remarkably eager and able to escape into make-believe "worlds," Goldwyn's imagined target-consumer shared uncanny resemblances with G. Stanley Hall's teenage girl.

Films starring mythologized young actresses in roles that broached female transformation and romantic awakening (such as Cinderella, "the daughter of an earl," or the bride of "a cowboy") thus directly spoke to a female demographic originating from diverse backgrounds. This complex female audience included middle-class schoolgirls—whose dreams of stardom reflected a personal desire for peer admiration, social recognition, and self-beautification—as well as Goldwyn's targeted wage-earning girl who, "tired of [her] work-a-day life," sat in the theater dreaming of film stardom as the ultimate panacea to all her day-to-day economical struggles and unfulfilled romantic fantasies.[75]

The trade and popular presses often captured the subtle nuances differentiating these two groups of girls' affective investment in movie fandom. We find valuable insight into working girls' dreams of film glory in a nationwide competition. From October 1915 until December 1916, one of the leading film fan magazines, *Photoplay*, and the recently developed "photoplay maker" World Film Corporation decided to capitalize on female adolescents' longing for stardom by organizing the "'Beauty and Brains' Contest." This nationwide competition promised to send "half a score of American Girls to become moving picture stars." All the female readers had to do was mail "a profile picture and a full face study," as well as a "letter of not more than 150 words stating: 'Why I would like to be a photoplay actress.'"[76] Although open to girls of all professional and personal backgrounds, I suggest that the "'Beauty and Brains' Contest" tapped into dreams of social ascendance and economical improvement intrinsically linked with the rise of a class of working girls.

Published monthly starting in December 1915, the 150-word autobiographical narratives submitted by the participants suggest that fan girls rooted their aspirations for stardom in a quest for more lucrative employment and rewarding class status: "One girl wrote that she is training to become a nurse 'but if successful in this contest it will be 'Goodnight Nurse.' [...] One girl who has been 'everything [...] from typist to drawing room dilettante; from kitchen to office and store; from underling to boss, [...] now wants to be a camera queen."[77]

In addition, the competition addressed fan girls' main fear about stardom: that the lack of stage experience would minimize their chances of succeeding in the motion picture business. In December, an ad compared the hopeful movie-struck fans to "unskilled young women leaping into stellar roles [such as ...] Mae Marsh,

Anita Stewart, Mabel Normand, [...], and many other film stars" also in their teens when they gained film fame.[78] A July editorial introduced the eleven winners as "daughters of destiny [...] forecast[ing] the new type of player: the native player, the player whose first and only study is the shadow stage, and who brings to it no prejudices of the theatre."[79] By presenting these examples of inexperienced girls' rise to stardom, *Photoplay* invited female contestants to identify with such manufactured narratives of rags-to-riches transformation underpinning most actresses' circulated texts. In fact, such comparative rhetoric implicitly promised that by simply entering the contest, any anonymous fan girl regardless of her class standing could suddenly become "a notable actress of extraordinary individuality and powers."[80]

Although eligible to girls of all walks of life, this promotion of instantaneous female stardom spoke most directly to working girls. In fact, the magazine maintained that, similar to many of their fans, stars like Normand or Marsh had once struggled in menial jobs but thanks to being "discovered," "today are enjoying fame and fortune in the profession."[81] In other words, most of rags-to-riches star texts suggested that, through overnight film stardom, working girls could instantly shed their wage-earning struggles and enter a luxurious lifestyle marked by aggrandized self-worth, personal comfort, and magnified social respect.

Nonetheless, cinema's fantasy of transformative self-betterment equally resonated with middle-class girls. In an attempt to classify the effects of movie watching in younger audiences, in the late 1920s university sociologist Herbert Blumer conducted a survey of almost two thousand high school and college-level students across the country. This ambitious research, supported by the Payne Fund and commissioned by the Motion Picture Research Council, resulted in a book titled *Movies and Conduct* (1933). Within its pages we find a repository of girls' first-person accounts describing their adolescent engagement with motion pictures. These testimonies are accompanied by the interviewee's age, ethnicity, and educational standing. Positioned as confessional reminiscences, the autobiographical reports shed some light on how middle-class American schoolgirls, unencumbered by working pressures, internalized the myth of female stardom. Consistently, the girls regarded the late 1910s/early 1920s as the formative time in their lives when movies impacted them the most. A majority of girls confessed to having been drawn to young actresses, and that such admiration often took the form of imitation. A "white, high-school senior," admitted that after

> each movie, I think there is a great tendency to try to act like the girl you have just seen. Clara Bow has been my ideal girl, and I have tried to imitate some of her mannerisms. The way she wears her hair, [...] how she rolls her eyes, [...] and all her little actions. I have learnt from the movies how to be a flirt, and I have found out that at parties and elsewhere the coquette is the one who enjoys herself the most.[82]

In the same vein, a "Female, 17, white, high-school junior" linked her imitative fan behavior to the "girls in the movies." The high-schooler confessed that she only copied the female stars because they "were always beautiful and lady-like and so I tried to be too." [83] A twenty-year-old "college sophomore" concurred, claiming that "one learns from the movies something in the best ways of portraying one's charms," the reason she constantly mimicked actresses' "graceful" posture and "good appearance."[84]

Curiously, by the late 1920s schoolgirls still elected the girlish Pickford of 1910s fairy tales as their favorite star and role model. A "Female, 19, Jewish, white, college sophomore" spoke of watching *The Poor Little Rich Girl* (1918) "three times, and as a result let my hair grow and put it up in rags every night [... and] became an ardent Mary Pickford fan."[85] Another nineteen-year-old Jewish girl explained that she had learned "the difference clothes may make in appearance" by seeing Mary Pickford in *Daddy Long-Legs* (1919) "parade for five scenes, barelegged, in dark brown cast-offs, pig-tailed, and freckle-faced."[86] Finally, a "Female, 20, white, college sophomore" selected fairy tales starring Pickford and Clark as her preferred genre, remarking that after seeing

> "'Pollyanna,' 'Mrs Wiggs of the Cabbage Patch,' and others [I] acted just as they [the film heroines] had done. I wanted mom to cut my hair and curl it as Pollyanna's was. I even wanted to be struck by an automobile so that I could enjoy the experiences of being a heroine like Pollyanna."[87]

In short, grounding their imitative relation with girlish actresses in a desire for social refinement, self-betterment, and public recognition, on the one hand Blumer's schoolgirls articulated a productive rapport with female stars that prioritized amusement, peer accolades, personal grooming, and an enhanced taste level. Working girls' testimonies, on the other hand, tended to equate movie stardom with professional advancement and economical improvement.

Regardless of fan girls' different backgrounds, however, in the end discourses on female stardom tapped into the ubiquitous American dream of miraculous metamorphosis that had for so long underscored the country's national identity as an inclusive safe haven, the mythical land of opportunities where hard-working migrants and free-thinking immigrants strove to become their most optimal selves. Similarly, the message channeled through many of the young actresses' star texts suggested that any girl—regardless of her class, experience, or personal background—could be magically made anew, ultimately transformed into someone better: from Jane Doe into "Miss Movie," the queen of filmdom heights. Not coincidentally, female stars—like real-life princesses turned queens—usually shed their birth name once they reached celebrity status. In such a manner Gladys Smith became the "Princess of Photoplays," Mary Pickford; Juliet Shelby, "the fairy of filmdom," Mary Miles Minter; and little Augusta Appel, the Cinderella-ish Lila Lee.

## Conclusions

The emergence of a movie star system focused on the promotion of deified "picture personalities" coincided with a renewed interest in mythologized female figures, either fictional fairies or real-life princesses. Such intersection allowed an inchoate "princess culture" to transcend the localized constraints of the page and the stage, taking over America's collective imagination via mass-marketed cinema. As a reflex of such widespread cultural proclivity, a burgeoning film industry produced girl stars—young-looking, curly-haired, and sweet-mannered performers—whose fabricated biographies repeated legible narratives of rags-to-riches transformation that mirrored the tales of popular fairy tale heroines. As a way to reinforce a homogeneous cohesion between a player's lived identity and her body of work, these girl stars only played virginal heroines on the cusp of adulthood who either underwent magical metamorphoses or miraculously improved in social standing, often through matrimonial completion or a third party's fantastic intervention.

Further, these altered biographies and screen characterizations targeted a specific female demographic, imagined by press agents and magazine writers, as young, dreamful, and at times also wage earning. Although it is easy to suppose that mass-produced representations of girls as star-struck fans and fairy tale stars created an understanding of girlhood as derivative and superficial, girls' responses to the star system's fabricated discourse on female stardom suggest otherwise. By utilizing the new film fan magazines as a public venue where they explored their intimate dreams of class ascension and self-betterment; by deriving pleasure from usurping the fairy tale identities portrayed on stage and on screen; by re-appropriating actresses' movie characters as productive role models; and finally, by participating in the drafting of their own star texts, fan girls and girl stars were far from passive instruments of a new film culture. Their agency at times may have been obscured by the saccharine connotations associated with the figures of diminutive fairies and dispossessed princesses, as well as with the economical goals of a male-dominated movie industry. However, girls' agency—in the shape of female fans' assiduous patronage and passionate self-identification, and of female stars' professional acumen and film labor—helped to enable that collapse between audiences' fascination with adolescent girlhood, fairy princesses, and the emergence of an institutionalized motion picture world, markers that so crucially influenced American culture in the 1910s.

## Endnotes

1. Shorey, Jerome. 1918. "Do You Believe in Fairies?" *Photoplay* (September): 47, italics mine.
2. *Philadelphia Times*. 1917. "Varied Femininity in New Photoplays." (April 24).
3. *The New York Dramatic Mirror*. 1916. "The Stellar Doll." (July): 13.
4. Shorey, "Do You Believe in Fairies?" 47.
5. "Thelma." 1922. Audrey Chamberlin Scrapbook Collection, Vol. 45: 100. Margaret Herrick Library, Academy of Motion Picture Arts and Sciences Los Angeles.
6. Hall, G. Stanley. 1911. "The Budding Girl." In *Educational Problems*, Vol. 2. New York: D. Appleton Co.: 1–2.
7. Hall, G. Stanley. 1911. *Educational Problems*, Vol. 1. New York: D. Appleton Co.: 39, 363.
8. Shorey, Jerome. 1917. "Princess of the Dark." *Photoplay* (April): 132.
9. See: Hansen, Miriam. 1994. *Babel and Babylon: Spectatorship in American Silent Film*. Cambridge, MA: Harvard University Press; and Stamp, Shelley. 2000. *Movie-Struck Girls: Women and Motion Picture Culture after the Nickelodeon*. Princeton, NJ: Princeton University Press.
10. See: Enstad, Nan. 1999. *Ladies of Labor, Girls of Adventure: Working Women, Popular Culture, and Labor Politics at the Turn of the Twentieth Century*. New York: Columbia University Press; and Peiss, Kathy. 1986. *Cheap Amusements: Working Women and Leisure in Turn-of-the-Century New York*. Philadelphia: Temple University Press.
11. For more information on early-twentieth-century visual culture's intersection with means of mechanical reproduction, see: Higonnet, Anne. 1990. "Feminine Visual Culture in the Age of Mechanical Reproduction." In *Berthe Moriset's Images of Women*. New York: Harper & Row; Chaney, Leo, and Vanessa R. Schwartz. 1995. Eds. *Cinema and the Invention of Modern Life*. Berkeley: University of California Press; Garvey, Ellen Gruber. 1996. *The Adman in the Parlor: Magazines and the Gendering of Consumer Culture, 1880s to 1910s*. New York: Oxford University Press; and Singer, Ben. 2001. *Melodrama and Modernity: Early Sensational Cinema and Its Contexts*. New York: Columbia University Press.
12. Stanley Hall seminally described "the budding girl" as "no longer a little girl, but by no means yet a young woman, nor is she a cross between or a mixture of the two, but a something quite unique and apart." "The Budding Girl," 1.
13. See: deCordova, Richard. 1990. *Picture Personalities: The Emergence of the Star System in America*. Urbana: University of Illinois Press.
14. Historian Beverly Gordon argues that in late-nineteenth-century Anglo-American culture, "'fairyland' functioned as a code word, implying something appealing and magically transformed. "[… Everyday] girls were particularly encouraged to cultivate the sentimental fairytale ideal." Gordon, Beverly. 2006. *The Saturated World: Aesthetic Meaning, Intimate Objects, Women's Lives, 1890–1940*. Knoxville: University of Tennessee Press: 40–41.
15. Hall, "The Budding Girl," 1.
16. Other popular fairy anthologies included Andrew Lang's *Fairy Books of Many Colors*, a series of twelve collections of fairy tales published between 1889 and 1910, and illustrated by renowned artists H. J. Ford and Lancelot Speed. In 1910 alone, French-born Edmund Dulac illustrated two popular British anthologies focused on young fairy princesses: Mrs. Rodolph Stawell's *Fairies I Have Met* and *The Sleeping Beauty and Other Fairy Tales*.

17. Meaningfully, all these texts would be turned into motion pictures throughout the 1910s.
18. Smith, Fred J. 1913. "Have You a Little Fairy in Your Play?" *The New York Dramatic Mirror.* (March 12): 18. The slogan was popularized by Ivory Soap.
19. For more information on the generic specificity of fairy tales, see the foundational works by Frye, Northrop. 1957. *Anatomy of Criticism; Four Essays.* Princeton, NJ: Princeton University Press; and Todorov, Tzvetan. 1975. *The Fantastic: A Structural Approach to a Literary Genre.* Ithaca, NY: Cornell University Press.
20. *The New York Times.* 1916. "Children Act 'Snow White.'" (December 28): 9.
21. *The San Francisco Chronicle.* 1917. " 'Snow White' Is Scoring Success." (February 18): 24.
22. Davies, Mary Carolyn. 1915. "The Gift of Forgetfulness," *Motion Picture Magazine* (November): 93.
23. Smith. 1913. "Have You a Little Fairy in Your Play?," 18.
24. Peterson, Elizabeth. 1915. "Discovered—The 'Homey' Girl." *Motion Picture Classic* (March): 33.
25. *The Day Book* 1913. "Pretty Princess Must Give Up Love to Bring Royal House Together." (February 22): Image 27.
26. *The Day Book.* 1916. "Danish Princess May Wed Prince of Wales—She's War Nurse Now." (May 05): Image 31.
27. *The Day Book.* 1915. "No 'War-Brides' in Royal Family, No Husbands for Royal Ladies." (March 01): Image 21.
28. *The Salt Lake Tribune.* 1912. "A Royal Heartbreaker." (May 26): Image 41; and *The Salt Lake Tribune.* 1912. "No Princess Scorned Me—Now Let Me Love." (September 15): Image 33.
29. *The Day Book.* 1917. "Newest Photographs of Europe's Most Beautiful Royal Family." (March 16): Image 23.
30. *The New York Tribune* "Fairy Play by Rumania Queen Has Brilliant Opening in Paris." 1920. (August 22): 12.
31. *Photoplay.* 1917. (July): 159; Hamilton, Laurel S. 1916. "He Queered Himself," *Motion Picture Magazine* (April): 85; *The Washington Post.* 1917. "The Cousins' Letters." (April 29).
32. "The Cousins' Letters." 1917.
33. *The Washington Post.* 1917. "The Cousins' Letters." (January 28).
34. *The Day Book.* 1912. "May Get Palaces Rather Than Footlights." (October 22): Image 13.
35. *The Day Book.* 1914. "Nation-Wide Hunt For Princess Ends." (April 04).
36. *New York Tribune.* 1920. "Fairy Play By Rumania Queen":12.
37. *Cinderella. Exhibitor's Herald* (1914).
38. Smith. 1913. "Have You a Little Fairy in Your Play?" 18.
39. Pickford fully expresses her distaste for the film rendition of *A Good Little Devil* in her autobiography. Pickford, Mary. *Sunshine and Shadow.* 1955. New York: Doubleday and Co.
40. Interestingly, in 1916, fan magazine *Picture Progress* noted that by playing Cinderella's inner life so effectively, "Mary Pickford has perhaps proved a different theory about dreaming than usual, for it is her acting of dreams and not the dreaming that has made many things come true [...] (including the biggest salary ever paid to a girl)." *Picture Progress.* 1916. (August): 72.

41. *Motion Picture News*. 1917. "Cleveland to Judge Two 'Snow Whites.'" (January 6): 103.
42. "Snow White Press Book." 1916. (December 22). Washington DC: Library of Congress.
43. In fact, Elsie Albert co-wrote, co-directed, and played more fairy princess roles in her short film career (1910–1917) than many popular young actresses. From 1913 to 1914 alone, she starred in *The Sleeping Beauty*, *Beauty in the Beast*, *Golden Locks and The Three Bears*, as well as *For The Heart of a Princess*, *Such a Princess*, and *The Love of Princess Yolande*, all fairy tale shorts produced by Rex/Universal and directed by her husband, Harry C. Matthews.
44. Gunning, Tom. 1990. "The Cinema of Attractions: Early Films, Its Spectator and the Avant-Garde." In *Early Cinema: Space, Frame, Narrative*. Eds. Thomas Elsaesser and Adam Baker. London: British Film Institute: 56–61.
45. Milne, Peter. 1915. "Cinderella." *Motion Picture News* (January 9).
46. *The Morning Telegraph*. 1916. "Realism Marks Picture." (December 24).
47. Graves, George W. 1917. "Snow White." *Motography* (January 13): 97.
48. Tinee, Mae. 1917. "Please Come with Us to Fairyland!" *Chicago Daily Tribun*e (January 9): 14, italics mine.
49. Desch, Frank H. 1919. "Cinderella." *New York Tribune* (Match 30): 5.
50. "Tess of the Storm Country." Audrey Chamberlin Scrapbook Collection. Margaret Herrick Library, Academy of Motion Picture Arts and Sciences, Los Angeles.
51. Smith. 1913. "Have You a Little Fairy In Your Play?," 18.
52. Legend has it that Clark's film performance would also become the blueprint for Walt Disney's famous animated princess depicted in *Snow White and the Seven Dwarfs* (1937). For more information on Clark's Snow White and Disney's movie, see: Kaufman, J. B. 2012. *The Fairest One of All: The Making of Walt Disney's Snow White and the Seven Dwarfs*. San Francisco: Walt Disney Family Foundation Press.
53. Johnson, Julian. 1918. "The Shadow Stage." *Photoplay* (December): 67.
54. For more information on the manufactured elision between players' everyday and screen persona, see: deCordova, Richard. 1990. *Picture Personalities*.
55. Murdock, Julia. 1913. "Julia Murdock's Gossip." *The Washington Times* (June 13): 8.
56. *The Tattler*. 1919. "The Truth about Mary Pickford." (June): 10.
57. *Photoplay*. 1918."Lila Lee—and Truthful Publicity." (October): 75.
58. Ibid.
59. Bartlett, Randolph. 1917. "There Were Two Little Girls Named Mary." *Photoplay* (February): 38.
60. Shorey. 1918. "Do You Believe In Fairies?," 47.
61. Drake, Annie Grace. 1916. "Mary Miles Minter, The Fairy of Filmdom." *Motion Picture Magazine* (May): 140, 143.
62. Murdock. 1913. "Julia Murdock's Gossip," 8.
63. Peltret, Elizabeth. 1917. "The Girl Outside." *Photoplay* (July): 141.
64. Kingsley, Grace. 1917. "Extra Girls Who Became Stars." *Photoplay* (April): 68.
65. This is true of all three girls. Pickford had a younger sister, Lottie, as well as a brother, Jack, who achieved limited success on the screen; Marsh supposedly was introduced to Griffith through her older sister, "Love" Marsh; and Talmadge's younger sister, Constance, also became a well-known actress in the late 1910s/mid-1920s.

66. Doherty, Edward. 1930. *The Rain Girl: The Tragic Story of Jeanne Eagels*. Philadelphia: Macrae & Smith Co.: 87.
67. Doherty. *The Rain Girl*, 86.
68. *The Day Book*. 1914. "Who's Who on the Films." (December 10): Image 13.
69. *Motion Picture Magazine*. 1915. "Brief Biographies of Popular Players." (November): 114.
70. Johnson, Julian. 1917. "Our Screen Stars and Their Stars." *Motion Picture Magazine* (January): 93.
71. *Picture Progress*. 1916. (August): 72.
72. *Motion Picture Magazine*. 1918. (August): 51.
73. According to Susman, the twentieth-century concept of "personality" came to substitute that of nineteenth-century "character" as the leading distinguishing feature in the social arena. Susman has suggested that, while "character" intrinsically depended on personal sacrifice and accomplishment, "personality" stemmed from the quick growth of a superficial media culture. Simply put, if "character [was] either good or bad; personality [was only] famous or infamous." Susman, Warren. 2003. *Culture as History: The Transformations of American Society in the Twentieth Century*. Washington, DC: Smithsonian Books: 277.
74. Goldwyn ad. 1920. *Photoplay* (June): 2.
75. As Enstad has noted, "The movie-struck fantasy was a dream of lavish recognition [... that] imaginatively combined women's workplace struggles with [...] fantasies of romance, adventure, and sudden changes in fortune that characterized working ladyhood." *Ladies of Labor*, 183–184.
76. *Photoplay*. 1915. "Beauty and Brains." (October): 47.
77. Photoplay. 1915. "Beauty and Brains." (December): 54–55.
78. Ibid. 46.
79. *Photoplay*. 1916. "Youth: An Editorial." (July): 23.
80. *Photoplay*. 1915. "Beauty and Brains." (December): 54.
81. Ibid. 55.
82. Blumer, Herbert. 1933. *Movies and Conduct*. New York: Macmillan Company: 63.
83. Ibid. 80.
84. Ibid. 45.
85. Ibid. 33.
86. Ibid. 76.
87. Ibid. 60.

CHAPTER NINE

# JAPpy: Portraits of Canadian Girls Mediating the Jewish American Princess and Identity

REBECCA STARKMAN

Growing up Jewish in Toronto, a city with a large Jewish population, I have had the Jewish American Princess (JAP)[1] stereotype as an established fixture in my social world. However, the degree to which this stereotype has mediated my own identity as a Jewish woman is unclear. A few years ago, I sat with a friend in United Bakers, a popular Jewish restaurant, where we discussed my need for a new winter coat. I was interested in the Canada Goose–brand parka,[2] which had emerged at that time as the latest JAP status symbol. We discussed the social meanings associated with this item of clothing, forcing me to consider the possibility that people would judge *me* to be a JAP if I wore this coat. How would it make me feel to be considered a JAP? Would wearing a Canada Goose parka be enough to actually *make* me a JAP? Was the possibility of being labeled a JAP enough to deter me from buying this coat altogether? In sum, just how does the JAP stereotype mediate my identities? This dilemma spurred me to explore the role of the sociocultural stereotype of the JAP in the lives of Jewish girls and women.

The Jewish American Princess (JAP) is a complex and emotionally loaded stereotype. Emerging out of the quickly rising Jewish middle class in post–World War II America, the JAP stereotype represents the epitome of an overindulged and materialistic Jewish girl. As a term employed by both Jews and non-Jews over the past sixty years, the *American* Jewish princess also circulates in Canada. Canadian and American Jewish communities are very similar in their histories of immigration and their experiences as minority groups within a dominant Christian culture. My research, however, examines the complex social reality of the JAP for *Canadian* Jewish girls alone.

The following discussion presents qualitative research conducted with Jewish high school–age girls in Toronto, Canada, exploring the role that the JAP stereotype plays in Jewish girls' identity negotiations. In this chapter I argue that individual interpretations of the JAP stereotype influence individual performances of identity. In this way, the JAP stereotype mediates identity by serving as a reference point for identity performance.

My analysis is informed by Third Wave feminist thought and sociocultural approaches to identity, and uses Daniel Yon's (2000) research metaphor of the *portrait* as the mode of analysis. The first section of this chapter outlines the historical evolution of the JAP stereotype and the theoretical tools used to analyze the data. I then focus on portraits of three participants, Lily, Lauren, and Leah, in order to illustrate the complex ways in which the JAP stereotype mediates identity.

## The Evolution of the Jewish American Princess Stereotype

According to historians, folklorists, and other scholars, the stereotype of the Jewish American Princess, in its classic construction, depicts a Jewish woman as sexually frigid, assertive, self-centred, and above all else, excessively materialistic—the ultimate consumer (Byers 2009; Dundes 1985; Newhouse 2005; Prell 2003). In response to the offensive nature of the JAP label, the phenomenon of JAP-baiting on college campuses across the United States,[3] and the popularity the stereotype had reached by the mid-1970s (Prell 1998), Jewish feminists launched an aggressive deconstruction of the term, leading to its decline in the early 1990s (Beck 1992).

The Jewish feminist deconstruction of the JAP stereotype establishes the term as conclusively negative, and presents two perspectives from which to interpret the purpose and the perpetuation of the JAP stereotype. The first is to see the JAP within the context of the historical persecution of the Jewish people, wherein the JAP stereotype can be understood as a modern form of anti-Semitism (Appel 2008; Beck 1992; Klagsbrun 1987). While anti-Semitism began to be seen as politically incorrect by some in North America after the Holocaust, negative perceptions of Jews found new, less overt forms of expression. The label JAP represents one of the key mechanisms of this subtler form of anti-Semitism. Looking at the specific words that constitute the stereotype, *American* and *Princess* can be equally negative or positive, depending on the context. It is only the modifier *Jewish* "that changes the princess from magically or potentially spoiled to money grubbing, power hungry, and manipulative … [and] 'American' to mean obsessed by upward mobility and ostentatious displays of (newfound) wealth" (Appel 2008, 47). Jewish feminist scholars have argued that the JAP label can also be understood to reflect sexist and misogynist views for the way it degrades and specifically vilifies women and girls (Prell 2003; Medjuck 1988; Schnur 1987). In practice, these scholars maintain that the "JAP picks up on the combined negative attitudes toward Jews and women" (Schwalb and Sedlacek 1989, 11).

After a hiatus in the 1990s, the JAP stereotype has reemerged in North American popular culture—from movies to TV shows and novels to print articles[4]—and reappeared among Canadian and American youth. According to Rabbi Julia Appel (2008, 47), the meanings of the JAP label no longer neatly correspond to those first identified by feminist scholars. Unlike the scholarship on the JAP phenomenon written by Second Wave feminists from the 1970s and 1980s, the recent literature by young Jewish writers (Appel 2008; Belzer 2001; Newhouse 2005; Stone 2005) explores their negotiation with the stereotype. Their new millennial writings represent a significant shift in the understandings and usages of the stereotype.

## Third Wave Feminism and the Sociocultural Approach to Identity

Tenets of Third Wave[5] feminist thought constitute the overarching theoretical perspective guiding this research. My work follows feminist scholars who begin their social analysis with the recognition that women and girls experience injustices on account of their gender (LeGates 2001). Unlike First and Second Wave feminist theory, Third Wave understandings take a more individualized approach to the interpretation and the expression of feminist values and goals (Heywood and Drake 1997). Third Wave feminism, moreover, conceptualizes identity and experience as fluid, evolving, multiple, layered, complex, and contradictory. Approaching the study of the JAP stereotype using a theoretical perspective that intentionally affords flexible understandings of identity and experience, and that serves to amplify multiple girls' voices,[6] encourages rich interpretations of this label.

Complementing the Third Wave feminist framework, this work is also informed by a sociocultural approach to understanding identity as contextually constructed and performed. Penuel and Wertsch (1995) and Brown and Tappan (2008) reject the notion that an essential self serves as the basis for identity construction, positing instead that identity is constructed by the social context that links the social and the individual. Extending sociologist Lev Vygotsky's original premise that identity does not stem from an essential self, Brown and Tappan (2008) look to the social and cultural environment for concepts that mediate an individual's performance of identity. This sociocultural approach to identity recognizes an irreducible and productive tension between the individual and her social context. It creates the conceptual space for individuals to appropriate, transform, and resist the cultural concepts available to them. The interplay between the individual and the social helps to illuminate the place of social, historical, and cultural processes in the formation and transformation of individual identities.

Sociocultural understandings of identity provide an entry point for exploring how cultural concepts (such as words, stereotypes, jokes, images, and media texts) mediate identity. Within this framework I approach the JAP stereotype as a cultural concept. Penuel and Wertsch (1995) and Tappan (2005) argue that cultural concepts can serve as both an "empowering" and a "constraining" means for identity formation. "Empowering tools" provide individuals with an appealing set of ideas and behaviours to embody. "Constraining tools" limit the range of roles available to individuals in their identity performances. In these ways, the JAP stereotype functions as a cultural concept that serves both empowering and constraining roles in my participants' identity performances.

In keeping with the emphasis on identity set out in the theoretical framework, I have also employed research methodology designed to enhance the study of identity. This chapter draws on interview data from my 2010 qualitative study exploring how Canadian Jewish girls experience and understand the JAP stereotype. I carried out in-depth, semi-structured interviews with six Jewish girls attending Jewish high schools in Toronto in order to explore the ways that Jewish girls negotiate their self-understandings and mediate their identity performances in relation to the JAP stereotype. I employ Daniel Yon's (2000) *portrait* as the method of data analysis. Utilized as a research metaphor, the portrait represents a "snapshot" designed "to capture a moment" in time or a "particular pose" of an individual (Yon 2000, 144). Following Yon's (2000) approach, I reconstituted the interviews into individual portraits of each girl's identity-based experience. These portraits reveal the ways in which the JAP stereotype mediates aspects of my participants' identity negotiations.

The *portrait* is an appropriate metaphor for use here because it allows for the analysis of data in a way that reflects the complex and intersectional nature of identity. In this chapter, I argue that the JAP stereotype mediates identities by functioning as a reference point in identity performances. *Portrait* analyses of my interviews demonstrate how participants positioned their identity performances with reference to the JAP stereotype. Each of my six interview participants presented a unique understanding of the JAP stereotype, resulting in correspondingly nuanced identity-based portraits. No two participants discussed the JAP in the same way, leading me to analyze their narratives as distinct entities. I have selected the three portraits that are the focus of this chapter because they present the broadest range of identity positions vis-à-vis the JAP stereotype, including affiliations with, rejections of, and ambivalence about components of the JAP stereotype. While these three portraits make up only half of the JAP-based identity narratives garnered through my research, they illustrate the ways that my participants leveraged their understandings of the JAP stereotype in order to accomplish their identity goals.

## JAPpy Portraits

Before analyzing the portraits of JAP-related identity, it is useful to summarize the JAP stereotype as my participants presented it. When asked individually to describe the attitudes and behaviours of a JAP, my participants mentioned many of the same traits, but established different hierarchies of importance for these characteristics. My participants appeared to be in agreement that the JAP exclusively wears brand-name clothing and accessories, is excessively materialistic, is self-centred, and *girly*. As outlined by Lily, "JAPs are all about what labels they're wearing," indicating that donning specific designer labels is a key defining feature of the JAP stereotype. Furthermore, following Spencer (1989), I also characterize JAP style as constituting a uniform. Spencer's (1989, 333) now 20-year-old description of a JAP as a girl who wears "an oversized sweater or sweatshirt; … tight, dark stirrup pants; high-top Reebok sneakers; … [and] designer bags and wallets" has strong similarities to my participant Barbie's description that JAPs "wear a Free City[7] sweatshirt, with leggings and like your UGGs[8] folded over." The differences between the two descriptions illustrate that JAP style reflects the time and place, while always relying on entrenched style components, resulting in the perception of a JAP uniform.

In terms of attitude, my participants described the JAP as excessively materialistic, as self-centred, and as *girly*. They defined the JAP's excessive materialism by her rampant consumerism. Lauren further specified that she "would never say that because someone has lots of money therefore they are a JAP," but instead found an attitude of entitlement and the tendency to "flaunt" one's material possessions to indicate a JAPpy attitude. My participants also described the JAP as self-centred, best summarized by Emma in saying that "the JAP thinks 'I am the most important thing in my world, and everything revolves around me.'" Finally, the JAP is seen as a "girly-girl" who expresses a "more feminine side." Leora expanded the meaning of "girly" to include an interest in feminine activities like clothing and makeup. Emphasizing designer clothing and accessories coupled with materialistic, self-centred, and girly attitudes make up the key components of the JAP stereotype.

## Lily: 'Part JAPpy': Inherent and Optional Identity

This portrait depicts how for Lily, constructing a JAP-related identity is an inherent aspect of being a Jewish girl in Toronto today, while also demonstrating how the stereotype is one that must be actively managed when outside of the Jewish community. Lily was a student in grade 12 at the Jewish Academy (JA) at the time of our interview. The JA is a co-educational Jewish secondary school serving families of all Jewish denominations in the Toronto area. During our conversation Lily spoke frankly about her experiences "within" the Jewish community. Lily described herself as frequenting synagogue regularly and attending Jewish day school since she was little. These spaces seem to have had significant influences on her identity as a young Jewish woman and her perceptions of the JAP stereotype.

Lily explained that her parents bought her all of the material goods she desired. She listed popular electronics, clothing, and footwear as the most coveted items. This pattern of material consumption is the norm for her peer group. For this reason, Lily characterized herself as "a little JAPpy." She has "JAPpy parts," but is not a "full-blown JAP." The aspects of her identity that Lily identified as JAPpy are derived from her consumption of status-laden material goods. Lily attributed her position as a consumption-based JAP as "just the nature of things," referring to her upbringing and community—of "how [she's] grown up and where [she] goes to school, and what [she] does in [her] spare time that makes [her] some form of a JAP." Lily saw JAPpyness as inevitable and intrinsic to membership in the Toronto Jewish community. "I don't really see it as anything bad or good, the way I've been brought up it was *bound* to happen," she explained, referring to her regular synagogue attendance and studies at Jewish day schools. She framed her JAPpy side as something she "could not have changed." Lily's attribution of her JAPpy traits as a by-product of Toronto's Jewish culture seems to absolve her from taking any responsibility for this persona.

At the same time, Lily described actively mediating her performance of being a Jewish girl when outside the Jewish community. While embracing particular status symbols around other Jews, Lily downplayed these markers when among non-Jews for fear of being labeled a JAP. While early in the interview Lily asserted that she did not actively distance herself from the JAP stereotype, her position changed as she realized through our conversation the many ways she did modify her behaviour daily to downplay her JAPpyness. In a public space like the Toronto subway system, Lily worried about the negative associations that stemmed from carrying particular status symbols. She feared that in public, strangers would assume that all Jewish girls who sported status symbols are JAPpy. She feared the generalization of all Jewish girls as rich, spoiled, and entitled. Consequently, Lily moderated her use of a Coach-brand purse[9] when she "purposefully picked out a hidden one, the one without the logos all flashing." She also purchased fake UGG boots instead of real ones. And to avoid strangers from thinking, "Oh, that girl is a little bratty, JAPpy girl on her Blackberry,"[10] she hid her cellphone in her bag. The longer we talked she thought of additional examples of how she avoided giving off the impression of being spoiled or JAPpy when outside the Jewish community.

Lily's reported decision to embrace JAPpyness when around Jews and to downplay it among non-Jews provides strong evidence for Penuel and Wertsch's (1995) theory that cultural entities—like the JAP stereotype—have fluid and contextually derived meanings. The meaning of the cultural concept is largely determined by how it is understood and used in a particular situation. For Lily, in the school context where "everyone looks the same" and her fellow students appreciate the JAPpy status items, the JAP stereotype served to increase social status and belonging. In contrast, Lily believed that outside the Jewish community the JAP stereotype held negative implications for Jewish girls among gentiles who might assume that all Jewish girls own expensive goods and display them in an entitled way. This alternate understanding influenced Lily's identity performance in such a way that she mediated her presentation while in public spaces outside of her Jewish neighbourhood. She hid her cell phone, carried less conspicuous purses, and tried to avoid speech that might be construed as sounding spoiled. Lily's portrait illuminates the ways in which the meanings of the JAP stereotype are shaped by its contexts and subsequently determine the extent to which this cultural notion mediates identity.

## Lauren: 'Not a JAP!': Individuality and Identity

This portrait of JAP-related identity comments on the JAP stereotype as a symbol of social conformity, and Lauren's subsequent oppositional presentation of herself as an *individual.* Lauren was also a student in grade 12 at the JA at the time of our interview. Lauren attended a public school prior to starting at the JA for high secondary, framing her experiences with the JAP stereotype differently from those participants who attended Jewish day schools for their entire education. From our conversation, Lauren seemed very self-aware. As we discussed her experiences with the JAP stereotype, she often added reflexive commentary about her own tendencies and how she felt about them.

Before I even asked, Lauren declared that she *was not* a JAP! She added that she "would be *extremely* offended if someone called [her] a JAP, or said that [she] was a JAP … [she] feels strongly about that." From the beginning of our conversation Lauren contextualized her understanding of the JAP stereotype in terms of social conformity. She perceived the JAP as someone who is "not an individual," someone who "conforms to whatever their friends are doing, wears what they wear, and adopts the sort of language that they use." This portrait explores how, unlike Lily, Lauren constructed her identity in opposition to the JAP whom she regarded as displaying a highly undesirable trait of social conformity:

> I see myself as having individual values and I feel like if I were to classify myself as a JAP it would almost be degrading. I feel like I would be like lowering myself, like belittling my role in society to being part of a group, and not seeing myself as an individual person, but rather just seeing myself as a group of girls. And that's *not* how I see myself. Like I see myself as an individual.

Believing in the importance of being an individual, Lauren rejected the JAP stereotype for its premise that all Jewish girls dress and act in the same ways.

Lauren's negative assessment of the JAP stereotype mediated her identity in ways that were not always free of conflict. In one sartorial instance, her desire for comfort led to a collision between her belief in individuality and her disdain for conformity. Lauren recounted a story about a "JAPpy" Free City–brand sweatshirt she received from her mother as an illustration of how she sought to resolve the conflict. This was a "horrible" gift because Lauren actually *liked* the JAPpy sweatshirt because it was "really comfy." Even though she only wore the sweatshirt around the house and "didn't want to wear it to school," just wearing it at all led to "an internal dilemma." Lauren came to the conclusion, "I like this sweatshirt so I'm going to wear it. Not because everyone else is wearing it but just because I like this sweatshirt!" Then at summer camp, believing that other campers shared her belief that people should feel free to be themselves, Lauren wore the same JAPpy sweatshirt expecting it to go unnoticed. Much to her surprise, when her peers reacted she speculated that "they were thinking in their heads 'oh my god, like what a JAP, like I can't believe she's wearing that sweatshirt.'" Lauren subsequently decided not to wear the sweatshirt that identified her as a status-seeking JAP again.

During our interview, Lauren presented herself as an individual who actively opposed social conformity—and who wanted to be seen that way. For her, the JAPpy sweatshirt signified obedience to the social conformity she despised. Lauren thus constructed her identity by resisting the conventionality that threatened her non-conformist core. In this way, the JAP stereotype mediated her identity performances by positioning it in opposition to who she was. The intensity of Lauren's belief in individuality resonates with the Third Wave feminist understandings of identity as individual and contextual. At the same time, Lauren's somewhat inflexible necessity to express her individuality in this story does not reflect Third Wave feminists' willingness to accept contradictions in constructions of the self.

While Lauren described investing a great deal of energy separating herself from JAP-identified commodities, she concluded the interview by stating that "not being a JAP" was *not* part of her identity: "I wouldn't say that I am consciously making an effort not to be a JAP all the time." However surprising, given the intensity by which she described her reactions and subsequent actions to the Free City sweatshirt, her clarification reveals the limitations of a sociocultural approach to identity construction that values specific moments and contexts in which cultural tools are taken up in identity negotiations. The story about the Free City sweatshirt represents only one occasion on which Lauren reported taking up the JAP stereotype as a means through which to mediate her identity performance. At that particular time, Lauren used the JAP discourse and its representation in that context of social conformity to establish herself as an individual who chose to follow her own clothing styles. It is important to bear in mind that this is one story that she told me, and not a reflection of the totality of Lauren's engagements with the JAP stereotype. Nevertheless, within this one narrative, Lauren's active negotiations do provide evidence of her deep awareness of the JAP stereotype and how she engages with it in the construction and performance of her identity.

## Leah: Half-JAPpy: Intentionally Complex Identity

Leah was 16 and a student in grade 11 at the Mesorah Academy for Girls (MAG) at the time of our interview. MAG is an all-girls Jewish high school catering to families who affiliate with Orthodox denominations of Judaism in Toronto. Leah was talkative and often seemed older than her age. She clearly loved to read and made numerous references to classic literature during our conversation. Leah was quick to answer my questions, as if the answer was already formed in her head; she was only waiting for someone to ask her opinion on the matter.

To Leah, the Jewish American Princess was a "girly-girl" invested in beauty culture, dressing well, and behaving in particularly feminine ways. Leah considered herself a "half-JAP" because she too liked to wear designer clothes, walked and talked in *feminine* ways, and enjoyed being girly. This characterization of the girly-girl is also found in Rebecca C. Hains's (2012, 157) research on girls and Girl Power; Hains offers similar descriptions of the "girly-girl" as one who emphasizes feminine clothing and high heels, and as a girl who ultimately performs normative femininity. At the same time as labeling herself as *girly*, Leah also described herself as a "nerd" and a "smart girl." Pomerantz and Raby (2011) situate the image of the smart girl within dominant post-feminist[11] and neoliberal[12] politics and values. Within this context, the smart girl is part of a new discourse of female academic success that is built on the assumptions that feminist interventions in schools have enabled girls to succeed scholastically, and the view that girls can have it all through hard work and personal choice. The following portrait illustrates how Leah fused the JAP and the smart girl identities in ways that both challenge and reinforce seemingly antithetical constructions.

Leah described how smartness had always been her baseline for understanding herself, until her budding physical maturation forced a shift in her sense of self. Prior to grade 5, Leah considered herself to be the "the biggest nerd" with "zero JAPpyness." In grade 5 she "got boobs before everyone else," and boys started looking at her differently. Leah described having to re-work how she understood herself. Her newfound interests in fashion and beauty contributed to an emerging JAPpy sense of self. "I am girly, I like designer things, I like nice clothes, I wear high heels," explained Leah who has also found it challenging to "figure out how to balance the fact that [she is] a ginormous nerd and a little bit of a JAP." In this statement Leah pits being a nerd against being a JAP, as two opposing states. Here she sets the foundation for her critique of the socially constructed binary she experiences between smartness and JAPpyness.

Describing the process of balancing her JAP with her nerd identities, Leah demonstrates how the JAP stereotype can mediate identity as both an empowering and as a constraining tool for self-expression. Leah claimed that the nerd label reinforced her passion for reading and helped her to assert her intelligence among her peers. However, she found shortcomings in the nerd stereotype for it did not provide prescriptions for especially girly behaviour. The JAP stereotype, on the other hand, represents Leah's desire to act in a girly manner, focused on beautiful clothes and dressing up. By including JAPpyness in her self-description, the stereotype functions as an enabling cultural concept that gives Leah the framework to indulge in more feminine expressions and performances. Leah turned to the JAP stereotype in order to compensate for the gender constraints of the nerd. Doing so, Leah creatively adapted the JAP for her own identity construction purposes.

At the same time, by challenging the presumption that girly-girls cannot also be smart, Leah utilized the JAP stereotype as a tool to support her identity as a nerd: "I like making people challenge what they think. Like I hate the idea that if you're a girl, and you dress well, and you are slightly attractive, you can't be smart." As Leah presented herself in our interview, the JAP stereotype mediated performances of her intelligence. Leah's explanation illustrates how she used the stereotype of the JAP, capitalizing on the elements of that entity that present girls as unintelligent or only capable of being interested in material consumption, to confuse those around her and challenge their assumptions about who or what a "smart girl" is. In this description, she intelligently and imaginatively weaved the two discourses together into her identity as smart *and* girly. Leah defined herself as a "living contradiction," emphasizing the need she felt to highlight the assumed paradox of being both a nerd and a JAP. The JAP stereotype is a critical component in mediating Leah's identity as intentionally complex and contradictory. She reported taking up the JAP stereotype in identity construction very consciously in that she used her "JAPpyness or femininity to prove that [she] can like high heels *and* [she] can read textbooks." She "like[d] using the two of them together."

Did Leah feel that these two seemingly contradictory aspects of her identity were in conflict with each other? She presented a well-processed sense of self, alluding to having "issues" identifying herself as a JAP and a nerd at an earlier time in her life, "but not anymore." "[Now] that is a part of my identity and I am OK with that." Contextualizing her own understanding of identity, Leah explained that she could either ignore the JAPpy parts of herself, or she "could use it to [her] advantage." Depending on the situation, Leah appears to capitalize on the JAPpy aspects of her self-presentation to accomplish other goals. Leah's intentional description of herself as a "living contradiction" strongly resonates with Third Wave feminist understandings of identity. Like Lauren, Leah's desire to establish herself as an individual fits within the Third Wave feminist approach to identity as unique and varied. However, unlike Lauren who was uncomfortable with inconsistencies in how she understood herself, Leah suggests that she has no qualms about living with "different paradoxes" in how she presents herself. Leah explained that exhibiting contradictory traits in being both JAPpy and nerdy never bothered her until others challenged her, calling her "confusing." To those who challenge her, Leah responded by asking them, "What's your point?" declaring, "We are all different things." In our conversation, Leah presented herself as someone who accepts herself fully. Obviously influenced by contemporary notions of girlhood, her beliefs echo the Third Wave feminist approach to accepting identity-based contradictions, and providing space to cultivate and explore those contradictions. The confidence and self-assuredness Leah exuded to me is a model for those who feel compelled to eradicate conflicting aspects of their identity, trying to achieve a cohesive, seamless state of self-expression. Leah makes her alternative—embracing the "lived messiness" (Heywood and Drake 1997, 8) of being a girl today—seem much more appealing when she explains that "you could either ... be ashamed of being a JAP…. Or you could be like, this is a part of who I am, if you don't like it, it's *so* your problem…. Deal with it."

Within the taxonomy of girlhood, the girly-girl persona is often positioned as the standard of girlhood, from which all other performances of girlhood are differentiated (Hains 2012). From this perspective, the nerd or the smart girl can be understood as a type of girlhood that deviates from the norm, and which Leah might understandably feel the need to justify her performance of. Leah has built her identity in a way to integrate the JAP stereotype, representing the smart girl, the inherently less valuable social identity, as supported by the normative girly-girl. The ways in which the JAP stereotype serves to mediate Leah's composite identity as both JAPpy and smart illuminate her broader identity goals of performing her self-described "confusing" and contradictory female identity.

## Making Meaning

These portraits illustrate a spectrum of complex ways that the JAP stereotype mediates the identity performances of Jewish girls. According to the ways they presented themselves to me, none of my participants unequivocally identified as a Jewish American Princess. At the same time, they did indicate resemblances, to widely varying degrees, to certain elements of the stereotype. Lily wondered whether she was partly a JAP simply by virtue of her upbringing in the Jewish community. Lauren acknowledged that despite eschewing the JAP label, she liked the Free City sweatshirt, a JAP status symbol. Finally, Leah saw her feminine and girly side as easily fitting within the JAP stereotype. It is clear from these portraits that positioning oneself in relation to the JAP stereotype is not as simple as either identifying as a JAP, or not.

The JAP stereotype encompasses a wide range of behaviours and attitudes, resulting in a continuum of characteristics to which girls respond. These portraits illustrate the multiple meanings of the JAP stereotype and demonstrate how these then mediate identity performances in varied ways. The Jewish girls in this study did not take up the JAP stereotype in relation to their identities in a uniform way. Instead, as evidenced by these snapshots of JAP-related identities, they apply their own unique interpretations of the discourse in their identity expressions. This creative process highlights the interplay between the individual and the social context outlined in the sociocultural approach to identity formation. The respective uses of the stereotype both support and challenge aspects of the JAP stereotype, illustrating how a cultural concept can be transformed through identity performances.

What is especially interesting about these portraits is how they illuminate the contradictions inherent in identity. As a controversial social stereotype, the JAP elicits a wide range of emotional and intellectual responses. The portraits above reveal the often-contradictory nature of these responses. The openness with which my participants frame their varied perspectives on the JAP-related identity suggests an affinity with the Third Wave approach to identity as encompassing contradictions and ambiguity (Heywood and Drake 1997; Mann and Huffman 2005). The Third Wave feminist lens provides the necessary framework to accommodate these complex self-understandings.

Together, these three portraits of JAP-based identity contribute to our understanding of the role of consumption in determining how the JAP stereotype manifests in the social lives of these Jewish girls. Materialism and status goods are obviously related to the JAP stereotype because of the materialism attributed to the stereotype. Going further than merely referencing materialism, though, these portraits describe experiences, attitudes, and patterns of consumption that result from the presence of the JAP stereotype in individual girls' lives. Mary Douglas's (1992) analysis of consumption provides a useful framework for understanding how my participants' JAP-based identity portraits illustrate the relationship between the stereotype and materialism. Douglas (1992, 22) argues that "people use consumption to say something about themselves and about their families and their localities," and we therefore need to look at the consumption patterns of goods as symbolic or indicative of whole structures of meaning. In this way, material goods act as "rank markers" in their capacity to reveal the social positionings of the consumer (Douglas 1992, 28). Consumer goods' capacity to function as rank markers effectively drives consumption patterns as a vehicle for communicating who is a social insider versus a social outsider. That other members of a social group accept these messages illustrates how the consumption of specific goods mutually constructs the social meaning of those items. Lily, Lauren, and Leah all discussed how the purchasing of specific brand-name goods establishes one as a Jewish American Princess. They differ in their reactions to being labeled as a member of this social group. Lily and Leah presented reasons they are comfortable with consuming rank markers of the JAP social position, while Lauren firmly established herself as outside of this social position by rejecting the JAP rank markers. Either way, all three described their consumption patterns as determining where they fall in relation to the JAP stereotype. In this way, these three portraits together provide insight into the significant role that consumption plays in shaping the experience of the JAP stereotype today.

The JAP stereotype functions as a cultural concept, available to Jewish girls in their social environments as a set of ideas they can utilize in expressing aspects of their identity. To explain the uniquely individual ways my participants utilize the JAP stereotype, I examined the intersections in their experiences. Each participant stands at a unique intersection of peer, gendered, religious, and communal experience. She has crafted her own understandings of what it means to be a girl and to be Jewish. These understandings are inextricably linked to her identity as a Jewish girl. It therefore follows that her usage of the JAP stereotype as a tool to express individual identifications is necessarily distinctive as well. The portraits I present in this chapter have aimed to illustrate how Lily, Leah, and Lauren took up the JAP stereotype in individual ways, to express their truly individual experience of configurations of the gender, religion, and social influences in their lives.

In many ways, my participants exercised their individual power to resist the narrow definitions of Jewish girlhood imposed by the JAP stereotype. Through their creative interpretations of aspects of the stereotype, they are actively contributing to its evolution. The meaning of the cultural concept, here the JAP stereotype, is modified, adapted, and affected each time it is used in direct reflection of the individual who uses it and the context in which it is employed. It is in these moments of utilization that the cultural tool is shaped, where its meanings change, and its resulting power to define and order categories of being is shifted.

## Endnotes

1. In this chapter, I use the full term *Jewish American Princess,* and its acronym JAP, interchangeably. It is important to note that my participants referred to the entity almost exclusively as *JAP*.
2. The down-filled winter parkas offered by this Canadian company are available in bright colours, have real fur collars, and include posh details like fleece wrist cuffs and a wire inside the edge of the hood to shape the hood to the wearer's head. They are priced approximately between $550 and $700 CDN.
3. *JAP-baiting* is the catch-all term used to refer to acts of verbal harassment, public humiliation, and the overall targeting of young women labeled as JAPs on university campuses during the 1980s (Spencer 1989).
4. Clothing referencing the Jewish American Princess is in wide circulation. For example, in 2004 the clothing chain Urban Outfitters sold a T-shirt with the phrase "Everyone loves a Jewish girl" surrounded by dollar signs (Judkis 2012). The main character in the movie *Marci X* fits the JAP persona, along with the prevalence of JAP characters in *Barney's Version*, a 2010 comedy-drama film set in Montreal, Canada. Furthermore, the Style and Bravo networks have also joined the JAP bandwagon. The Style Network recently put out a casting call for a new show called *JAP Squad.* In June 2013, Bravo aired its new reality show, *Princesses: Long Island,* featuring six Jewish women in their late 20s. Modeled after the shows *Jersey Shore* and the *Real Housewives* series, the show follows the women through their consumption and primping-filled days in their quest to find a Jewish husband.

5. Third Wave feminist thought fits within the well-known metaphor of *waves* in feminist theory. See Mann and Huffman (2005) and LeGates (2001) for details on the feminist waves.
6. The seminal anthology *Third Wave Agenda: Being Feminist, Doing Feminism* (Heywood and Drake 1997) provides the foundation for my understanding and usage of Third Wave feminist theory.
7. Free City is a line of lounge clothing, focusing on sweatshirts and sweatpants in bright colours with bold graffiti-style graphics of birds and hearts. The sweatshirts and sweatpants are sold for an average of $150 to $300 CDN.
8. UGG is an Australian company that makes sheepskin boots lined with fur. They have a signature flat sole and wide rounded toe, and are sold for $200 to $300 CDN per pair.
9. This brand of accessories is well known for its purses that feature the label "Coach" prominently etched or appliqued on the body of the purse, often in numerous places. The handbags are sold for an average price of $300 to $500 CDN.
10. The BlackBerry is a line of *smart* phones that are sold by mobile phone carriers in Canada. As a *smart* phone, the BlackBerry is equipped to send email and browse the internet, and has its own instant messaging program called *BlackBerry Messenger* that was a popular means of social communication amongst my participants.
11. Pomerantz and Raby (2011, 549) describe post-feminism as the "popular idea that girls and women no longer need—or want for—feminist politics."
12. The authors outline neoliberal politics as emphasizing "individualization, personal choice, and the belief that structural inequities are personal problems" (Pomerantz and Raby 2011, 549).

## References

Alperin, Mimi. 1989. "JAP Jokes: Hateful Humor." *Humor, 2*(4): 412–416.

Appel, Julia. 2008. "The Princess Diaries." *Bitch, 38*: 47–51.

Baum, Charlotte, Paula Hyman, and Sonya Michel. 1975. *The Jewish Woman in America*. New York: Dial Press.

Beck, Evelyn Torton. 1990. "Therapy's Double Dilemma: Anti-Semitism and Misogyny." *Women & Therapy, 10*(4): 19–31.

Beck, Evelyn Torton. 1992. "From 'Kike to Jap': How Misogyny, Anti-Semitism, and Racism Construct the Jewish American Princess." In *Race, Class, and Gender*, ed. M. Anderson and P. H. Collins, 87–95. Belmont, CA: Wadsworth.

Belzer, Tobin. 2001. "On Being a Jewish Feminist Valley Girl." In *Yentl's Revenge,* ed. Danya Ruttenberg, 181–188. Seattle, WA: Seal Press.

Booker, Janice L. 1991. *The Jewish American Princess and Other Myths*. New York: Shapolsky.

Brown, Lyn Mikel, and Mark B. Tappan. 2008. "Fighting Like a Girl Fighting Like a Guy: Gender Identity, Ideology, and Girls at Early Adolescence." In *The Intersections of Personal and Social Identities*, ed. M. Aazmitia, M. Syed, and K. Radmacher, 47–59. San Francisco: Jossey-Bass.

Byers, Michelle. 2009. "The Pariah Princess: Agency, Representation, and Neoliberal Jewish Girlhood." *Girlhood Studies: An Interdisciplinary Journal, 2*(2): 33–54.

Chayat, Sherry. 1987. "JAP-Baiting on the College Scene." *Lilith, 17*: 6–7.

Douglas, Mary. 1992. "Why Do People Want Goods?" In *Understanding Enterprise Culture,* ed. S. H. Heap and A. Ross, 19–31. Edinburgh, Scotland: Edinburgh University Press.

Dundes, Alan. 1985. "The J.A.P. and the J.A.M. in American Jokelore." *Journal of American Folklore, 98*(390): 456–475.

Gold, Nora. 1998. "Canadian Jewish Women and Their Experiences of Sexism and Anti-Semitism: Results from Phase One of a National Study." *Selected Papers in Canadian Studies.* Occasional Paper #21.

Hains, Rebecca C. 2012. *Growing Up with Girl Power.* New York: Peter Lang.

Heywood, Leslie, and Jennifer Drake. 1997. "Introduction." In *Third Wave Agenda: Being Feminist, Doing Feminism,* ed. Leslie Heywood and Jennifer Drake, 1–20. Minneapolis: University of Minnesota Press.

Judkis, Maura. 2012. "Urban Outfitters: All Its Recent Controversies, Explained." *The Washington Post*, The Style Blog, March 29. http://www.washingtonpost.com/blogs/arts-post/post/urban-outfitters-all-its-recent-controversies-explained/2012/03/29/gIQAP2lDjS_blog.html

Klagsbrun, Francine. 1987. "JAP: The New Anti-Semitic Code Word." *Lilith, 17*: 11.

LeGates, Marlene. 2001. *In Their Time: A History of Feminism in Western Society.* New York: Routledge.

Mann, S. A., and D. J. Huffman. 2005. "The Decentering of Second Wave Feminism and the Rise of the Third Wave." *Science & Society, 69*(1): 56–91.

Medjuck, Sheva. 1988. "From Self-Sacrificing Jewish Mother to Self-Centered Jewish Princess: Is This How Far We've Come?" *Atlantis, 14*(1): 90–97.

Nathan, D. 2009. "The (Self-Proclaimed) J.A.P." *New Voices,* May 18. http://newvoices.org/2009/05/18/0074-2/

Newhouse, Alana. 2005. "The JAP: Reclaim Her or Reject Her?" *Lilith, 30*(2): 28–30.

Penuel, William R., and James V. Wertsch. 1995. "Vygotsky and Identity Formation: A Sociocultural Approach." *Educational Psychologist, 30*(2): 83–92.

Pomerantz, Shauna, and Rebecca Raby. 2011. "'Oh, She's So Smart': Girls' Complex Engagements with Post/Feminist Narratives of Academic Success." *Gender and Education, 23*(5): 549–564.

Prell, Riv Ellen. 1998. "Cinderellas Who (Almost) Never Become Princesses: Subversive Representations of Jewish Women in Postwar Popular Novels." In *Talking Back: Images of Jewish Women in American Popular Culture,* ed. Joyce Antler, 123–138. Hanover, NH: Brandeis University Press.

Prell, Riv Ellen. 1999. *Fighting to Become Americans.* Boston: Beacon Press.

Prell, Riv Ellen. 2003. "Rage and Representation: Jewish Gender Stereotypes in American Culture." In *American Jewish Women's History: A Reader*, ed. P. Nadell, 238–255. New York: NYU Press.

Schneider, Susan Weidman. 1987. "From the Editor." *Lilith, 18*: 2.

Schnur, Susan. 1987. "Blazes of Truth." *Lilith, 17*: 10–11.

Schwalb, Susan, and William Sedlacek. 1989. *Student Attitudes toward 'JAPs': The New Anti-Semitism*, 9–89. College Park: Maryland University Counseling Center.

Spencer, G. 1989. "An Analysis of JAP-Baiting Humor on the College Campus." *Humor, 2*(4): 329–348.

Stone, Miriam. 2005. "The Shame of the JAP." *Lilith, 30*(2): 31.

Tappan, Mark. 2005. "Domination, Subordination and the Dialogical Self: Identity Development and the Politics of 'Ideological Becoming.'" *Culture Psychology, 11*(1): 47–75.

Yon, Daniel. 2000. "Urban Portraits of Identity: On the Problem of Knowing Culture and Identity in Intercultural Studies." *Journal of Intercultural Studies, 21*(2): 143–157.

CHAPTER TEN

# If I Were a Belle: Performers' Negotiations of Feminism, Gender, and Race in Princess Culture[1]

REBECCA C. HAINS

For most of Disney's history, movies such as *Snow White and the Seven Dwarfs* and *Cinderella* were part of Disney's panoply of family films. The films' title characters were beloved by children and parents alongside other iconic Disney characters, such as Pinocchio and Bambi. In 2000, however, executives in Disney's consumer products division changed their marketing strategy, grouping feature film princesses into a separate, unified, gendered line. This new Disney Princess brand successfully positioned three- to five-year-old girls as an audience for all things princess: The Princess brand is now worth far more than the sum of its parts. Today, preschoolers avidly consume Disney Princess films, dolls, dress-up clothes, and other toys, prompting a surge in other brands' princess-themed products for young girls (Orenstein 2011).

In the years before and after the Disney Princess launch, Disney films' representations of gender and race have been subjects of scholarly critique (Baker-Sperry and Grauerholz 2003; Beres 1999; Do Rozario 2004; Dundes and Dundes 2000; England, Descartes, and Collier-Meek 2011; Giroux 1998; Pewewardy 1996/97; Stone 1975; Trites 1991; Tucker 2009; Wiltz 2009). Within this literature, however, a gap exists: Professional performers' work portraying princesses has been overlooked. Hundreds of women have played Disney Princesses in stage shows at Disney parks, on cruise ships, and in ice shows, as well as in the Broadway musical versions of *Beauty and the Beast* and *The Little*

*Mermaid.* Disney also provides opportunities for women to perform as princesses in unscripted positions. These include "face characters"[2] at Disney theme parks, with whom park visitors may converse individually and pose for photographs. They also appear in Disney parades, visit ill children (e.g., through the Make-A-Wish Foundation), and attend expensive "character dining" sessions on Disney property.

Beyond Disney's empire, professional performers also portray generic, public domain counterparts of Disney's Princesses at children's birthday parties. These performers and their employers make it clear they are unaffiliated with Disney, but Disney has so completely colonized children's fairy tales that most children can't tell Snow White from *Snow White* or Beauty from Belle—a situation Zipes (1994) characterized as Disney's "cultural stranglehold on the fairy tale" (p. 72).

In this chapter, I wish to add to the critical literature on Disney's Princess portrayals by considering professional performers' negotiations of princess culture. I consider this work feminist in nature, as I critique Disney's gender portrayals and lack of diversity while foregrounding women's voices regarding their performance experiences. My own performance background prompted my interest in this topic: In addition to being a media studies professor, I am a professional classical singer, frequently performing soprano solos in classic oratorio works (e.g., Beethoven and Mozart) with regional symphony orchestras. I sometimes also foray into amateur and small-scale professional musical productions, in which I must make sense of characters whose actions and decisions I may find problematic. Therefore, as I set about this research project, I wondered: How do the women who portray Disney and Disney-style princesses negotiate the problematics of princess culture in their work?

## Literature Review

Before answering this question, it is important to specify the precise natures of the Disney princesses' problems. Feminist scholars have argued that the princesses are too skinny, too buxom, too girly, too passive, too helpless, and too often white.[3] To modern sensibilities, the princess films' formulaic dependency on romance narratives offers a further affront: Many dislike Disney's lesson that heteronormative romantic relationships solve all problems. Additionally, Disney's films about princesses of color have often featured regressive stereotypes: For each step forward, it seems, they have also taken a step back.

## Femininity, the Romance Narrative, and Female Strength in Disney Princess Films

Disney based most of its princess films upon folk tales. Written centuries ago in eras with different cultural norms, folk tales brim with sexist content. Unfortunately, in U.S. culture, the most-reproduced fairy tales are those in which the prioritization of feminine beauty is a particularly central theme, such as *Snow White* and *Cinderella*. Baker-Sperry and Grauerholz (2003, 723) problematized this, noting that the beauty ideal "may operate as a normative social control for girls and women," drawing their attention and resources (such as time and money) away from other pursuits in favor of performing normative femininity. Kay Stone (1975, 44) similarly argued that while folk tales too often featured passive, pretty heroines, North American cultural gatekeepers exacerbate the issue: Stories about passive heroines "jump[ed] from twenty percent in the original Grimm collection to as much as seventy-five percent in many [North American] children's books." Walt Disney's versions of these same heroines further "amplified" their worst stereotypes, so that taken together, "the popularized heroines of the Grimms and Disney are not only passive and pretty, but also unusually patient, obedient, industrious, and quiet" (Stone 1975, 45)—worse for modern audiences than their predecessors.

In addition to presenting passive prettiness as a feminine ideal, the Disney Princess films consistently present romantic relationships as the solution to the heroines' problems. For example, *Snow White and the Seven Dwarfs* (1937) featured a full-fledged romance, exaggerating the prince's role compared with the folk tale. The prince appeared early in the film, and only his kiss could break the Queen's spell—unlike the folk tale, in which he appeared later and Snow White awakened when a dwarf stumbled with her coffin (Zipes 1994, 88–89).

In more recent Disney films than classics such as *Snow White and the Seven Dwarfs* (1937), *Cinderella* (1950), and *Sleeping Beauty* (1959), Disney has made its heroines stronger in response to changing U.S. cultural expectations for girls and women, cleaving less strongly to traditionally feminine gender roles (England et al. 2011, 562). Thus, in *The Little Mermaid* (1989) and *Aladdin* (1992), Ariel and Jasmine did not accept their lots without protest; they asserted that they did not want what their fathers wanted for them. Their narratives quickly undercut their purported empowerment; however, both passed quickly from father to prince, in transactions denying them opportunities for independence. Giroux (1998) argued that in the overarching narrative of *Aladdin*, Jasmine was more an object of Aladdin's desire and a means to his success than an individual with agency in her own right. Likewise, Ariel served as a "metaphor for the traditional housewife-in-the-making narrative" (Giroux 1998, 59); as Dundes and Dundes (2000) argued, the wedding scene in *The Little Mermaid* made it clear that Ariel is never truly free. Interestingly, Hans Christian Andersen's *The Little Mermaid* was no romance, but rather a Christian allegory about salvation in which the title character fails in her quests to gain a human soul and dies. By reimagining *The Little Mermaid* to focus on Ariel's self-actualization via romance, Disney introduced modern sexist notions into the story (Trites 1991).

*Beauty and the Beast* (1991) also offered an updated heroine: Rather than being obsessed with romance, Belle was obsessed with reading and had strength and aspirations that were absent from the original fairy tale. Yet as with *Snow White* and *The Little Mermaid,* Disney introduced a romance narrative into *Beauty and the Beast,* into which all Belle's previous interests became subsumed. This romance's unfolding raised scholarly concern, for the Beast battered and abused Belle in scenes resembling real-life patterns of domestic violence (Beres 1999; Media Education Foundation 2001). Belle's union with the Beast thus perpetuated the primacy of romance in Disney's worldview, with a horrible suggestion that even domestic violence can lead to love. Giroux (1998, 60) lamented that despite Belle's strength, "In the end, Belle simply becomes another woman whose life is valued for solving a man's problems," much like Jasmine.

## Race Representation in Disney Princess Films

For decades, critics complained that Disney symbolically annihilated girls of color, excluding them from the screen (Tuchman 1978). Jasmine's debut in 1992 marked the first Disney Princess of a non-European ethnicity in Disney's then fifty-five-year feature-film history. Disney continued making progress in race representation with *Pocahontas* (1995), *Mulan* (1998), and *The Princess and the Frog* (2009), which featured strong female leads who were Native American, Chinese, and African American, respectively. Jasmine, Pocahontas, and Mulan were all incorporated into the Disney Princess brand upon its creation in 2000 (even though Mulan is not actually a princess). Yet despite this progress, these films were riddled with problems.

For example, *Mulan* invented a form of female oppression (matchmaking) that did not historically exist in China (Media Education Foundation 2001), with the effect of making Mulan's China seem more oppressive of women than it was—and making Western culture seem more enlightened by comparison. Also, while Terry (2010) argued that *The Princess and the Frog* effectively redressed the racist attributes of earlier Disney films such as *Song of the South,* popular press critics have argued that *The Princess and the Frog* stereotyped people of color and the voodoo religion (Tucker 2009). Wiltz (2009) even charged Disney with giving too little screen time for Tiana in her human form. This concern was reasonable, given prior criticisms that in Disney films set in locales calling for Black characters, people were entirely absent: Disney presented anthropomorphized animals (as in the case of *The Lion King*, set in Africa), instead (Media Education Foundation 2001).

As with the classic princess films that came before them, the source materials that Disney chose to dramatize bore some, but not all, of the blame for these newer films' problematic content. *Pocahontas* is a key example: A real historical figure who played an important political role in her society, Pocahontas has been appropriated for centuries for neocolonialist rhetoric, made to symbolize the New World presented as a demurely idealized "Indian Princess" dedicated to serving White interests; appropriations of her story have marginalized other Native Americans' experiences with colonialism (Pewewardy 1996/1997). In *Pocahontas*, Disney continued this tradition of erasing Pocahontas's real political importance—and further, it retrofitted her story into the romance narrative mold. It also rendered some other Indians not as people, but as anthropomorphized animals and plants (such as Grandmother Willow) (Pewewardy 1996/1997). Even more troubling is Disney's revisionist history: *Pocahontas* also included an original song about "savages" that Pewewardy found racist and offensive, and which the Media Education Foundation (2001) noted misrepresented the European invasion of Native American culture as a mere misunderstanding, one in which *both* sides viewed the other as savages. Inexplicably, the film concludes with the English explorers leaving the Natives in peace.

In sum, previous scholarship indicates that despite Disney's apparent efforts to respond to critical concerns in their newer films, Disney Princess narratives remain problematic, presenting women in regressive, subordinate roles, valued primarily for their appearance and finding fulfillment in romance. Furthermore, after ignoring people of color for decades, Disney ultimately showed less than adequate sensitivity once it began depicting people of color, introducing problematic ideas and grafting romance narratives onto these stories, as well. How, then, do performers who live with these characters negotiate these issues?

## Theory and Methodology

In this chapter I specifically consider the experiences of women who have portrayed Belle (the Disney character) and Beauty (her generic counterpart) because for these characters, a remarkable range of performing opportunities exist. They include:

- Belle in a twenty-five-minute-long stage musical version of the film in Disney's Hollywood Studios, called *Beauty and the Beast—Live on Stage*, which debuted simultaneously with the film in 1991.
- Belle in a Broadway musical production, first produced in 1994, which has since toured nationally and been produced regionally by professional theaters.[4]
- The face character Belle in Disney parks, tasked with meeting and greeting park guests and performing in parades and the like.
- Belle in other performances, such as the *Disney on Ice* shows produced by Feld Entertainment, which tour internationally, and on Disney cruise ships.

For this chapter, I conducted individual interviews with eight women about their experiences as Belle and, beyond the Disney family, as Beauty. I recruited participants in 2010 and 2011 for a broader study on princess culture, for which I interviewed fifteen performers. I also spent several days conducting field observations of Disney face characters while they interacted with guests at Disney parks in Orlando, and I even found employment for several months as a performer at children's birthday parties, immersing myself in girls' princess culture.

I therefore relied on snowball sampling to recruit participants. Recruiting was challenging, as there is a relatively small pool of potential interviewees (several hundred in the United States) who are difficult to identify and locate. Furthermore, Disney management discourages employees from discussing their experiences with those who would publish on the topic, so many of those I did locate declined an interview. The eight interviewees featured in this chapter are:[5]

**Adriana**, age 43, African American. Played Belle in a regional theater production of the Broadway musical *Beauty and the Beast.*

**Alice**, age 30, European American. Played Belle in two regional theater productions of the Broadway musical *Beauty and the Beast* and at Disney's Hollywood Studios theme park stage production of *Beauty and the Beast—Live on Stage.*

**Avril**, age 37, European American. Played Beauty at various children's birthday parties.

**Brooke**, age 29, European American "with a lot of Native American heritage." Played Belle in Disney's Hollywood Studios theme park stage production of *Beauty and the Beast—Live On Stage.*

**Camille,** age 34, European American. Played Beauty at various children's birthday parties.

**Lena,** age 25, European American. Played Beauty at various children's birthday parties.

**Naomi,** undisclosed age, African American. Played Belle in three regional theater productions of the Broadway musical *Beauty and the Beast.*

**Olivia,** age 22, Asian and European American. Played Belle in a *Disney on Ice* show.

I interviewed the performers individually via telephone (and one via an exchange of several emails); the telephone conversations lasted between 45 minutes and 1.5 hours. All interviews followed a semi-structured discussion guide, focused on the performers' personal views about princess culture and the performative aspects of their work. A research assistant transcribed these interviews; the eight interviews listed above yielded transcripts totaling nearly 90,000 words. In conducting my analysis, I used an emergent coding method to document the larger themes within these interviews.

I conducted my research from the interdisciplinary perspective of feminist cultural studies, within the broader rubric of media studies (Lister and Wells 2001). By adopting a feminist theoretical framework, I take a political stance regarding women's and girls' societal subordination, including their depiction in mass media. I seek to understand how the women in this study resisted domination, in ways small or large, as they enacted race and gender in the specific contexts of their performances (see Denzin and Lincoln 1998, 26–27). The fact that my interviewees are relating not experiences with the performativity of everyday life (Butler1997) but rather with performance in the traditional sense (i.e., on stage) is intriguing: They are not just performing gender as socially expected of them, but actually mediating Disney's interpretation of femininity as embodied by the princesses. As such, Butler would argue that they can distance themselves from these professional performances, maintaining a separate identity from that with which they disagree about the princess ideal:

> In the theatre, one can say, "this is just an act," and de-realize the act, making acting into something quite distinct from what is real. [...] [T]he various conventions which announce that 'this is only a play' allows strict lines to be drawn between the performance and life. (Butler 1988, 527)

This differentiation suggests that if the princess performers disagree with the authorial intentions that they have been hired to embody, they might find opportunities for resistance through small but meaningful acts, or micro-tactics (de Certeau 1984, xv).

In presenting my data, I draw from the feminist ethnography tradition that foregrounds women's voices, quoting their words amply, rather than summarizing their perspectives in academic terms (Abu-Lughod 1993). Although feminist ethnographers sometimes avoid analysis and concluding commentary to steer clear of the "interpretive/analytical mode being questioned by the very construction of narratives" (Abu-Lughod 1993, xvii–xviii), I offer analysis of my interviewees' words to better illuminate emergent themes regarding the performers' experiences with gender, race, and feminism. Drawing from dialogic theory (Newcomb 1991), I consider not just how the performers negotiated Belle, but also how these negotiations related to the encoding of femininity and other traits in other princess characters.

## Negotiating Princess Culture: Performers' Perspectives

In analyzing the transcribed interviews for major themes, I wished to understand how the performers negotiated their characters and whether they brought to their performances an awareness of princess culture's problematic aspects. Predictably, some did while others did not; interestingly, the interviewees with the most critical outlook were two of the three who performed at children's birthday parties. They offered explicitly feminist perspectives about their work.[6]

## Feminist approaches to performing princess culture

Perhaps because they were not bound by pre-set dialogue or a requirement to mimic an established Disney character,[7] Lena's and Camille's feminist intentions permeated their work at children's birthday parties—subverting many cultural expectations of fairy tale princesses. For example, Lena asked me: "Have you ever heard that line, or seen people like—there's this shirt that says, 'This is what a feminist looks like'?" I replied with a laugh, "Yes, I love that shirt." Lena used that concept as a launching point for her perspective on performing at princess-themed birthday parties:

LENA: To me, being a feminist doesn't mean a certain set of rules. To me, it means doing what you want and being who you want to be without other people having particular, you know, expectations of you, I guess? As a woman? And so, you know, it's being—dressing up as a Disney princess or pretending that you're a princess shouldn't mean inherently that you're

| | |
|---|---|
| | an airhead [laughs] or that you're superficial. You know what I mean? Or that finding a husband is the only thing that's important to you. And I think that is the crux of the feminist thing for me. It's like, I can dress up and I can look this way because it's fun and still have, you know, goals and interests and you know, be intelligent and all that other stuff. |
| INTERVIEWER: | Right. |
| LENA: | So, it's not—it's kind of like disproving that expectation that all there is to being a princess is, like, being pretty and nice. |

Lena's strategies for accomplishing this goal included introducing topics of conversation beyond the stereotypes, in an effort to make the characters "more three-dimensional" and to try to "squeeze in values." She explained:

| | |
|---|---|
| LENA: | I definitely stay true to the character [I am playing], but I definitely embellish on that when I'm at the parties and stuff. |
| INTERVIEWER: | Like in what ways do you embellish? |
| LENA: | Um ... well, I know one of the things that we started to talk about before was how, you know, when I'm with them, I make it a point not just to be like ... not to just say superficial things. "I like your hair!" and "I like your dress!" [Smiles in voice] You know? "Pink is my favorite color, too!" I sort of say things like, I ask them about creative stuff ... like, "I like to sing, do you like to sing? Do you sing in school?" You know, "Do you like to dance? Do you study any dance forms?" That kind of thing. Or, I'll transition into things like, "Have you read my story?" You know, "Do you like to read? I like to read." You know, I say—I try to kind of ease in stuff like that. |

Lena also explained that when children complimented her beautiful dress, she would often reply, "This is my party dress because I'm at your birthday and I wanted to dress up," and perhaps additionally comment, "I certainly wouldn't be wearing this dress if I was going to be exercising!" Lena also engaged older children in conversations about the political power and responsibilities of princesses. She even worked to undercut the "love at first sight" narrative that dominates princess culture, arguing that Disney's vision "isn't a practical portrayal of relationships." Thus, when children asked whether her prince was handsome, she responded: "He is very handsome to me. What people think is attractive is different to every person and it's always been important to me that, you know, a guy is intelligent and thoughtful."

Camille had similarly feminist goals during her work at children's parties. Like Lena, she also identified as a feminist, which she defined as follows:

CAMILLE: For me, being a feminist means not accepting anything less than equal treatment by and compared to my male counterparts; advocating for women's rights; making conscientious decisions about how I present myself to the world versus allowing others to decide that for me, and encouraging younger women to do the same.

Camille drew upon her feminist conscience at various moments during her work at children's birthday parties, carefully portraying Beauty and her other princess characters as "self-determining individuals, not passive people who let other people decide what they did or who they were."

CAMILLE: I would try to infuse a bit more self-initiative and strength of character into the dialogue to show that I didn't just sit around waiting to be rescued. For example, I would talk about going out and doing volunteer work, or leading a park cleanup crew while Prince Charming would be home in the castle kitchen making dinner. Who knows if the kids got the message, but I got an appreciative laugh from many moms!

Given feminist concerns about the beauty ideal in young girls' lives, Camille was cognizant of not just her status as a role model, but of the potential impact of her conversations about beauty with her young partygoers—for as was the case at Lena's parties, children inevitably wished to converse about being pretty.

CAMILLE: No matter who I portrayed, one thing I always made sure to do was to reaffirm the party guests' self-worth. There is so much marketing out there that gets girls thinking they have to look like the princesses to be pretty. Whenever there were guests who, unlike many of the other kids at the party, weren't in mini princess gowns, I would make sure to gush over them just as much, and when it was time for the makeup boutique, I would whisper to each girl that she didn't need makeup to be beautiful. Who knows if that stuck with them; it helped placate my feminist side.

INTERVIEWER: What were the makeup boutiques like?

CAMILLE: Our party bags would be filled with games, props, etc., including a big makeup bag with glittery eyeliner sticks, liquid eye liner, blush, pink lipstick, and "fairy dust" to sprinkle on the kids' cheeks. I would always whisper to each girl, "You don't need makeup to look beautiful—this is just for fun!" I would do that because the feminist in me was worried about what kind of message the makeup boutique was sending.

In these ways, Camille and Lena worked to negotiate their contradictory positions as feminists who were performing as stereotypically normatively feminine princesses. Recognizing that by embodying princess characters like Beauty they might be perceived as implicitly approving of what they represented, they developed their characters far beyond what was found on the page, and with tremendous divergence from their more popular Disney counterparts.

## Negotiating female strength

The performers who appeared as Belle had markedly different experiences from Camille and Lena. I could not locate any face character performers who had portrayed Belle to interview for this chapter; all worked from a script, limited to the words on the page. They therefore relied upon small but meaningful shifts in characterization (in tone and line delivery and so on) to shape the characters they portrayed and in some cases engage in resistant micro-tactics—giving, for example, a character more strength or self-assurance than Disney as corporate author seemed to intend based on the original feature film.

In reviewing the performers' explanations of how they characterized Belle, a major theme emerged: To some degree, nearly all took note of Belle's relative strength. Although none expressed critical perspectives like Camille and Lena did—in fact, several sounded surprised and disconcerted to hear about Peggy Orenstein's book, *Cinderella Ate My Daughter* (2011), which critiques princess culture—as performers, they seemed more interested in playing a strong character than a weak one. Presumably, their choices in these areas had an impact on the experiences of their audience members.

Adriana offered an excellent discussion of the types of decisions she could make as a performer about her character's apparent strength. While preparing to play Belle in a regional production of *Beauty and the Beast*, Adriana watched the film. She recalled, "I recognized right away that I wasn't going to be the Belle that was in the movie." She explained:

ADRIANA: I recognized that I wanted Belle to be ... um ... a little bit more mature. Just a little bit more. Um, not because she's lived life, but because she reads so much. And she absorbs so much. Because that was the only way I could make sense of a young woman who would go to an enchanted forest with a half-man, half-beast and not have a nervous breakdown.

INTERVIEWER: Okay.

ADRIANA: It was the only way I could make sense of that. She was very wise and highly intellectual, and she liked to investigate. Plus, too, her father was a scientist. So she looked at her enchanted forest, or her enchanted castle and thought, "There's gotta be a reason for this. I've read things about enchanted castles—many things about enchanted castles—so this doesn't surprise me. I didn't think it was real, but there's gotta be a reason why this is real."

INTERVIEWER: Right.

ADRIANA: And so I made her a little bit more intelligent and a little bit more, um, mature. And … but, she was very fun-loving. The other thing I did was, I made her challenge the Beast. She was much stronger.

INTERVIEWER: Oh, good!

ADRIANA: Much stronger, um, you know. I found the movie was kind of a little bit weepy. Um, and I just thought instead of her being weepy about not being able to see her father and being with this ogre who's yelling, I just thought that she'd be a little angry about it. And that she was determined to not let it take her over. And that she'd get to the bottom of it. And, um, the way I was able to get away with that, is that there were about four places in the movie where she could, just—where I could pull out my best Carol Burnett, who is my hero. Carol Burnett is my hero and I can imitate her, like, nothin'. So I pulled out my best Carol Burnett on those times that the prince and Gaston sings his song. We blocked it so that he was kind of, yanking me around the stage. Tossing me here, tossing me in the other arm and I just had that Carol Burnett face, you know, every time he did it. I backed up and looked into his eyes with my eyes really big, and the kids would just howl with laughter. [Interviewer laughs appreciatively.] So because I had my four very, very silly moments, like, when the Beast comes in and he says, "You will join me for dinner!" And she says, "I'm not hungry." And I made her a little pouty about it. But then she said something to him about, you know, yelling and he says, "Why can I not yell?" in her face. And the line is that "Because it's rude," but I had her lean in to him so he would lean all the way back into a back bend and I said, "Because it's ruuuuuuuuuuuuuuude!" And I just kept saying "rude" and then I went, "Ugh!" And the kids just lost it. So they didn't mind when she was strong. […] But, that's the only thing I changed. I just made her a little more mature and a little stronger.

These details emphasize that Adriana used tactics such as body language and intonation to characterize Belle as mature and strong—and as far from a "weepy" girl as possible.

In Alice's case, during the twenty-five-minute *Beauty and the Beast—Live on Stage*, she had much less room to effect Belle's character. Whereas Adriana could stretch bits of Belle's dialogue, the twenty-five-minute show Alice performed in was on an automated track. In viewing the show, I witnessed that only Belle's and Gaston's voices are live; the rest are pre-recorded. Even the dialogue is musically underscored; the performers had to keep up with the recording at all times. Therefore, while performers like Alice could use intonation and body language to influence characterization, they lacked flexibility.

| | |
|---|---|
| ALICE: | There's not a whole lot of time. I mean, you do what you can within the time constraints, but really, in terms of the lines of the songs and the talking lines, they all have to be delivered in that set time. So it really came more to the way that you might say a line and all, and like I said, I really didn't have much trouble at *Beauty and the Beast* with that. I mean, I felt like I was able to give her a really strong portrayal and I think part of that, too, is just owing to the fact that there's not … I mean, there's just not very much. So there wasn't very much opportunity for real development, but on the flip side, there wasn't real much opportunity to make her that weak, either. You know what I mean? |
| INTERVIEWER: | Yeah. |
| ALICE: | It wasn't, you know, it wasn't a choice I felt I actively had to make. Now, I've seen—oh, gosh, probably at least eight to ten other girls do the stage show that we did. You know, training subs and coming in on off days and watching shows and all that. And I would say that, I mean everyone has a different portrayal of it, and yes […] within that framework, you can play it either very sweetly and a little bit on the weak side, versus really, you know, strong. And I would say I tended toward the strong side. But there were lots of other girls that just sort of, were very princess-like. If that kind of makes sense. |

In other words, Alice did not recall the choice to be more "strong" than "weak" and "princess-like" as a conscious one, but without much reflection on the matter, she performed a stronger Belle than did some of her colleagues.

Interestingly, whether a Disney performer experienced Belle as a strong character seemed related to her prior performance experiences. Some had performed as princesses who were even stronger than Belle, and they had to soften themselves to portray Belle, while others had the opposite experience. For example, Alice recalled feeling more at home with Belle than other characters she had played at Disney's parks. Alice struggled at first to articulate why, but ultimately she realized she could more easily be strong while playing Belle than as other characters, such as Cinderella.

| | |
|---|---|
| ALICE: | I'm having trouble figuring out the way to really say this clearly, but you know, that Cinderella doesn't have to be someone who's real helpless, or ... so dainty and fragile that, you know, there's no chutzpah behind her. You know? It was easier with Belle. Belle just has a lot of gumption as a character, written into her story. But Cinderella, you know, can go sort of either way! [Laughs] And I didn't want [my characterization of her] to go the way that they wanted me to go! |

In contrast, Brooke had played roles such as Pocahontas prior to appearing as Belle in Disney's twenty-five-minute production. She had to work on being more "princess-y," or delicate and ladylike, when she transitioned out of Pocahontas and into Belle:

| | |
|---|---|
| BROOKE: | Well, Belle's very much more princess-y than Pocahontas is. You know, she's very—Pocahontas is very earthy, and it's all about that. Also, when learning the voice, I talked differently when I was Pocahontas than I did as Belle. Lowering the voice, um, more of an open-throated approach to it, versus Belle which is a little bit more pinched and refined. Because even though she's not like a Snow White and very prim and proper, she's still a French lady. She's—she was—Belle was actually based on a young Katharine Hepburn as she was in *Little Women*, when she played Jo in *Little Women*. |
| INTERVIEWER: | Oh! |
| BROOKE: | That's what a lot of Belle—Belle's characteristics and mannerisms were based on her. Also the um, ballerinas from Degas—the way she walks. Belle walks with the music, and she walks with a dancer's turnout in her feet. |
| INTERVIEWER: | Ooh. |
| BROOKE: | And so ... so those were the things. Whereas, Pocahontas moves more like a gazelle and when she jumps and waits and runs. So those were extremely different characteristics. [Laughs] And it's funny, when I went over to train for *Beauty and the Beast*, they had to "de-Poca" me, as they said. |
| INTERVIEWER: | [Laughing] De-Poca you! |

BROOKE: Yeah, they had to put my feet back together [laughs], you know, and make sure that I wasn't standing too distant, and that my gaze was not up above the ... up above the clouds as it is with Pocahontas, so.

INTERVIEWER: Right.

BROOKE: So those ... I mean, I can probably talk for hours about the differences between the two and the basis for them and things of that nature. Because that's something I studied a lot. Um, you know, why does she move this way; why does she talk this way?

Brooke explained she learned these facts through independent study and research to facilitate her own character development. In her experience, despite Belle's strengths, she was not as strong as Pocahontas.

Like Brooke, Olivia found Belle to be a gentler character than others. In addition to playing Belle in the *Disney on Ice* show, Olivia also previously played characters such as Mulan. She explained:

OLIVIA: All the princesses had much different demeanors. You know, Mulan was much stronger and Belle was much softer and I think that, um, it definitely, you had to work on different, different types of skating and play your strengths and weaknesses. Like, I think that I'm more of a strong skater, so I had to work on like, the softness of the more demure demeanor of Belle when I did that.

In this way, playing the "demure" Belle with "softness" required Olivia to work against her natural tendency toward strong skating, which had been such an asset for Mulan, who is a warrior. Olivia noted that despite this preference, she derived more enjoyment from playing Belle because of the relatively higher amount of skating Belle did. "Plus," she added with a smile in her voice, "you got to wear a prettier dress when you were Belle."

## Addressing Race Representation

In exploring princess culture's problematic aspects, the intersection of gender and race must be considered. Disney's representations of race have been regarded as problematic for many years (Giroux 1998; Hurley 2005; Lacroix 2004), and prior to the premier of *The Princess and the Frog* in 2010, no African American Disney Princesses existed.

Given this history, Naomi's and Adriana's experiences as African American women portraying Belle are noteworthy. Belle is represented on screen and in Disney parks as a light-skinned, green-eyed brunette, and Naomi and Adriana's race presumably could have hindered their audience members' enjoyment of their performances. (Consider that after the release of the film *The Hunger Games*, audience members protested the inclusion of African American actors portraying characters they had presumed to be white in the books; some even claimed it had "ruined" the film for them [Stewart 2012].) In their respective interviews, however, Naomi and Adriana felt their performances as Belle in professional productions of the *Beauty and the Beast* musical were warmly received, with significance for audience members and themselves.

| | |
|---|---|
| INTERVIEWER: | What was the reception like for your work? Any particular reviews stand out or comments or anything? |
| NAOMI: | Um, I don't usually read reviews, although I heard they were pretty good. I was actually quite surprised, because I didn't know, being African American, I didn't know if the kids would be coming with their arms crossed like little ... you know? [Laughs] |
| INTERVIEWER: | Mmm hmm. |
| NAOMI: | You know what I mean? But, I was so pleasantly surprised. I'd come out the stage door even dressed in my normal clothes and they'd all be like, "Oh! Belle!" You know? It was just actually really encouraging because I was like, "Oh these kids ... they don't care. They don't ... all they want is the story." And it's never even occurred to them ... you know, all they wanted to do is meet Belle. And [...] they had me go to the Barnes & Noble and, like, to a bank and read the book. The storybook. |
| INTERVIEWER: | Oh! |
| NAOMI: | Dressed in my Belle costume to read the storybook to, like, kids who wanted to come. |
| INTERVIEWER: | Oh, that's sweet. |
| NAOMI: | And I was like, here I am, holding this book, and I'm dressed as Belle. And clearly the girl in the book does not look like me. And they're just transfixed. And you could not tell them that I was not the real Belle. [Laughs] |
| INTERVIEWER: | [Laughs] |
| NAOMI: | You know what I mean? So, I really loved that. I really think it just goes to show how open-minded, um, kids are before, you know, society puts labels on things and people. |
| INTERVIEWER: | Right. |
| NAOMI: | It was really cool. |

INTERVIEWER: Yeah, I think that's really beautiful and great that they just didn't bat an eyelash at it.

NAOMI: Yeah. And I mean, also because I've never had any kid come up to me and go, "Why don't you look like the real Belle?" Or something … never once. And I would always come out after the show and sign autographs [in my everyday clothes] and say hi to the kids and all that stuff. It was amazing. They were none the wiser.

For Naomi, then, being accepted both onstage and off as "the real Belle" was wonderful. Performing prior to the release of *The Princess and the Frog*, Naomi was uncertain what her reception would be—whether audience members would willingly suspend their disbelief in her portrayal of such an iconic character. In the end, she was pleased and amazed by the children's open-mindedness and admiration of her as Belle. The acceptance she experienced underscores the importance of giving young children diversity in their role models—before the societal practice of labeling "things and people," as Naomi put it, forms stereotypes in children's minds.

Adriana reported similar experiences of unqualified acceptance from her young audiences. Asked what it was like to perform such an iconic Disney character, she explained,

ADRIANA: I wasn't even thinking about it being a Disney princess or anything. I didn't recognize that it was a Disney princess until the kids, until the audiences got there. And they were screaming and, you know, one of my most memorable moments is when I had to take my place in the dark—and after the narrator tells the story of what happened to the prince and why he was cursed, there's a slow light that comes up on a pin spot on my face as I'm reading a book leaning up against a wall. And there was this little three-year-old in the second row, right in front of me who gasped and said, "Oh! Belle!"

INTERVIEWER: Ooh!

ADRIANA: And didn't even notice that my skin was brown, that I had long braids. I was Belle! Because of the dress, that little person automatically saw Belle. And I just thought, "That's just beautiful."

Once Adriana realized how strong and positive a reaction young audience members had to her performance as Belle, she decided to break with the theatrical tradition of changing into her everyday clothes to meet audience members. Instead, she would change into Belle's iconic blue dress so that the children could experience her once more as Belle.

| | |
|---|---|
| ADRIANA: | Afterwards [...] I would come out in that dress and they would just, "Belle! Belle! Belle! Will you sign my—Belle! Belle!" And nobody noticed my skin was brown. It was just Belle. And it was *just* so sweet! And then my other favorite story is there's this little Black girl who went to a predominantly White school. And her mother brought her back to me after the show to meet me because she was in school and her mother and her father always called her a princess. "You're a little princess; you're a little princess." And in the playground that week, in the playground, she said, "I'm a little princess. That's what my mommy and daddy says." And the other little girl said to her, "You can't be a princess! You're Black." |
| INTERVIEWER: | Ooh. |
| ADRIANA: | "There are no Black princesses." Seven years old. "There are no Black princesses." And she was crushed. And so then her mother found out about the *Beauty and the Beast*, she saw the story and she saw my picture, the one that I sent you in the paper. And she was, "Eureka! I have to bring my daughter to this, to see this woman play this." So she brought me, and the whole time she's telling me this story, the little girl was just looking up at me with those, with this awe. And I'm trying not to lose it, and the director cried, and she said, "That's why we do this." She said, "You," she pointed to the little girl, she said, "you're the reason why Adriana is here and I hired her to do this role. You are the reason why." And I gave her a big hug and I said, "You are just so sweet." And she said, "You sing so nice! You sing so nice." And she went to go, "Bye princess!" And she just waved at me, and I was like, "Okay. That's it." |

Adriana's on-stage appearance as a Disney princess who happened to be African American—without comment, with neither apology nor fanfare—seems to have been an important instance of inclusivity for the seven-year-old girl who had faced discriminatory taunting related to Disney's exclusion of African American characters. Adriana's performance countered the girl's classmates' belief that Black girls cannot be princesses, and meeting a child to whom this inclusivity mattered nearly moved Adriana to tears.

Naomi similarly felt her portrayal of Belle made a positive difference for young audience members of color. She recalled:

| | |
|---|---|
| NAOMI: | There was one little girl that I actually invited back stage. She was dressed as Belle and she was a little Black girl. [...] And I saw this girl and she was so cute, and so I told stage management to have ushers bring her back after the show because I wanted to meet her and take a picture. And it turns out it was her birthday! [Laughing] |
| INTERVIEWER: | Oh my gosh! |
| NAOMI: | And she was so excited to come back stage and to meet me and everything. And I stayed and talked, you know, and talked to her for a little bit, so—that was a fun moment. |
| INTERVIEWER: | That is so adorable! [Laughs] |
| NAOMI: | Isn't it? Yeah. [Laughs] I think it's especially cool for, um [...] kids of color to be able to come to a show and see a Disney princess that looks like them, because before *The Princess and the Frog*, there was no Black Disney princess. |
| INTERVIEWER: | Right. |
| NAOMI: | It always kind of touched me when I could see people in the audience of color, because I know when I was a kid, I would have loved to do something like that. |

Naomi concluded, "I'm so glad I had the great experience I did, as far as the kids being so open to me. It was a great experience; I really loved doing it every time."

## Conclusion

In this chapter, I have discussed how the performers I interviewed drew upon their own perspectives—including their understandings of feminism, their feelings about female strength, and their positionality as women of color—in their performances as Belle (the Disney character) and Beauty (the public domain character). When they desired to do so, the performers were able to mediate the messages of princess culture, using micro-tactics to shift them toward more empowering, egalitarian messages.

The performers' ability to produce these shifts in their performances was both enabled by and in spite of the messages contained in the original fairy tales and the Disney films, which feature both empowering and problematic content. For performers playing Belle, the musical's script and the film offered insights into Belle's intelligence and her interest in books; this helped justify Adriana's more mature interpretation of Belle. But Belle could also be read as more "princess-y," more normatively feminine, than more recent counterparts such as Mulan and Pocahontas. Performers could characterize her as more delicate, if they so desired, possibly reinforcing feminine beauty ideals that critics found too prevalent in Disney's Princesses.

Naomi's and Adriana's reported experiences also support the practice of race-blind casting. Given audience members' apparent willing suspension of disbelief regarding the African American performers' skin tone in the full-length musical production of *Beauty and the Beast*, Disney executives might wish to consider race-blind casting of Belle and/or other princess characters on its properties in the future. I have witnessed that the cast of the twenty-five-minute *Beauty and the Beast* stage show can be quite diverse; in one performance I saw, many villagers in the cast were portrayed by people of color, despite their exclusion from all scenes in the film. What would it take to open up more opportunities for performers of color in leading roles in the parks—to institute race-blind casting there, as well?[8]

In conclusion, the small but meaningful changes individual performers can bring to children's off-screen experiences as they "meet" their favorite Disney Princesses can have a positive effect, serving as a subtle critique of mainstream princess culture and Disney's cultural production strategies. Although this chapter features the recollections of only eight interviewees about their performative experiences with princess culture, the thoughtful and detailed nature of the interviewees' responses to my questions affords a glimpse of the range of experiences, strategies, and perspectives that princess performers bring to their work, despite the often stereotypical nature of the characters they portray. If desired, there is room for interpretation, even resistance—especially for performers portraying unscripted characters.

## Endnotes

1. Note: An earlier version of this chapter was presented at the annual meeting of the Association for Education in Journalism and Mass Communication in Chicago in 2012. The author would like to thank AEJMC's Cultural and Critical Studies Division and their blind peer reviewers for their feedback.
2. These performers are called "face characters" to differentiate them from fully costumed performers playing characters like Mickey Mouse, whose faces are covered.
3. For example, scholars have interrogated the Disney Princesses' representations of race (Giroux 1998; Hurley 2005; Lacroix 2004); their marketing and merchandising (Brockus 2004); their reception by or effects upon children (Beecher 2010; Blaise, 2005; Hayes & Tantleff-Dunn 2010; Wohlwend 2009, 2012; Yeoman 1999); and the significance of the princesses' cultural dominance (Brockus 2004).
4. In contrast, the Broadway musical version of *The Little Mermaid* has still not embarked on a national tour as of March 2014.

5. Note: All names are pseudonyms, and some additional details have been changed to better ensure the interviewees' anonymity.
6. Note that although several of the interviewees approached their princess performances with a feminist conscience, none took on this work specifically as an opportunity to subvert the dominant ideologies encoded in the Disney versions of the princesses. They took their positions as performers as a matter of practicality, suggesting that the mundane (having to earn money to live) can become a means of infusing one's feminist perspective into the performance of the princess role.
7. Indeed, the performers who appeared as Beauty were, like performers from most reputable birthday party companies, respectful of Disney's trademarks and therefore deviated substantially from the Disney story.
8. A former Disney parks casting director told me that race-blind casting of princess characters will never happen, because the parks' casting directors strive to closely match potential princess performers with the original animated characters, but I feel it is an interesting question nevertheless.

## References

Abu-Lughod, Lila. 1993. *Writing Women's Worlds: Bedouin Stories*. Berkeley: University of California Press.

Baker-Sperry, Liz, and Lori Grauerholz. 2003. "The Pervasiveness and Persistence of the Feminine Beauty Ideal in Children's Fairy Tales." *Gender and Society, 17*(5): 711–726.

Beecher, Bronwyn. 2010. "No, I Won't Marry You! Critiquing Gender in Multiliteracies Fairytale Play." *Canadian Children, 35*(2): 15–24.

Beres, Laura. 1999. "Beauty and the Beast: The Romanticization of Abuse in Popular Culture." *European Journal of Cultural Studies, 2*(2): 191–207.

Blaise, Mindy. 2005. "A Feminist Poststructural Study of Children 'Doing' Gender in an Urban Kindergarten Classroom." *Early Childhood Research Quarterly, 20*: 85–108.

Brockus, Susan. 2004. "Where Magic Lives: Disney's Cultivation, Co-creation, and Control of America's Cultural Objects." *Popular Communication, 2*(4): 191–211.

Butler, Judith. 1988. "Performative Acts and Gender Constitution: An Essay in Phenomenology and Feminist Theory." *Theatre Journal, 40*(4): 519–531.

Butler, Judith. 1997. *Excitable Speech: A Politics of the Performative*. London: Routledge.

De Certeau, Michel. 1984. *The Practice of Everyday Life*. Berkeley: University of California Press.

Denzin, Norm, and Yvonna Lincoln (Eds.). 1998. *The Landscape of Qualitative Research: Theories and Issues*. Thousand Oaks, CA: Sage.

Do Rozario, Rebecca-Anne C. 2004. "The Princess and the Magic Kingdom: Beyond Nostalgia, the Function of the Disney Princess." *Women's Studies in Communication, 27*(1): 34–59.

Dundes, Lauren, and Alan Dundes. 2000. "The Trident and the Fork: Disney's *The Little Mermaid* as a Male Construction of an Electral Fantasy." *Psychoanalytic Studies, 2*(2): 117–129.

England, Dawn Elizabeth, Lara Descartes, and Melissa Collier-Meek. 2011. "Gender Role Portrayal and the Disney Princesses." *Sex Roles, 64*(7–8): 555–567.

Giroux, Henry. 1998. "Are Disney Movies Good for Your Kids?" In *Kinderculture: The Corporate Construction of Childhood*, ed. Shirley R. Steinberg and Joe L. Kincheloe. Boulder, CO: Westview Press.

Hayes, Sharon, and Stacey Tantleff-Dunn. 2010. "Am I Too Fat to Be a Princess? Examining the Effects of Popular Children's Media on Young Girls' Body Image." *British Journal of Developmental Psychology, 28*(2): 413–426.

Hurley, Dorothy L. 2005. "Seeing White: Children of Color and the Disney Fairy Tale Princess." *Journal of Negro Education,* 74(3): 221–232.

Lacroix, Celeste. 2004. "Images of Animated Others: The Orientalization of Disney's Cartoon Heroines from *The Little Mermaid* to *The Hunchback of Notre Dame*." *Popular Communication, 2*(4): 213–229.

Lister, Martin, and Liz Wells. 2001. "Seeing Beyond Belief: Cultural Studies as an Approach to Analyzing the Visual." In *Handbook of Visual Analysis,* ed. Theo van Leeuwen and Carey Jewitt, 61–91. London: Sage.

Media Education Foundation. 2001. *Mickey Mouse Monopoly: Disney, Childhood, and Corporate Power* [DVD]. Northampton, MA: Author.

Newcomb, Horace. 1991. "On the Dialogic Aspects of Mass Communication." In *Critical Perspectives on Media and Society,* ed. Robert K. Avery and David Eason, 69–87. New York: Guilford Press.

Orenstein, Peggy. 2011. *Cinderella Ate My Daughter: Dispatches from the Front Lines of the New Girlie-Girl Culture.* New York: HarperCollins.

Pewewardy, Cornel. 1996/97. "The Pocahontas Paradox: A Cautionary Tale for Educators." *Journal of Navajo Education.* http://www.hanksville.org/storytellers/pewe/writing/Pocahontas.html

Stewart, Dodai. 2012. "Racist *Hunger Games* Fans Are Very Disappointed." *Jezebel,* March 26. http://jezebel.com/5896408/racist-hunger-games-fans-dont-care-how-much-money-the-movie-made

Stone, Kay. 1975. "Things Walt Disney Never Told Us." *Journal of American Folklore, 88*(347): 42–50.

Terry, Esther J. 2010. "Rural as Racialized Plantation vs Rural as Modern Reconnection: Blackness and Agency in Disney's *Song of the South* and *The Princess and the Frog*." *Journal of African American Studies, 14,* 469–481.

Trites, Roberta. 1991. "Disney's Sub/Version of Andersen's *The Little Mermaid*." *Journal of Popular Film & Television, 18*(4): 145–152.

Tuchman, Gaye. 1978. "Introduction: The Symbolic Annihilation of Women by the Mass Media." In *Hearth and Home: Images of Women in the Mass Media*, ed. Gaye Tuchman, Arlene Kaplan Daniels, and James Benét. New York: Oxford University Press.

Tucker, Neely. 2009. "Disney Introduces First Black Princess, Tiana, in *The Princess and the Frog*." *The Washington Post,* April 19. http://www.washingtonpost.com/wp-dyn/content/article/2009/04/16/AR2009041603139.html

Wiltz, Teresa. 2009. "The Froggiest of Them All: Is Disney Hedging Its Bets, Afraid of Letting Too Much Blackness Play Front and Center on the Big Screen?" *The Root*, December 11. http://www.theroot.com/views/froggiest-them-all

Wohlwend, Karen E. 2009. "Damsels in Discourse: Girls Consuming and Producing Identity Texts through Disney Princess Play." *Reading Research Quarterly, 44*(1): 57–83.

Wohlwend, Karen E. 2012. "'Are You Guys *Girls*?' Boys, Identity Texts, and Disney Princess Play." *Journal of Early Childhood Literacy, 12*(1): 3–23.

Yeoman, Elizabeth. 1999. "'How Does It Get into My Imagination?' Elementary School Children's Intertextual Knowledge and Gendered Storylines." *Gender and Education, 11*(4): 427–440.

Zipes, Jack D. 1994. *Fairy Tale as Myth / Myth as Fairy Tale*. Lexington: University Press of Kentucky.

# Part IV
# The Royal Cultures and Imagined Princess Cultures

CHAPTER ELEVEN

# Princess Sissi of Austria: Image, Reality, and Transformation

PHYLLIS S. ZRZAVY AND HELFRIED C. ZRZAVY

Princess Elizabeth of Wittelsbach (1837–1898)[1], later Empress Elizabeth of Austria, continues to be one of the preeminent figures that characterizes the international princess culture. Popularly known as "Sissi," Elizabeth became known "as an exceptional beauty and a popular 'people's Empress' around whom a mythology has arisen that continues to lend the figure of Sissi ... a great deal of mystique and appeal" (Wauchope 2002, 170). The inscrutability and charisma of Elizabeth's life story have blossomed into a veritable veneration, as "Princess Sissi" has firmly established itself as a mediating figure in the imaginations and identities of girls in Austria and Germany, indeed in other countries in Europe and around the world.

In the popular imagination, Elizabeth is a tragic historical figure associated with forestalled feminist and egalitarian tendencies of nineteenth-century Europe as well as an idealized princess figure who could easily fit into the Disney-fied canon of Sleeping Beauty, Cinderella, and Beauty and the Beast.

Indeed, for the youngest girls in Europe, there is an animated cartoon series, a co-production of the German, French, and Italian national television services, which is devoted entirely to Elizabeth. *Sissi* explores her early life and courtship, replete with coloring books depicting Sissi as the princess at the perfect intersection of youth and beauty, Franz Joseph as the handsome prince, and Archduchess Sophie as the evil mother-in-law (Stumpf). For slightly older girls, there is a Sissi Barbie doll, a Zapf-made Sissi doll with a horse, a Sissi PEZ dispenser—next to

Mozart the only historical figure so honored in the European PEZ market—and a Princess Sissi–themed book trilogy for young readers written by Gaby Schuster (Schuster 1998a, 1998b, 1999).

Older girls growing up in Europe can continue to nurture princess fantasies with a wide variety of Sissi swag, including ready-made Sissi hair pieces that can be worn with Sissi costumes during *Fasching*, or carnival. For young eligible females, a princess fantasy can find its expression in one of the many Sissi-styled wedding dresses which range in price from €1,000 to more than €4,000 (examples are Jolie, Modekarussell, and Cinderella Brautkleid). But the Sissi princess market extends far beyond the "princess" years into merchandise that is targeted at more mature women. Collectible Sissi porcelain figurines and platters abound in Europe, as do collectible boxes and a variety of Sissi-branded beauty products and fragrances (examples are Maison De Haute Parfumerie Nicolas De Barry, Marc De La Morandiere)

Wherever the private market has not already cultivated a pop culture image of Elizabeth, national governments have stepped in to commemorate Sissi as a royal figure. In the past fifteen years alone, not one but two jubilee years were dedicated in Austria to her memory, the first in 1998, which commemorated the centennial of her death in 1898, and the other in 2012, which celebrated the 175th anniversary of her birth. Both anniversaries were accompanied by television specials (Wagner-Roos 2012) and a plethora of new biographies, some of them extolling Elizabeth's independent lifestyle as the quintessence of the modern woman (Hamann 1997; Haslip 2000; Sinclair 1998). Newspaper reports, magazine articles, and website entries compared Sissi's life with the tragic life of Princess Diana who died in 1997 (Supp 1998; Silverstar, "Lady Diana and the Empress Elisabeth"). There are several websites, webpages, and even a Facebook page devoted to Sissi (among many others: Futter, Unterreiner, Brandt and Wilkes, Mahon, Alexandra) which has caused some fans to complain in the blogosphere that "so much has been written about Sisi[2] that she has been practically elevated beyond the realm of reality. Some call this phenomenon a cult of personality" (Schmid 2012). In 1998, the Austrian postal service issued a new commemorative stamp in Elizabeth's honor, which was followed in 2012 by the issue of an entire commemorative stamp book (Steiniger-Mocnik 2012).

There were special museum exhibits dedicated to Sissi. The Villa Hermes on the outskirts of Vienna offered an exhibition around the theme "Elisabeth—Schönheit für die Ewigkeit" ["Elizabeth—Beauty for Eternity"]. There were specially guided tours and historical-interpretive walks through the inner-city districts of Vienna called "Kaiserin Elisabeth—die seltsame Sissi" ["Empress Elisabeth—the Mysterious Sissi"]. To attract the younger crowd, there was even a marionette play in the Castle Schönbrunn in Vienna called "Sissis Geheimnis" ["Sissi's Secret"]—and these were just some of the special attractions dedicated to Sissi during the anniversary years.

There is also a regular series of events that is dedicated to what some think is a veritable Sissi cult. There is a Sissi museum in the Hofburg in Vienna allowing the public a glimpse of the Imperial apartments. The famous portrait of Elisabeth by Franz Xaver Winterhalter, which shows her at age twenty-eight in her ball gown and with diamond stars in her hair, was extensively, and expensively, restored in honor of her birthday ("Aufhängung Des Winterhalter-Porträt Von Sisi"). A permanent Sissi-themed tour in the carriage museum at Castle Schönbrunn in Vienna shows off the horse carriages in which she used to travel as well as the horse-drawn hearse that was employed for her funeral procession. The Museum of Technology in Vienna has on display the specially converted Ringhoffer salon and sleeper car that Elisabeth used to travel by train (Winkler). The Imperial Furniture Collection in Vienna's seventh district has a special "Sissi path" that shows off the Habsburg furniture that was used for the sets of the *Sissi* movie series. Other museums devoted to the life of the princess can be found in Bad Ischl in Austria where Sisi's husband Franz Joseph had an imperial villa built in the shape of the letter *E* for Elisabeth. Unterwittelsbach and Possenhofen, both located in Bavaria, Germany, also have permanent museums dedicated to Elisabeth. There are numerous statutes and large-scale memorials dedicated to Sissi in Vienna and Salzburg, in Bad Kissingen in Germany, in the towns of Szeged and Gödöllö in Hungary, in the cities of Meran and Trieste in Italy, and on the Mediterranean island of Corfu off the west coast of Greece.

Curiously, Sissi made medical history in 1998, one hundred years after her death, by having a psychiatric disorder named after her—the controversial Sissi syndrome, a special form of depression that is masked by hyperactivity (Bauer, Hilscher, Faust). And finally, there is the 1992 musical, which is simply titled "Elisabeth." It is the most successful German-language musical of all time and has been seen by more than ten million spectators. It has been translated into seven languages and has been performed in Europe in Austria, Germany, Switzerland, Italy, Hungary, the Netherlands, Sweden, Finland, and as far away as South Korea and Japan. In 2012, the musical was revived in Vienna at the Theater an der Wien, the site of its world premiere, for the quartoseptcentennial celebration of Elisabeth's birthday.

Over time, the public image of Empress Elizabeth, who spelled her own name as "Sisi" not "Sissi," has been carefully constructed through the process of museum curation, a selective process at best which leaves many questions about the real life of the former Empress unanswered and open to interpretation. Add to that the thick, century-old patina of mediated images, popular culture treatments, and commercial kitsch, and it has become nearly impossible to distinguish between Sisi, the historical figure, and Sissi, the amalgam of societal idealizations and receptacle of mirrored historical self-projections. While Sisi has been buried in the Vienna Kapuzinergruft, "Sissi" seems to have taken on an enduring life of her own.

Sissi's image has been irrevocably shaped by the movie trilogy *Sissi* (1955), *Sissi—Die junge Kaiserin* (1956), and *Sissi—Schicksalsjahre einer Kaiserin* (1957). The *Sissi* movies are shown annually at Christmas on Austrian, German, Dutch, and French TV and in 1998 were digitally restored to their original Agfa-color splendor and reissued in high definition. The trilogy is a Cinderella-like portrayal of the young princess, from her youth in Bavaria to her ascension to the throne at the age of sixteen, and her conflicted marriage to her cousin, the Austrian emperor Franz Joseph.

The movies, taken together as an ensemble piece, constitute an important historical artifact. Filmed on location in Allied-occupied Austria, the films were largely the creation of Ernst Marischka, the Austrian screen writer and director who wrote or co-wrote nearly one hundred movie scripts and directed twenty-nine films over the course of his career.

Marischka had first worked with the *Sissi* material in the early 1930s, soon after his brother Hubert had discovered a comedic play by Ernst Décsey and Robert Weil, writing under the pseudonym Gustav Holm. The title of the play was *Sissys Brautfahrt*, [*Sissy's Bridal Journey*]. The Marischka brothers turned the lighthearted drama into a libretto that the Austrian violinist and composer Fritz Kreisler used to score an operetta. The result of their collaboration was *Sissy*, which debuted in December 1932 in the Theater an der Wien in Vienna, with the renowned actress Paula Wessely in the title role. Even though the operetta was highly popular and was performed 289 times in a row, the swift and far-reaching implementation of anti-Semitic laws following Hitler's annexation of Austria made it illegal to continue to perform Kreisler's music. As a result of the performance ban, the rights to the successful *Sissy* operetta were sold to Columbia Pictures which remade it into *The King Steps Out*, a light comedy film directed by Josef von Sternberg (Lugmayr 2008, 89–90).

When Marischka revisited the *Sissi* material in the early 1950s, the external political and historical circumstances surrounding his rediscovery could not be more different from that of his first treatment of the subject. Following the defeat of Hitler in 1945, the Allied Powers occupied both Germany and Austria. Both countries were confronted with the horrors of Nazi extermination politics in the wake of the publicized liberation of concentration camps throughout the former Third Reich nations. While some could legitimately claim no direct knowledge of the atrocities that had been committed, neither country could escape the *Kollektivschuld*, or collective guilt, of silently condoning or acquiescing to the pogroms and other Nazi purification campaigns that had been directed at ethnic minorities. One of the first Allied initiatives after the military defeat of the Third Reich was the vigorous pursuit of *Entnazifizierung*, or denazification, a series of directives issued by the Allied Control Council in Berlin to rid the politics, societies, and cultures of Germany and Austria of any remnants of Nazi ideology.

This initiative included strict censorship of the entertainment media to counteract the intense Nazi propaganda that both countries had been exposed to for more than a decade. As a result, much of the German-speaking film industry, which once had rivaled Hollywood in innovation and creativity, retreated into the relative safety of non-controversial subjects, such as the *Heimatfilm* genre. The typical *Heimatfilm*, or homeland movie, extolled the beauty of the alpine landscape and fauna and the moral conduct of its noble protagonists, such as forest rangers, mountain guides, country doctors, and shepherds, all wrapped in simplistic plot structures of good-versus-evil or sentimental variations of boy-meets-girl tropes and conventions. Indeed, the three *Sissi* movies have been interpreted as prime examples of the *Heimatfilm* genre (Müller 2008). The trilogy has been the subject of a wide variety of analyses, including one that uses queer theory to locate it as an example of "queer rupture in the fairytale of benevolent power" (Schlipphacke 2010, 254).

Most of these interpretations are very well researched and definitely have merit. However, there can be little doubt that central to the deeper reading of the *Sissi* trilogy and to the understanding of these movies in their proper cultural and historical contexts figures the concept of *Vergangenheitsbewältigung*. Literally translated, this term signifies the practice, predominantly situated in Germany and Austria, of attempting to cope with, or to get over, their shared past and joint culpability for the atrocities committed during the Third Reich. Peter Reichel (2007) characterizes *Vergangenheitsbewältigung* as

> der bis heute andauernde, konfliktreiche Prozess der Schuldbewältigung und Schuldverdrängung, des politischen Wandels, des trauernden Gedenkens, des öffentlichen Erinnerns und Vergessens, der historiographischen Deutung und Umdeutung, des Erfindens und Erzählens.
>
> [the continuing, conflict-laden process of coming to terms with guilt and the repression of guilt, of political change, of mournful remembrance, of public memory and of public amnesia, of historical interpretation and reinterpretation, of fabrications and telling of stories.]

The voice-over of the trailer for *Sissi* (1955) serves as an example of historical reinterpretation and selective public memory. It promised

> Ein Farbfilm der Anmut, der Jugend, der Romantik, und der Erfüllung einer großen Liebe! Mit dem einmaligen Zauber der Landschaft, von den bayrischen Seen bis Bad Ischl. Von der Wachau über die Donau in die Kaiserstadt Wien. Eine strahlende Schau der Lebenslust, echt und menschlich, volkstümlich und humorvoll… . Sissi, der Farbfilm mit unvergeßlichen Höhepunkten! Mit einer verschwenderischen Pracht der Ausstattung, im Rhythmus zündender Melodien, im Spiegel des Lichtes und der Farben!
>
> [A movie in color about grace, youth, romanticism, and the fulfillment of a great love. With the unparalleled magic of the landscape, from the Bavarian Lakes to Bad Ischl [a spa town in Upper Austria], from the Wachau [valley] of the Danube river to the Imperial City of Vienna. A sparkling film that expresses a zest for life, authentic and humane, folksy and humorous… . Sissi, the movie in color with unforgettable highlights, with a lavish grandeur of décor and with the rhythms of engaging melodies, in a mirror of light and colors!]

Significantly, the trailer ends with a prolonged, ten-second medium shot and fadeout of the tolling of the Pummerin in St. Stephen's Cathedral in the inner city of Vienna. The Pummerin is the largest swinging bell in Austria, the third-largest in Europe, the fifth-largest in the world. For Austrians, the Pummerin has long held a special place in their national consciousness. Because it was cast from cannons captured from Turkish invaders during the second siege of Vienna in 1683, it has become a lasting symbol of freedom, a national treasure comparable to the Liberty Bell in Philadelphia. The bell is inscribed with the Latin words *pax in libertate*, "peace in liberty," and is dedicated to the Queen of Austria.

The Pummerin is also popularly known as "the voice of Austria" and is tolled only about ten times a year, during high church holidays and at midnight on New Year's Eve. On rare occasions in Austrian history, the Pummerin was tolled for secular reasons, for example, to announce the end of wars. On May 15, 1955, the Pummerin rang to celebrate the end of the Allied occupation of Austria and the signing of the Austrian *Staatsvertrag*, which reestablished Austria as a free, sovereign, and democratic nation. It was that most recent tolling of the Pummerin that must have been fresh in the minds of moviegoers when the film was released in December 1955.

*Sissi*, the first installment in the film trilogy, perhaps most vividly exemplifies the storytelling aspect of *Vergangenheitsbewältigung*. The movie deals overtly with the broad theme of freedom and loss of freedom to an autocratic political regime. It deals with the issues of personal happiness and the subordination of personal happiness for the greater political good. And it deals with the excesses of bureaucracy and of an overly regulated state, sometimes to the point of preposterous absurdity.

But rather than reflecting on the burdensome linkages between Austria and Germany and their recent historical connections, in particular between Upper Austria, Hitler's birthplace, and Bavaria, the fulcrum of his rise to power, Ernst Marischka's *Sissi* provides the fiction of an alternative past, an avenue for diversion and reinterpretation. In lieu of bringing up memories of Hitler's Munich Beer Hall Putsch attempt and its aftermath, Marischka takes the viewer into a fictitious historical reality more than one hundred years earlier, to the carefree existence of a Bavarian-Austrian aristocratic family in the stylistically bucolic environs of Possenhoffen at Lake Starnberg. Theirs is a life of leisure, one of physical comfort and security, of hunting sports in the wooded mountains and of beer- and wine-toasting *Gemütlichkeit* at home. In short, their world is, as the German saying goes, "in order."

The movie opens with a panorama pan shot of Lake Starnberg, rising slowly upward to the Bavarian Alps, and briefly resting on Castle Possenhofen proudly flying the Bavarian *Rautenflagge*, the traditional blue-and-white lozenge flag, from its roof. The camera cuts back to the lake view where four men on a raft harmonize a slow, traditional yodel song. They greet the lord of the house, Duke Max in Bavaria, who is fishing from a small boat dock, with a bow and: "Guten Mogen, königliche Hoheit!" ["Good morning, Your Royal Highness!"], to which Max responds with a jovial: "Grüß Euch Gott!" ["God may greet you!" a common form of greeting in Bavaria and Austria]. Just as Max returns their greeting, a big fish bites and he calls his six youngest children to help him haul in his catch. The children, three girls dressed in traditional *Dirndl* style and three boys in *Lederhosen*, the traditional Bavarian leather pants, excitedly run down the hill to the lake. As they get closer to the boat dock, they yell back to their mother that "Dad has caught a big fish," to which Max's wife, the Austrian-born Habsburg Duchess Ludovika, replies from an open window in the castle with a joyful: "Petri Heil!" a typical angler's greeting. Max lets one of his sons, Gackl, hold the fishing pole while he retrieves a landing net. But Gackl cannot hold on to the pole, falls into the water and lets the fish escape. Max uses the landing net to retrieve Gackl from the lake and the whole family returns to the castle for breakfast.

Though barely two minutes in length, this opening sequence provides an important foreshadowing of some of the film's major themes: nature as a symbol of freedom, both transcendental and indomitable; society, with its persistent stratifications that rank both the aristocracy and the lower classes; and the social order that is maintained by the articulated deference to inherited power, carefully counterbalanced by the expressed respect for the common man.

These themes continue through the breakfast scene, in which Ludovika chastises Max for his lumberjack-like table manners that appear to have rubbed off on the children: "Nicht einer hat ein Besteck benützt! Und warum? Weil Du immer mit den Fingern ißt!" ["Not one of them has used the silverware [to eat their breakfast]! And why? Because you always eat with your fingers!"] Ludovika is concerned that her oldest daughter Helene, called Néné, is at the right age for marriage but the only suitors who have shown up at the castle are of an undesirable class, such as the son of an innkeeper in Vienna.

At that moment, Mr. Johann Petzmacher, the innkeeper's son, enters the scene with news from the court in Vienna. He reports that the entire court is still jittery over the assassination attempt on Emperor Franz Joseph I by the Hungarian nationalist János Libényi and adds, jokingly, "Der einzige Mann in der Hofburg is die Soferl" ["The only man in the imperial palace is Soferl"]. Affronted by the lack of ceremonial manners of her husband's visitor, Ludovika insists that Petzmacher correct his disrespectful address of the Emperor's mother, Ludovika's sister, to "her Imperial Highness, the Archduchess Sophie." The embarrassing situation is resolved when the butler serves a red wine vintage 1849, the year imperial absolutism was reestablished in Austria after the liberal revolutions that had rocked the foundations of the Habsburg empire in 1848. "Wenn Dir der nicht schmeckt, dann schmeckt Dir keiner" ["If you don't like this one, you won't like any."], Max remarks in an obvious reference to the reestablishment of order by the monarchical forces.

This correction of the conduct of Duke Max's guest is significant because it sets up an intriguing reversal of the typical male-female dichotomy with regard to courtly ceremony. While both male and female characters are shown seeking a stable political order, the male characters are, uncharacteristically, cast as generous, less interested in maintaining strict social decorum than are the female characters. The only exception to this convention in the *Sissi* films, which boldly brushes against the history of the movie audiences who had lived through the male-dominated Nazi dictatorship, is Sissi herself who is portrayed as a tomboyish girl of natural grace and beauty.

Sissi is introduced to the film audience in the scene immediately following the wine-tasting sequence. Sissi rides, sidesaddle, a wild black mare up the steep mountain meadow. While her mother Ludovika is worried about her safety and admonishes her to be careful, her father encourages her to jump the horse over a high hedge of red roses. "Sporen geben!" ["Use the spurs!"], Max yells and when Sissi completes the jump, he adds, admiringly: "Ein

Prachtmädel!" ["What a girl!"]. As a reward for being daring, Sissi is invited by her father to go on a hunt.

Sissi's gentler communion with nature is invoked after the riding scene. She dismounts her horse and immediately proceeds to take care for her menagerie of animals, a pair of birds in an open-air cage and, in a specially fenced-off area in the yard, a young orphaned deer. Sissi's compassion toward animals is paralleled by her easy demeanor around the family servants, Herr Mittermeier, the aged groomsman, and Mrs. Stoeckl, the maid who suffers from arthritis but continues to work in the garden for the Duke's family. Sissi is portrayed as the paragon of the benevolent young patrician, one who cares little about social status differentiations but instead engages others on the basis of their humanity, a serene country princess who is placed against the backdrop of the idyllic fauna and flora of rural Bavaria.

The film's pacing picks up as Ludovika receives a letter from the imperial palace in Vienna, informing her that the Archduchess Sophie has chosen her oldest daughter Néné as the bride for her son Franz Joseph. A cut to the palace introduces the second main narrative, that of life at the Habsburg court in Vienna. From the moment of his introduction—Franz Joseph conducts state business at his desk with his grandmother Maria Theresa's oversized portrait above him—it is clear that the Emperor is completely governed by Sophie, whom he addresses by the formal German personal pronoun "Sie."

Sophie explains to Franz Joseph that the time has come to get married since his status as a bachelor is starting to create political problems for the monarchy.

> "Schon zu viele Mächte haben ihre Fühler bei mir ausgestreckt. Ablehnungen könnten nur zu politischen Verwicklungen führen… . Deshalb habe ja ich die Wahl für Dich getroffen! Eine Wahl, die kein Land verletzt und keines bevorzugt."
>
> ["Already, too many nations have sent out their feelers to me. Continued rejections can only bring about political complications… . That is why I have made a choice for you! A choice that does not affront any nation nor shows preference for any country."]

In the marriage-planning scene, Marischka provides two historical touchstones to which Austrians of the 1950s could readily connect. The first is the—in Austria well-known—Latin motto of the Habsburg family: *Bella gerant alii, tu felix Austria, nube!* ["Others may wage war but you, happy Austria, marry!"]. It refers to the practice of the Habsburg dynasty, well-honed since the end of the Middle Ages, to secure both political and geostrategic security through carefully constructed matrimonial projects that promised to yield a variety of territorial, financial, military, or religious advantages. This stood in sharp contrast to the more recent history of the Austro-Bavarian alliance that had been based on a military power grab by Adolf Hitler.

The other is the Freudian constellation of the domineering mother figure who exerts control over her son's sexuality by choosing not only the timing of his marriage but also the identity of the bride. For the dutiful son in the movie, it is supposed to be a supremely insipid choice of a woman, one who "neither affronts nor shows preference"—an easily controlled, silent partner who will bend to the rule of the court without difficulty and not assert any independent thought. This very overt depiction of sublimation, a classic Freudian defense mechanism, must have been quite intriguing to Austrian film audiences since any references to psychoanalytic theories were strictly forbidden under the Nazi regime. Freud's books were publicly burned and psychoanalysis branded an undesirable "Jewish science." The reintroduction of Freudian thought, apart from its cinematic value, constitutes another instance of *Vergangenheitsbewältigung* in the *Sissi* movie, an example of public memory restored.

The middle part of the *Sissi* movie follows the traditional narrative arc of the Cinderella story. Ludovika takes Néné to Bad Ischl to meet her future husband. Sissi, who is not intended to be part of the engagement celebrations, leaves the villa where she is staying with her family and accidentally encounters the Emperor on the road to Bad Ischl. Franz Joseph thinks she is a commoner but is taken with her, not knowing that the girl who presents herself as "Liesl von Possenhofen" is, in reality, Néné's sister. Dreading the engagement ceremony, he sets up a last affirmation of his personal freedom by arranging a rendezvous with "Liesl," promising to go on a hunt with her.

This scene replicates a scene earlier in the movie in which Sissi's bravura, jumping the rose hedge with her horse, was rewarded with an idyllic hunting trip into the Bavarian Alps with her father. Both scenes reaffirm the visual metaphors of German idealism and attempt to reclaim, from Nazi distortions, the culturally contested principles of *Stammboden*, or inner rootedness, and *Naturverbundenheit*, or closeness to nature. The exact parallels between the two scenes are not coincidental, as other researchers have observed. Erica Carter notes that these two sequences in the movie reiterate "a standard *topos* from sentimental literature … that balance and inner harmony derive … from human communion with nature" (Carter 2010, 84). Nadja Krämer adds: "The visual constellation represented by the two scenes foreshadows Franz's [the future husband's] replacement of Maximilian [the father]."

Duke Maximilian Josef of Bavaria is the male role model who thus serves as an ostensibly uncompromised basis of German identity, assuring national continuity along with untainted renewal within the emerging postwar German democracy (Krämer 2012, 353).

In a very overt manner, therefore, these two scenes, and the analogous codes with which they are inscribed, serve the purpose of *Vergangenheitsbewältigung* as a self-conscious form of historical reinterpretation.

But there is a second parallel, this one involving a linguistic particularity. In the hunting rendezvous scene with Sissi, Franz Joseph dismisses and sends home the entire hunting party to have greater privacy with the putative country girl whom he knows as Liesl of Possenhofen. As the hunters bid their farewell, they extend the traditional huntsman's greeting: "Waidmann's Heil!" translated as "Good hunting!" in the subtitles, to which Franz Joseph responds with "Waidmann's Dank!" subtitled "Hunter's thanks." Just as Ludovika had greeted Max's fishing in the opening scene with a jovial: "Petri Heil!" the hunters in this scene appear oblivious to the fact that the expression "Heil!" had taken on another, more sinister dimension in the years of the Third Reich. Common German parlance has used the word "Heil" in only four combinations ever: "Petri Heil!" the fisherman's greeting, "Waidmanns Heil!" the hunter's greeting, and the two Nazi-connected "Sieg Heil!" and "Heil Hitler!" greetings. Ernst Marischka's use of two of the four forms of "Heil!" within a span of less than forty-five minutes in the original *Sissi* film manifests itself as a strategy of contestation and linguistic co-optation that unmasks and upsets the code of domination during the fascist years and returns the words to more of a naturalized sense of linguistic evolution and continuity.

Equally important is the conscious reclaiming of German music in the original *Sissi* movie. Throughout, there are short pieces of incidental music that recall the Bavarian tradition of beer drinking and merrymaking songs as well as other traditional pieces of folk music and harmonizations. In the hunting scene with Franz Joseph, which "Liesl" leaves abruptly after she realizes that the Emperor is about to be engaged to her sister Néné, Sissi leaves behind a zither, much in the same way that Cinderella leaves behind a slipper in the Cinderella fairy tale. Symbolically, nature and culture unite in this filmic metaphor.

The second half of *Sissi* is interpolated with several music pieces that resonated well with audiences. For example, the announcements of the imperial guests at the state dinner, which is to serve as the engagement ceremony for Franz Joseph, is underscored by Chopin's Polonaise in A Major, the "Military" Polonaise, the same music that had been used during World War II to score victory announcements in weekly newsreels. There are Strauss waltzes and quadrilles, polkas and marches aplenty, including Johan Strauss's "Radetzky March," which serves as the soundtrack to the Emperor's introduction to the public of Sissi as the future Empress from the balcony of the Imperial villa in Bad Ischl.

Ten of the last fifteen minutes of the movie, which build up to a dramatic wedding finale, are shot without any dialogue whatsoever. Instead, the camera follows Sissi on her Danubian boat voyage from Passau to Vienna, joyfully waving at the crowds that have gathered at river's edge to welcome the Emperor's future bride. After a brief scene set in the Schönbrunn palace, there is a prolonged sequence of the Imperial bridal procession through the streets of Vienna, again without any dialogue, but with a crescendo of bell-ringing that culminates in Bach organ music as Franz Joseph and Sissi enter St. Michael's Cathedral. The final scene of the movie shows the marriage being consecrated by the bishop of Vienna, accompanied by a rendition of Händel's "Hallelujah Chorus" sung by the Vienna Boys Choir. The film ends with the last phrase and the fermata of the "Hallelujah Chorus" accompanying a slow vertical pan shot of the three-story Baroque high altar where the camera rests briefly on the Eye of Providence in the canopy before fading to black.

The accentuated emphasis on Austrian cultural iconography in the second half of the movie—from the expansive views of the Hofburg and Schönbrunn palaces to the close-ups of the Imperial horse carriage, from the ornate uniforms of the imperial army officers to the musical formality of the cotillion—forms a cinematic pastiche that evokes the ideal self of the Habsburg past. As Margarete Lamb-Faffelberger and Franz-Peter Griesmaier (2002) have observed, the post-war film industry played to a self-understanding of the Austrian nation as a *Kulturnation*, a highly cultured nation. "This image was created to support Austria's national and cultural identity formation during its restoration years in the 1950s. Austria's political and cultural elite proclaimed the Second Republic as a modern continuation of the Habsburg-Austria." Quoting the Austrian poet and novelist Alexander Lernet-Holenia, Lamb-Faffelberger and Griesmaier contend that the thrust of *Vergangenheitsbewältigung* in Austria was not progressive in nature but rather reactionary: "We only need to continue where the illusions of a mad man interrupted our dreams. In fact, we do not need to look forward but back" (Lamb-Faffelberger and Griesmaier 2002, 1). In that sense, Ernst Marischka's first *Sissi* film fulfilled its mission with aplomb.

The second and third *Sissi* movies, *Sissi: The Young Empress* (1956) and *Sissi: The Fateful Years of an Empress* (1957), continue the story of the young bride at the court in Vienna. They chronicle Sissi's increasing involvement in Austrian politics, her central role in achieving the *Ausgleich* with Hungary in 1867, her near-fatal illness and recovery, and her final political act, the *rapprochement* with the renegate regions of Lombardi and Venezia in Italy.

The main narrative arcs of the second and third movies develop roughly along the same lines as the first. Even whole scenes appear to be repeated, with only some minor variations. In the first movie, Sissi rides her horse wildly through her family's estate. In the second film, she rides dangerously through the Prater, the Imperial hunting grounds between the Danube river and the Danube canal east of Vienna's historic city center. In the third movie's opening scene, Sissi is shown to participate with Count Andrassy in a stylized fox hunt in Hungary.

The beauty of the Bavarian and Austrian woods as a touchstone of unspoiled nature in *Sissi* is replaced by the unspoiled vistas of the Karawanks mountain range in the Austrian Alps and the Puszta grassland on the Great Hungarian Plain in *The Young Empress*. The visual splendor of the Mediterranean locations on the islands of Madeira and Corfu dominates in the *The Fateful Years of an Empress*.

The iconic tension between Archduchess Sophie and Empress Elizabeth —mother and wife competing for the attention, if not affection, of Franz Joseph—is retained as a recursive movie theme. This conflict comes to a head when the Emperor's mother insists on taking over the education of her first-born child and Sissi temporarily leaves the court and her husband. In the third movie, the conflict with the mother-in-law is resurrected when Sissi, having been diagnosed with consumption, overhears Sophie advising her son to think about who, after Sissi's impending death, his next wife is going to be.

The second, court-focused narrative from the first film finds its counterpart in Sissi's successful engagement of the Hungarian rebellion in the second movie. Through personal charm and persistence, and against the will and political sentiment of Archduchess Sophie, Sissi manages to win over the leader of the Hungarian rebellion, Count Andrassy, who becomes the ambassador of her cause among his people. The last five minutes of *Sissi: The Young Empress* again build up to a filmic spectacular similar to the wedding scene in the first *Sissi* film; this time, the movie ends with the extended portrayal of the pomp and circumstance that surrounds the coronation of Franz Joseph and Sissi to King and Queen of Hungary. This type of ending is a unique feature of the *Sissi* films. In the analysis of one reviewer, the films' endings "with [their] long, elaborate scenes of spectacle, *tableaux vivants* of royal display … engage in a temporal stretching that interrupts the flow of the narrative," which serves to "suspend the story in a manner that privileges an atemporal allegorical pleasure over historical continuity" (Schlipphacke 2010, 233).

The end of *The Fateful Years of an Empress* follows the same trusted formula. An extended musical scene in the La Scala Opera building first centers on the Italians singing, in protest, Giuseppe Verdi's "Chorus of the Hebrew Slaves" and then resolves into a prolonged gondola procession along the Grande Canale in Venice. The silence in this scene, in which the Italians refuse to cheer the royal pair in disdain of their visit, is "worse than an assassination attempt," in Franz Joseph's words. Once again, there are long stretches without dialogue in which the mise-en-scène is carried entirely by the visuals. It is Sissi's reunion with her daughter that turns the silent masses of onlookers into a cheering crowd of royal supporters. Having thus won over the Italian spectators, the Imperial couple is shown, in a long shot, processing to Saint Mark's Basilica as the population joins in singing "Gott Erhalte Franz Den Kaiser" ["God Keep Franz, Our Emperor"], the imperial Austrian national anthem that was well known to Austrian and German contemporary audiences as "Deutschland, Deutschland Über Alles," the German national anthem. Thus the trilogy concludes, in stark contrast to the actual, disastrous union between these two nations during World War II, on a positive representation of the literal and figurative marriage between Germany and Austria.

There is a third narrative strand that interweaves all three *Sissi* films. It is the central role that bureaucracy played in the Habsburg Empire. The movies portray the unique Austrian obsession with complicated titles among public officials at the lower levels of the state bureaucracy at which inequality in social rank based on occupational status was an immanent part of the system. This lower tier of the bureaucracy is personified in the farcical character of Oberst Böckl, who advances from local gendarme in *Sissi* to head of Sissi's personal security detail in *The Fateful Years of an Empress*. Böckl is the Austrian everyman, at once narrowly defined by the rules of courtly etiquette and yet buoyed in his successive elevations in military rank by the always-present bureaucratic career escalator that rewards loyalty over talent or merit. As arcane and occasionally absurd the system may appear to the modern observer, post-war Austrians found in it what they looked most for in the state—stability. Even modern sociological researchers have confirmed a "Habsburg effect" in the former countries of the Austro-Hungarian Empire that is based on the lasting perception among the public that the Habsburg bureaucracy was considered fairly honest and generally high-minded, producing "genuine citizen-state interactions" and resulting in formal cultural norms that prevail even today (Becker et al. 2011, 1–3).

At the highest levels of bureaucracy, audiences were reminded that the emperor and his family were deemed unapproachable, kept in the rarefied air of the archaic court ceremonial. Sissi does not willingly nor successfully adapt to the Viennese court manners. In *The Young Empress*, Sissi is ordered by Archduchess Sophie, through an intermediary, to learn her part of the rules of Spanish court ceremony by heart: "Neunzehn Seiten? … Schön. Ich werde mich bemühen, diesen Unsinn auswendig zu lernen" ["Nineteen pages? … All right, I will make an effort to commit this nonsense to memory."] Sissi also frequently speaks of equality, a topic that is anathema to a dynasty that requires *tiefe Reverenz*, deep public bowing on bended knee as a symbol of submission, from all of its subjects. In a scene with Count Julius Andrassy in *The Young Empress*, Sissi seeks to reassure the former leader of the Hungarian secession movement who has just been pardoned by an Imperial amnesty:

> Ich werde auch in Zukunft alles tun, um Ungarn Österreich, und damit auch dem Kaiser, näher zu bringen und um Ihrem Land die Gleichberechtigung wiederzugeben. Damit aber das Wort "Gleichberechtigung" kein leeres Wort sei, möchte ich Sie und alle aus dem Exil heimgekehrten Ungarn mit ihren Damen zum nächsten Hofball einladen. Wir wollen an diesem Tag die Stunde feieren, die unsere Herzen einander nähergebracht hat.
>
> [Also in the future, I will continue to undertake everything possible to bring Hungary closer to Austria and to the Emperor to ensure that your country will regain its status of equality. To make certain that the word "equality" not remain an empty phrase, however, I want to invite you, and all exiled Hungarians and their wives who have returned home, to attend the next imperial ball. On that day, we will celebrate the hour that has brought our two nations' hearts together.]

Here, too, Marischka shows a unique sensitivity toward *Vergangenheitsbewältigung* by accentuating what would resonate positively with Austrian audiences. Sissi, who as a Bavarian country princess is viewed as a near-morganatic consort to Franz Joseph by the court in Vienna, is ultimately portrayed as the politically wiser force whose *rapprochement* maneuvers with the Hungarian resistance harken back to the glory days of the waltzing Congress of Vienna during the post-Napoleonic era. So powerful has this public image become that it has found its way into official accounts of Sissi's life. In the words of one of Sissi's biographers: "The great gift of Empress Elizabeth [was] to create an image of concern for all, which would unite the nine nations … ruled by her husband, the emperor of Austro-Hungary" (Sinclair 1998, 207). In the movie, Sissi's tempering influence as an outsider to the monarchy is portrayed as providential. As Duke Max philosophizes in a dialogue with Duchess Ludovika in *Sissi: The Young Empress*: "Schau, ich glaube, das ist alles Schicksal … daß unsere Sissi Kaiserin geworden ist. … Umsonst geschieht nichts auf dieser Welt. Wahrscheinlich hat sie irgendeine Mission zu erfüllen." ["Look, I think that is all a matter of fate … that our Sissi became Empress of Austria. … Nothing in this world happens without reason. Perhaps she has to fulfill some sort of mission."]

Whether declared or undeclared, *Sissi*, the movie trilogy, fulfilled a mission of its own, that of easing Austria's difficult transition from totalitarian militarism and the crimes against humanity that had been committed under fascist dictatorship to post-war neutrality and democracy. The making of the movies themselves provided a welcome second chance for many of the actors and production workers who had previously collaborated with the Nazi regime, perhaps none more so than Marischka's chosen cinematographer Bruno Mondi. Mondi had previously gained fame as the cinematographic genius behind the 1940 film *Jud Suess*, a particularly vile example of Joseph Goebbels's Third Reich indoctrination campaign. Mondi's *Jud Suess* has been characterized as "one of the most notorious ... pieces of anti-Semitic film propaganda produced in Nazi Germany" (Cull 2003, 205); to this day, the film's screening is restricted to academic researchers or instructional presentations and its distribution continues to be banned in Germany (Marek and Harmann 2010). Exactly why Marischka chose Mondi for the *Sissi* films remains unknown but the movies' undisputable success among German-speaking audiences in the post-war years speaks to the possibility that, among many, motives of personal redemption and national *Vergangenheitsbewältigung* may have intertwined.

The *Sissi* movies continue to rank among the most successful Austrian-made film productions in history. An estimated twenty-five million moviegoers watched these movies in the German-speaking countries alone. The *Sissi* trilogy was later translated and synchronized in several major languages and has led to an international, film-induced tourism boom (Peters et al. 2011) that, in its economic impact on the Austrian economy, rivals or perhaps even surpasses that of the *Sound of Music* tourism phenomenon. Financially lucrative in its box office success and secondary commerce, the *Sissi* series provided the additional benefit of alleviating national guilt. In the words of one reviewer: "Although there were other films with similar themes and similar settings, it was this series of films ... that did ... much to promote a positive and uncontroversial image for Austria both at home and abroad" (Wauchope 2002, 172).

The German political theorist and philosopher Mark Arenhövel has observed that any country that embarks on the transition from dictatorship to democracy and, in the process, attempts to establish a measure of accountability for past abuses or crimes against humanity, faces a series of profound judicial and political dilemmas during the initial phase of democratization.

> Zu einem häufig noch grundlegenderen Konflikt wird der Umgang mit der Vergangenheit, mit "Erinnerungskonflikten" und "Konflikterinnerungen," welche die gesamte Gesellschaft durchziehen... . Dieser Prozeß der Erinnerungsarbeit, die sich zwischen reueloser Amnesie, Amnestie und schmerzhafter Anamnese bewegt [hat Relevanz] für die Stabilität und Konsolidierung einer jungen Demokratie. (Arenvögel 2000, 7)

> [The handling of the past, of both "conflicts of memory" and "memories of conflict," frequently becomes a much more profoundly contested field that can permeate an entire society... . This process of actively engaging history, which spans the gamut from remorseless amnesia to amnesty and painful anamnesis, [has relevance] for the stability and consolidation of any young democracy.]

The powerful image of Sissi, as created and mediated in the Ernst Marischka trilogy, and the largely uncritical fandom that it has engendered since the release of the films nearly sixty years ago, has acted as a lasting transformative agent on the self-understanding of central Europe's past, especially since the *Sissi* movies are shown annually at Christmas on Austrian, German, Dutch, and French TV. Rather than supporting the difficult engagement with history through a concerted national process of self-reflective *Vergangenheitsbewältigung*, the films have provided an easily embraced diversion from the need to confront recent history. It remains to be seen whether this mnemonic trend will be challenged by the rising movement toward unification that requires serious debates about Europe's recent historical heritage, or whether the past will remain relegated to the ready-made, theme-park version of illustrious Habsburg glory that Marischka's *Sissi* movies have helped create.

## Endnotes

1. Note: In this chapter, the authors refer to Princess Sissi as both "Elisabeth" and "Elizabeth." "Elisabeth" is the original German spelling of her name; UK writers use both "Elisabeth" and "Elizabeth"; and American writers tend to prefer "Elizabeth." In this chapter, the authors alternate between both variants in order to use the form found in the originating source (German/British/American).
2. "Sisi" is the way that Elizabeth spelled her own name. "Sissi," more often than not, refers to the mediated historical persona of Sisi.

## References

Alexandra. "Kaiserin Elisabeth Von Österreich." The Royal Correspondent. Accessed February 10, 2014. http://royalcorrespondent.com/2012/12/23/kaiserin-elisabeth-von-osterreich/

Arenhövel, Mark. 2000. *Demokratie und Erinnerung: Der Blick zurück auf Diktatur und Menschenrechtsverbrechen*. Frankfurt am Main: Campus.

"Aufhängung Des Winterhalter-Porträt Von Sisi." News release. Hofburg Wien. Accessed February 14, 2014. http://www.hofburg-wien.at/en/nc/services/press-information/archiv/press-information-2012/press-information-detail-2012/artikel/aufhaengung-des-winterhalter-portraet-von-sisi.html

Bauer, Martin. "Sissi-Syndrom." Sissi-Syndrom. Accessed February 8, 2014. http://www.uni-protokolle.de/Lexikon/Sissi-Syndrom.html

Becker, Sascha O., Katrin Boeckh, Christa Hainz, and Ludger Woessmann. 2011. "The Empire Is Dead, Long Live the Empire! Long-Run Persistence of Trust and Corruption in the Bureaucracy." CESifo Working Paper Series No. 3392.

Brandt, Jürgen, and Uli Wilkes. "Sissi | Historisch." Sissi | Historisch. Accessed February 16, 2014. http://www.sissi.de/historisch

Burg, Katerina von. 1995. *Elisabeth of Austria: A Life Misunderstood.* Chippenham, Wiltshire, UK: Windsor Publications.

Carter, Erica. 2010. "Sissi the Terrible: Melodrama, Victimhood, and Imperial Nostalgia in the Sissi Trilogy" In *Screening War: Perspectives on German Suffering*, ed. Paul Cooke and Marc Silberman, 81–101. Rochester, NY: Camden House.

Cinderella Brautkleid. "Brautkleid Sissi." Advertisement.–Prinzessin Hochzeitskleid Im Wäsche-Look. Accessed February 10, 2014. http://www.cinderella-traumkleid.de/brautkleider/hochzeitskleid_rueschen.html

Cull, Nicholas J., David Culbert, and David Welch. 2003. *Propaganda and Mass Persuasion: A Historical Encyclopedia, 1500 to the Present.* Santa Barbara, CA: ABC-CLIO.

Faust, Volker. "Ist Die "neue" Depressionsform Des Sisi-Syndroms" Eine Ess-Störung?" Accessed February 8, 2014. http://www.psychosoziale-gesundheit.net/psychiatrie/sisi.html

Futter, Nikolaus. "Das 100. Todesjahr Der Kaiserin Elisabeth 'Sisi'" Home.html. Accessed February 16, 2014. http://www.sisi.at/

Hamann, Brigitte. 1997. *Sissi: Kaiserin Elisabeth von Österreich.* Köln: Taschen.

Haslip, Joan. 2000. *The Lonely Empress: Elizabeth of Austria.* San Diego, CA: Phoenix.

Hilscher, Christian. "Sissi-Syndrom / SISI-Syndrom." Sissi-Syndrom (SISI). Accessed February 8, 2014. http://psylex.de/psychologiebuch/lexikon-psychologie/sissi-syndrom.html

Jenny, Hans A. 1998. *Sissi: Liebe, Tragik und Legenden: Zum 100. Todestag der Kaiserin Elisabeth.* Basel: F. Reinhardt.

Jolie. Advertisement. Luxus Sissi Brautkleid 2013 2014–Kleider Online Bestellen. Accessed February 10, 2014. http://www.modekarusell.eu/product_info.php?products_id=67960

Krämer, Nadja. 2012. "Models of Masculinity in Postwar Germany: The *Sissi* Films and the West German *Wiederbewaffnungsdebatte.*" In *A Companion to German Cinema*, ed. Terri Ginsberg and Andrea Mensch, 341–378. Oxford: Wiley Blackwell.

Lamb-Faffelberger, Margarete, and Franz-Peter Griesmaier. 2002. "Introduction." In *Literature, Film, and the Culture Industry in Contemporary Austria*, ed. Margarete Lamb-Faffelberger, 1–7. New York: Peter Lang.

Lugmayr, Saskia. 2008. "Die 'Sissi'-Trilogie von Ernst Marischka," Diplomarbeit, Universität Wien.

Mahon, Elizabeth. "Scandalous Women." The Lonely Empress: The Life of Elisabeth of Austria. Accessed February 10, 2014. http://scandalouswoman.blogspot.com/2009/12/lonely-empress-life-of-elisabeth-of.html

Maison De Haute Parfumerie Nicolas De Barry. "L'eau De L'impératrice Sissi–L'indomptable–Un Parfum Qui Vous Donnera une Personnalité Libre, Fantaisiste Et Entière." Accessed February 17, 2014. http://www.maisonnicolasdebarry.com/catalogue/les-parfums-historiques/l-eau-de-l-imperatrice-sissi-the-indomitable.html

Marc De La Morandiere. "ELISABETH D'AUTRICHE – HONGRIE." Advertisement. Parfum « Sissi » Par Marc De La Morandiere. Accessed February 17, 2014. http://www.elisabethdautriche.fr/?p=7276

Marek, Michael, and Sarah Harman. 2010. "'Jud Suess' Causes Controversy Second Time Around." *Deutsche Welle*, September 22. http://www.dw.de/jud-suess-causes-controversy-second-time-around/a-6033357

Marischka, Ernst. 1955. *Sissi.*

Marischka, Ernst. 1956. *Sissi: The Young Empress.*

Marischka, Ernst. 1957. *Sissi: The Fateful Years of an Empress.*

McVeigh, Joseph. 2007. "Popular Culture in Austria, 1945–2000." In *A History of Austrian Literature 1918–2000*, ed. Katrin Kohl and Ritchie Robertson, 247–263. Rochester, NY: Camden House.

Modekarusell. Advertisement. Luxus Sissi Brautkleid 2013 2014–Kleider Online Bestellen. Accessed February 10, 2014. http://www.modekarusell.eu/product_info.php?products_id=67960

Müller, Sabine. 2008. "'Finally a Human Being in This Palace': How 'Sissi' Deals with the Past." In *New Readings: Europe in the 1950s: The 'Lost' Decade?* ed. Claire Gorrara and Heiko Feldner. Vol. 9, Cardiff Schools of European Languages, Translation, and Politics. http://ojs.cf.ac.uk/index.php/newreadings/issue/view/5

Peters, Mike, Markus Schukert, Kaye Chon, and Clarissa Schatzmann. 2011. "Empire and Romance: Movie-Induced Tourism and the Case of the Sissi Movies." *Tourism Recreation Research, 36*(2): 169–180.

Reichel, Peter. 2007. *Vergangenheitsbewältigung in Deutschland: Die Auseinandersetzung mit der NS-Diktatur in Politik und Justiz* (2nd ed.). München: Verlag C.H. Beck oHG.

Schlipphacke, Heidi. 2010. "Melancholy Empress: Queering Empire in Ernst Marischka's *Sissi* Films." *Screen, 51*(3): 232–255.

Schmid, Angelyn. 2012. "The Most Beautiful Woman in Europe." Weblog entry, January 14. http://www.heartsthroughhistory.com/the-most-beautiful-woman-in-europe/

Schuster, Gaby. 1998a. *Sissi, eine Prinzessin für den Kaiser*. Bindlach: Loewe Verlag.

Schuster, Gaby. 1998b. *Sissi, im Dienst der Krone*. Bindlach: Loewe Verlag.

Schuster, Gaby. 1999. *Sissi, Schicksal einer Kaiserin.* Bindlach: Loewe Verlag.

Silverstar. "Emperor Franz Joseph I (1830–1916) and Empress Elisabeth (Sissi) (1837-1898)–Page 2–The Royal Forums." The Royal Forums RSS (web log). Accessed February 16, 2014. http://www.theroyalforums.com/forums/f210/emperor-franz-joseph-i-1830-1916-and-empress-elisabeth-sissi-1837-1898-a-16503-2.html

Sinclair, Andrew. 1998. *Death by Fame: A Life of Elisabeth, Empress of Austria.* New York: St. Martin's Press.

"Sisi (Elisabeth Empress of Austria) Her World and Her Legend | Facebook." Facebook. Accessed February 10, 2014. http://www.facebook.com/pages/Sisi-Elisabeth-Empress-of-Austria-her-world-and-her-legend/355768187767739

Steiniger-Mocnik, Theresa. 2012. *Sisi—Legende und Wahrheit.* Wien: Ferrytells Verlag und BeratungsgmbH im Auftrag der Österreichischen Post AG.

Stumpf, Michael. "KiKA–Fernsehen–Sendungen Von A-Z–Sissi." KiKA–Fernsehen–Sendungen Von A-Z–Sissi. Accessed February 10, 2014. http://www.kika.de/scripts/fernsehen/a_z/index.cfm?b=s&a=2&i=671

Stumpf, Michael. "KiKA–Spiel & Spaß–Malen–Ausmalbilder–Sissi." KiKA–Spiel & Spaß–Malen–Ausmalbilder–Sissi. Accessed February 10, 2014. http://www.kika.de/spielspass/malen/ausmalbilder/sissi/index.shtml

Supp, Barbara. 1998. "Schwestern in Schmerz: Mit Kitsch, Kult und Massentrauer jähren sich die Todestage von Prinzessin Diana und Kaiserin Sisi," *Der Spiegel*, August 17, 94–104.

Unterreiner, Katrin. "Vienna–Sisi–Empress Elisabeth–Sissi–Empress of Austria." Vienna–Sisi–Empress Elisabeth–Sissi–Empress of Austria. Accessed February 10, 2014. http://www.wien-vienna.com/sisi.php

Wagner-Roos, Luise. 2012. *Sisi—Mythos einer Märchenprinzessin*. ZDF broadcast, June 3.

Wauchope, Mary. 2002. "Sissi Revisited." In *Literature, Film, and the Culture Industry in Contemporary Austria*, ed. Margarete Lamb-Faffelberger, 170–184. New York: Peter Lang.

"Weltpremiere: Sky Zeigt Sissi-Trilogie in Echtem HD Auf Sky Christmas HD." News release. Accessed February 8, 2014. http://www.hdtv-pro.de/hdtv-sender/weltpremiere-sky-zeigt-sissi-trilogie-in-echten-hd-auf-sky-christmas-hd-7190.html

Winkler, Thomas. "Hofsalonwagen – Technisches Museum Wien." Technisches Museum Wien. Accessed February 9, 2014. http://www.technischesmuseum.at/objekt/hofsalonwagen

CHAPTER TWELVE

# Dedicated to Princesses: The Marriage Market and the Royal Revelations of Ancien Régime Fairy Tales

REBECCA-ANNE C. DO ROZARIO

Once upon a time, fairy tales were written for princesses, and authors of fairy tales lived in close proximity to those princesses. During the reign of the Sun King, Louis XIV, a vogue for fairy tales swept the salons and the court itself. Fairy tale authors such as Marie-Catherine d'Aulnoy, Catherine Bernard, Henriette-Julie de Murat, Marie-Jeanne Lhéritier de Villandon, and Charles Perrault wrote about princesses to an almost obsessive degree. They wrote about beautiful princesses, ugly princesses, wise and cunning princesses, passive and rather stupid princesses. While at court, a princess was a political commodity, one with little agency in a royal marriage market. In the tales, however, a princess might subvert her political objectification and become the centre of her own narrative, whether or not that narrative had a happy ending.

Many fairy tale authors of this period of the Ancien Régime were female. Their tales are generally longer and more socially complex, contain extensive detail about fashions and politics of the time, and focus on the agency of female characters, whether princesses or powerful fairies, the latter wielding more authority than kings. Yet, the tales of women writers failed to make the fairy tale canon and have been obscured by the works of male authors, including their contemporary, Charles Perrault, and later authors and collectors including Jacob and Wilhelm Grimm, Hans Christian Andersen, Andrew Lang, and, eventually, Walt Disney and his studio.[1] The gradual exclusion of women writers from the fairy tale canon can be attributed to the privileging of spare and simple tales ostensibly, though not always reliably, representing folk authenticity, and the operation of the male literary establishment itself.[2]

This chapter builds on recent work on the publication history of fairy tales and the tales of seventeenth-century France in particular. In investigating this area of the fairy tale, a more comprehensive understanding of the history of the princess in the fairy tale can be understood, both through the earlier royal context of such tales and their promotion of marital freedoms over commodification. Such understanding sheds new light on the tales produced today. Disney's Rapunzel, for example, who knocks a strange man out with her frying pan in *Tangled* (2010), isn't such a far cry from Lhéritier's heroine, Finette, who threatens a lecherous prince with a hammer in "L'Adroite Princesse, ou les aventures de Finette" ("The Discreet Princess; or, the Adventures of Finette") (1695). While Disney may commodify Rapunzel, churning out dolls and other merchandise, the princess's narrative trajectory toward freedom of marital choice—she can choose to wed a thief rather than a prince—echoes the desires of princesses from tales of the seventeenth century. Knowing that princesses were not always passive, too, allows contemporary readers to question the continued popularity of such authors as the Grimms and Lang.

This chapter focuses on a selection of tales including Perrault's "Cendrillon; ou la petite pantoufle de verre" ("Cinderella; or, The Little Slipper Made of Glass") (1697) and "Riquet à la houppe" ("Riquet with the Tuft") (1697), d'Aulnoy's "Finette Cendron" ("Cunning Cinders") (1697) and "Le Nain Jaune" ("The Yellow Dwarf") (1697), Murat's "Le Sauvage" ("The Savage") (1699), and Bernard's "Riquet à la houppe" ("Riquet with the Tuft") (1696). These tales critique and ratify issues of beauty, marital commodification, and female agency.

## Royal Contexts

Early fairy tales from the pens of Giovan Francesco Straparola (1550–1553) and Giambattista Basile (1634–1636), authors who pioneered literary tales in Europe, frequently present the reader with a hapless peasant marrying a princess or a cunning woman from the urban classes marrying a king, ignoring the rigid social hierarchies that would have made such marital arrangements inconceivable at the time. The royals in these early tales are often figures of bawdy humour and parody. Nancy Canepa says, "Above all, Basile's royal figures appear as flesh-and-blood human beings caught up in the same passions, headaches, and rituals of everyday life as their lowly co-protagonists" (Canepa 1999, 112). The tales of Basile and

Straparola critique society by revealing superstitions about and attitudes toward fashion, pregnancy, marriage, and much more.

However, they were succeeded by authors who wrote instead within the orbit of the Sun King. Louis XIV corralled his nobles in Versailles in order to achieve greater control over their activities. Fairy tales published under his reign became mirrors of court life. D'Aulnoy heralded the oncoming vogue for fairy tales in Paris with her tale "L'Île de la Félicité" ("The Island of Happiness") in 1690. She, like many of her peers, was an aristocrat and Paris's glittering network of salons rallied around the fairy tale genre as a source of entertainment and rebellion against restrictions imposed upon female aristocrats.

While fairy tales often deal in love and marriage, the tales published at this time revealed the political context that accompanied a princess's amorous adventures. Love might be a particularly romantic notion, but it could be used politically by these aristocratic women, actually subverting the patriarchal structures of property, inheritance, and even diplomacy that relied on the economic and civic arrangement of marriages. According to Joan DeJean, "In early modern Europe, the marriage of an aristocratic woman was always a thoroughly political matter: it was understood by all concerned that she was first and foremost a commodity" (d'Orléans 2002, 3).[3] Love, therefore, could disrupt a woman's commodification if she was able to follow her desire.[4] Writers such as d'Aulnoy and Murat led unconventional married lives themselves and were repeatedly embroiled in scandal, often involving lovers and accusations of debauchery, while other authors such as Bernard and Lhéritier chastely refrained from marriage in their pursuit of literary careers.[5] The tales told by these female authors deal with princesses who must either subvert or take control of their commodification in the marriage market.

Perrault was himself sympathetic to his female peers and, indeed, Lhéritier was his near relative and her preface to the tale "Marmoisan," addressed to Perrault's daughter, praises the work of "that erudite man" (Bottigheimer 2012, 131).[6] Perrault's work nonetheless entered the fairy tale canon to the exclusion of his female peers, including Lhéritier, in part because Perrault himself was a member of the male literary establishment and his fairy tales were presented as ostensible retellings of simple folklore with passive, domestic princesses. Yet, while Perrault titled his most famous collection *Histoires ou contes du temps passé* (1697) under the guise of 'old Mother Goose,' his tales, like those of his female peers, in fact include extensive detail of prevailing courtly fashions and innovations. Perrault spent almost two decades as an inspector of royal buildings, giving him great familiarity with and access to Versailles, in particular, and the material extravagance necessary to a royal court. Perrault may suggest his tales are bygone and originate from the "ordinary people," but this assertion is undercut by the details (Bottigheimer 2012,

126). Interior design and fashion of the day are described. At this point in history, Paris was leading the way in fashion and elite culture and this is evident in Perrault's tales.[7]

In "Cendrillon; ou, La petite pantoufle de verre" ("Cinderella; or, The Little Slipper Made of Glass"), the stepsisters sleep in rooms that have parquet floors, fashionable beds, and full-length mirrors. Parquet floors had become popular in the 1600s, and Louis XIV installed these in Versailles in 1684. Likewise, the full-length mirror recalls the innovation of Versaille's *Galerie des Glaces* (Hall of Mirrors), completed in 1684. The mirrors appear in Perrault's "La barbe bleue" ("Bluebeard"), too, with the heroine and her friends admiring the furniture in Bluebeard's house, especially the full-length mirrors with frames of glass and gilt metal. "What more perfect symbol could be found for the dazzling reign of the Sun King than this prestigious hall," explains Sabine Melchior-Bonnet, "where court members dripping with jewellery could look at and admire themselves and one another from head to toe in all their splendor?" (Melchior-Bonnet 2002, 46). Versailles, though not named, effectively serves as the background for Perrault's Cinderella tale, particularly for her visits to the ball where the prince presents Cinderella with oranges and citrons, alluding to Versailles's orangery. Perrault's pen also lingered upon other aspects of the culture, fashion, and commercial interests of Parisian elites. References to the styles and processes of dress required to attend the ball, the details of particular laces, dress styles, including the mantua, the wearing of patches, and the popularity of hairdressers also allude to court fashions and feminine dress habits of the time.

While Perrault asserted that his "tales (*contes*) take us inside the most humble households," his descriptions of the fashions and architecture of humble homes and citizens are vague (Bottigheimer 2012, 126). Basile and Straparola had elaborated on the conditions of poverty. Straparola's "Constantino Fortunato" relates how destitution gives his young hero a dreadful complexion while Basile's young hero in "Cagliuso" exhibits rough manners. In "Le maître chat; ou, Le chat botté" ("The Master Cat; or, Puss in Boots"), by contrast, Perrault begins with the business of inheritance: "neither the solicitor nor the notary were called in: their fees would soon have eaten up the whole of the miserable inheritance" (Perrault 2009, 115). Unlike his predecessors, Perrault shifted attention from the conditions of poverty to the economic and professional implications of poverty, and in so doing focused more on contrasting middle- and upper-class practices of inheritance.

Likewise, Perrault's "Le petit poucet" ("Hop o' My Thumb") begins with a humble woodcutter and his unusually fertile wife. Perrault speaks of a famine, perhaps referencing one of the recent famines experienced in France, but quickly reveals that the main reason for the family's hardship rests with the failure of a local lord to pay his debt to them. The tale concludes with a bourgeoisie moral about making one's fortune in public service, much as Perrault himself did. Perrault's attention to matters of property and ownership sits oddly with his assertion that the tales are of humble origins.

Perrault suggested that the tales of his collection, coming from the homes of commoners, were nonetheless instructive to the princess to whom he dedicated the volume. Élisabeth-Charlotte d'Orléans (1676–1744) was Louis XIV's niece, a nineteen-year-old who had recently inherited the title of Mademoiselle from her older sister. Perrault explained, "The desire for this knowledge has driven heroes, and heroes of your race, as far as huts and cabins to see firsthand what nobles and monarchs must understand to be well educated" (Bottigheimer 2012, 126). In fact, Perrault's tales themselves were far more instructive about the fashions of Paris with which Mademoiselle herself was familiar.[8]

Female authors likewise dedicated their tales to princesses and also their peers; Lhéritier, for instance, dedicated "L'Adroite Princesse, ou les aventures de Finette" ("The Discreet Princess; or, the Adventures of Finette") (1696) to fellow author Murat. Nadine Jasmin thus notes, "An obviously female cast of characters predominates in the tales' dedications" (Raynard 2012, 42). D'Aulnoy dedicated Volume 1 of *Contes des Fées* (*Tales of the Fairies*) to Madame, Elisabeth Charlotte, Princess Palatine, Duchesse d'Orléans, sister-in-law of Louis XIV, mother of Mademoiselle, the dedication placing her fictional fairy tale courts in direct commune with the actual court:

> Here are queens and fairies, who after having given happiness to whoever was the most charming in their times, are coming to the court of Your Royal Highness to seek for whoever is the most famous and loveable in ours. They know that France possesses a great princess all of whose actions must serve as examples, and who combines marvelous goodness and generosity with the nobility of the most majestic blood: they know, Madame, that all the virtues have equally competed to form the heart, the spirit, and the person of Your Royal Highness. (Bottigheimer 2012, 170)

D'Aulnoy not only places her characters on par with Louis XIV's court, but she also expresses through them admiration for Madame, herself a formidable figure whose daughter and stepdaughters were married, like herself, according to political necessity.[9] Madame herself alluded to the link between fairy tale and court life and referenced her son's character in terms of fairy tales in which a baby is endowed by fairies with a range of noble and wonderful qualities only to be crossed by the seventh fairy, who was uninvited to the christening (d'Orléans 1984, 190).

D'Aulnoy set the frame tale of the volume at Saint Cloud, Madame's preferred residence. Anne E. Duggan notes, "Here d'Aulnoy implicitly associates the

Princesse Palatine and her husband with Rhea and Saturn, whose peaceful dominion contrasts with that of Jupiter—in other words, Louis XIV" (Duggan 2005, 230). By using Saint Cloud, d'Aulnoy shifted her tales from the orbit of Versailles. The frame tale thus alerted the reader to the very real royal context of the tales themselves and articulated a preference for the household of Madame.

## Cinderella and the *Mésalliance*

If we look at the Cinderella tales of Perrault and d'Aulnoy, their different approaches to the royal marriage market are especially discernable. The well-known tale describes the adventures of a dispossessed daughter who contrives to attend a ball, lose a shoe, and marry a prince. Perrault offers a Cinderella who is the daughter of a nobleman with no name other than an insult with which her stepfamily addresses her. It is through the efforts of a fairy godmother—a patroness, in effect—and her own docile obedience, that Cinderella is provided the material wherewithal to attempt the most splendid of matches. Perrault affixed the moral message that "Cinderella had learned from her [fairy godmother] how to behave / With such grace and such charm that it made her a queen" (Perrault 2009, 139).

The marriage of a prince at the time would have been a political matter and no mere nobleman's daughter, glass slipper aside, could have hoped for such a match.[10] Yet Louis XIV's 'secret wife,' the marquise de Maintenon, had risen from impoverished nobility to become the mistress and then morganatic wife of the king.[11] The idea that beauty and a pleasing disposition alone could lead to marital success at court consequently underwrites Perrault's tale. His earlier heroine, Griselda, has an even more dramatic marital trajectory from shepherdess to princess, but her virtues are severely tested by her husband in order to determine her worth. The tale reveals disturbing attitudes to marriage. For instance, the Prince repines that the choice of a wife is difficult for men since appealing, young, and virtuous girls develop independent minds once married. Perrault's statement in the introductory verse specifically disdains the women of Paris: "For as we have consistently been shown Patience is what their husbands need" (Perrault 2009, 9). Versailles was indeed home to a number of unruly wives, some of whom were writing their own fairy tales, and a good portion of the cause does lie in their marital circumstances.

D'Aulnoy was one such unruly wife and her Cinderella heroine arranges her own marriage. D'Aulnoy had been married to a man thirty years her senior, and she and her mother became embroiled in a plot to have him arrested and executed for treason, resulting in their exile before she returned to Paris to be celebrated as an author. Yet while d'Aulnoy champions a woman's agency, it is specifically an *aristocratic* woman's agency. D'Aulnoy does not approve of the *mésalliance*, a marriage of unequal rank. As Duggan notes, "In her tales, d'Aulnoy responded to Perrault's degrading images of women as well as to the *mésalliance* and social climbing prevalent in the academician's tales" (Duggan 2005, 241).[12] Thus while Perrault's heroine presages the cavalcade of upwardly mobile Cinderellas into the twenty-first century, including the Grimms' heroine, simply the daughter of a rich man, and Disney's, daughter of a gentleman, d'Aulnoy's Cinderella is a princess by birth and bears the name Fine-Oreille or Finette. Her parents, a king and queen, have managed the kingdom poorly and are consequently overthrown, a perhaps cheeky reference to the problems of the French economy under Louis XIV and an early portent of the revolution that would occur in the following century. Finette seeks the aid of her fairy godmother, Merluche.[13] Although patronage is common to both tales, there is a further patina of courtliness and negotiation to the exchanges in d'Aulnoy's version, including Finette's "three respectful curtsies to her godmother" (d'Aulnoy 2001, 455).

After a series of adventures, during which Finette kills an ogre couple to claim their chateau, only for her sisters to reduce her to a kitchen slut, Finette never actually meets the prince at the ball.[14] He simply finds her red velvet slipper and pines with love for it.[15] The prince does not then enter into a marriage with a woman of unknown birth: Finette is a princess and the court celebrates her queenly appearance. Indeed, when Finette comes to the palace to claim her shoe, she agrees to marry only after she has told her story and established her royal pedigree. She further negotiates the marriage by insisting that her future in-laws, who had coincidentally absorbed her native country, restore her parents to their kingdom. Thus Finette takes over the negotiation of her own marriage for political ends, through her own agency and by finding the prince attractive and acceptable. Neither prince nor princess contracts a *mésalliance*: Indeed, Finette forges an alliance with an obviously stronger kingdom and sets conditions by which her own family can regain their status.

D'Aulnoy's tale emphasises that Finette can act autonomously, negotiating a successful marital alliance that takes into account both the importance of rank and personal choice. Perrault's tale, conversely, promises the reward of a prince if a girl is simply appealing. It is this fairy tale promise that many of the female authors opposed and complicated.

## *"Le Sauvage,"* the Princess of Savoy and Fairies

Henriette Julie de Castelnau, the countess de Murat, moved in aristocratic circles, but her tales remove marriage from the preserve of kings to the patronage of fairies where female autonomy can be achieved. Murat's first fairy tale collections, *Contes de Fées* (*Fairy Tales*) (1698) and *Les Nouveaux Contes des Fées* (*New Fairy Tales*) (1698) were both dedicated to Princess Marie-Anne de Bourbon, Louis XIV's illegitimate and favourite daughter, legitimised when she was three, married to the Prince de Conti, and widowed by the time of Murat's dedication. The princess would inherit the title of duchesse de La Valliére in her own right, never remarrying or having children. Sophie Raynard and Ruth B. Bottigheimer reflect: "Although Mme de Murat's scandal-ridden life made her unwelcome at the royal court, which by the 1690s was subject to the piety of Louis's morganatic wife Mme de Maintenon, she positioned her tales as high in the royal hierarchy as she possibly could by dedicating them to the Dower Princess" (Bottigheimer 2012, 199). Indeed, Murat was a lively member of Paris society through the '90s and her worst problems with the law occurred at the end of the decade when she was imprisoned after scandals that included purported lesbianism and debauchery.[16] The dedication of her collection to the daughter of one of Louis XIV's mistresses may not be altogether an act to attain respectability, as much as it was an understanding of marital power in the court as Louis XIV legitimised his children and, as they matured, wed them to legitimate royal members, a scandalous trend in the customs of the royal marriage market.

Murat took a different tack in dedicating *Histoires sublimes et allégoriques* (*Sublime and Allegorical Stories*) (1699) to *les fées modernes* (the modern fairies). As Elizabeth Wanning Harries suggests, it is apparent that she "deliberately mocks the kind of tale that Perrault produced, his 'Contes de ma mere l'Oye' that had been published only two years earlier" (Harries 2003, 57).[17] In her dedication, Murat admiringly and pointedly identifies the modern fairies as aristocratic peers rather than peasant tellers: "You are all beautiful, young, with a good figure, fashionably and richly clothed and housed, and you live exclusively in royal courts or in enchanted palaces" (Bottigheimer 2012, 203). The fairy tales are thus explicitly founded in court politics and customs, astutely linking her princesses to the princesses inhabiting contemporary Versailles and, more important, emphasising that the 'modern fairies' hold great rank, wealth, and beauty, enabling them to aid their protégés in the marriage market. The fairies of French fashion, in fact, exist apart and ostensibly above kings and queens, inhabiting their own kingdoms and estates from which they exert great influence.

In "Le Sauvage" ("The Savage") Murat places the heroine Constantine's birth in the context of the royal marriage market. The King of Terceres marries a princess whose father, the King of Cataracts of the Nile, had earlier arranged for her to marry the King of the Bitter Fountains, the name suggesting the unpleasantness of the proposed alliance. Unlike Louis XIV, who firmly insisted on the obedience of unwilling female relatives, the King of the Cataracts breaks the arrangement to accede to his daughter's wishes and she marries for love, despite the necessity of fighting a war as a result. The royal couple, however, produce "three most frightening monkey-faced girls" (Murat 2013, 202). The construction of daughters as marital commodities is once more foregrounded as the parents wonder, "What to do with such merchandise?" (Murat 2013, 202). The King dowers his daughters with the promise of an island kingdom for each husband, but still does no better than a trio of impaired knights for sons-in-law.[18] Physical appearance is a core concern in the marriage market, but deficiencies can be overcome through qualities of rank and money.

So far, the narrative of the tale has been a study of the princess as commodity in which the status quo of the marriage market dominates. After retiring, though, the King and Queen unexpectedly produce another daughter, Constantine, and immediately her marriage is a concern: "Richardin and Corianthe would have well wished to see her married off" (Murat 2013, 203). She is not merely beautiful, unlike her sisters, but adept at both male and female accomplishments.[19] Nonetheless, her value on the marriage market relies on factors outside her person and character, however desirable. With her father's retirement, her political significance and wealth are negligible. Her father chooses one of his officers "without wealth, without good looks and without wit," a proposal horrifying to both the Queen and Constantine (Murat 2013, 203).[20] The Queen, in fact, suggests that it would be better to allow Constantine to inherit his remaining wealth in her own right rather than be wed and Constantine herself would rather remain single than submit to a *mésalliance*.

Constantine evades her matrimonial fate by posing as a man, helped by a fairy who first appears "dressed as Diana is painted" (Murat 2013, 204). The fairy's sartorial reference to the virgin goddess is apt as young, unmarried women existed in a precarious state where independence from patriarchal control was difficult, often impossible, to achieve. A powerful female protector could provide the means to such independence.[21] The plot proceeds with Constantine, now the masculine Constantin, winning the love and respect of the King of Sicily and his sister. Typical of such cross-dressing tales, the princess, Fleurianne, falls in love with the masquerading Constantin/e. The King of Sicily, however, is pressed to arrange Fleurianne's marriage to Prince Carabut, heir of the King of the Canaries: "This prince was hump-backed and quite disagreeable, and the princess had no reason to be happy about it" (Murat 2013, 206). Fleurianne attempts to circumvent a distasteful union of appropriate rank *in favour* of a *mésalliance* with Constantin. "Le Sauvage" thus emphasizes the unstable female position in the marriage market as well as insisting that female desire should be addressed in the negotiation of marital arrangements. That Fleurianne and Constantine do take different positions in respect to their individual prospects highlights the latter point.

Murat, however, does not stay strictly within the realms of the fictional, but turns to actual marital arrangements in the court of Louis XIV at the time of her writing. Constantine flees Carabut's jealous revenge and comes across the chateau of the fairy Obligeantine. Dwelling upon the wonders of the chateau and its grounds, Murat rather cleverly situates Obligeantine's court in competition with Versailles. Constantine visits Destiny's study there, where she is introduced to the fate of France itself. Murat describes Louis XIV's qualities as a king—his armies, his wealth, his palaces, his family—but she then announces that "this was nothing in comparison" to the princess who travels to Versailles (Murat 2013, 211). Murat thus nimbly raises Marie-Adélaïde of Savoy, the princess who was travelling to wed Louis XIV's grandson, above the king. In fact, she quickly refers to her marriage as "the greatest event of our time," which, as Stedman notes, "subtly undermines Louis XIV's other political achievements" (Murat 2013, 212).

Murat juxtaposes her fairy tale tangle of marital arrangements with the actual marriage of a French princess, where the ostentatious display of the bride provided political leverage. Marie-Adélaïde of Savoy wed Louis, duc de Bourgogne, as part of the Treaty of Turin (1696). Describing the arrangement, Murat wrote that the marriage put "an end to a cruel war by bringing peace to an infinite number of powers united by jealousy against this flowering empire" (Murat 2013, 212). Marie-Adélaïde was escorted to Paris and afterward wed in true fairy-tale style, becoming one of Louis XIV's most beloved female relations.[22] While the virtues of the bride and groom are celebrated in her fairy tale, Murat nonetheless acknowledges that the marriage is foremost a political act. Obligeantine carries Constantine herself to Versailles where, rendered invisible by a magical herb, they participate in the ceremonies. They even enter the royal bedroom: "They saw the prince and the princess get dressed, get undressed, and go to bed" (Murat 2013, 213). The dressing and undressing of royal persons was a complex spectacle to which specific nobles and royals were privileged to attend, participants accorded roles such as the passing of chemises according to their rank. This privilege was particularly valued on the wedding night.[23] The heroine's participation in the celebrations focuses attention on the bride, but while the youthful Marie-Adélaïde is exalted, she is an exhibition of royal bridehood.

By contrast, in the fairy tale, the refusal of marriage has led to war, underscoring what happens when the bride does not uphold her political role. While Constantine is visiting the kingdoms of the real world, so to speak, the King of Sicily is fighting wars consequent to his sister's rejection of Prince Carabut's proposal. Obligeantine, however, quickly orders matters with a series of marriages.

Constantine is wed to the King, and Fleurianne is wed to a 'savage,' who is actually King of the Loving Islands.[24] The latter is positioned as an opposite to the King of the Bitter Fountains, referenced at the beginning of the tale. The fairy organises the match between Fleurianne and the king on the basis of Fleurianne's worth—"beneath this horrible appearance is a prince worthy of you"—and awaits Fleurianne's consent (Murat 2013, 217). Further, the King's monstrosity is explained as his own plight, a consequence of another fairy's unwanted love, and his transformation is not reliant upon Fleurianne's hand in marriage, thus forcing her pity, but upon the marriage of Constantine and the King of Sicily.[25] Obligeantine arranges alliances between kings and queens, but her choices are made in accordance with the desires and worth of each princess.

The tale ends with Obligeantine going one step further and redeeming Constantine's sisters by making both the princesses and their husbands attractive. Murat doesn't dismantle the marriage market, but she does reorganise it and place it under female jurisdiction, permitting female desire to be articulated and fulfilled.

## Riquet: Tales of Beauty and Marriage under Duress

Beauty played a crucial role in the royal marriage market, especially for women. Jo Eldridge Carney notes of the position of queen: "Her body as aesthetic object was also subject to official scrutiny, public commentary, and royal standards. The queens who came to the throne through political marriage rather than inheritance were vetted with especial care; beauty was a primary criterion for royal suitability, though it could be trumped by a prospect's political or financial assets" (Carney 2012, 98).[26] As Carney suggests, the king's appearance was also significant, but not to the same degree. Since most royal marriages were arranged without even a prior meeting between the key participants, princesses and princes relied on portraits and the accounts of ambassadors. Physical appearance thus became key and tales like d'Aulnoy's "Le Nain Jaune" ("The Yellow Dwarf"), "La Princesse Rosette" ("Princess Rosette"), and "La *Biche* au bois" ("The White Doe") feature portraits as prominent objects in the romances of protagonists, highlighting the significance of physical appearance in making a marital choice.

The politics of marriage and physical appearance are played out in competing tales of Riquet, an ugly goblin-like figure who contracts a marriage with a beautiful princess lacking in intellectual gifts. Catherine Bernard's "Riquet à la houppe" ("Riquet with the Tuft") (1696) and Perrault's "Riquet à la houppe" ("Riquet with the Tuft") (1697) both tell the tale of how Riquet promises the princess intelligence if she agrees to marry him in a year's time. The tales have no apparent precedent, but Perrault includes his among his 'Mother Goose tales,' while Bernard's "Riquet à la houppe" is included in her novel, *Inès de Cordoue* (1696). While Perrault's tale ends with the princess readily agreeing to the marriage and Riquet's transformation into a handsome husband, Bernard's tale ends with Riquet wreaking revenge on his adulterous wife by turning her handsome lover into an ugly creature indistinguishable from himself. On the one hand, Perrault's tale of contractual marriage apparently promises the fulfilment of romantic desire, a piece of wishful thinking by which even the most hideous husband could be rendered beautiful and desirable if only his wife loved him. Bernard's tale, on the other hand, promotes the emotional difficulties of such a marital arrangement. Her heroine, Mama, not only retains a handsome lover for the first part of her marriage, but also suffers the ignominy of living with two equally hideous husbands. Riquet is not transformed into a handsome husband, but transforms her lover into his image, Bernard ending the tale, "But perhaps she hardly lost anything there. In the long run lovers become husbands anyway" (Bernard 2001, 721).

The context for Bernard's tale sheds further light on the constructions of beauty and marriage represented. Bernard dedicates her novel to the baby Prince de Dombes, son of one of Louis XIV's legitimised sons, the Duc de Maine, and Anne-Louise-Bénédicte de Condé, a princess of the blood. Considering the tale's focus on physical perfection and its opposite, it is notable that the Duke was known for a pronounced limp resulting from one shorter leg, while the Duchess's arm was lame. Furthermore, the Duchess, daughter of the royal house of Condé, who bore the popular epitaph 'Madame Gunpowder,' was ashamed of her match and not at all faithful to her husband, drawing her into a ready parallel with Mama (Buckley 2008, 370). Bernard places the tale itself at the point in her novel at which two female rivals at the Spanish court tell tales. The storytelling is overseen by the queen, herself French, who suggests the topic of love. The ladies of the court create the rules of the storytelling: "That the adventures always be unexpected (*contre la vray-semblance*) but the sentiments always natural" (Bottigheimer 2012, 157). The criterion that contextualises the tale, therefore, while appearing to divorce the tale from the realities of the marriage market, actually focuses the tale on the emotional ramifications of that market.

Bernard and Perrault treat the ramifications of women's submission to the marriage market quite differently. Harries observes that "Bernard's tale is about the dangers for women in fairy-tale marriage patterns, the patterns that Perrault both reproduces and mystifies" (Harries 2003, 38). Mama is introduced as the daughter of a nobleman who "experienced a domestic calamity that poisoned all the treasures that made up his fortune" (Bernard 2001, 717). Immediately, Mama is contextualised with her father's treasures, commodifying her. Bernard states Mama's beauty plainly and without hyperbole, but explains that her stupidity makes her appear awkward and unattractive, thereby indicating that beauty and intelligence are interconnected. Mama's lack of intelligence sets her on a path to discover what she is lacking, even if, as Bernard suggests, she isn't intelligent enough to understand that she is lacking intelligence.

Perrault, conversely, punishes an excited queen at the birth of her twin daughters. The fairy, who in the tales of female authors would take control of the marriage market to benefit women, here acts in favour of the patriarchal marital system. She first attends Riquet's birth, promising him intelligence despite his ugliness, and the ability to make his wife intelligent. She then curbs another queen's happiness in her new and beautiful daughter by rendering the baby unintelligent, promising only that she would be able to bestow beauty upon her lover. Of course, the fairy is orchestrating the match between the children, but her motivations are to serve Riquet and punish the Queen through her daughter. The fairy consequently disappears, as does the Queen, for by the tale's end, it is the father who permits his daughter to wed Riquet, the Queen unmentioned, the work of the fairy only referenced retrospectively. The tale's conclusion further erases female desire and autonomy: "On the very next day the wedding took place, as Ricky the Tuft had foreseen, and according to the orders that he had given long before" (Perrault 2009, 150). In short, the marriage is represented as entirely choreographed by the prince, any appearance of the princess's desire or the fairy's dealing erased.

Bernard's Mama, by contrast, becomes intelligent through her own efforts, albeit the intelligence is still provided by Riquet, and uses that intelligence to further her own ends contrary to Riquet's, specifically in relation to love and marriage. Her ultimate failure is orchestrated by the patriarchal status quo. She can only retain her acquired intellectual autonomy by marrying Riquet and her compromise—retaining her lover and intellect through this *mésalliance*—only leads to her own unhappiness, or, indeed, horror. Riquet is not a prince of her world, but the king of gnomes and inhuman. Mama is carried away to an underworld and ultimately there is no escape from marriage for her. Like many a royal princess, she is severed from her single life, forced to conform to the conditions of a foreign court. This could be quite a brutal process.

D'Aulnoy's "Le Nain Jaune" ("The Yellow Dwarf") published in the fourth volume of her *Les Contes des Fées* (1697), could well be counted beside these tales of Riquet, although the villain is a dwarf rather than an actual Riquet. "Le Nain Jaune" is particularly focused on the consequences of removing a bride from her world and marrying her to a monstrous figure. D'Aulnoy did not embed her tale in a juxtaposition of beauty and intelligence, however. Her heroine, Toutebelle, is simply a spoilt beauty whose history parallels that of Louis XIV in a variety of ways. The Queen, her mother, is a widow like Louis XIV's mother, Anne. The Princess appears regularly in the costume of Pallas or Diana, just as Louis XIV famously appeared as Apollo. There is an apparently impudent inference that Toutebelle is the female equivalent of Louis XIV himself, providing a gendered critique of the marital treatment of royal figures.[27]

Indeed, d'Aulnoy's tale follows and lampoons royal behaviours. When the Princess turns fifteen, her portrait is sent to a number of kings with the aim of securing a good alliance. D'Aulnoy describes the kings as charmed, some to comic extremes: "Some fell ill, others lost their wits, and those fortunate enough to maintain their health and senses rushed to her court" (d'Aulnoy 1989, 459). Those who retain their sanity after viewing her portrait spend lavishly on courtly entertainments and all verse and prose of the period is written about Toutebelle: "All the bonfires were made with these compositions, which burned and sparkled better than any other sort of fuel" (d'Aulnoy 1989, 459). The exaggeration of love for Toutebelle is countered by Toutebelle's own resistance to marriage. She takes up the more common male position of opposition to marriage and appears to take delight in critiquing the kings, content to remain happy in her single state.[28] At this point in the narrative, the marriage market is absolutely in feminine control and the Queen's speeches confirm that she has the power to bestow a husband upon Toutebelle, rather than to bestow Toutebelle upon a husband. Toutebelle nonetheless says to her mother: "Please permit me, madam, to enjoy my serene indifference. If I were to change, you might be very sorry" (d'Aulnoy 1989, 460). The Queen interprets this as a threat of *mésalliance* and travels to consult a fairy. Toutebelle's disavowal of marriage, even a marriage organised to honour her rank and desires, creates the quandary of the tale.

Yet, it is the dwarf of the title who forces a marital alliance, once more placing the blame for women's unhappiness on patriarchy. On her way to see the fairy, the Queen is beset by lions. The yellow dwarf offers to save the Queen if she arranges to wed Toutebelle to him: "I'll accept her out of charity" (d'Aulnoy 1989, 461). Although his wording provides him with the power in the arrangement, upon seeing his estate, being a low, thatched cottage in a field of nettles, the Queen realises the *mésalliance* to which she herself has condemned her daughter. Worried about her mother's consequent despondency, Toutebelle likewise seeks out the fairy and is likewise forced to rely on the dwarf to save her from lions. Two key statements are made by Toutebelle. She asserts that her mother's sadness is caused by her failure to find a husband she considers worthy of a princess. Toutebelle is vain, but the emphasis is on finding a husband worthy of her rank. Toutebelle, discovering her mother's deal, then insists that the Queen would have spoken to her "for I'm far too interested in this affair for her to arrange my engagement without seeking my consent beforehand" (d'Aulnoy 1989, 463). Toutebelle confirms that she has a voice in her own marital fate and cannot be unwillingly wed. Unfortunately, the threat of being eaten by lions forces her hand and she agrees to the *mésalliance.*

Toutebelle does not surrender, however, but forges a rival alliance through marriage with the King of the Gold Mines, one of her many admirers, to evade the *mésalliance.* D'Aulnoy remarks: "Her vanity was as great as ever, and she was still fully convinced that nobody in the world was suitable enough for her" (d'Aulnoy 1989, 464). Nonetheless, Toutebelle makes a point of becoming familiar with her future husband, a luxury most princesses of Louis XIV's court were not granted. Even the beloved Marie-Adélaïde of Savoy's access to her future groom was restricted leading up to their wedding. The result of such social intercourse is that Toutebelle does come to return the love of her King. She may have chosen him initially as the most powerful, and in light of his name, most wealthy, alliance, but over time she does find him to be an agreeable lover. Unlike Perrault's heroine, who comes to love Riquet, Toutebelle makes an informed choice at the outset and, furthermore, d'Aulnoy does not bless this relationship with a happily-ever-after.

D'Aulnoy's tale, like Bernard's, ends in an unhappiness that confirms the suffering of women in marriage. In initially defying the patriarchal organisation of the marriage market, Toutebelle, like Mama, is doomed. In this case, the dwarf and fairy intervene to enforce the prior contractual obligation and, despite the aid of a siren, the denouement of the tale leads the dwarf to kill the King. Toutebelle immediately dies in grief. Bernard and d'Aulnoy do not, in these particular tales, celebrate the happy ramifications of marriage based on love and mutual compatibility of rank and wealth. They do not celebrate the successful outcome of the articulation of female desire. The heroines of their tales ultimately fail in their attempts to oppose patriarchal constructions of marriage. However, they do highlight the unhappiness that results from *mésalliance* and the alienation of the wife once in her husband's power. As Harries (2003) suggests, their tales express the dangers women encounter within the marriage market.

Perrault's tale, in contrast, ostensibly rewards his heroine's obedience in exploiting the rules of the marriage market with a happily-ever-after. In this way, Perrault cemented the now popular fairy tale path from rags to riches. It was not a new path; outspoken, active heroines such as Basile's Viola had already happily married into royalty. The change that Perrault brought was to celebrate the beautiful, passive, domestic heroine, rewarded for her submissive, appealing behaviour toward her prince. While his female peers wrote their tales with a view to promoting female desire and action in the marriage market of Europe's courts, Perrault paved the way for heroines of popular social standing who could only be satisfied with a mass-produced prince.

Male authors came to dominate the genre of the fairy tale, as Perrault's female peers were increasingly displaced, much like d'Aulnoy's Finette herself. The Grimms took up the passive, domestic ideal represented in Perrault's portraits of heroines like Griselda and Cinderella. Their princes belong to rather bourgeois royal courts, distanced from their contemporary counterparts by the assertion of folk origins and German romanticism. Maria Tatar remarks of the hero: "He may not marry a peasant's daughter, but the castle in which he finally takes up residence has the distinct odor of the barnyard" (Tatar 2003, 99). Disney in the twentieth century restored the castle as an idealistic image of itself, aptly aping Ludwig II's Neuschwanstein Castle, itself inspired by German romanticism. Disney's early princesses did household chores and sewed their own dresses, all the while waiting, apparently, for their prince to come. Disney's Princesses are now promoted as aspirational figures for the masses, their fairy tale ancestors, cunningly negotiating political and personal alliances, quite forgotten.

In the past few decades, more and more 'commoners' have married into Europe's royal families and almost always the media headlines these marriages as fairy tales. These are very different fairy tales from those produced by the female authors of Louis XIV's court, who would have looked askance at such *mésalliances* and disputed the marketing of passive princesshood as a feminine ideal. Yet, the court of Louis XIV has passed away: Indeed, a revolution overturned the carefully prescribed hierarchy of rank and privilege he presided over. Nonetheless, the tales remain as energetic reminders of the wilful princesses who refused to be treated as commodities in an entrenched royal marriage market.

## Endnotes

1. See, for example, Elizabeth Wanning Harries's excellent study of this trend, *Twice Upon a Time: Women Writers and the History of the Fairy Tale* (2003).
2. The growing conviction of fairy tale as suitable matter only for child readers likewise impacted upon the formation of the canon, excluding the more adult themes that were elaborated not only by d'Aulnoy and her contemporaries, but also earlier authors like Straparola and Basile.
3. DeJean's remark contextualises the life of Anne-Marie-Louise d'Orléans who, due to her high rank and independent wealth, was able to resist the imposition of a political marriage arranged by her cousin, Louis XIV. She wrote in favour of a society in which women retain autonomy and her example may well have influenced the female authors of fairy tale.
4. However, the use of love to destabilise the aristocratic marriage market could itself be destabilised through opportunistic marital arrangements. Authors like d'Aulnoy did not seek to undo the system of aristocratic rank; they simply wished to avoid being used as a marital commodity within that system.
5. Sophie Raynard edits a collection of biographies of fairy tale authors in *The Teller's Tales* (2012).

6. There is apparently no evidence of Perrault's daughter beyond this preface.
7. Donna Bohanan, for instance, notes: "Foreign responses to French—that is, Parisian—style, positive and negative, not only denoted a growing awareness of France as trendsetter but also set the standardization for elite material culture" (Bohanan 2012, 4). DeJean posits of Louis XIV's reign: "By its end, his subjects had become accepted all over the Western World as the absolute arbiters in matters of style and taste" (DeJean 2005, 2).
8. Perrault places Mademoiselle in the context of the tales themselves: "Never did a fairy of past time give a young creature more gifts, and gifts more sublime, than you got from nature" (Bottigheimer 2012, 126). Perrault's close relative and fellow fairy tale author, Marie-Jeanne Lhéritier, also dedicated poems to Mademoiselle.
9. Madame railed against suggestions to marry her daughter to Louis XIV's illegitimate (though later legitimised) son, the Duke of Maine. Later, her son did marry one of Louis XIV's illegitimate daughters, to her chagrin. Madame did not view the illegitimate offspring as being of equitable rank to her own children and resented the political pressure imposed on her to consent to such alliances.
10. Cinderella's kind efforts at marrying her stepsisters to high-ranking noblemen echo the nepotism of court life, even the levels at which Perrault operated.
11. Duggan further suggests that "d'Aulnoy's critique of domineering lower-ranking women recalls seventeenth-century perceptions of Françoise d'Aubigné, the marquise de Maintenon" (Duggan 2005, 209). Aptly, d'Aulnoy dedicates her own collection to Madame, herself not a fan of Louis XIV's mistresses and their children and particularly antagonistic to their proposals for the marital arrangements of her own children. Jennifer M. Jones notes, "She was certainly not content with the illegitimate power that their beauty had enabled them and their children to attain at court" (Jones 2004, 50).
12. Duggan offers an extensive reading of *mésalliance* in the tales of Perrault and d'Aulnoy and asserts that in d'Aulnoy's work, "characters who attempt to elevate themselves through marriage or usurp in any way a noble identity are referred to pejoratively as 'peasants'" (Duggan 2005, 208).
13. The name translates as something rather like 'dried cod.' D'Aulnoy, unlike Perrault, names the fairies and provides them with distinctive narrative arcs and backgrounds.
14. 'Kitchen slut' simply references her low standing within the household and consequent disorder of personal appearance.
15. It's tempting to think that d'Aulnoy might be ironically referencing Louis XIV's choice of red-heeled footwear. The King was very proud of his legs and enjoyed wearing good shoes. The reference also plays on Basile's "The Cat Cinderella," in which the King gives a fulsome oratory upon finding his love's lost patten (overshoe).
16. Geneviève Patard's examination of the evidence brings her to "a single conclusion: Murat wrote her 1690s words from Paris and not from a forced rustication. [...] Her 1690s residence in Paris agrees with the social dimension of the fairy-tale vogue, which spread within the sophisticated sphere between Paris and Versailles" (Raynard 2012, 82).
17. Her mockery rests, apparently, upon her reference to ancient fairies: "the most considerable results of their art were just weeping pearls and diamonds, blowing emeralds into handkerchiefs and spitting rubies" (Bottigheimer 2012, 203). She appears to be addressing Perrault's "*Les Fées*" ("The Fairies"), but it is true that Lhéritier's "*Les*

*enchantements de l'éloquence; ou, Les effects de a douceur*" ("The Enchantments of Eloquence") is a variant on this theme. The mockery rests, perhaps, more properly in how Perrault approaches the tale. Where Lhéritier focuses on the nobility and eloquence bestowed on the heroine, Perrault simply focuses on the docile virtues of the heroine, whose birth is indeterminate.

18. Physical infirmity is described as "disgraced by nature" (Murat 2013, 202). As the tale suggests, physical deformity is not merely an issue of appearance, but bodes ill for future offspring, endangering the family line. At the time, with many royal families closely related, inbreeding resulted in physical and mental problems for heirs. Charles II of Spain is often cited as such an example.
19. Murat is equitable in the importance she places on both male and female accomplishments, concluding that Constantine's achievements in both render her perfect.
20. Straparola's equivalent heroine, Constanza, is vocal on the issue of "an inferior marriage" and tells her father, "I shall never take a husband unless, like my three sisters, I can wed a king of rank equal" (Straparola 2001, 161).
21. The single Lhéritier, for instance, found a wealthy patroness in the duchesse de Nemours, whose own wealth was a result of inheriting her mother's fortune.
22. Louise d'Auneuil, a cousin of Murat, incidentally dedicated her fairy tale collection, *La Tiranie des fées détruite* (*The Tyranny of the Fairies Destroyed*) (1702), to her.
23. Owing to the youth of the bride and bridegroom, the bedding was a ritual and the marriage was consummated years later.
24. Murat curiously names her tale after this last-minute protagonist, one who really has little to do with her heroine's narrative, but whose back story suggests a tangled web of romantic and marital interests among the fairies.
25. Many "Beauty and the Beast" tales feature beasts who rely upon the love of the heroine to turn them into princes. Murat, on the other hand, specifically denies Fleurianne's love as a condition of the savage's transformation.
26. Carney makes a study of d'Aulnoy's "Gracieuse et Percinet" ("Gracieuse and Percinet") as an example of "the tradition of rivalry between a queen and a would-be queen" (Carney 2012, 95).
27. Holly Tucker posits: "With such direct references to the long-awaited births of daughters to childless couples, the *conteuse* uses her tales to rethink the male-dominated traditions that had long placed the survival of the monarchy on shaky ground by asking the not-so-simple question: What if Anne had given birth to a daughter instead?" (Tucker 2003, 97).
28. Fairy tales frequently feature princes who are unwilling to wed, including the prince of Basile's "The Three Citrons," who will relent only if he finds a wife as beautiful as a piece of ricotta.

## References

Bernard, Catherine. 2001. "Riquet with the Tuft" [1696]. In *The Great Fairy Tale Tradition: From Straparola and Basile to the Brothers Grimm*, trans. and ed. Jack Zipes, 717–721. New York: W. W. Norton.

Bohanan, Donna J. 2012. *Fashion Beyond Versailles: Consumption and Design in Seventeenth-Century France.* Barton Rouge: Louisiana State University Press.

Bottigheimer, Ruth B. (Ed.). 2012. *Fairy Tales Framed: Early Forewords, Afterwords, and Critical Words.* Albany, NY: SUNY Press.

Buckley, Veronica. 2008. *Madame de Maintenon: The Secret Wife of Louis XIV.* London: Bloomsbury.

Canepa, Nancy L. 1999. *From Court to Forest: Giambattista Basile's* Lo cunto de li cunti *and the Birth of the Literary Fairy Tale.* Detroit: Wayne State University Press.

Carney, Jo Eldridge. 2012. *Fairy Tale Queens: Representations of Early Modern Queenship.* New York: Palgrave Macmillan.

d'Aulnoy, Marie-Catherine. 1989. "The Yellow Dwarf" [1697]. In *Beauties, Beasts and Enchantment: Classic French Fairy Tales*, trans. Jack Zipes, 459–476. New York: NAL Books.

d'Aulnoy, Marie-Catherine. 2001. "Finette Cendron" [1697]. In *The Great Fairy Tale Tradition: From Straparola and Basile to the Brothers Grimm*, trans. and ed. Jack Zipes, 454–467. New York: W. W. Norton.

DeJean, Joan. 2005. *The Essence of Style: How the French Invented High Fashion, Fine Food, Chic Cafés, Style, Sophistication, and Glamour.* New York: Free Press.

d'Orléans, Anne-Marie-Louise, Duchesse de Montpensier. 2002. *Against Marriage: The Correspondence of La Grande Mademoiselle*, trans. and ed. Joan DeJean. Chicago: University of Chicago Press.

d'Orléans, Elisabeth Charlotte, Duchesse d'Orléans. 1984. *A Woman's Life in the Court of the Sun King: Letters of Liselotte von der Pfalz, 1652–1722*, trans. and intro. Elborg Forster. Baltimore: The Johns Hopkins University Press.

Duggan, Anne E. 2005. *Salonnières, Furies, and Fairies: The Politics of Gender and Cultural Change in Absolutist France.* Newark: University of Delaware Press.

Harries, Elizabeth Wanning. 2003. *Twice Upon a Time: Women Writers and the History of the Fairy Tale.* Princeton, NJ: Princeton University Press.

Jones, Jennifer M. 2004. *Sexing La Mode: Gender, Fashion and Commercial Culture in Old Regime France.* Oxford, England: Berg.

Melchior-Bonnet, Sabine. 2002. *The Mirror: A History*, trans. Katharine Jewett. New York: Routledge.

Murat, Henriette-Julie de. 2013. "The Savage, a Story," trans. Allison Stedman. In *Marvelous Transformations: An Anthology of Fairy Tales and Contemporary Critical Perspectives*, ed. Christine A. Jones and Jennifer Schacker, 201–218. Peterborough, Ontario, Canada: Broadview Press.

Perrault, Charles. 2009. *The Complete Fairy Tales* [1697], trans. and intro. Christopher Betts. Oxford, England: Oxford University Press.

Raynard, Sophie. (Ed.). 2012. *The Teller's Tale: Lives of the Classic Fairy Tale Writers.* Albany, NY: SUNY Press.

Straparola, Giovan Francesco. 2001."Constanza/Constanzo" [1550/1553]. In *The Great Fairy Tale Tradition: From Straparola and Basile to the Brothers Grimm*, trans. and ed. Jack Zipes, 159–167. New York: W. W. Norton.

Tatar, Maria. 2003. *The Hard Facts of the Grimms' Fairy Tales* (2nd ed.). Princeton, NJ: Princeton University Press.

Tucker, Holly. 2003. *Pregnant Fictions: Childbirth and the Fairy Tale in Early-Modern France.* Detroit, MI: Wayne State University Press.

# Contributors

**Diana Anselmo-Sequeira** earned her doctorate in Visual Studies from the University of California, Irvine. She is currently finalizing her dissertation on girl fandom and American cinema from the 1910s. Her work has been published in the journals *Spectator* and *Luso-Brazilian Review,* the anthology *Transnational Horror Across Visual Media,* and is forthcoming in *Cinema Journal.*

**Guillermo Avila-Saavedra** is an Assistant Professor in Communications and Media Studies at Salem State University. He received an MA in Advertising from Michigan State University and a PhD in Mass Media & Communication from Temple University. His research interests include the relation between media representation and identity, intercultural and international communication, and Latino issues in the media. His work has been published in, among other journals, *Mass Communication and Society*, *Communication Quarterly*, and *Media, Culture & Society*.

**Megan Condis** is an Assistant Professor in the English department at Stephen F. Austin State University. She works on gender discourse in popular culture including film, comics, and video games. She is also the Managing Editor for *Resilience: A Journal of the Environmental Humanities.* She is currently revising her dissertation, "The Politics of Gamers: Identity and Masculinity in the Age of Digital Media." You can find her online at megancondis.wordpress.com.

**Rebecca-Anne C. Do Rozario** teaches at Monash University. She is interested in fairy tales, fantasy and children's literatures, and musical theatre, having published work in such journals as *Children's Literature*, *Musicology Australia*, *Marvels & Tales* and *Women's Studies in Communication*, and in collections including *The Gothic in Children's Literature: Haunting the Borders*.

**Miriam Forman-Brunell** is a Professor of History at the University of Missouri-Kansas City. She is the author of *Made to Play House: Dolls and the Commercialization of American Girlhood* (1993; 1998) and *Babysitter: An American History* (2009). Forman-Brunell served as Guest Editor of the doll-themed issue of *Girlhood Studies: An Interdisciplinary Journal* (2012) and editor of *Girlhood in America: An Encyclopedia* (2011), co-editor of *The Girls' History & Culture Readers: The Nineteenth and Twentieth Centuries* (2011), and co-editor of *Dolls Studies: The Many Meanings of Girls' Toys and Play* (2014).

**Rebecca Hains** is an Associate Professor of Communications at Salem State University. She is the author of *Growing Up With Girl Power: Girlhood On Screen and in Everyday Life* (2012) and *The Princess Problem: Guiding Our Girls Through the Princess-Obsessed Years* (2014). She has published essays in anthologies including *Mediated Girlhoods: New Explorations of Girls' Media Culture* (2011) and *Geek Chic: Smart Women in Popular Culture* (2007), as well as journals such as *Girlhood Studies: An Interdisciplinary Journal*, *Women's Studies in Communication, Popular Communication*, and *Popular Music and Society*. For more information, visit rebeccahains.com.

**Ilana Nash** is an Associate Professor of Gender and Women's Studies at Western Michigan University. She is the author of *American Sweethearts: Teenage Girls in Twentieth-Century Popular Culture* (Indiana University Press, 2006). She is the owner of the Girls Studies Discussion List and serves on the advisory board of Girl Museum (www.girlmuseum.org).

**Diana Nastasia** is an international lecturer and scholar. In her home country of Romania, she taught at the Romanian-American University, the University of Bucharest, and the National University for Political Studies and Public Administration. In the United States, she has taught at several universities and colleges in North Dakota, Missouri, and Illinois. She has published chapters in books such as *The Palgrave International Handbook on Women and Journalism* (Palgrave 2013) and *The Walk of Shame* (Nova 2013), and articles in publications such as *Controversia: The International Journal of*

*Discussion and Democratic Renewal* and *Triple C* (*Cognition, Communication, Co-operation*).

**Kirsten Pike** is an Assistant Professor in Residence in the Communication Program at Northwestern University in Qatar. Her teaching and research interests include girls' media culture, feminist media studies, and critical/cultural studies of television. Her research appears in such places as *Girlhood Studies: An Interdisciplinary Journal*, *Mediated Girlhoods: New Explorations of Girls' Media Culture*, *Television & New Media*, *Reality Gendervision: Sexuality and Gender on Transatlantic Reality TV*, and the *Encyclopedia of Gender in Media*.

**Rebecca Starkman** is a doctoral student in Curriculum Studies & Teacher Development at the Ontario Institute for Studies in Education at the University of Toronto. Her research explores the intersections of gender, religion, and schooling, focusing on the experiences of religious students within public educational institutions. Rebecca's previous research project, *Revisiting the Jewish American Princess: Jewish girls, the J.A.P. discursive stereotype, and negotiated identity*, was conducted while completing a Master of Arts at Brock University.

**Charu Uppal** obtained her PhD in Media Studies from Pennsylvania State University. She has taught at Indiana University in Bloomington, Clarion University in Pennsylvania, Pennsylvania State University, and at The University of South Pacific in Fiji. Her research interests include the representation and formation of cultural identity in the developing world in the global era, and the role of media and technology in mobilizing citizens towards political and cultural activism. Dr. Uppal currently teaches at Karlstad University, Sweden.

**Karen E. Wohlwend** is an Associate Professor of Literacy, Culture, and Language Education at Indiana University, Bloomington. She is the author of *Playing Their Way into Literacies: Reading, Writing, and Belonging in the Early Childhood Classroom* (2011), *Literacy Playshop: New Literacies, Popular Media, and Play in the Early Childhood Classroom* (2013), and a forthcoming book with Carmen Medina: *Literacy, Play, and Globalization: Converging Imaginaries in Children's Critical and Cultural Performances* (in press for 2014). Wohlwend's articles have appeared in *Reading Research Quarterly*, *Gender and Education*, *Journal of Early Childhood Literacy*, *Language Arts*, and *Contemporary Issues in Early Childhood*, among others.

**Phyllis Scrocco Zrzavy**, PhD, is Professor of Mass Communication at Franklin Pierce University in Rindge, New Hampshire. Her research area of interest is women in media representations. She serves on the editorial board of the *Journal of Media Literacy Education* and is a member of the Academic Advisory Board for *Annual Editions: Mass Media*. She is the author, previously, of "Women, Love and Work: The Doris Day Show as Cultural Dialogue" in Mary F. Dalton and Laura R. Linder, eds., *America Viewed and Skewed: Television Situation Comedies* (SUNY Press, 2005).

**Helfried C. Zrzavy**, PhD, is a native of Vienna, Austria. He serves as the Technology Integration Specialist at Contoocook Valley Regional High School in Peterborough, New Hampshire.

# Index

## A

## D



## E

## F



## G

## H



## I

## J



## K



## L



## M

## Q



## R

## S



## T

## U



## V



## W



## Y



## Z

Sharon R. Mazzarella
*General Editor*

Grounded in cultural studies, books in this series will study the cultures, artifacts, and media of children, tweens, teens, and college-aged youth. Whether studying television, popular music, fashion, sports, toys, the Internet, self-publishing, leisure, clubs, school, cultures/activities, film, dance, language, tie-in merchandising, concerts, subcultures, or other forms of popular culture, books in this series go beyond the dominant paradigm of traditional scholarship on the effects of media/culture on youth. Instead, authors endeavor to understand the complex relationship between youth and popular culture. Relevant studies would include, but are not limited to studies of how youth negotiate their way through the maze of corporately-produced mass culture; how they themselves have become cultural producers; how youth create "safe spaces" for themselves within the broader culture; the political economy of youth culture industries; the representational politics inherent in mediated coverage and portrayals of youth; and so on. Books that provide a forum for the "voices" of the young are particularly encouraged. The source of such voices can range from in-depth interviews and other ethnographic studies to textual analyses of cultural artifacts created by youth.

For further information about the series and submitting manuscripts, please contact:

SHARON R. MAZZARELLA
School of Communication Studies
James Madison University
Harrisonburg, VA 22807

To order other books in this series, please contact our Customer Service Department at: